Language, Ontology, and Political Philosophy in China

SUNY series
in
Chinese Philosophy and Culture

David L. Hall and Roger T. Ames, editors

Language,
Ontology,
and
Political Philosophy
in China

Wang Bi's Scholarly Exploration
of the Dark (*Xuanxue*)

Rudolf G. Wagner

State University of New York Press

Published by
State University of New York Press, Albany

For information, address the State University of New York Press,
State University Plaza, Albany, NY 12207

Production by Micheal Haggett
Marketing by Fran Keneston

Library of Congress Cataloging-in-Publication Data

Wagner, Rudolf G.
    Language, ontology, and political philosophy in China: Wang Bi's scholarly
exploration of the dark (*xuanxue*) / Rudolf G. Wagner
        p. cm. — (SUNY series in Chinese philosophy and culture)
    Includes bibliographical references and index.
        ISBN 0–7914–5331–6 (alk. paper) — ISBN 0–7914–5332–4 (pbk. : alk. paper)
        1. Philosophy, Chinese — 221 B.C.–960 A.D.   2. Metaphysics.   3. Wang Bi, 226–
249.   I. Title: Wang Bi's scholarly exploration of the dark (xuanxue).   II. Title.   III.
Series.

B126.W284 2002
181'.11 –dc21

                                                                        2002070719

                    10 9 8 7 6 5 4 3 2 1

Contents

Preface   vii

Introduction   1

1 Discerning the That-by-Which:
   The Language of the *Laozi* and the *Lunyu*   5
   A Plea for a History of Understanding   5
   The Consensus: The Ineffability of the Sage's Thinking   7
   The Radical Position   10
   Developing Reading Strategies   15
   The Discussion about Language and
      the Thinking of the Sage in Wei   44
   The Structural Contradiction of the Confucius Texts:
      Talking about That-Which-Is-Dark   56
   The Logical Deduction of the Unnameability of
      That-by-Which the Ten Thousand Kinds of Entities Are   57
   The Deduction of the Possibility of Limited but
      Sufficiently Grounded Propositions about That-by-
      Which the Ten Thousand Kinds of Entities Are   60
   Traces of the That-by-Which Found by the Confucius Texts
      within the Structures of Discernible Entities: Antinomy and
      Negation   62
   Grasping Aspects of the That-by-Which   69
   An Explanation of the Images [Xiang of the *Zhouyi*]   80

2 Wang Bi's Ontology   83
   The Framework of Analysis   83
   Wang Bi's Inquiry into the That-by-Which   88
   Wang Bi's Approach   91
   The Binary Structural Organization of Entities   98
   The Order of the Ten Thousand Kinds of Entities   108
   The One and the Many   121

The Dao   125
The Dark   144

3 Wang Bi's Political Philosophy   **148**
The Actual and Perpetual Crisis of Human Society   148
The Causes of the Crisis   153
Operating the Return: The Sage   177
Sagely Politics as Public Performance   199
Wang Bi's Philosophy: An Ideology?   213

Notes   217
Bibliography   243
Index   255

Preface

It has taken many years, and several other books, to finish this work of which the present book is the third and last volume. In fact, the writing of this book took as many years as Wang Bi, its subject, lived, namely twenty-three. My gratitude for the spiritual and material support of this book and its critical discussion has accumulated. The core ideas were developed in 1971 in Berkeley, where I spent a wonderful year as a Harkness Fellow. The first of many drafts of an extrapolative translation of the *Laozi* through the Wang Bi *Commentary* was begun then, and continued in the following year in Berlin with a habilitation grant from the German Research Association (DFG). A position as assistant professor at the Free University of Berlin began a long detour. My education had been exclusively in the field of classical Chinese studies, while the focus of the Berlin Institute was modern China. While gaining some expertise in this new field, my work on Wang Bi remained active, but on the back burner. After the job in Berlin had run its course in 1977, I worked part time as a science journalist and consultant on Chinese agriculture and finished the first full draft of this book. In 1980, I submitted it (in German) as a habilitation thesis, and it was passed in 1981 with my late teacher, Professor Wolfgang Bauer (Munich), and Professor E. Zürcher (Leiden) as external referees. Cornell University was generous enough to invite me as a fellow into its Society for the Humanities in the same year, which resulted in a book on Taiping religion. In the subsequent years, I was a research fellow at Harvard University and a research linguist at University of California, Berkeley, working on two books on the politics of modern Chinese fiction. Only small segments of my Wang Bi study were published in English during these years. In 1987, I began to teach at the University of Heidelberg in Germany at an institute in urgent need of a major development effort. A stipend from the Stiftung Volkswagenwerk made possible another year at Harvard, working now on the English version of this book. In the meantime, scholarship had been revived in mainland China, and a sizable amount of new work had emerged. I was relieved that my core arguments seemed solid enough to survive, thus I developed new sections, such as the analysis of Wang Bi's commentarial strategies, the reconstruction and critical edition of the texts, and the chapter on textual transmission, while reworking all of the rest. In short bursts of feverish work between long stretches of other equally feverish work, my project finally was completed.

This study follows two others that have already been published, because of the broad-mindedness and long-term view with which State University of New York Press has been willing to support publications in Chinese philosophy. These include *The Craft of a Chinese Commentator: Wang Bi on the Laozi* (State University of New York Press, 2000) and *A Chinese Reading of the* Daode jing: *Wang Bi's Commentary on the* Laozi. *With Critical Text, and Translation* (State University of New York Press, 2003).

Much of the emotional cost of such a project is not borne by the author but by those on whom this kind of work imposes painful deprivations. My older daughter, Martha, was born in 1971. When I eventually told her that the manuscript was now completed, she seemed unbelieving. Since the day she was born, this manuscript had hung over her head with the eternal and never fulfilled promise that, after one last effort, it would be finished. I thank her, her sister, Tina, and their mother for their many years of bearing the burden of this work with me, and I apologize for the ensuing deprivations and disruptions that they endured.

My thanks to the foundations and universities that have generously supported this work at various stages, such as the German Research Association (DFG), the Stiftung Volkswagenwerk, and Cornell University, Harvard University, and the University of California, Berkeley, which offered me research opportunities; to the members of the research group "Text and Commentary" in the Institute of Chinese Studies in Heidelberg, who gave much-needed spiritual support and critical advice; and to Dr. Johannes Kurz and Holger Kühnle, who during the last stages, helped as research assistants to finish the manuscript and the bibliography. In addition, Florence Trefethen eventually applied her firm and gentle pen in an effort to make my English more understandable and economical.

Last, Catherine Vance Yeh, with her unflinching optimism and support, is thanked for this book's eventual completion. I wish to dedicate this volume to her.

Heidelberg, November 2000

Introduction

Wang Bi did not have much of an appetite for philosophers who, belonging to a given "school" of thought, would then proceed to read the bequest of the Sages in light of their school's teaching. He certainly did not think that he himself was properly described by being assigned to one of the schools. He, like many of his peers and admirers, rather wanted to be defined by the object of their inquiry and judged by the contribution they made. Their main discovery was the intrinsic "darkness" of "that by which," *suoyi* 所以, the ten thousand kinds of entities are, and their main contribution was to discover this darkness not as a sad limitation of the human mind and of human language in their capacity to conceptualize something excessively complex but as a constituent feature of the That-by-which itself.

I take this term *That-by-which* from the opening statement in Wang Bi's analysis of the "Structure of the Laozi's Subtle Pointers":

It is generally true with regard to

that by which things are created that by which achievements are brought about . . .[1]

夫

物之所以生 功之所以成

Wang Bi does not nominalize the *suoyi*/that-by-which, but he avoids with this innocuous formula the use of some overdetermined older concept. I have decided to follow his track and, to avoid a Western philosophical term that I would have to refashion beyond recognition, I adopted the awkward but fairly precise noun "That-by-which."

The relationship between the That-by-which and the ten thousand kinds of entities is one between the One and the Many. This was thought of as the universal and stable model that an ideal ruler was to follow in his intrinsically unstable relationship with the "Hundred Families" of society; the ensuing question of how the constituent aspect of the "That-

1

by-which," namely, its "Darkness," could be enacted by the ruler moved Xuanxue from pure philosophy of Being to political philosophy and of praxis. When the interpretations of Wang Bi and others were made into assigned university reading in the Southern Dynasties since the fifth century, they were not subsumed under some existing or adapted school name such as "Taoism" or the modern "Neotaoism" now sometimes used for them, but their work was defined by the object of their exploration and thus was referred to as Xuanxue, the Scholarly Exploration of the Dark.[2] Wang Bi's exploration of the Dark is the subject of this book.

This book comes at the end of a lengthy expedition that set out to secure a solid basis for the analysis. The fruits from this expedition are now available in a volume containing a critical edition, plus an extrapolative translation of Wang Bi's *Laozi* text, his *Laozi* commentary, and the surviving long bits of his exploration of the "subtle pointers" of the *Laozi*, the *Laozi weizhi lüeli*,[3] and in another volume that analyzes the craft of Wang Bi as a commentator.[4] In this manner I felt I had done all I could to provide myself and the reader with material that would permit a solidly based critical dialogue about the philosophical inquiry of Wang Bi presented here. It also made for much brevity in the present work, for many of the often tantalizingly difficult details in matters of textual philology and extrapolative translation have been discussed in these other volumes. The texts as they are used here will very often deviate substantially from what is popularly referred to as "the Wang Bi edition" (which sadly is anything but a Wang Bi edition), and the translations also follow my analysis and reasoning detailed there. The reader is kindly asked to consult these works for more detailed reference.

The discovery of the "Dark" as a constituent feature of the That-by-which, or condition for the possibility of the ten thousand kinds of entities, seems to foreclose any further talk about the latter and to mark the end of discursive philosophy. Wang Bi confronted the problem as a philosophical one that would not allow cheap solutions. The first chapter deals with his analysis of the necessary collapse of definitory language in the face of the Dark, his analysis of the uses of language made by the Sages and the warnings they gave about its unreliability, the ensuing tentative nature of their pointers, and the reading strategy appropriate for their understanding.

While prevented by the very Darkness of the That-by-which to apply a definitory hammer, language is still able to make meaningful heuristic statements about aspects of it. The second chapter explores the ontology into which Wang Bi develops and transforms the *Laozi*'s forays. The term ontology is here used pragmatically in its meaning of "study of the Being of entities." Again, Wang Bi combines a ruthless search for what "by necessity" is true about the That-by-which that enables it to be the condition for the possibility of all entities, with an exceedingly careful and probing reading of the available statements in the *Laozi* but also the *Zhouyi* (especially the *Xici* and the *wenyan*) and the *Lunyu*. His approach is guided not so much by a "purely philosophical" interest than by an interest in the consequences this analysis will have in the realm of political philosophy, a general direction that he certainly shares with the texts he is analyzing (at least in his reading of them). The systematic manner in which Wang Bi maps the relationship between the One and the Many and the conditions under which the One can be the One of the Many and not one among the many provides the groundwork for his political philosophy.

Wang Bi translates the general logic prevailing in the relationship between the One and the Many into a normative guideline for the management of human society in which the ideal ruler is to model himself after the hardly gratifying features of the One in order to achieve a stability of the entire body politic—social order and security for his throne. Following the *Laozi*'s procedure, he presents the ideal ruler, the Sage, as the person able to live up to this standard. As opposed to the stable ontological relationship between the One and the Many, the relationship is essentially unstable in history and society. In a close reading of the *Laozi*, Wang Bi extracts a highly sophisticated understanding of the dynamics of a political body and outlines the manner in which the Sage, by modeling himself after the That-by-which, is able to prevent this body from exploding into chaos and civil war. The *Laozi* was written during a time perceived by contemporaries as tumultuous, the Warring States period. Wang Bi again lived in a time when the Han empire had just collapsed into three separate states, each vying for supremacy, with intermittent fighting. It was easy to depict an ideal ruler keeping the state in order at some utopian past where order had never collapsed. But what about a body politic corroded as much at the top as at the bottom, and where the hopes for a return of one of the Sages of old had long been given up? Taking his lead from a few fragmented thoughts in the *Laozi* and supplementing this with arguments proffered in other texts that he associated with the same philosophical enterprise, Wang Bi develops a strategy of a public performance of rule modeled on the That-by-which that is thrilling in its originality and even modernity, and that shows at the same time a keen understanding of the dynamics of a body politic under duress.

Since Tang Yongtong's pioneering work, a number of summary studies have been written in Chinese on the Scholarly Exploration of the Dark, but there are still few detailed studies of individual works and authors. Since in many cases the philological problems have not even been tackled, these overviews could not base themselves on a rich body of previous work but as a rule proceeded by going through all that they considered important without being able to spend too much time on individual problems and texts.

The relationship of detailed studies and such overall studies is a complex one, and in many cases a bold outline written without all of the facts at hand can focus and guide detailed studies, while in others a single, detailed study can derail the consensus that had been plodding along for decades. The present work clearly falls into the realm of detailed studies, and it does not attempt to give a summary treatment of Xuanxue. At the same time it hopes, through the careful analysis of a narrowly circumscribed body of historical material of high sophistication, to arrive at broader conclusions, and I would like to flatter myself with the thought that these might even be of interest to the political scientist and to the philosopher of our days.

Chapter 1

Discerning the That-by-Which: The Language of the *Laozi* and the *Lunyu*

A PLEA FOR A HISTORY OF UNDERSTANDING

Many decades ago, Feng Youlan suggested dividing the history of Chinese philosophy into two great ages—the age of the philosophers, *zixue shidai* 子學時代, which lasted until Liu An (d. 122 B.C.E.), the Prince of Huainan, and the age of the study of the classics, *jingxue shidai* 經學時代, which he saw beginning with Dong Zhongshu (176–104 B.C.E.) and ending with Kang Youwei (1858–1927). Few would doubt the importance of the early Han shift in Chinese philosophy, even while disagreeing with Feng Youlan's lumping the entire remainder of Chinese philosophy into a single category because, as he said, "there was no other basic change with regard to politics, the economy, and society."[1] He set these two stages up on a then-current model of European history of philosophy in which the short age of the philosophers such as Plato and Aristotle is said to be followed by the long centuries of scholasticism. He then transferred a common disdain for European scholastic thinking, that it mostly "poured new wine into the old bottles," to the Chinese tradition of commentaries to the classics, which thus came under the general heading of secondhand thinking. China, however, failed to move early on to the third and very innovative phase of Western philosophy that began with Descartes, and did so only when confronted with Western post–Cartesian thinking.

Feng thus imported a very particular view of the history of European philosophy developed mostly in the Protestant countries, which stressed *urtext* and originality to the detriment of orthodox ("Catholic") tradition and commentary. In a direct transfer of these orientalist presumptions, Feng Youlan's age of the study of the classics thus only "poured new wine into old bottles," and therefore it deserved less attention. Feng Youlan thus devotes one volume to the 300-plus years of the age of philosophers, and one to the 2,000-odd years of the latter age. In this view, Chinese thinking during the latter age was second hand and ephemeral in nature. Evidence is the subordination of philosophy under the classics of old that is manifest in the preferred form of this age, the commentary.

Seeing the beginning of this second age mostly in terms of a politically enforced orthodoxy, neither Feng Youlan nor later prominent historians of Chinese philosophy have pondered the historical pessimism written into the shift between the two ages or the change in mentalité that this involved. Perhaps because of this imported devaluation of the second age, comparatively few serious studies on philosophers of this second period have appeared that have focused on their relationship to the classics. And while we have, since the beginning of the twentieth century, been flooded with Chinese "histories" of just about everything from literature to eclipses of the sun, even a simple history of Chinese commentary literature has not been written, not to mention such pressing studies as a history of understanding, of hermeneutics, or of the change in the mentalité of the class of scholars who would spend their lives understanding and making understood not the world, Being, or their own thoughts but the obscure messages left behind by others, whom they elevated to the unattainable rank of Sages.

Such studies would move beyond the anecdotical evidence collected by scholars such as Pi Xirui 皮錫瑞[2] (1850–1908) on the history of the study of the classics, beyond the constructs of linear development of the commentary form, as presented by Ishida Kōdō 石田公道,[3] and beyond the few abstract quotations about the hidden meaning of the classics and the way to handle them assembled by Feng Youlan himself, and more recently by Yu Dunkang 余敦康.[4] They would join in the large project once begun, and not continued, by Kaga Eiji 加賀榮治,[5] actually studying the commentaries and related writings, their craft, their implied assumptions, and their explicit philosophy.

Focusing, as I do in this book, on a commentator of the *Laozi* who is not only already part of a long history of commentaries but also engages in some lively trade and polemics with his predecessors, I am thus forced to provide a sketch of this historical background in the full awareness and ardent hope that some scholar better equipped for this task will quickly make this portrayal obsolete with a full and reasoned study.

Instead of a dilettante outline of a history of understanding, which also would involve solving problems of textual dating, I shall present the tradition through the perspective of Wang Bi himself. He was not a historian of philosophy but a philosopher. The options presented by various earlier texts such as the *Zhuangzi*, the *Laozi*, the *Lunyu*, or the *Zhouyi* did not enter his intellectual universe in a sequential, or possibly even a logical, historical order but simultaneously as options of thinking, and possible solutions to philosophic problems. I shall therefore try a systematic exposition of those options definitely known and pondered by him or likely to have been at his disposal. Into the first category I would put texts such as the *Lunyu, Laozi, Zhouyi, Zhuangzi, Chunqiu,* and *Zuozhuan,* to which he refers explicitly and which were part of the curriculum of educated youths at the time; into the second, I would put texts such as the *Wenzi, Huainanzi,* or *Yinwenzi,* which in great likelihood were present in his own library and read by him, but where it can only be inferred that he knew them from allusions and an occasional unmarked quotation.

THE CONSENSUS:
THE INEFFABILITY OF
THE SAGE'S THINKING

The Master said: "Writing does not fully express what is said. What is said does not fully express what is thought." 書不盡言 言不盡意.[6]

This famous, often-quoted statement from the *Xici* is not a general statement about the inequities of the written and spoken language. It is followed by a question: "Is one accordingly unable to see the thinking of the Sages?" 然則聖人之意 其不可見乎. Thus the "what is thought," *yi* 意, of the Master's phrase refers to the thinking of the Sages. The "Sages" are a very limited number of individuals whose appearance must be counted as a world event. They qualify for this category by virtue of their insight into the ultimate things that make for the order of the universe, hence, of society, often referred to by the general name of "Dao." This insight, the "Master"—that is, Confucius, who himself is seen as the last of these Sages—says, cannot be fully expressed in spoken language, which in turn cannot be fully expressed in written characters.[7]

Wang Baoxuan has justly pointed out that this statement by the Master is not the actual argument but in the context of the *Xici* passage only affirms a commonly accepted truth.[8] The actual argument comes after this passage and deals with the devices used by the *Zhouyi* to circumvent the problem of language and writing. It will be dealt with later. In a more explicit translation, the Master's statement thus reads:

> The Master said: "[It is true that] writing does not fully express what is said [by the Sages about the Dao], and that what is [thus] said does not fully express what is thought [by the Sages about the Dao]."

Merely reaffirming a commonly held assumption, the *Xici* passage does not have to give a reason for this ineptitude of the spoken and the written word. The same is true for the *Laozi*. The statements again are well known. As to the Way, the *Laozi* says (in Wang Bi's reading), "A way that can be spoken of is not the eternal Way" [1.1]. And the *Laozi* 41 ends with the blunt statement: "The Way is hidden and nameless." The *Laozi* repeats the description of the Way as *wu ming* 無名, "nameless," in 32.1: "The Eternal of the Way is Namelessness" 道常無名. In these statements, the difference made in the *Xici* between the written and the spoken language is blurred in the general term *ming* 名.

The Sages themselves are enabled by their knowledge of the Dao to perform the same role in society that the Dao performs in the cosmos as a whole. As a consequence, the trouble language has in dealing with the Dao is repeated in its dealing with the Sages. The *Lunyu* (in Wang Bi's reading) is quite explicit about language's inability to "name" and define the Sages. It quotes Confucius as saying:

> Great indeed is Yao being the ruler! Immeasurable he is! Only Heaven is great, and only Yao was modelled after him. So boundless he [Yao] is, that none of the people were able to define him! 大哉堯之爲君也! 巍巍乎唯天爲大, 唯堯則之. 蕩蕩乎民無能名焉.[9]

The term *great* here has the meaning of "absolute," "beyond all measure," and thus "indefinable." The same is true for Heaven as for the Dao. Consequently, the Sage Yao, whose only measure is Heaven itself, is undefinable by means of language. So is Confucius in the eyes of his contemporary and later admirers. In Wang Bi's reading, *Lunyu* 9.2 begins:

> A villager from Daxiang said: "Great indeed is Confucius. So widely learned is he that there is nothing [specific with which] to complete a definition [of him]." 大哉孔子博學而無所成名.[10]

Wang Bi comments: "[His being widely learned, but there being nothing with which to complete a definition of him] is like harmonious music that emerges out of the eight musical instruments, but the eight instruments are not its [the music's] definition." In this context, Confucius becomes undiscernible. He himself states as much: "There is no one to discern me 莫我知也夫," and ends a description of himself with the words "as to discerning me, there is only Heaven!" 知我者其天乎.[11] True to the statement imputed to Lao Dan in the *Zhuangzi*, that "he who knows does not speak," Confucius himself finally claims, "I want to be without words" 予欲無言, and he answers the shocked question of his students about what they were to transmit if he did not leave a verbalized teaching for them:

> What words does Heaven make? The four seasons roll on and the hundred [kinds of] animals are born. What words does Heaven make?![12]

From Wang Bi's commentary to this passage, we see its pivotal importance for his understanding of the Sage's communications. Wang Bi comments:

> [Confucius'] saying "I want to be without words" means that he wishes to bring the root to light 明本 [that is,] to bring up the root and [thus] to encompass [all] branches [springing from it] 舉本統末 and thus show the Ultimate of the entities 示物之極. Were [he] to establish words and hand down teachings with the purpose of penetrating to the [true] nature [of entities], abuses [of these words and teachings] would end up by proliferating. Were [he] to rely on hints and to transmit instructions, the situations [in which they would be used] would end up by being vexatiously complex. Thus he is searching for the insuperable control that is in the Dao,[13] and therefore he cultivates the root and discards the words and practices the transformation [of others] by modeling [himself] on Heaven.
>
> Seen in the strictest terms, the "heart of Heaven and Earth" [mentioned in the *Zhouyi* hexagram Return, *fu* 復] becomes visible in [their] not speaking. As cold and warm [seasons] follow each other in due order the unspoken orders [of Heaven] are acted out in the four seasons. How would Heaven [,as *Mengzi* 5A5 says,] "repeatedly [give orders]?"[14]

Wang Bi makes it clear that this statement by Confucius is a sigh of resignation. He might wish to make do without words, but in fact he talked all day, and he knew he would have to. With the advantage of hindsight, Wang Bi can well argue that what has been made into "the teachings" of Confucius has suffered from the double jeopardy of whimsical interpretation and changing circumstances of application. Confucius continues talking and acting, well aware that language might be an unreliable medium of philosophic communication but accepting that it is irreplaceable. The statement is thus a warning by Confucius himself that his utterances should not be reified into some textbook teaching, and it is a guide showing the insightful how to read the Master's words and acts. "Seen in the strictest terms" 以淳而觀, however, the real control 御 over the entities is achieved through not meddling, that is, not speaking.

For Wang Bi's *Laozi*, the Sage who embodies the Dao also defies language. "If the Great [the Sage] is at the top, those below know [only] that he exists [but cannot define him]"[15] 大上，下知有之 [17.1]. "Those in antiquity who were well-versed in the Way were recondite and abstruse, so deep that they could not be discerned" 古之善爲道者微妙玄通深不可識 [15.1].

There is thus a consensus across these texts that the Dao of the Sages cannot be simply expressed in language. The classics are supposed to be aware of this problem and to be efforts of the Sages to circumvent the limits of language while continuing to make use of it.

THE RADICAL POSITION

The above-mentioned statements are defensive. They concede the impossibility of expressing the Sages' thinking while proposing alternative strategies or being inserted into texts whose structure has to be viewed as such an alternative strategy. While the surviving sources do not seem to permit the reconstruction of the horizon of discussion within which these statements became defensive, some surviving passages in the *Zhuangzi*, possibly from a later age, maintain what might have been the original proposition about the ineffability of the Dao in a counterattack against well-established alternative strategies.

The first passage comes from a section in the "Tianyun" chapter 天運 in the outer chapters of the *Zhuangzi*, which Graham has grouped together into the "Dialogues of Lao Tan and Confucius":

> Confucius said to Old Dan: "I have studied the six classics, the Songs, Documents, Rites, Music, Changes, and Annals in my opinion for quite a while, and I am quite familiar with all their

details; with this knowledge, I introduced myself to seventy-two princes; discoursing about the Dao of the former kings, I threw light on the traces [left behind] by [the Dukes of] Zhou and Shao [in these classics], but not one prince saw anything he could snap up for his use. Really! Isn't it [because] the Dao is difficult to explain that people are hard to convince?[16]

The argument is "late" primarily in that it presupposes a previous discussion of the issue.[17] The difficulties of getting access to the Way of the former Sages have already been experienced. The classics have already been described as a way to attain this access. The *Zhuangzi* passage takes issue with this form of access, which possibility is claimed primarily by the Ru, and it does so ironically by having the highest authority for the Ru, Confucius himself, declare his frustration with the effort. In this remark, Confucius defines the classics as the "traces" of the dukes of Zhou and Shao. What caused these traces is the "Dao of the former kings," which the two dukes followed and thus encoded into the classics left behind. In his discourses for the princes, Confucius does not extrapolate this Dao of the former kings from the configurations of these traces but throws light on these available traces by making use of the Dao of the former kings. This presupposes that he knows the Dao of the former kings, and that this knowledge enables him to make these traces meaningful. It is not made clear whether he knows their Dao by being a Sage himself or as a result of his studying the classics, but evidently he intends eventually to make the classics the guidebooks from which the princes might "snap up things for use." Although Confucius is thoroughly familiar with the classics, he somehow does not manage to convince the princes. Owing to the fact that although the "traces" are there, the Dao remains hard to explain, Laozi answered:

> What luck that you did not meet a prince [setting out to] establish [true] order in the world [and trying to use you and your teaching for it]! Because the six classics are [but] the obsolete traces of the former kings—how should they be that by which these traces were made? 夫六經, 先王之陳迹也, 豈其所以迹哉 [Guo Xiang comments: "That by which the traces are made is the true nature [of beings]. As they [the former kings] relied on the true nature of the other beings, the traces of this are the six classics"]. Now what you are talking about [in holding forth on the classics] are still [just those] traces. Traces, however, are brought about by shoes; how could the traces be the shoes? 今子之所言猶迹也夫迹履之所出而迹豈履哉[18]

Laozi's statement describes the classics from two perspectives, their genesis and their decoding. They are, it is true, as Confucius calls them, the traces of the former kings. Confucius, however, made efforts to illuminate these traces to the point of providing the ruler with some accessible matter imbued with the Way. These efforts were frustrated, and Confucius even understood that the relationship between the Way of the former kings and the linguistic configuration of the traces they left in the classics was far less close than he had thought. Laozi picks up this thought and drives it to its natural conclusion. He maintains that what caused these traces, the practice of the former kings, is irretrievably gone. The traces are just *chen* 陳, "obsolete," like the obsolete and exhausted ether, *chen qi* 陳氣, which, according to the *Suwen* 素問, the sick person has to "push out" for the disease to be cured.[19] The traces cannot operate as a pointer to something beyond themselves. By attaching himself in his own oral explanations to the written classics that he studied so meticulously, Confucius attached himself to the obsolete part of the event of the former kings, the empty tracks. The image chosen here by the *Zhuangzi* does not do justice to the passage. When Laozi says, "Traces, however, are brought about by shoes; how could the traces be the shoes?" he invites the thought that, in fact, much about the shoe can be discovered by a careful study of the traces. The Dao, however, is not a shoe, nor anything as neatly definable, and Laozi's description of the workings of the Dao immediately following this sentence makes this quite clear. We thus have to read the intention of this statement by Laozi against the words actually used in the statement. The passage accepts the claim that the classics are the traces of the Dao of the former kings, and it operates in the hierarchical sequence of written word/spoken word/meaning familiar from the *Xici*. But by arguing that this Dao is elusive, it denies the possibility of talking about those traces as a way of getting access to this Dao.

The second *Zhuangzi* passage also comes from a section in the outer chapters that Graham considers "related" to the inner chapters. It runs:

> The [form] in which the world cherishes the Way is the written form 書. As the written form is nothing else but the spoken word [written down], it is the spoken word which has [in fact] something to be cherished. That which is cherished in the spoken word is the thinking 語之所貴者意也. Thinking has something it is about 意有所隨. What thinking is about cannot be transmitted by words 意之所隨不可以言傳也; but on account of that [object of thinking] the world cherishes the words [indicating the thinking] and transmits [them] in written form 而因世貴言傳書. Although the world cherishes them

[the written words], I still think they do not qualify for being cherished because their [the written words'] being cherished is not the cherishing of IT [that is, of what the thinking is about, namely, the Dao] 世雖貴之, 我猶不 足貴, 爲其貴非其貴也. That is why what can be seen when one looks at it is shape and color; what can be heard when one listens for it is name [spoken term] and [musical] tone. How sad that worldly people consider shape and color, name and tone sufficient to get a feeling for THAT [what the thinking is about]! 悲夫, 世人以形色 名聲爲足以得彼之情! As, however, shape and color, name and tone are definitely not sufficient to get a feeling of IT, "he who knows does not speak, and he who speaks does not know" [as the *Laozi* says in 56.1 and 56.2], and so how should the world [ever] learn about it?[20]

Graham translates the key phrase 爲其貴非其貴也 "because what is valued in them is not what is valuable,"[21] and Watson, "what the world takes as value is not real value."[22] Both agree in relating the two *qi* 其 to the same noun, namely, "words," and attributing two different grammatical functions (verb and noun, respectively) and meanings to the two *gui* 貴. My own translation also assumes that the repetition of *qi gui* 其貴 is a play on words, but I assume that the two *qi* 其 refer to two different objects—the first to the written words, *shu* 書, with whom the entire argument started, and the second to what these ultimately are supposed to be about, the Dao. In this sense, "the cherishing of them [the *shu* 書] is not the cherishing of IT [the Dao]." In the preceding lines, the text made the argument that written characters only reproduce spoken words, which in their turn only refer to thinking, which itself refers to something unnamed and later called "THAT" 彼.

The argument of the text is not dealing with language in general but is directed against the attachment of the world to the written, verbalized, and thought forms of the Dao, which in fact "cannot be transmitted by spoken words [not to mention written characters]." The second part of the argument generalizes the first. We are not only dealing with language in all its specificity but with the objects of all the senses that again are characterized by specificity. This specific world altogether does "not qualify to get a feeling of THAT," and therefore, "he who knows [about THAT] does not speak."

The hierarchy written word/spoken word/thinking of the Sage, already familiar from the *Xici* passage quoted above, is here extended one further step with the argument that thinking is about something, which itself cannot be transmitted by words, a similar position to that found in the previous passage, which also denied access to IT through the written traces of the former kings. While the *Xici* only argues that the thinking of the Sages cannot be exhaustively presented, *jin* 盡, through words, the two *Zhuangzi* passages quoted here maintain that there is no way at all to "transmit" the content of this thinking through words and writing. Strictly speaking, as he "who knows [about the Way of the Sages] does not speak," "how should the world ever learn about it?"

The next passage directly follows the previous one, and the two are linked by their theme:

> Duke Huan was reading a book on top of the hall; wheelwright Bian was chipping a wheel at the foot of the hall. He put aside his mallet and chisel and went up to ask Duke Huan: "May I ask whose words my lord is reading?" The Duke answered: "The words of the Sages." "Are Sages still alive?" "They have already died." "But then what you are reading are but the dregs of men of antiquity!" 古人之糟魄!
>
> Duke Huan answered: "How can it be that a wheelwright criticizes my reading books? If you have an explanation you'll get away with it; if not, you die." Wheelwright Bian said: "Your subject sees it from the perspective of your subject's business. If, in chipping a wheel, I am too slow, [the chisel] slides and does not grip. If I am too fast, it bites and won't budge. Not too slow and not too fast, you've got it in your hand and it responds to the heart, my mouth cannot articulate it, there is a knack somewhere in the middle of all of this 有數存焉於其間. Your subject is unable to teach it [even] to your subject's son, and your subject's son also is unable to receive it [even] from your subject [his own father]. That is why I have been at work for seventy years always chipping wheels [without ever having myself replaced by my son]. The men of old died together with those things that could not be handed down. Thus what you are reading are just the dregs of the people of old."[23]

The key points of this conversation match the passages from the *Zhuangzi* that I have already quoted. The written form is but a sad record of the words spoken, only the "dregs" left from the Sages of antiquity, another expression for the "obsolete traces of the former kings." Their Dao "cannot be handed down"; they took it into their graves. Still, like the wheelwright himself, the Sages had this Dao, and to attain it remains a distinct possibility, but it cannot be attained through the verbal mediation of teaching and learning, writing and reading. The only access to this Dao is through the spiritual practice and exercise described in other passages and here for wheelwright Bian. These *Zhuangzi* passages see no possible access to the Way of the old Sages through the verbal dregs left behind in the classics.

This, however, is what Confucius and Duke Huan are trying to do in the *Zhuangzi* passages quoted above. The *Zhuangzi* mounts the most formidable polemic against this assumption by ridiculing attempts to extrapolate the Way of the former Sages from their sorry dregs, the classics, and by adding one more, ultimate layer of remoteness to the *Xici* list, what thinking is about. Still, the *Zhuangzi* argues against what was and remained to the end of the third century C.E. the common assumption, namely, that the classics (including the *Laozi*) were texts of a special kind coded in a highly sophisticated manner, which managed to purvey a glimpse of the Dao to those who knew how to read them.

DEVELOPING READING STRATEGIES

All three texts for which Wang Bi wrote his commentaries and outlines implicitly, explicitly, and repeatedly stress the inability of language and hence cognition to "name," that is define, the last things.

The *Zhouyi* consists of two parts, the *jing* 經 and the *zhuan* 傳. The former contains the hexagrams with the *tuan* and *xiang* as well as the line statements, the latter, the commentaries appended to all of these statements and inserted into the main text by Wang Bi, as well as additional interpretive material such as the *Xici*, which remains in separate chapters. Generally speaking, the *jing* part is considered older and directly related to prognostication, while the *zhuan* are more interpretive and philosophical.[24] As a communication construct, the *Zhouyi* makes ample use of nonverbal devices, whether graphic/structural (hexagrams, trigrams) or relational (lines, their positions, and the dynamics of their relationship). The wording used to explain the meaning of the different clusters is grammatically and terminologically diffuse, seemingly full of allusion and metaphor. Its particular meaning is established in a complex interplay with the nonverbal structural context of the hexagram or line to which a given statement refers. At the same time, the statements are firm and definite enough to evoke the impression of systematic thinking of an impenetrable depth. The silent structure and the textual surface of the *Zhouyi* can both be read as an implicit commentary on the insufficient potential of verbal and/or written communication and as explorations of alternative and more complex forms of expression. The actual use of these devices thus suggests an implicit theory about the limits of language in dealing with such elusive and complex matters. The above-quoted passage from the *Xici* A thus continues with a statement about the particular strategy used by the *Zhouyi* to circumvent this problem.

> The Master said: "[It is true that] writing does not fully express what is said [by the Sages about the Dao], and that what is [thus] said does not fully express what is thought [by the Sages about the Dao]."
>
> [Question:] "Is one accordingly unable to see the thinking of the Sages?" 然則聖人之意 其不可見乎?
>
> The Master said: "The Sages set up the images in order to fully express [their] thinking, and set up the hexagrams in order to fully express what is actual and what is false. It was through appending [written] statements [to both, in the form of the *guaci* and the *yaoci*] that they fully expressed what they [intended to] say 聖人立象以盡意設卦以盡情偽繫辭焉以盡其言. They made it flexible as well as comprehensive in order to fully express what is beneficial 變而通之以盡利. They drummed and danced about it in order to fully express the spirit 鼓之舞之以盡神.[25]

The two statements carry high authority, because the "Master" is commonly assumed to be Confucius.[26] The entire passage is not a general statement on language but on the language of the *Zhouyi* as a means of expressing "the thinking of the Sages." The second statement of the Master, however, makes the entire complex verbal and nonverbal structure of the *Zhouyi* an attempt to circumvent the accepted limitations of writing and speaking in expressing the Sages' thinking. Accordingly, the *Zhouyi* as a whole *is* in fact the thinking of the Sages. In the presentation of the *zhuan*, especially the *Xici*, the *Zhouyi* code is based on the code of the universe, and thus the *Zhouyi* contains all of the mysteries of the universe's operation, and there is enough language to justify a transition from a cosmological to an ontological reading of the *Zhouyi*. In short, the thinking of the Sages as present in the *Zhouyi* is focused on the only subject matter deserving the thoughts of the Sages, the Dao 道, but the Dao has a role both in the universe and in society.

The first statement by the Master in this *Xici* passage about written and spoken words and the thinking of the Sage does not exactly match the second with its series of measures taken by the Sages themselves to overcome this limitation of language.[27] For the expression of the Sages' thinking, images are set up, and for the full expression of their spoken words, the "Appended Statements," *xici*, are made. There is, however, no counterpart in the first part to the phrase that they "set up the hexagrams in order to fully express what is actual and what is false," nor to the last two phrases on making "it flexible as well as comprehensive" and on drumming and dancing about it.

The *Zhouyi* thus describes its own form of communication as being the result of the insight into, and the acceptance of, the inability of language to fully express what is thought by the Sages. It accepts this insight and claims to be in fact a structure that can at the same time respect this rule and circumvent it through a different use of language and sign. The appended statements, *guaci* and *yaoci*, which make written statements indicating the content of the hexagrams and their individual lines, are here said to "fully express" what the Sages said, and the images *xiang* 象—that is, the specific form of the hexagram—are said to "fully express" what the Sages thought. The *Xici* states that but does not explain why these appended statements should be able to fully express what the Sages said, while regular writing cannot do so. The same is true for the images or symbols in relation to the Sages' thinking. Both symbols and appended statements of the *Zhouyi* have their point of reference beyond themselves in a hierarchy that leads from the "Appended Statements" to spoken words, from spoken words to symbols, and from them to thinking.

The appended written statements do not mean what they say, they do not define a given object, they are not co-determinous with their object but point beyond themselves to "spoken words,"[28] and they get their content only from this referral. They differ from regular written statements by being "appended" and thus structurally signaling that they have their point of reference beyond themselves. Through this interaction they are able to develop with great economy a more complex form of communication that evokes the richness of oral communication. These spoken words again do not define their object but are there to point to and elucidate a still more refined form of communication, the symbol, which again does not in itself define but becomes the ultimate pointer, indicating where the meaning is and getting its own content not from itself but from this interaction. In this manner, a four-tiered structure of communication is developed to mediate between the immediately accessible written language and the ultimately targeted thought, with the result that this thought is being "fully expressed" without ever appearing in the manifest verbal or nonverbal structures of the *Zhouyi*.

The *Zhouyi* does not describe itself as a book consisting of a text and one or more commentarial layers added by a sequence of commentators. What might be seen as different strata of the text with the later strata commenting on the earlier ones, whose meaning had become unaccessible or whose point of reference had to be adjusted to new concerns, is depicted within the *Xici* as a historic creation to which a sequence of Sages contributed, the final product eventually enabling them fully to express their thinking without ever directly putting it into the inept media of symbol, speech, or writing.

There was a common assumption that the Sages of old shared the same thought and purpose.[29] For this reason it is not necessary to specify which Sage's thinking went into this or that passage. They can be referred to by a collective name, indifferent as to singular and plural, "Sages." By linking the structure and content of the *Zhouyi* to this "thinking of the Sages," *shengren zhi yi* 聖人之意, the *Xici* established a unity for the text that is certainly not evident on its surface.

The self-referential *Xici* statement about the crafting of the *Zhouyi* is thus at the same time a statement about reasons for its complex structure and a guide for the reader about how to approach and handle this structure without undue reification. It advises him or her that the textual surface has a multilayered, referential character unified by an underlying thinking, and that the immediately accessible text is in itself unreliable and possibly trivial and meaningless, because it is thrice removed from the meaning. The reader is instructed to remember that the writing and the words themselves are unable to express the Sages' thinking, and that only by handling the specific forms of writing, words, and symbols as tentative, tenuous, and referential will he or she be able to reach this meaning. This explanation of the *Zhouyi* form of communication and Sagely communication altogether has dramatic consequences. By defining these communications as those by the Sages, they become impregnated with high meaning perfectly independent of the often overwhelming triviality that the surface text might seem to exude. At the same time, they open a wide window of opportunity for the specialists able to handle such arcane matter. While this construct provides much freedom for the commentator by loosening his or her ties to the surface text, it also establishes a demanding and rigid framework of analysis by requesting a unified and unforced explanation of the entire body of Sagely communication, and it lays upon the reader the heavy responsibility and challenge to access the thinking of the Sages, which precludes any frivolousness in the operation. In *Lunyu* 16.8, Confucius himself is said to have called the words of the Sages "fearsome." Kongzi said:

> The Junzi has three [things] he fears: He fears the orders of Heaven, he fears the Great Man, and he fears the words of the Sages.

The Great Man is identified with the Sage in the *Wenyan* to the first *Zhouyi* hexagram. What makes these three fearsome is that all are hard to fathom. In fact, Wang Bi's senior contemporary, He Yan, comments on the last phrase:

> What is deep and far-reaching, impossible to easily understand and fathom are the words of the Sages.[30]

Huang Kan's 皇侃 (488–545) subcommentary to this passage states that "the 'words of the Sages' means writings left behind by the Sages [in the form] of the Five Classics as well as the official records"[31] 五經典籍. In this reading, the words left behind by the Sages present a fearsome challenge even to a Junzi because of the difficulty of their subject and the awkwardness of language. There is no question, however, that these texts contain and express the truths discovered by the Sages.

While the *Lunyu* contains statements by Confucius on the Sages, it is mostly a record of the *acta, verba et gesta* of Confucius and some of his disciples. Its anecdotal and aphoristic form of hundreds of very short, unrelated individual pieces again is a possible implicit commentary on the limits of language in describing the Master's thinking and what he embodied. A systematic and defining description would by necessity run afoul of the rule that Confucius is as undefinable as the thinking of the Sage is according to the *Xici*, and thus tentative, suggestive, contradictory statements and anecdotes might be read as hints at what language cannot define in its entirety.[32] This implicit level of form and structure is again supplemented by explicit statements about the insufficiency of language when dealing with the Sages and their thinking, some of which have been quoted above.

The form of the *Lunyu* thus becomes another attempt to deal with a unified, undefinable subject—the Sage and his thinking—by using language in a nondefining, referential way. Confucius himself develops the principles for this form. He claims "only to transmit and not create [new things himself]" [*Lunyu* 7.1]; this might presuppose a great diversity in what he transmitted. At the same time he claims against Zengzi, who obviously is holding forth on the diversity of the Master's teachings, "My Way has one [single motive] to thread through it" or, in Wang Bi's reading, "My Way has the One to thread through it" [*Lunyu* 4.15]. The surface of the Master's *acta et gesta* again is unreliable; they do not get their rhyme and logic from their relationship with each other but from their common point of reference beyond themselves, namely, the Sage and what he embodies.

Confucius continues to speak and act, since no other communication seems to be available. He does not write a book, and this no-book is his most elaborate statement on language and philosophy. But he is seen as rearranging what were to become the classics in a manner so as to transform them into philosophic signposts. As Yang Shixun 楊士勛 (Tang) writes in his subcommentary to the *Guliang Commentary to the Chunqiu*: "What Confucius edited are called the classics. The classics, *jing* 經, are what is constant, *chang* 常. Being the great work of the Sage, they are constantly to be revered and used. That is why they are called classics."[33] Confucius claims a unity of thinking in the midst of great formal diversity of the different classics with his comment about the *Shijing*, that its 300 songs "could be summed up by one single statement [taken from it]" 一言以蔽 之 [*Lunyu* 2.2].

His students, however, always have the impression that what he means is different from what the surface of his words and actions seems to suggest. The Master will give largely different answers to the same question; he will throughout refuse to define his terms. His personality seems to be such that the students constantly have the feeling that he is withholding something from them, to the point of asking the Master's son what Confucius was saying in the intimacy of his home [*Lunyu* 16.13] and maintaining, as Zigong did, that they only have the writings for their perusal but failed to get to hear what the Sage thought in the depth of his heart "about human nature and the Way of Heaven" 性與天道 [*Lunyu* 5.13].

The controversy about the proper reading of this passage shows the interpretive pressure to which readers and commentators subjected the text. The entire passage runs in Huang Kan's *Lunyu jijie yishu*: 子貢曰夫 子之文章可得而聞也. 夫子之言性與天道不可得而聞也已矣. He Yan comments on the first phrase: 章明也文彩形質著見可以耳目循. "Zhang 章 means clear. The ornamentation of patterns and the particulars of form are manifest and [thus] it is possible to perceive them with one's eyes and ears." He Yan thus deviates from the Han readings by separating *wen* 文 and *zhang* 章 and in reading the latter as a verb. The first phrase thus has to be read: "The texts of the Master are clear, [therefore I] am able to perceive them." These "texts" [patterns], whether read in He Yan's manner or together as *wenzhang*, in the manner of Zheng Xuan, were seen since the Han dynasty as a reference to the classics, an opinion shared by Huang Kan.[34]

The classics put together by the Sage are thus clear and readable to one like Zigong. The second sentence marks the difference from the first; what is said about these two items even Zigong does not get to hear. This must refer to the "words," *yan* 言, of the Master. Following Huang Kan's reading, the "Master's words" are "what the *wenzhang* are talking about" 言即文章之所言也. Thus 夫子之言 has to be rendered, "[But] what the

Master is talking ABOUT," namely, as Huang Kan "translates" it, "the pointers the six classics are talking about" 六籍所言之旨. The next part, 性與天道, seems to have been read by He Yan as "human nature and the Way of Heaven," with the common point that both are elusive and not manifest, and therefore even Zigong is unable to perceive them. The translation would be, "[But] what the Master is talking about [in these texts], [namely] human nature and the Way of Heaven [I am] perfectly unable to perceive!" Zigong perceives the texts that have been handed down, but it seems impossible to grasp the deep and subtle things to which they might point.

There were, however, two more readings of this passage, one of them definitely earlier than He Yan. This has been mentioned by Qian Daxin 錢大昕 (1728–1804): "Some say 性與天道 is like saying 'nature is in agreement with Heaven'" 性與天合. He gives some examples for this reading from the *Hou Hanshu*, the separate biography of He Yan's senior contemporary, Guan Lu, quoted in the *Commentary to the Sanguo zhi* and the *Jinshu*.[35] This would result in a translation: "[But] as in the words of the Master [his] nature is in agreement with the Way of Heaven, one is unable to hear [= understand] them." A third reading known from a critique of the previous reading in Yan Shigu's *Commentary to the Hou Hanshu* identifies *xing* 性 as an adverbial *ziran* 自然: "When the *Lunyu* quotes Zigong as saying . . . [above quotation] this means that he [Confucius] does not talk about human nature 性命 and the Way of Heaven, but the scholars have misread this, 學者誤讀, and explain it as 'Kongzi's words spontaneously ['in their nature'] agree with the Way of Heaven" 孔子之言自然與天道合.[36] This last reading seems well in tune with Xuanxue thinking after He Yan and Wang Bi. We see already before Xuanxue started to flourish that the readers were looking for passages in the Lunyu that would explain the Master's use of language and guide the reader to the deeper levels beyond the surface. Zigong's confession that he was unable to understand these deeper meanings served as a warning to the later born about the formidable obstacles in their way.

By including seemingly trivial incidents and statements of the Master, lifted through this inclusion onto the level of major if not easily perceptible wisdom, the *Lunyu* could be seen as a conscious attempt to provide a glimpse of its elusive object by exploding the limitations of language and expanding the means of discourse far beyond simple words. As a record of the Master's performance, it translated his own statements on language into devices of textual structuring. The explicit statements about the undefinability of the Master and his teaching in the *Lunyu* again serve as a guide for the reader to stay focused on the absent center of the text. The easy shimmer of the surface, however, has made this a painfully difficult enterprise for the Master's students, and more so for later commentators.

At the same time, the *Lunyu* could be only a weak and awkward attempt at preserving the traces of what seemed irremediably lost with the death of the last of the Sages. Ban Gu (d. 92 C.E.), who more than anyone else was depressed about the finality of the Sagely dispensations,[37] opens his preface to the book catalogue in the *Hanshu* with the words:

> Since Zhongni [= Confucius] is no more, the subtle words have been cut off 仲尼沒而微言絕. Since the 70 disciples [of Confucius] have departed, [even] the overall meaning [of what Confucius had to say] has become confounded 大義乖. That is the reason why the *Chunqiu* [interpretation] became divided into five [different strands], the *Shi[jing]* into four, and [even] the *[Zhou]yi* has several school traditions. With the conflicts of the *Zhanguo* period, correct and false [theories] were contending here and there, and the sayings of the different philosophers were bubbling forth in utter confusion. When it came to the [establishment of the] Qin dynasty, they loathed this [situation], and thus proceeded to burn and destroy [these] works, with the result [however] of stultifying the black-haired people. Once the Han dynasty had fully established itself [a few decades after its founding in 206 B.C.E.], it changed the destructive [course] of the Qin [which it had continued during the first decades], proceeded to collect writings and records in a great way, and broadly opened the road for presenting manuscripts [to the court]. When it came to the time of Filial Emperor Wu (reg.140–86 B.C.E.) the manuscripts [previously collected] had deteriorated [again] and the bamboo slips [previously collected] were coming apart [again] [with the result] of the rituals being in decay and the music collapsing. The emperor cried out in desperation "I am truly upset!" Thereupon he instituted a policy of storing books, assigned officials for the writing [= copying] of manuscripts, and down to the sayings of the philosophers handed down [by their students] everything was put into the Secret Archive [= Imperial Library].[38]

First, the original dispensation of "subtle words" ceased, then even the broad meaning got thwarted, and eventually the texts themselves were destroyed. The manuscripts and scrolls that were left and had been recollected deteriorated again. Since Emperor Wu, the Han dynasty did its best to have the surviving texts collected, and Emperor Cheng (reg. 32–8 B.C.E.)

proceeded to have them edited by specialists under the direction of Liu Xiang and his son. But while Ban Gu clearly praises these emperors for their actions and mentions that Liu Xiang gave a summary of the purport 指意 of each book after the editing had been completed, the presence of competing commentaries of the classics during his own lifetime prompts a wide lacuna in his description: Ban Gu pointedly fails to mention that the "broad meaning" of the Sage's dispensation had been recovered, or that people had arisen who were capable of uttering "subtle words" in their own right. In his eyes, the Han scholars, all their seeming reliance on the classics notwithstanding, could definitely not claim even a general understanding of Confucius' "subtle words."

In a similar vein, King Zhang, known for his attempts at recovering some of the lost meaning through the imperially sponsored interpretation meeting in the White Tiger Hall, complained in an edict in 83 C.E. about the danger of losing contact with the Sage's subtle words altogether:

> The Five Classics are in shambles; the longer the time separating [us] from the Sage grows, the more the *zhangju* 章句 commentaries forget [the meaning] of [his] statements, so that errors and doubts are [ever more] difficult to correct, and it is to be feared that the subtle words of the late Master [= Confucius] will become completely cut off [from us] 恐先師微言將遂廢絕, and will cease to be the means by which to venerate antiquity and to search for the truth of the Way.[39]

The term *weiyan* 微言, "subtle words," in the sequence of this quotation expanded to a complete *weixue* 微學, "scholarly study of the subtle [words of the Sage]," here refers to oral communication in all the complexity of its contextuality and interaction with other elements such as intonation and gesture, of which the written form is at best a distant and uncouth relative. The term *weiyan* 微言, which might have become a standard attribute of Confucius' communications through Ban Gu's much-read statement, is used in both cases for the Master's elusive oral statements. It might have been taken from an anecdote reported in the *Lüshi chunqiu* 呂氏春秋 and the *Huainanzi* about a conversation between Duke Bai and Confucius, where it refers to a communication beyond words and symbols, as might be used among Sages.[40] It seems that, already toward the end of the Former Han, the earlier optimism of fully comprehending the Sage's teaching gave way to a feeling that his essential teachings were being lost, and that the mushrooming *zhangju* commentaries were more a symptom of this loss than a remedy for it.

With its eighty-one unlinked short *zhang*, the *Laozi* in its turn repeats core features of the structure of the two other texts. Each *zhang* starts anew and takes another angle or example. In addition to this implicit comment on defining and systematic language as a tool of Sagely articulation, the *Laozi* is most explicit in its assessment of language's capabilities in dealing with ultimate things. The statements are well known.

The *Laozi* does not restrict itself to this purely negative description. Thirty-three times the *Laozi* uses the expression *wei* 謂, "[I] call." The standard form, twenty-four cases, is "this [I] call . . . ," 是謂, to be followed by an expression. In the large majority of the thirty-three cases, namely, twenty-five, the expression following the *wei* 謂 refers to a quality of the That-by-which, or the Sage who embodies it. In a number of cases the term following *wei* contains the word *xuan* 玄, "dark," or similar expressions, with no other purpose than to indicate the darkness and abstruseness of the object under consideration, namely, that it cannot be defined by a "name," *ming* 名. From this record, Wang Bi does have a case to impute a conscious use of the term *wei* 謂 to the *Laozi*. As opposed to *ming* 名, a "definition," *wei* 謂 is a way of speaking that does not claim to define its object in its entirety. In many cases the term following the *wei* is not found elsewhere in this meaning. The standard translation "is called . . . " therefore has to be replaced by an "[I] call . . . " Wang Bi will develop this factual use of the term *wei* 謂 in the *Laozi* into a core feature of his philosophy of language, claiming in the process that he is only making explicit the *Laozi*'s implied insights. *Laozi* 25.4 f. says about the "entity that completes out of the diffuse," mentioned in 25.1, that "I do not know its name" and give "it the style 'Way'" and [only] "[when] forced to make up a name for it, I would say '[it is] great'." The term *zi* 字, translated here as "style," stands for *wei* 謂. With the proviso that these are only "ways of speaking," the *Laozi* in fact makes possible a rich communication about the Dao by language. It should be mentioned, however, that the *Laozi* is not absolutely consistent in maintaining the terminological difference between *wei* 謂 and *ming* 名.[41]

The *Laozi* then proceeds to spell out again the makeshift nature of the language used for them. "As they were undiscernible, [I] say, when forced to give a sketch of them: Hesitant [they were] as if crossing a [frozen] river in winter, undecided . . . , formal . . . , brittle . . . , genuine . . . , vast . . . , murky . . ."[15.3]

Beyond these properly announced "ways of speaking," the *Laozi* also uses a great deal of metaphoric and/or onomatopoetic language concerning ultimate things, indicating (in Wang's reading) their diffuseness and inaccessibility in terms of language. The basically untranslatable expressions for the Dao and the Sage who embodies it such as "Vacant it is, alas, still" 寂兮寞兮 [25.2], "deep" 淵兮 and "immersed" 湛兮 [4.1], "intangible it is, but still it exists" 綿綿若存 [6.1], the terms *fine* 微, *inaudible* 希, and *smooth* 夷 [14.1], the "undecided he is" 猶兮 [17.6], or the "vague, ah, diffuse, ah" 恍兮惚兮 and "secluded, ah, distant, ah" 窈兮冥兮 [21.3, 21.4] all merge (in Wang Bi's reading) into the general expression of un-definability. Wang Bi has a case, because the *Laozi* itself gives this basic definition in 15.1, quoted above, and in 14.2, "this One, . . . dim it is and impossible to name" 繩繩兮不可名. All the wealth of onomatopoeia, metaphor, structure, syntax, and makeshift expression is based on the assumption spelled out in the *Xici* that written and spoken words cannot fully express the thinking of the Sage. In Wang's reading, *Laozi* 35 ends with the words:

> Music and fragrant food cause [even] a passing customer to stop. The words [however], uttered about the Way indeed are stale; they are without taste! Looking for it, one cannot manage to see it; listening for it, one cannot manage to hear it; making use of it, it is impossible to exhaust it.

These explicit statements and actual linguistic devices again have to be read—through Wang Bi—as directions to the reader about the proper way of handling the text, because all the denials do not lead to aphasia. The constant reminders about the makeshift character of the statements and terms are to undermine the reader's spontaneous trust in and attachment to the reliability of the surface text and to force him or her into a different strategy of reading; this, all particular differences in the communication devices notwithstanding, is in principle similar to the suggestion in the *Xici* passage above.

The three texts commented upon by Wang Bi unanimously imply and explicitly state the impossibility of defining and thus recognizing in specific terms the Dao and the Sage who embodies it. At the same time, they do not opt for abandoning language as an avenue of communication about the Dao and for an awed silence as the only proper response,[42] although this option was available. They develop particular linguistic, structural, and narrative devices to evoke and point to that which in itself defies definition. The *Zhouyi*, *Lunyu*, and *Laozi* were certainly seen in the third century as being the most philosophical, but they were not considered singular exceptions in terms of the problematic they were addressing. Both the textual structures and the explicit arguments detailed above were present in other texts.

The story of Confucius' editing the classics has made them, despite their often diffuse or trivial surface, into further attempts to deal with the same elusive object. The *Chunqiu* and the *Shijing* may serve as examples.

In the three early traditions, the *Chunqiu* was constructed as a text written against the background of another text, namely, a book of rules for entries into the court's register. A few decades after Wang Bi, Du Yu 杜預 (222–284) systematized this approach, which he described in the preface to his edition and commentary on the *Chunqiu* and *Zuozhuan*.[43] This book of rules seems never to have existed, but its rules can be inferred from the standard practice of the *Chunqiu* itself, and from ritual sources such as the *Zhouli* and the *Liji*.

The explicit statements of the *Chunqiu* are thus only one part of its textual structure; there are things described in the text that should not be, and other things are not stated that one might have expected. And there are also things said in one manner that normally would be stated in another. All of these and more deviations from the "book of rules" hint at the actually intended meaning that the bare surface text would be hard put to yield on its own. In another reading strategy, the *Chunqiu* is read against an equally imaginary book of Yin/Yang/*wuxing* connections, which allows, indeed requires, the controlled translation of the text verbiage into cosmological speculation.

Confucius' presumed editing of the *Shijing*, along with some anecdotes about his strategies of reading the songs, has led to a reading strategy encoded in the *Great Preface*; this again sees the symbolic structures of the textual surface as merely a series of pointers to a different and sociopolitical level of thinking and meaning grounded in the same elusive Dao.[44] In short, the entire body of the classics was seen as unreliable in its textual surface, understandable only in terms of its reference to some higher thinking and meaning whose complexity defied the simplistic contours of language, spoken or written.

The explicit statements about the language of the classics were, rather than complete novelties, a systematization of or reaction to prevailing opinion. Quoting passages from the *Shijing* or the *Zhouyi* in diplomatic or argumentative contexts with a meaning perhaps derived from the textual surface but certainly not immediately evident is well documented from such thinkers as Confucius or Mengzi and such sources as the *Guoyu* or the *Zuozhuan*. To be able to go beyond the textual surface and understand this level of discourse was considered the hallmark of a true scholar. When Zigong, upon hearing Confucius stating the maxim "poor, yet delighting in the Way; rich, yet a student of ritual," quoted the *Shijing* line "as thing cut, as thing filed, as thing chiseled, as thing polished," he claimed that this line referred to the same qualities. In the original context, the surface text of the line seems to describe the beauty of a lover. Zigong's capacity to dissociate himself from this surface text and to see its possible meaning

for the Junzi prompts Confucius' praise: "Now I can really begin to talk
with you about the *Shijing*."[45] Zigong's reference could claim legitimacy
from a commonly accepted reading strategy of the *Shijing* and from the
possibility of reading the entire poem as a metaphor for the self-cultivation
of the Junzi, so that its context would be preserved.

The transformation of certain texts into classics, however, also opened
the way to take them as vast storehouses of maxims for any given situation,
to decontextualize individual statements, and thus to alter their meaning
by inserting them into new contexts. This prompted an exchange in the
Mengzi about the relationship between the overall meaning of such a passage and the particular wording. It produced a maxim that has been of
key importance for later commentators when they were confronted with
seeming nonsequiturs in the surface text, or even passages that did not
seem to fit their overall assumption of the classics' meaning.

Xianqiu Mang questioned the unity of meaning of the classics by
referring to a passage in the *Shangshu* 尚書 in which Emperor Shun is
displeased at seeing his father among the other officials facing north during
the audience; this indicates that he does not see his father as his subject.
Xianqiu Mang then quotes from the poem *Beishan* 北山 from the *Xiaoya*
section of the *Shijing*—a poem that, according to a probably older tradition reported in the *Lüshi Chunqiu*, had been written by Shun himself,[46]
with the words: "In All Under Heaven there is no [place] that is not the
king's land. To the borders of the land, there is none who is not the king's
subject." From this it follows that Shun's father is Shun's subject. This
would leave the classics in contradiction with each other.

In his answer, Mengzi recontextualizes these lines. "That ode definitely
does not mean this 是詩也非是之謂也. It [means] laboring so much in the
king's business one has no opportunity to nurture one's father and mother.
It [means] all of this is the king's business [which should be taken care of
equally by all the grandees], but I alone [am to use my] talent to labor [at
it]."[47] In fact, Xianqiu Mang had left out the line, "The grandees are not
treated equally; I alone am considered qualified to labor in [his] business,"
which confirms Mengzi's reading. From this reinsertion into the original
context it follows that Shun cannot be the author, and that the meaning
of the core clause, "there is none who is not the king's subject," refers
specifically to the other grandees who owe the king their share of services.
In the context of the poem's intention, in which a grandee complains that
he alone is to shoulder all of the king's business, the reading imposed by
Xianqiu Mang is not plausible.

The *Mengzi* then proceeds to spell out a rule for explaining the
Shijing:

That is why those explaining the *Shi* should not on account of a character do harm to a phrase, and not on account of a phrase do harm to the intention [of the poem]. 故說詩者不以文害辭, 不以辭害志. By matching the thinking to the intention—that means to get it! 以意逆志, 是爲得之! [But] if only by means of the phrases 辭 [one matches the intention], there [,to give an example of what would happen,] is that ode The Milky Way, which says "of the black haired people left from Zhou, there is not one left." If we believe this wording, this would mean that no people [at all] are left in Zhou![48]

The example deals only with the second possible mistake, namely, taking the phrasing at face value. The Han dynasty *Mengzi* commentator, Zhao Qi 趙岐 (108–201), points out that the intention of this ode is "to lament the fact that, for the people stricken by natural disaster nothing is left." The wording "there is no one left" thus is literary hyperbole. To take it verbatim would miss or "harm" its intention. We can assume the same with the relationship of *wen* 文 to *ci* 辭. An individual word, or rather, Chinese character, should not get in the way of the consistency of the phrase.[49]

But how does one "match the thinking to the intention" to get it? In the *Mengzi*, it is not absolutely clear whose *yi* 意, "thinking," this is. Is it some general "meaning" encoded in the poem itself, which one has to extract from studying the "intention," which one gets from studying the general meaning of the "phrases," the content of which again is constructed on the basis of the overall meaning of the individual characters? Zhao Qi, for his part, clearly identifies the *yi* 意 as being that of the scholar studying the poem. He says: "People's feelings are not far apart. If with one's thinking 意 one meets the intention of the poet, that is getting what really there is in the [poem]."[50] This reading is supported by the idea that the "thinking" should "meet," *ni* 逆, the intention of the poem, which suggests a meeting from outside.

Mengzi envisages a very complex process of "getting" the "intention" of the *Shijing* odes. Radically speaking, the individual characters are unreliable to the point of getting in the way of the phrases. The phrases are unreliable to the point of getting in the way of the intention. And the intention itself is not spelled out. Individual characters do not have their intrinsic meaning but derive it from their smooth functioning in the context of entire phrases, which in turn are composed of characters. The phrases do not have their intrinsic meaning but derive it in the context of the overall intention, which itself is not stated. The reader thus has to go through the hermeneutic circle of constructing the overall intention on the basis of the available characters and phrases, and then go back to read the phrases in light of the intention, and the characters in light of the phrases.

Mengzi is dealing with the *Shijing*, but his argument does not hinge on its being a text containing the thinking of the Sages but rather on the structure of lyrical communication which, like philosophic communication, handles its absent subject matter through devices that disappear in their particularity in the process of pointing beyond themselves. In practical terms, the Mengzi statement enjoins the reader not to attach himself or herself to the surface verbiage in his or her search for meaning. The reading guidelines outlined by Mengzi, with his stratified move from characters to phrases to intention, largely coincide with the *Xici* statement on the coding of the *Zhouyi* with its appended phrases, words, symbols, and thinking of the Sage. This parallel is stressed by Zhao Qi himself who reads Mengzi's *wen* 文 as *wenzhang* 文章, which "one adduces to bring up an event" 引 以興事 and the *ci* 辭 as "the words sung by the poet," identifying in this manner *wen* 文 as the written and *ci* 辭 as the spoken form.[51]

Zhao Qi also gives a fine example of the close links between the strategies with which a scholar decodes other texts, the presumed strategies he or she uses for coding his or her own texts, and the strategies to be developed by his or her readers to decode these texts. In fact, he must be credited with the discovery of a method later made famous by Leo Strauss in his study of Machiavelli's *The Prince*. Strauss writes:

> We must read him [= Machiavelli] according to those rules of reading that he regarded as authoritative. Since he never stated these rules by themselves, we have to observe how he applied them in reading such authors as he regarded as models. His principal author being Livy, we must pay attention to the way in which he read Livy. His manner of reading Livy may teach us something about his manner of writing.[52]

Zhao Qi tells us in the preface to his *Commentary on the Mengzi* that Mengzi "particularly excelled in the *Shi[jing]* and *Shu[jing]*."[53] His famous statement, "of the 'Completion of War' [chapter of the *Shu*] I accept two or three sections, not more," shows that while he might have been a good student of it, it was not his favorite text; he suggested a similar reading technique for the *Shu* as for the *Shi* when he said, "To completely trust the [surface text of the] *Shu* is worse than having no *Shu* at all."[54] As to Mengzi's own writing, Zhao says:

> Mengzi was particularly good in [using] metaphor, *piyu* 譬喻, [so that] without [his] pressing the phrases, thinking was con-

veyed all on its own. 辭不迫切而意已獨至. He said, "Those
explaining the *Shi* should not on account of a character do
harm to a phrase, and not on account of a phrase do harm to
the intention [of the poem]. 說詩者不以文害辭, 不以辭害志.
By matching of the thinking to the intention—that means to get
it!" 以意逆志, 是爲得之矣! These words probably were in-
tended to alert the later born to deeply strive for his [Mengzi's]
thinking by way of explaining his [Mengzi's] text, and they do
not only pertain to explaining the *Shi*[*jing*]. 斯言殆欲使後人深
求其意以解其文不但施於說詩也.[55]

Zhao Qi extracts his own strategy for reading the *Mengzi* from Mengzi's strategy of reading the *Shijing*. He links Mengzi's coding system to the
triad writing/words/meaning in the first part of the *Xici* statement, and thus
merges the terms *zhi* 志, "intention," and *yi* 意, "thinking," separated in
Mengzi's statement, and he proclaims his own commenting strategy to be
based on the implications hidden by Mengzi in his words about the *Shijing*.
Zhao Qi also takes care of the fact that Mengzi did not write poetry, all
of his metaphors notwithstanding. Modeling himself on Confucius' return
from Wei to Lu to edit the *Shi*, *Shu*, *Zhouyi*, and *Chunqiu*, Mengzi

withdrew from Qi and Liang and set to write about the Way
of Yao and Shun. This was how this great worthy imitated the
Sage [Confucius]. When the crowd of seventy [of Confucius'
disciples] gathered to collect the sayings of the Master, and
made the *Lunyu* out of it, this *Lunyu* was the hub of the Five
Classics 五經之錧鎋 and the throat [through which] the six
arts [had to pass] 六藝之喉衿也. Mengzi's book took this
[*Lunyu*] as a model.[56]

As I have indicated above, the *Lunyu* itself warned in many statements as well as in its form about the inadequacy of language, making it a
communication as elusive and important as the *Shijing*. By suggesting this
twofold model of *Shijing* and *Lunyu* for the *Mengzi*, Zhao Qi reiterated
the structural similarity between their two forms of communication.

The criticism implied in Mengzi's words against those who let the
words and the phrases get in the way of the phrases and the intention, respectively, is taken up in Zhao Qi's polemics against readers of the *Mengzi*
who fell into the same trap:

The crowd of explainers, however, [disregard this hint of Mengzi and] time and again pick out [a phrase here and a phrase

there] to explain him [i.e., Mengzi's thinking], and, to boot, their explanations are in many cases erratic and don't agree with each other. 多乖異不同.⁵⁷

The *Mengzi* argument about language and meaning in the *Shiji* was appropriated by authors such as Dong Zhongshu for the *Chunqiu*. While Mengzi remains fairly technical and pragmatic in his analysis of the *Shijing*'s language, a passage from the *Zhuangzi* approaches the problem of language and Dao from a philosophical angle. It does not repeat the claim of the *Zhuangzi* statements already quoted that no way whatsoever can lead from the written word to the Dao. The passage is from Chapter 26, one of the miscellaneous chapters. In the period between the end of the Han dynasty and the beginning of the Tang dynasty, this short piece became, in the particular spin given to it by Wang Bi, one of the most widely used statements on the relationship between words and thought. While the *Zhuangzi* passages already quoted are comfortable in their rejection of all linguistic communication on the Dao of the Sages as dregs and obsolete traces, they fail to account for the fact that they themselves are part of an extensive written communication precisely about the Dao of the Sages. The following passage begins to deal with this difficulty.

> The fish weir is the means to arrest a fish. Once one has caught the fish, one forgets about the fish weir. The snare is the means to arrest a hare. Once one has caught the hare, one forgets about the snare. Spoken words are the means to arrest a thought. 言者所以在意. Once one has caught the thinking, one forgets about the words. 得意而忘言. Where will I find a man who forgets about words to talk with him? 吾安得夫忘言之人而與之言哉?⁵⁸

In a later reading, the statement lumps into the category "words" both the written and spoken forms, separated in the other examples as in the first *Xici* statement, and confronts them with *yi* 意, "thinking." In fact, the statement does not refer to the classics or to some other text as being a trap; from the last sentence it is clear that it refers to oral communication. This "thinking" again appears as the end of the process, and not as in the *Zhuangzi* passage about the "world's" preference for writings about the Dao, where thinking—insofar as it is thinking about—was merely the most ethereal pointer to that which eludes specificity. The text is part of a series of fragments. There is no immediate context to establish the kind of thinking envisaged by the text. The general context of the *Zhuangzi*, however, and the particular context of the discussion on words and thinking in this work and others strongly suggest that again we are concerned with the problem of articulating the Dao. While this passage does not go as far as the second *Xici* statement with its possibility to "fully exhaust" the thinking, it establishes a connection between these words and the "catching" or "getting" of the thinking.

The imagery of the fish weir and the fish suggests a radical difference between the two, as well as the pure instrumentality of the words in the process. The weir is designed to arrest the fish, which means that some understanding of the fish's nature must go into the design. At the same time, the weir is no relation of the fish; it is not similar to it, but only an instrument to catch something radically different from itself. This is different from the relationship between the written and the spoken word in the second *Xici* statement.

It should be remembered that the Dao is not a fish and not a hare, slippery and elusive as these might be. Even after it has been "caught" in the trap, the Dao cannot be put into a basket and taken home. This is where the "forgetting" comes in.

The statement seems pragmatically reasonable. Once the fish is caught, one might forget about the weir. It has served its function. But in this sense, one might also not forget about the weir; forgetting it or not has no bearing upon one's having caught the fish. As the Dao, however, is no fish, the only thing one really has in one's hand to hold onto, define, and describe after having caught the fish is still the weir. Thus the forgetting of the weir becomes as necessary a part in catching the Dao as the use of the weir. Only by using the weir can one catch the Dao; only by forgetting the weir will what one has caught actually be the Dao and not the weir. The *Zhuangzi* does not develop this argument, which will be done by Wang Bi, but from the last sentence we gather that he was well aware that the forgetting of verbal traps was an essential, and not an incidental, part of their successful use. At the same time, the presence of the trap, as opposed to the ongoing unspecificity of the Dao, made it a natural candidate for the mind to hold onto as a notion and object of discourse. Thus it will be exceedingly hard to find someone able to keep in mind the instrumentality of language in a discussion of the last things, to the point of understanding that only in its disappearance will its elusive object manifest itself. Therefore, *Zhuangzi*'s desperate question: "Where will I find a man who forgets about words to talk with him?"

As opposed to the other statements, this passage opens a way out of silence as the only form of communicating about the Dao. Silence again, it should be remembered, is a specific act of speech, meaningful only in the rejection of the possibility implied in a question about the Dao, namely, that it could be answered by specific words and terms. The most famous example is Vimalakīrti's Buddhist "lion-roar" silence in response to Maitreya's question.[59] In this sense, silence, rather than being the simple absence of speech, is a particular escape from the entrapments of speech, and it belongs to the same category as the other "ways out," described in the *Xici* passage and in this *Zhuangzi* statement. Consequently, silence is not replaced by "later," more complex uses of nondefining language, but it remains one of the possible acts/acts of speech about the Dao.

Still, the differences between the various positions remain important. The *Xici* claims the invention of a technique to "fully exhaust" the thinking of the Sages by written plus structural communication, without entering into a discussion of what is to happen to the devices used in getting at this thinking. Wang Bi was to link the *Zhuangzi* passage on the fish trap to the *Xici* statement and thus transform the former into a statement about reading the classics.[60]

These statements of the *Zhuangzi* about language are analytic. But being a disquisition on the potential of language, they turn into what may be considered the philosophical bases for *Zhuangzi*'s own handling of language which with its stories, riddles, and dark statements, constantly undermines the reader's trust in the validity and reliability of the textual matter at hand; the understanding of the strategies guiding the *Zhuangzi*'s use of language in turn provides the strategies for the reading of this text, consisting as it does of writing and language about the Dao that is not a fish.[61] There are two positions in the *Zhuangzi*; both have been used in later discussions. For the reading of his text, the passage presently under consideration is more important, because it shows that verbalized communication about the Way is possible, but only for someone who, in the process of using words, forgets about all those aspects that are alien to their signifying something beyond themselves.

The *Wenzi* and the *Huainanzi* take up the problem from a different angle. The *Wenzi* writes:

> Laozi says: "He who undertakes affairs acts in accordance with the changes. [As] changes arise out of [the circumstances] of time, he who knows about time does not have a constant way of acting." That is why [it is said in *Laozi* 1.1] "A way that is able to be the Way is an inconstant Way, a name that is able to be the name is an inconstant name." Writings are what sayings bring about. 書者言之所生也. Sayings come forth from the knowledgeable, [but] what the knowledgeable do not know is the inconstant Way. 言出於智, 智者不知, 非常道也. [Thus]

a name that is able to be the name is not contained in books. 名可名, 非藏書者也. "Having heard [= learned] much, one's reasoning will be exhausted; it does not compare to keeping to the middle."[62]

In the following lines, the *Wenzi* quotes from *Laozi* 20 and 19 the famous statement that the abandonment of learning, sageliness, and knowledge will do no harm. In this *Wenzi* passage, the "knowledgeable" are clearly perfectly ignorant as to the inconstant nature of the Dao, while those who "know about time" understand this nature. This passage accepts the triad writing/spoken word/thinking, but only as a dead-end road. The essence of the Dao is inconstancy and change, and therefore the names can be only temporary, in accordance with the circumstances of time. Two elements enter here: an argument against those who claim that solutions for society's problems can come only from returning to old rules contained in the old books, especially the "classics"; and a more cosmological understanding associated with thinkers such as Dong Zhongshu and with the *Huainanzi*, that changes in the seasons and in the constellations of the heavenly bodies constantly alter the circumstances of action so that no fixed parameters can be set. This thinking also prompts the translation of the first line of *Laozi* 1, given above. In this argument the Dao itself is in constant change, and therefore can be described at any given moment in a definite manner, but no definitions are valid across changes in time. The problem of language is thus greatly diffused. The *Wenzi* returns to the same thought in Chapter 2, where it includes a more explicit argument against learned readers:

Laozi says: By just helping the destitute and supporting those in distress, a reputation is being created. By just promoting benefit and warding off damage, achievements are completed. [But] if the time is not [plagued] by disasters, even a Sage will have nothing on which to exert his capacity, and if high and low are on good terms with each other, even a worthy will have no way to establish his achievements. That is why the Supreme Man in his ordering [of society] cherishes capacity and holds on to the Way, promotes truthfulness and rejoices in dispensing grace; concerning his unlimited knowledge he refrains from speaking and does not talk about it, and there is no one in All Under Heaven who knows how to appreciate his not speaking. Thus [,in view of the fact that as *Laozi* says in 1.1,] "the Way that is able to be the Way is an inconstant Way, a name that is

able to be the name is an inconstant name," what is written on
bamboo and silk and carved into metal and stone and can be
transmitted among men are just the crude [external aspects] of
it [the Way]. The Three Emperors and Five Kings were different in their affairs but of the same mind; they walked different
roads, but in the same direction. But the latter-day scholars do
not know what unites the Way and what is the core of capacity;
they hold on to the manifestations [in words] of definite affairs
[of the former Sages] and hold forth on them from their high
pedestal [read 危 for 跪 with *Huainanzi*], and although they are
widely learned and have heard much, they cannot avoid confusion.[63]

The differentiation between those truly knowledgeable and the knowledgeable bookworms was not easy to keep, because the same term was
used. This becomes evident if the first *Wenzi* text quoted above is compared
to its close parallel in the *Huainanzi*.

Wang Shou shouldered his books and went to visit Xu Feng in
Zhou. Xu Feng said: "Someone doing affairs moves according
to changes; changes arise out of [the circumstances] of time.
That is why he who understands time has no constant way of
acting. Writings are what sayings bring about; 書者言之所出
也; as sayings come forth from the [seemingly] knowledgeable,
[only] the [seemingly] knowledgeable hoard writings." 言出
於知者, 知者藏書. Whereupon Wang Shou burned the books
and danced about them. This is why Laozi [*Laozi* 5.4] says:
"By multiplying the words, the reasoning will [only] come to
naught; this does not compare to keeping to the middle"![64]

In this text, the difference between those who know about the changing
circumstances of time and have, in the *Wenzi*'s words, "unlimited knowledge" and the "knowledgeable" is not made clear. There is a memory of
this differentiation, however, in the phrase "the knowledgeable hoard
writings," which only makes sense if these knowledgeable have no real
knowledge, and this is confirmed by the *Laozi* quotation that argues against
making words and thus against the rattling of these pseudo-knowledge-
able. D.C. Lau, seemingly unaware of the parallel passage in the *Wenzi*,
follows a reading of this story given in the *Hanfeizi* and suggests a radical
change, namely, to add a *bu* 不 before the *cang* 藏, which would turn "the
knowledgeable hoard writings" into "the knowledgeable do not hoard

writings."[65] In view of the unanimous textual tradition of the *Huainanzi*
here as well as of the *Laozi* quotation, this does not make much sense. The
Hanfeizi significantly ends his story with another *Laozi* quotation. This
Huainanzi passage actually confirms Sun Xingyan's (1753–1818) earlier
argument that the *Huainanzi* took large parts from the *Wenzi*.[66] The passages in the conversation given by *Huainanzi* look like arguments that
have already been made. The actual story is about Wang Shou's burning
the books and dancing around the pyre as a sign that he is dissociating
himself from his earlier existence of a bookworm who was unaware that
the inconstant nature of the Way ensured that his books could not possibly
contain anything of real value. The passage operates with the familiar triad
of writing, spoken words, and the thinking of the "knowledgeable." With
its claim that "someone doing affairs is moving according to changes," it
undermines the possible validity of books, which can contain the thinking about only one moment of this change and cannot retain this value
for other moments. There still is a Dao that the truly knowledgeable can
understand, but its essence is inconstancy and defies fixation into eternally
valid writings.

The polemic against the classics as a language of eternal validity is
even more explicit in the following *Wenzi* passage, written in interlocking
parallel style:

If the governing of a state has something Eternal, it is that the benefit for the people will be its basic [concern];	If the political teaching has the Way, it consists in the execution of orders being esteemed (read 右 for 古).
As long as there is benefit for the people, [government] does not have to imitate the old.	As long as government affairs are properly taken care of, [political teaching] does not have to follow [established] customs.

That is why the Sage's

laws change with circumstances;	rituals transform with customs; clothing and instruments [for rituals] each are adapted to their use.

laws and systems each fit their purpose.

That is why

it is unavoidable that the old should be changed.	following [established] customs does not count for much.

To recite the books of the old kings does not compare to listening to their words; listening to their words does not compare
to getting that on the basis of which they spoke. Once one has
gotten that on the basis of which they spoke, words are not
capable of saying [what it is]. 誦先王之書不若聞其言，聞其言
不若得其所以言，得其所以言者言不能言也.
    That is why [it is said in *Laozi* 1.1]: "A way that is able to
be the Way is an inconstant Way, a name that is able to be the
name is an inconstant name." That is why that which the Sages
base themselves on is called the Way, and what they do is called
affairs. The Dao is like the metal and stone [musical instru-
ments]; their timbre cannot be changed. The affairs are like the
lute; once the tune is over, the timbre of the sound is changed.
    The laws and regulations, rituals and music are the instru-
ments of [state] order, but not that by which [state] order is
brought about. That is why [as *Zhuangzi* 42/17/6 says] it "is
not possible to talk with a country squire about the highest
Way; he is mired in [prevailing] customs and bound to [prevail-
ing political] teaching."[67]

The familiar dichotomy of the spoken and written word takes on a
new meaning here. The spoken word refers to a given situation; the written word decontextualizes statements by making them permanent so that
they can attain a validity far beyond their actual application. That which
"makes" the Sages "speak" is ineffable; "words are not capable of saying
[what it is]." The reason is that there is not an unchanging entity beyond
reality, but an impermanence that precludes giving a permanent name to
it. At any given moment it can be defined and translated into timely action. Still, as the comparison with drums and stones indicates, it has some
unchanging timbre underlying whatever particular tune might be played
at any given time.
    The passage again has a close parallel in the *Huainanzi*, which has all
of the elements of the *Wenzi* text—the general statement, its application by
the Sage, the conclusion in the first pericope about the written and spoken
words by the Sage, ending with the quotation from the *Laozi* 1, and the
comparison with musical instruments; but it illustrates all of these with
examples. After giving some examples of changing rituals, the *Huainanzi*
writes (parallels to the *Wenzi* are indicated by brackets <>):

Thus, neither ritual nor music ever remained unchanged. That
is why the Sage regulates ritual and music, but is not regulated
by it.

<If the governing of a state has
something Eternal, it is that the
benefit for the people will be its
basic [concern];

If the political teaching has the
Way, the execution of orders
has highest priority.

As long as there is benefit for the
people, [government] does not
have to imitate the old.

As long as government affairs
are properly taken care of, [polit-
ical teaching] does not have to
follow the old [customs].>

As to the demise of the Xia and Shang, they went under while
not changing their laws. As to the rise of the Three Dynasties
[of Xia, Shang, and Zhou], they became overlords while not
mimicking what had been handed down.

<That is why the Sage's

laws change with circumstances;

rituals transform with customs;
the clothing and the instruments
[for rituals] each are adapted to
their use.

the laws and systems
each fit their purpose.

That is why

it is unavoidable that the old
should be changed.

following [established] customs
does not count for much.>

The hundred streams have different sources, but all render
themselves to the same sea. The Hundred Families have different occupations, but all contribute to social order. Only when
the kingly Way crumbled, the *Shi[jing]* was made; only when
the house of Zhou went into decline and ritual and justice fell
apart, the *Chunqiu* was written. The *Shi[jing]* and the *Chunqiu*
are the glory of learning, but both are the product of a declining age. When the Ru [Confucianists] follow these [products
of a decrepit age] in order to give guidance to [our] time, how
could [what they can achieve in this way] ever match the bloom
of the Three Dynasties? They consider the *Shi[jing]* and the
Chunqiu the Way of old and cherish it, but there still is the
[much more glorious] time when neither *Shi* nor *Chunqiu* had
been made! The crumbling of the Way does not compare to its
completeness; <to recite the books of the old kings does not
compare to listening to their words; listening to their words
does not compare to getting that on the basis of which they

spoke. Once one has gotten that on the basis of which they
spoke, words are not capable of saying [what it is]. That is why
[it is said in *Laozi* 1.1] "a way that is able to be the Way is an
inconstant Way; the name that is able to be a name is a inconstant name.">

The *Huainanzi* then goes back to the original argument about the
necessity to change laws and rituals, and it describes the Duke of Zhou,
who behaved in three completely different ways according to the times,
playing first the "capable son" for King Wen, then the "capable military
man" for the infant King Cheng, and finally the "capable minister" once
Cheng had come of age. The *Huainanzi* concludes, generalizing the observation made about the "Sage" Duke of Zhou:

> <That is why that on which the Sages base themselves is called
> the Way, and what they do is called affairs. The Dao is like
> the metal and stone [drums]; their timbre cannot be changed;
> the affairs are like the lute; once the tune is over, the timbre
> is changed. The laws and regulations, rituals and music are
> the instruments of [state] order, but not that by which [state]
> order is brought about.> Thus that humaneness is taken for
> the woof and justice for the warp is something that does not
> change for ten thousand generations. But as to people's check-
> ing the potential [of humaneness], and circumstances' looking
> out for what [justice] might be utilized, this can be done even
> with daily changes. How should there be an eternal law under
> Heaven? Proper order becomes possible by adaption to contem-
> porary affairs, by keeping to human principles, by following
> Heaven and Earth, and by sacrificing to spirits and gods.[68]

With regard to language, the two texts have two propositions in common. First is that the basis on which the Sages make their words in which
they proclaim what should be valid at a given time and in a given context
cannot be articulated, and therefore is not to be found in the words written
in the classics. Second is that the classics are strictly irrelevant, because
what can be found there is only of antiquarian interest. The *Huainanzi*
adds a third element in saying that the classics are in fact products of
a declining age, perhaps attempts to stem a further decline. If anything
might be worth imitating, it would be the time "before" there was either
a *Chunqiu* or a *Shi*.
   Both texts are written against a counter-text associated with the Ru.
The Ru claim that the texts administered by them are the only valid basis

for social order, and they aim to establish their specialty routines of textual, canonical interpretation as the basis of all matter—political, ethical, and philosophic. Both texts argue that while a basic "temperament" is maintained unchanged, actual political measures should fit the changes of the time. The Sagely dispensations of antiquity receive validation by being described in terms of cosmic and seasonal changes, while the claim for the eternity of the written word is denounced as antiquarianism and uninformed nostalgia for a time that had, in fact, been far from ideal.

While the counter-text targeted by the *Huainanzi* might be the *Gongyang* or *Guliang Commentary on the Chunqiu* with their antiquarian bent, Dong Zhongshu's *Chunqiu fanlu* 春秋繁露 managed to integrate the interpretative needs of the new Han dynasty for a unified dispensation with the imperatives of a textual reading that was well enough argued to convince others. He maintained the validity of the classics as a basis of political philosophy but created a much greater leeway for analysis by arguing that these texts were "difficult." For example, he said about the *Chunqiu* that, "as its statements embody the subtlety of Heaven, they are difficult to understand" 其辭體天之微, 故難知也.[69] Against a challenger who pointed out inconsistencies in the *Chunqiu*, he argued:

> The poems [from the] *Shi* you hear have no clear-cut speech 所聞詩無達詁, the [*Zhou*]*yi* [you hear] has no clear-cut words 易無達言, and the *Chunqiu* [you hear] has no clear-cut statements. 春秋無達辭.[70] One [has to] follow the changes and follow the meaning and unify [them] in order to act in accordance with Heaven's [commands]. 從變從義 而一以奉天.[71]

With this argument, Dong Zhongshu in no way undermined the authority of the canonical texts. The opposite is true. With the blunt statement, "Affairs all follow the[ir] names, and the names all follow Heaven" 事各順於名, 名各順於天,[72] he made it quite clear that the subtle concepts used by the Sage were much closer to the ultimate cause of entities, Heaven, than was reality itself, and that reality only "followed" these Heaven-ordained "names which are that by which the Sages explored the intentions of Heaven."[73] Their study, the interpretation of the canonical texts, thus provided the only access to truth.

Fixing the construction of the meaning of a text is a difficult process. Dong Zhongshu is not talking about varying exegeses, that is, an instability of the text in its interaction with the reader, but of an intrinsic instability in the textual surface of speech, words, and phrases. "In discussing events nothing is more important in the *Chunqiu* than the intention, *zhi*

志," he writes.[74] This intention is that of the historical actors and does not necessarily become visible in their action. According to the *Gongyang* and Dong, the *Chunqiu* will list someone as a murderer because he did not prevent a murder or did not persecute the murderer with a vengeance when he should have done so.

> People of old had a saying: "If you do not know the future, look at things past." Now the *Chunqiu*, taken as a field of study, consists in talking about the past to throw light on the future.[75]

This is the "subtlety of Heaven," encoded in the *Chunqiu*, which makes it so hard to understand. The linguistic surface looks bland for the stupid: "If one lacks the ability to investigate [the *Chunqiu*], it is as if there was nothing to it." But for those able to handle this complex communication, every word is full of meaning:

> For those who have the ability to investigate [the *Chunqiu*], there is nothing that it lacks. That is why, if those who work on the *Chunqiu* understand one [positive] feature and link it in multiple ways perceive one lacuna 見一空 and fill it amply, All Under Heaven is fully [explored].[76]

Obviously, the *Chunqiu* scholar will deal not only with the manifest features, *duan* 端, of the text but also with the meaning of its "non-writing," with specific absences of descriptions or terms normally expected. For these, Dong Zhongshu introduces the term *kong* 空, "empty space" or "lacuna." This duplication of the text into present and absent text, which is at the basis of all three *Chunqiu* traditions, greatly enhances the reader's chances to homogenize the textual message. In another passage, Dong Zhongshu describes in some detail the painful processs of decoding the *Chunqiu*, which enables the reader to completely "read out" and eliminate certain passages:

> The *Chunqiu*'s treatment of the events of 12 generations is superabundant with the Way of men and complete as to the Way of kings. The model is spread out throughout the 242 years. By putting together similar things a pattern is established and what does not fit [this pattern] is not in conformity with antiquity. That is why those dealing with the *Chunqiu* penetrate that which homogenizes it 合, search for the connections, compare

what is similar in it, pick out its classes [of similar things and events], check its connections, and wipe out its repetitions.[77]

The process of reading the text in all its hallowed authority is strained by the imperatives of homogeneous and applicable knowledge. This involves, as Yu Dunkang says, quite "brazen" interventions into the text,[78] beginning with the duplication of present and absent text and ending with the establishment of a master pattern, deviations from which will be considered negative and repetitions excised. The linkage of the meaning of the text to the Heaven-ordained changes means that the difficulty in reading the classics is not the ineffability of the ultimate but the changing contexts within which the texts must operate and to which they must constantly be adapted. There is no ultimate unified meaning but a constant pattern of change on which to draw for lessons about the future. In a more generalizing manner, Dong Zhongshu takes the hint from Mengzi's treatment of the *Shijing*'s language and applies it to the *Chunqiu*.

> The words are not able to achieve this [to communicate the complex thought of the *Chunqiu* about the fundamental injustice of wars, and the occasional necessity to wage them], all is in what [the *Chunqiu*] is pointing at. 辭不能及皆在於指.

In this sense,

> he who sees what [the *Chunqiu*'s expressions] are pointing at, will not put the weight on the [particular] words, and only if he does not put the weight on its [particular] words, will it be possible to go along with it [the *Chunqiu*] on the Way." 見其指者不任其辭不任其辭然後可與適道矣.[79]

Access to the Dao, as embodied in the *Chunqiu*, is thus dependent on not staying tied to the words that are to provide this access. Wang Bi was to develop this thought further, which is close to the fish trap argument in the *Zhuangzi*.

Present as options for Wang Bi, we have thus:

- the radical position that maintains that the language of the classics does not and cannot provide any access to the thinking of the Sages;

- the position that stresses the referential quality of written words, spoken words, symbols, and even thoughts, imputing to the classics complex devices to circumvent the limits of defining language;

- a position that claims that change or inconstancy is a feature of the Dao itself, so that an antiquarian search for an unaltering meaning of the Dao in the classics starts out from a misapprehension of the Dao's nature; a correct understanding would lead to a reading of the classics that is adapted to the requirements of the time and circumstances. While this latter reading also stresses the difficulty in understanding the classics and polemicizes against an antiquarian misunderstanding of them, it fails to provide a philosophic reason for their form and the ensuing difficulty in understanding them. Through Dong Zhongshu's espousal of this approach, this reading is closely linked to the political uses of classical learning during much of the Former and Later Han dynasties. By shifting the problem from language to the Dao itself, it also refocused attention away from language, so that theoretical discussions about language's capacity to handle the thinking of the Sages are rare in Han literature.

With the end of the Han dynasty and the removal of imperial patronage from the approach pioneered by Dong Zhongshu continued by the Later Han,[80] a revival of many of the pre-Qin schools and discussions occurred.[81] In the meantime, however, a number of important changes had occurred that made this revival a new beginning.

- Han cosmology had put the exploration of a unified system of the world onto the agenda, which would explain the operations of nature and society through one common mechanism.

- This mechanism was thought to be perfectly known to the Sage who had made the classics, and thus could be extracted from a reading of these classics.

- The classics had become the main source of truth, so the importance of their proper understanding had grown immeasurably.

- The various attempts at a unified explanation of the classics—sometimes even with direct imperial intervention, as in the discussion in the White Tiger Hall in 79 C.E.—had in fact led to a profusion of different and internally rather inconsistent interpretations based on ever more complicated constructs and, to boot, a plethora of textual variants and new texts, the *chanwei* texts, that all claimed to contain the true or secret teaching of the Sage. The profusion of these variant readings undermined this line of inquiry philologically. The end of the Han undermined it politically.

THE DISCUSSION ABOUT LANGUAGE
AND
THE THINKING OF THE SAGE IN WEI

The new post–Han discussions about language took up the pre-Qin discussions. In pre-Qin times, however, language had barely been a topic in itself and had been confined to random remarks; after the end of the Han, language was reconsidered in light of the dramatic new importance given to the classics during the long centuries of the Han dynasties. We now see efforts to broach the subject of language's ability to express the thinking of the Sage in a much more theoretical and systematic manner. This development is paralleled in the field of lyrics, where the first theoretical treatises appear at about the same time dealing with the "particle of art" beyond literature's pragmatic uses.[82]

The positions outlined in the *Zhuangzi* and the *Zhouyi* were among the first to resurface. Probably before the end of Wendi's reign in 226,[83] the following controversy is reported in He Shao's biography of Xun Can 荀粲 (ca. 212–240 C.E.) to have taken place among the young scions of the famous Xun 荀 clan from Yingchuan, descendants of Xunzi:

> [Xun] Can's brothers all argued on the basis of the Ru techniques 儒術, and Can alone loved to talk about the Dao.[84] He maintained that, as Zigong 子貢 claimed, "the words of the Master concerning human nature 性 and the Way of Heaven 天道 [we] are unable to hear" [as reported in *Lunyu* 5.13], the Six Classics, although [as opposed to the Master himself] still around, were definitely nothing but the dregs of the Sage.
>
> His older brother Wu objected: "As the [*Zhou*]*yi* also says: 'The Sage[s] set up images in order to fully [express their] thinking, and appended [written] statements [to them] in order to fully [express what they] had said'; how can one say that one is not able to hear and see the subtle words 微言 [of the Sage]?" [Xun] Can answered: "The subtlety of the ordering principle 理之微者 cannot be brought out through images of things 物象. If now [the *Zhouyi*] speaks about [the Sages'] setting up images in order to fully [express their] thinking, [it remains true that] these [images] will not penetrate to the meaning beyond the images,[85] and if [it speaks about the Sages] appending [written] statements in order to fully [express what they] had said, [it remains true] that these will not speak about

that which is beyond such appendages. Thus the thinking beyond the images 象外之意 and the words beyond the appendages 繫表之言 remain definitely hidden and do not emerge.[86]

As detailed elsewhere, the *Lunyu* itself already records the apprehen-
sions of the Master's students, that his true teachings were inaccessible
or incomprehensible to them.[87] Xun Can refers only to the best-known
example, the Master's teaching on human nature and the Way of Heaven.
To him, these are the only relevant topics. He interprets Zigong's remark as
saying that the Master's thinking about these issues could not be expressed
in terms of language and thus links it to the discussion about the ability of
language to express the Sage's thinking. In fact, this statement by Zigong
proves to him with the authority of a "classic" that the Sage, well aware
of the iniquities of language, did not leave his insights on the core issues
to be written down. This line of argument is even more radical than that
of the most radical *Zhuangzi* passages, which do, like Wheelwright Bian,
describe an alternative access to the Dao. Xun Can's argument furthermore
has the strength of an insight encoded into the behavior of the Sage himself.

His brother does not deny that human nature and the Way of Heaven
are the most revelant topics. He was, however, attached to the "techniques
of the Ru," that is, the technique of interpreting the classics by means of
the Yin-Yang *wuxing* system dominant during the Han. One other brother,
Xun Yi 荀顗 (205–274), in fact defended this system of interpreting the
Zhouyi against the challenge of Zhong Hui 鐘會, who argued against
Zheng Xuan that "the *Zhouyi* has no overlapping trigrams."[88] This attachment would mean that Xun Wu, like Xun Yi, was reading the terms *human
nature* and *Way of Heaven* within the cosmological model, where "Way
of Heaven" regularly refers to heavenly portents of luck and distress.

Both brothers agree that the mysteries of the universe or of Being [and
not moral or ritual details] are at the core of the Sage's thinking. Xun Wu
uses the phrase "the subtle words [of the Sage]" 微言 for these teachings
of the Sage, going back to Ban Gu's lament discussed earlier. For him, the
Ru techniques are quite capable of getting at the subtle words of the Sage.
He counters his brother's classical quotation from the *Lunyu* with one
from the *Zhouyi*, namely, the statement in the *Xici* that the structures of
the *Zhouyi* have been set up for the very purpose of fully expressing the
subtle words of the Sage, so that their study is the proper access to the
Dao. He reiterates the claim made by the *Xici* concerning the form of the
Zhouyi and extends it by implication to the other classics.

Xun Can counters, now on the authority of his own argument, that
the structure made up of symbols and appended statements, although

capable of a higher complexity than simple written words, still remains bound to the confines of the objects used in symbols and the terms used in the appended statements, and thus it is unable to express "the subtlety of the ordering principle" 理之微. The traditional notions of "human nature and the Way of Heaven" dealing with the human world and the cosmos, respectively, are now merged into the term *li* 理, which describes the de facto orderly arrangement of nature and society as well as the elusive principle on which it rests.[89] As the ordering principle, it must be "beyond" that which it orders and thus cannot be fully represented through it. It is thus "subtle" 微, a forerunner of the later word "dark," *xuan* 玄. The texts that had hitherto been read as ritual, moral, and historical guides, operating within a system of preset correspondences between nature and society, are being reconstituted here as inquiries into the fundaments of Being, whose seemingly innocuous form is due to their conscious attempt to circumvent the iniquities of language in dealing with this subject.

Xun Wu's reference to the *Xici* passage about the *Zhouyi*'s use of images and appended sayings as a means to express the thinking of the Sage is defensive. It concedes that this classic is the main source for these elevated thoughts and leaves leeway for a reading of this text as a philosophic work, while firmly rejecting the idea that the classics cannot provide access to the ultimate truth. Xun Can's second statement reinforces the notion that the only relevant topic is the principle ordering the ten thousand kinds of entities, but it seems to close off any avenue of reaching this principle through the reading of any of the classics. This lands him in a seemingly agnostic position, more radical than the *Zhuangzi*'s.[90] However, another section of He Shao's *Biography of Xun Can* quoted elsewhere says instead of the phrase that Can "loved to talk about the Dao," that "Xun Can was a capable conversationalist on the subject of the Dark and Remote," *xuanyuan* 玄遠, a statement reiterated by the *Shishuo xinyu*.[91] Obviously he was able to make statements on this "dark and remote" Dao or ordering principle and thus used some form of communicating about the Dao. Is Xun Can the first to claim that his own "subtle words" may match the meaning of the Sage?

Sources probably going back to the fourth century use the term *weiyan* 微言 for the philosophic aphorisms and statements made by philosophers such as Wang Bi during the *zhengshi* era (240–248). The *Jinshu*, for example, says:

The Director of the Imperial Secretariat Wei Guan 衛瓘 (220–291), a senior member of the [Jin] Court, had formerly partaken in discussions with the famous scholars of the *zhengshi* era [240–245]. When he met [Yue] Guang 樂廣 (252–304), he was

stunned by him and said: "For a long time the worthies [of the
zhengshi era, R.W.] are no more, and I was always afraid that
the subtle words would break off 恐微言將絕 until now when
I have again heard such words from you.[92]

In Wei Guan's view, the "famous scholars," *mingshi* 名士, of the
zhengshi era were able to produce such "subtle words" themselves. There
is a constant danger that these subtle words would "break off," a danger
already mentioned by Emperor Cheng and Ban Gu. The same thought
and terminology are found in a eulogy of the famously pale and ethereal
"jade man," Wei Jie 衛玠 (286–312), by Wang Dun 王敦 (266–324):

Formerly, Wang Fusi (= Bi) poured forth the "[opening] sound
of the metallic [instruments]" at the central court [in the Wei
capital] [to set the tone], and now you [Wei Jie] come up again
with the "[final] beat of the [musical] stone" beyond [= south
of] the river [Changjiang] [to conclude]. The continuity of
subtle words had been interrupted, but [now with you] the link
is restored. 微言之緒 絕而復續.[93]

The expression used here, Wang Bi's pouring forth "the [opening]
sound of the metallic [instruments]," *jinsheng* 金聲, and Wang Jie's "[final]
beat of the [musical] stone," *yu zhen* 玉振, comes from Mengzi's praise of
Confucius' ultimate perfection 集大成 as a Sage. The metallic instruments
set the tone of the musical sequence in the beginning, and the musical stone
concludes it. In the same manner, Confucius encompasses the beginning
and end of Sagehood.[94] Wang Dun is not claiming that either Wang Bi or
Wei Jie was Confucius' equal but does claim that the two together might
fill this role with their subtle words.

While the Han authors claimed that the generation of the "subtle
words" of the Sage's oral philosophic communication had ended with his
death, they mostly still implied that a memory of it was somehow alive,
so that there was only the "danger" of this insight's being lost altogether.
The scholars praising the *zhengshi* era, on the other hand, claimed that
such "subtle words" on ultimate things were spoken during that time,
perhaps matching the acumen of the Sage. In this line of thinking, the only
way the Sage's insights could be kept alive was by way of their reproduction through the very same forms he employed—the subtle spoken words
beyond all verbiage, namely, the famous "pure words," *qingyan* 清言, or
"pure conversations," *qingtan* 清談. Wang Baoxuan argues convincingly
that the reasons can be found here why these short bursts of oral philosophy were more highly appreciated during the Wei and Jin than written

tracts or even commentaries and brought more fame to their authors.[95] Confucius did not write a book but communicated—and could only communicate—his insights through "subtle words." The scholars of the Wei and Jin followed in his tracks.

There was constant apprehension that the chain transmitting these insights through the reiterated and ever-new creation of such words had broken or might break, and that the insights might be lost altogether. We find it in the efforts of Emperor Chengdi to improve the faltering understanding of the classics and in Ban Gu's efforts to list the works elucidating the classics, and it is revived in the rejoicing of Wang Dun and Wei Guan at the capacity of the *zhengshi* scholars and those emulating their model to generate "subtle words." As is shown elsewhere in this book, their appreciation of the Sage as an event of ontohistorical (*seinsgeschichtlicher*) importance did not prevent the brilliant young minds of the third and fourth centuries from playing with the idea that their own thinking might be of the same ontohistorical importance, and that one of them, or all, might qualify for the rank of a Sage, ushering in a new dispensation of Great Peace.[96] Wang Baoxuan has cited some sources that indicate that the "famous scholars," *mingshi* 名士, of this period not only saw themselves reaching the second highest level on Ban Gu's ninefold scale but even sometimes went so far as to consider themselves in many respects on a par with the last man on the highest pedestal, Confucius himself.[97]

From these later sources, we return to Xun Can's statement. He does not argue that the "subtlety of the ordering principle" is utterly inexpressible, he only argues that the constructs of the *Zhouyi* as depicted in the *Xici* cannot penetrate to the realm "beyond images" and "beyond words." The surviving historical records credit Xun Can with having been the first to stake such a haughty claim of being able, with his own words about the "dark and remote," to attain the Sage's insights that the classics could not transmit. Xun Can's importance lies in the vehement radicalism with which he defined the new dilemma, namely, the fundamental difficulty of language in dealing with the ontological basis of the ten thousand kinds of entities. This is no mere sigh about the limitations of language, no comment about the essential inwardness of sagely insight; his statement on the "subtlety of the ordering principle" marks the transition from the wisdom discourse of the pre-Qin period to the philosophic discourse of the Wei. Having defined the problem in a philosophic way, he proceeded to debunk the source that hitherto had been considered the one and only access to the Sage's insights, the classics. He radically questioned the capacity of the transmitted written record of the classics, of "the dregs of the Sage," to provide access to the core of his/their thinking. As a consequence of his own argument, he himself had to exclude the judgement, *lun*, and commentary as proper forms of philosophic inquiry.

His radical position, which "capable conversationalists [of his time] were unable to refute," as He Shao writes,[98] opened the way for a new and daring form of philosophic thinking. It also increased the pressure on the essays and commentaries dealing with the "dregs of the Sage" to prove that from these dregs ontological insights could indeed be gained, and that commentaries did not have to restrict themselves to word glosses or cosmological speculation.

Most later scholars, however, were not as exclusive as Xun Can. The "famous scholars" of the Wei and Jin did engage in the creation of "subtle words" but seem to have viewed them as only one of several possible ways of talking, acting, and thinking about the new problem of philosophy. Practically all of them also wrote commentaries and essays. Some, like He Yan, experimented with psychedelic drugs, perhaps to enhance their capacity to produce such "subtle words," many of which were collected at the time and eventually survived in the *Shishuo xinyu*.[99] Some also used metaphysical or landscape poetry,[100] painting,[101] calligraphy,[102] music, or handicrafts as a means of philosophic exploration, and the ultimate and most reduced form of philosophic communication became the humming of the sound *su* 嘯, which negated the articulation potential of even the "subtle words."[103]

For Wang Bi, however, writing just twenty years after this debate, Xun Can's triple radicalism in terms of the core of the Sage's thinking, the incapacity of the classics to transmit it, and the necessity to reapproach it through subtle words matching those of the Sage presented a formidable challenge to his project of reading the *Zhouyi*, the *Lunyu*, and the *Laozi*; a challenge greater than the tradition of the "Ru techniques," which at least conceded that the classics fully expressed the meaning of the Sages even if, in Wang Bi's view, they misconstrued them.

Xun Can was in close contact with many of the famous scholars of the time, among them Fu Jia 傅嘏 (205–255), Pei Hui 裴徽 (fl. 230–249), and Xiahou Xuan 夏候玄 (209–254), all of whom also had discussions with Wang Bi after Xun Can's death. In the development of the thinking about the language of the classics, Xiahou Xuan played a pioneering role. A relative of the ruling Cao family in Wei, he also was connected by marriage to the Sima clan. His personal name *xuan* 玄 was as much a philosophical program as his *zi* 字, which was *taichu* 太初 "ultimate origin." He ranked among the most brilliant intellectuals of the decades 230–250. The *Eulogies on the Gentlemen of the Jin* (Dynasty), *Jin zhugong zan* 晉諸公贊, claims that Xiahou Xuan wrote a *Dao De lun* 道德論,[104] but this should rather be read as a general title "A Judgment on Dao and De." The *Eulogies* give a list of such tracts that begins with Xiahou Xuan and Ruan Ji and then jumps down a generation to Yue Guang 樂廣 (253–304) and Liu Mo 劉謨. From this we may infer that Xiahou Xuan's tract was written before He Yan's, which is not mentioned here and must be dated about 247. For Ruan Ji, no tract entitled *Dao De lun* is listed elsewhere, and the reference is probably to his notes on the *Laozi* and the *Zhouyi*, the *Tong Lao lun* 通老論 and the *Tong Yi lun* 通易論, both of which are commonly dated in the *zhengshi* era (240–249).[105] From this it follows that Xiahou Xuan's tract predates those by Ruan Ji, He Yan, and Wang Bi and must have been written somewhere between 235 and 247 C.E. Neither the date of the text from which the the following quotation is taken can be ascertained, nor its title. In terms of content, it is likely to have been written during the 230s. The quotation is included in Zhang Zhan's early fourth century *Liezi* commentary on a phrase in the chapter on Confucius, where Confucius describes the only person who might be or might have been a Sage:

> Among the people of the West there is a Sage. He does not govern and [thus] there is no disorder; he does not speak, and [thus] is spontaneously trustworthy 自信; he does not reform [the people] and [thus what he wants] is done spontaneously [by them]. So vast is he that none of the people were able to give a name to him. 蕩蕩乎民無能名焉.[106]

The last statement by Confucius is a verbatim quotation from *Lunyu* 8.19, where Confucius says this about Emperor Yao, who "as a ruler" was "matching Heaven." By reassigning this text to the Sage from the West and by making his political program explicit, the *Liezi* brings out a potential in the *Lunyu* passage that had become buried under the honors piled on Yao as a founder of civilization. The excerpt from Xiahou Xuan's tract, which must have dealt with the *Lunyu* passage here, runs as follows:
Xiahou Xuan says:

Heaven and Earth endow by means of That-which-is-of-itself-what-it-is.	The Sage makes use of That-which-is of-itself-what-it-is.

That-which-is-of-itself-what-it-is
is the Way. The Way is fundamentally
without name.

That is why

Mr. Lao [= Laozi] says [in 25.6 about the "entity that creates out of the diffuse" and to which he gives the personal name "dao"] "only	Zhongni [Confucius] said about Yao [*Lunyu* 8.19] that he was "so vast that none of the people were able to give a name to him."

if forced to make up it a name for
it" [this would be "great"].

[But when Confucius] continues:[107] "Majestic" [Yao] is and
"completes achievements," [this means that] "forced to make
up a name for him,"he takes for a designation, *cheng* 稱,
[something] familiar to the world.
    [Because] how could it be that [Yao] had [in fact] a name but
one still had to say, "No one was able to give a name to him"? In
fact it is exactly because of his [/its] namelessness that he [/it] can
all-encompassingly be named with all the names in All Under
Heaven, but how should [anyone of them] be *his* [*its*] name?
    This should be sufficient to convey an understanding, but if
someone still does not grasp it, he would be like someone gaz-
ing at the lofty peak of Mt. Tai and saying that the original Qi,
yuanqi 元氣, was not vast and endless.[108]

Xiahou Xuan establishes the concept of Ziran 自然 as the That-by-
which allowing the forces regulating nature and society, that is, Heaven
and Earth, and the Sage, to function. There had been statements in the
Lunyu, the *Zhouyi*, and the *Laozi* about the Sage's taking Heaven as his
model, but the systematic stringency with which the parallel use of Ziran
by Heaven/Earth and the Sage is delineated here signals a new beginning,
the attempt at systematic philosophy. The terminological diffuseness, where
Ziran is identified with Dao and both correspond to Xun Can's "subtlety of
the ordering principle," is characteristic both of the groping after a proper
way of articulating philosophical issues and of the particular structure of
the problem that "fundamentally" does not allow for fixed names.
    Like Xun Can, whose criticism of the "techniques of the Ru" does not
come from a Daoist attachment but from a concern with the Dao beyond
the schools, Xiahou Xuan sees Confucius and Laozi as philosophers sharing the same insights about Ziran. He easily juxtaposes quotations from
the *Lunyu* and the *Laozi*, explaining one by means of the other. In this
manner, he also rejects Xun Can's absolutist statement about the classics,
because evidently the classical texts, if only read properly and stripped of
the interpretive constructions into which they have been forced, will provide proper ontological insight. The language used by at least the *Lunyu*
and the *Laozi* about the Dao is nondefining in a conscious sense. Because
of its unnameability, any way of talking about it with "designations familiar to the world" is legitimate. More detailed disquistions on the topic
by Xiahou Xuan do not survive, but from this short quotation a reading

strategy for these texts can be extracted that would take their insight into the nature of language and their ensuing strategies into account. Far from just being the "dregs of the Sage," they are carefully crafted philosophic texts for those who can read them. They give an idea of what is meant, as the peak of Mt. Tai might convey an idea of the immeasurable vastness of the Original Qi.

In the same commentary passage, Zhang Zhan quotes a lengthy excerpt from He Yan's 何晏 (ca. 190–249) "Judgment on Namelessness," *Wuming lun* 無名論. The biographical and bibliographical sources do not list a text by He Yan under this name. It must have come from the *Dao De lun* 道德論, the two tracts written by him on Dao and De, respectively, when he decided to scrap his *Laozi Commentary* after having heard Wang Bi explain this text; this situates these tracts in or shortly before 247.[109]

I.

Once someone is praised by the
people, he is one who has a name.   If there is no praise, he is one
                                       without name.

II.

                    If, however, one says [in view of the
                    act that] the Sage has

the name of being nameless   and   the praise of being without praise,

                    that the

nameless is the "Dao"   and   the praiseless is "great"

                    [as the *Laozi* does in 25.5 and 26.6,
                    where he gives it the *zi* "dao" and the
                    ming da, "great,"], one may [in this
                    sense] say

of him who is nameless that he has a
name,   and   of him for whom there is no
                                      praise, that he has praise,

                    but is the use [of these words] the
                    same [as when they are used] for
                    those who [in fact]

                                      can be praised and
can be named? [No.]

III.

This compares to [the fact] that [exactly] because of [being something] without anything that it has, it has everything that it has, but that within that which has what it has, it has to follow that which is without anything that it has, and thus to be different from that which has what it has. 此比於無所有故皆有所有矣而於有所有之中當與無所有相從而與夫有所有者不同. [Things] of the same category correspond to each other regardless of their distance; [things] of a different category will diverge from each other, regardless of their closeness [read 無近而不相違 for 無近而相違].[110] This compares to the Yang 陽 within the Yin 陰 and the Yin within the Yang—each of them strives after and follows its own according to the category of things [it belongs to, namely, Yang follows Yang, and Yin follows Yin]. The summer day is Yang; the [summer] evenings, however, are over the distance together with the winter days Yin. The winter day is Yin; the [winter] dawn, however, is over the distance together with the summer day Yang. Both are different from what is close [to them], and go together with what is distant. Once one has clearly understood this type of difference and congruence, one will be able to understand the theory of namelessness. Generally speaking, what is it that brings this [namelessness] about? The Dao, in fact, is that which has nothing that it has. 夫道者惟無所有者也. From [the great entities like] Heaven and Earth downwards, all [entities] have [something] they have. 自天地已來皆有所有矣. Thus, if one talks about them [Heaven, Earth, and so forth] in terms of the Dao, it is because of their being able again to make use of that which has nothing that it has. 然猶謂之道者以其能用無所有也. Therefore [del. 雖] [the fact that because of their] residing in the realm of that which has names their feature of namelessness disappears, is due to [the same process in which] because of their residence near [read 近 for 遠[111]] the Yang, it is forgotten that [the summer eves] by themselves belong to the distant category of Yin. 故處有名之域而沒其無名之象由以在陽之近體而忘其自有陰之遠類也.[112]

The two excerpts by Xiahou Xuan and He Yan show a common framework of discussion. They share an ontological agenda that includes the soteriological figure of the Sage, as well as a number of texts they consider

relevant to this discussion, and they have a common problem of hermeneutics—how to read these texts. We shall focus on this aspect.

He Yan begins with establishing a fundamental difference between
defining speech and the tentative use of expressions for the Sage who, as
the *Liezi/Lunyu* passage claimed, cannot be defined by a name and is thus
unspecific and unnameable. He Yan also works with the parallel Sage/Dao
by referring to the *Laozi*'s statements on the Dao in his discussion of the
"definition" of the Sage. He establishes two realms—the realm where
praise and fame can be meted out, and the realm where this does not apply.
The Sage is defined from the outset as he who is without fame and praise.
The two realms, however, are not neatly separated, because all possible
words belong to the realm of the specific; on the surface, the difference
between the description of a Sage and of a worthy minister can hardly be
perceived, although it is fundamental. This is precisely the problem with
reading the classical texts. Their surface seems innocuous enough to invite
a flat reading. Although these words about the Sage and the Dao appear in
the environment of similar words about minor and definable issues, they
are fundamentally different. The former speak about the unspeakable,
the latter about that which they can define. They require entirely different
reading strategies.

He Yan now proceeds to a two-tiered comparison. He first compares
this relationship between the nameable and the unnameable to the ontological relationship between the new philosophic concepts presented by
him here, *wu suo you* 無所有 and *you suo you* 有所有. Then, in turn, he
compares the relationship between these two with that between the summer
day and the winter dawn, and the summer eve and the winter day. The
second comparison is easier to crack, and we begin here. The summer eve
is close to the summer day, which is Yang. Far from being Yang, however,
the summer eve belongs to the same category as the winter day, which is
Yin. The same is true for the winter dawn and the summer day, both of
which are Yang. In the same manner, Heaven and Earth as well as the Sage
are residing among specific entities. They "have something they have,"
you suo you 有所有, but can fulfill their function within the entities only
by "following," *cong* 從, or "making use of," *yong* 用, the unspecific that
"has nothing that it has," *wu suo you* 無所有, defined here as the Dao,
and by being in fact different "in category," *lei* 類, from the surrounding
specific entities.

The last phrase is, sadly, corrupt. It runs:

Therefore [delete 雖] [the fact that because of their] residing in
the realm of that which has names their feature of namelessness disappears, is due to [the same process by which], because

of their residence near [read 近 for 遠] the Yang, it is forgotten
that [the summer eves] by themselves belong to the distant category of Yin. 故處有名之域而沒其無名之象由以在陽之近體
而忘其自有陰之遠類也.

I have offered my emendations. They are not based on manuscript or
quotation evidence but on textual logic. He Yan's text itself is struggling
with language in the attempt to create an instrument for the expression of
new thoughts. Therefore, such conjectures cannot even rely on standard
uses of terms, arguments, or grammatical patterns. If again we move from
the easier to the more difficult, we take the second part of the phrase first.
This second part argues that, because a summer eve with its Yin nature
is in such proximity to the summer day which is Yang, its Yin nature is
easily forgotten. In the same manner, as the nameless (Sage, and so forth)
is being stationed linguistically among the definable, its true nature of being nameless and undefinable is easily disregarded or "drowned," if we
translate 沒 in its original sense.

He Yan thus suggests a split in language. The defining language pertaining to the realm of that which "has something that it has," 有所有, and
the tentative language suggesting the radical otherness of that "which has
nothing that it has" 無所有. He discovers the reason why that which is
the basis of all the 有所有 specifics might be "forgotten" and "drowned":
it has, all its difference notwithstanding, neither linguistically nor onti-
cally another "place" 處 than in the midst of the overwhelming presence
of the specific. This fact is responsible for the misunderstanding of the
coded messages of the Sage and the forgetting of the dark root of the ten
thousand kinds of things.

Little of the writings of the Xuanxue scholars preceding Wang Bi survives. From the few fragments we have studied, it seems that most of the
important questions had already been developed or were in the process of
development when Wang Bi joined in. No one of the senior scholars such
as He Yan or Xiahou Xuan had devised a system or a school teaching
with its own social dynamics, so during these few years a rather unique
intellectual openness prevailed in which daring young newcomers such as
Wang Bi had a chance.

Wang Bi was familiar with the philosophical debates of his time and
took up many of these new ideas. He developed, however, what had been
tentative and still vague new notions into a highly sophisticated, detailed,
and cohesive analysis. We are concerned here with his writings on the
Laozi. In fact, his tract on the structure of the *Laozi*, the "Structure of the
Laozi's Subtle Pointers," *Laozi weizhi li lüe* (*LZWZLL*), devises a very
specific strategy of reading this text, based on an exact understanding of

the form of philosophic communication used here. Wang Bi assumes that the *Zhouyi* proceeds in quite a different way, and therefore his analysis of the structure of the *Zhouyi* deals with different, though not entirely unrelated, issues. The presentations of Wang Bi's theory of language, however, have been almost exclusively based on one section of his *Zhouyi lüeli* 周易略例, which develops *Zhuangzi*'s fish-and-hare-trap simile.[113] No study has been made of his rather more systematic attempts at unraveling the philosophic communication in the *Laozi* and the *Lunyu* and integrating them into the arguments in the *Zhouyi lüeli*.

Wang Bi's primary concern is not a general theory of language but the particular ways in which the Sage and his close second, Laozi, used it to deal with issues beyond the pale of language. His analysis is therefore no frivolous exercise but rather an attempt to save these texts from the charge of being just the dregs of the Sage and to make them accessible as philosophical texts.

THE STRUCTURAL CONTRADICTION OF THE CONFUCIUS TEXTS: TALKING ABOUT THAT-WHICH-IS-DARK

The texts for which Wang Bi wrote commentaries and structural analyses, the *Lunyu*, the *Laozi*, and the *Zhouyi*, can be read as explicitly and repeatedly stating the inability of cognition and language to "name," that is, define, the Way or the Sage.

Despite this insight into the elusiveness of their subject, the texts continue in their effort. Confucius cannot be defined and "named," but the *Lunyu* is a book about him. The *Laozi* claims that neither the Dao nor the Sage can be defined but continues to talk about them. The *Zhouyi* is described in the *Xici* passage quoted above as an attempt to circumvent the inability of the spoken word (and more so the written word) to express fully the thinking of the Sages through the most elaborately structured silent propositions contained in the relationships within the hexagrams.

Each one of the Confucius texts—and all three were read by Wang Bi as such—focuses on a certain realm of entities or structures through which to approach what is seen as their common dark object. As detailed in the chapter dealing with "The System of the Classics" in my *The Craft of a Chinese Commentator*, this was true for the entire body of the classics in the reading of Wang Bi and many of his contemporaries.[114] The *Shangshu* and *Chunqiu* took documents and history as their material; the *Shijing*, lyrics; the *Zhouyi* constructed its language in the hexagrams; and the *Lun-*

yu and the *Laozi* dealt with the Sage and the principle he embodied. The texts dealt with by Wang Bi share the structural feature of consisting of short and independent sections, a structure read by Wang Bi as a reaction to the shared insight into the limits of linear and systematic discourse.

Given the assumed abstruseness and elusiveness of the Dao and the Sage, the relevance of dealing with them at all might be questioned. What is the irritant forcing the philosopher to focus on them? After exclaiming that Yao was so vast that none of the people were able to name him, Confucius continues in *Lunyu* 8.19, "majestic he was [however] in his achievements!" What are juxtaposed here, namely, his majestic achievements and the incapacity of language to define him, might have deeper philosophical links. Obviously, Yao has the achievement of having created social order, and therefore it is as imperative as it is difficult to find out how he achieved it. In the same manner the Dao in all its abstruseness is assumed to be the basis, the "ancestor" of the ten thousand kinds of entities. The relevance and urgency to understand the Sage and the Way in times notoriously without either are directly proportional to the difficulties standing in the way of such an understanding.

THE LOGICAL DEDUCTION OF THE UNNAMEABILITY OF THAT-BY-WHICH THE TEN THOUSAND KINDS OF ENTITIES ARE

Wang Bi opens his "Structure of the *Laozi*'s Subtle Pointers" (*LZWZLL*) with the following argument:

It is generally true with regard to

that by which things are created— that by which achievements are
that [things] are necessarily created brought about—that [achieve-
out of the "featureless"; ments] are [necessarily] based
on the "nameless."'

The featureless and nameless is
[what the *Laozi* 4.1 calls] the "ancestor
of the ten thousand kinds of entities."[115]

Each of the two chains on the left and the right deals with one of the two great realms of entities. The first is that of material entities, *wu* 物, and the second encompasses social processes, usually referred to as "affairs," *shi* 事, from which the word here, "achievements," *gong* 功, is derived. Together they form the "ten thousand kinds of entities." In the ensuing passage, Wang Bi quotes further dispersed statements from the *Laozi* to insert into his systematic treatment of the elusiveness of this "ancestor":

[Being featureless,] it neither warms nor cools.

[Being nameless,] it neither [lets sound forth the notes] *gong* or *shang*.

[Even when] "listening for it," one is [still] unable to "hear it."

[Even when] "looking for it," one is [still] unable to perceive it.

[Even when] groping for it, one is [still] unable to identify it.

[Even when] going after its taste, one is [still] unable to get its flavor.

That is why [the *Laozi* says about the Dao]

"as a thing" it "completes out of the diffuse," as an "image" it is "without form";

as a "sound" it "has an inaudible tone," as a "taste" it is without flavor.

That is why it is able to be the "principle" and

the "master"

of all [different] categories of entities, to cover and permeate Heaven and Earth so that there is nothing that it does not thread through.

In these lines, Wang Bi systematizes into one stringent and unified chain of arguments propositions made by the *Laozi* in a variety of places. He uncovers in the terminology used by the *Laozi* in these different passages concerning "that by which" the ten thousand entities are a silently implied deep structure. The *Laozi* does indeed mention in different places the inability of the four senses to get hold of the Dao, and it also assumes the division of the ten thousand kinds of entities into two realms, for which it uses a variety of terms. But at no point are these two sets matched and systematized into an epistemological proposition as they are here.

Wang Bi has now made two propositions—that the shapeless and nameless is what the *Laozi* calls the ancestor of the ten thousand kinds of entities, and that this "ancestor," "master," or "principle" can be ancestor, master and principle of all the variegated ten thousand kinds of entities only *because* it is without feature and name and thus imperceptible to the senses. The second argument marks a dramatic advance. The undefinability of this ancestor is not the occasion for a distressed mystical sigh but is described as "necessarily" following from its function as the ancestor of the diversity of the ten thousand kinds of entities. The undefinability is not a function of the deficiency of language and cognition but of the structure of the ontological difference itself.

Still, Wang Bi needs to prove why the *wu*, the "things," should "necessarily" be created out of the featureless, and the achievements based on the nameless. He proffers this proof in the subsequent passage through a *reductio ad absurdum* of the opposite proposition.

[For the fact is,]

would it be warming, then it would not be able to cool.

would it [be tied to letting sound forth the note] *gong*, then it would not be able to [let sound forth the note] *shang*.

[This is so because]

a form necessarily has something that specifies it.

a note necessarily has [a place in the scale] to which it belongs.

That is why [according to the *Laozi* 41.13 and 41.14]

an image that has taken on form is not the "Great Image."

a sound that has taken on a note is not the "Great Sound."

The specificity of entities that is the basis for their being recognized and defined ("name") is illustrated by Wang Bi through the extremes of the antonyms warm/cool and *gong/shang*. It is a necessary consequence that the "ancestor"—if he be *one*—of both great realms of entities, which themselves are antonymic, and again are internally structured by antonyms, must be devoid of such specific features. Were this ancestor specifically to produce one of these entities, he would be bound by this specification and could not produce its opposite. It follows that the "that-by-which" mentioned in the first line must be characterized by the complete absence of any of the specific features of any entity in order to be able to be the "ancestor," "master," or "principle" of all. The argument is based on a single premise, namely, that a One be the basis of the ten thousand kinds of entities.

The necessary inability of language, insofar as it denotes and defines specific entities, to handle this "ancestor" of the ten thousand kinds of entities is thus not grounded in some insufficiency of language but in the ontological difference between the "That-by-which" of the ten thousand kinds of entities and these ten thousand kinds of entities themselves.

Wang Bi's basic approach is similar to Xiahou Xuan's and He Yan's, however, a difference is that he elaborates and proves what they observe. Wang Bi accepts the *Laozi*'s statements as based on a provable philosophic insight. His argument itself, however, is not deduced from the *Laozi* and not supported by any authority other than the stringency and strength of its own logic.

THE DEDUCTION OF THE POSSIBILITY OF LIMITED BUT SUFFICIENTLY GROUNDED PROPOSITIONS ABOUT THAT-BY-WHICH THE TEN THOUSAND KINDS OF ENTITIES ARE

In his famous exchange with Pei Hui, which must be dated at about 243 and thus well before the *Laozi* commentary, Wang Bi came out with the radical statement that "the Sage [= Confucius] embodies negativity. One is not able to explain negativity [by language]. Therefore [the Sage] did not explain anything about it." The term *negativity*, *wu* 無, is the most radically unspecific notion for the "That-by-which" in Wang Bi. At the same time, Wang Bi derided the *Laozi* for continuing to talk about negativity: "Therefore, that he [*Laozi*] obstinately talks about negativity is exactly his deficiency."[116] Wang Bi suggests that the Sage has other ways of communicating. Having once immersed himself deeper into the *Laozi*, he finds that this text is well aware of the pitfall and that it makes an effort at salvaging language as an instrument of communicating philosophic insight. Seen from the *Laozi commentary*, the harsh and bold statement in the discussion with Pei Hui has been mellowed, because Wang Bi's own enterprise focuses on saving language, philosophic language, as a limited but indispensable means of philosophic communication through the extrapolation of relevant philosophic insights from such texts as the *Laozi*.

Again, Wang Bi does not base this claim concerning the tentative viability of language for ontological discussion on the authority of the *Laozi*'s actual use of language. This viability must be grounded in the very same ontological relationship that prevents language from defining the "That-by-which." What, then, is the condition for the possibility of pointers to the "That-by-which" within the ten thousand kinds of entities?

Wang Bi continues:

If, however,

the Four Images did not take on form, then the "Great Image" would have nothing in which to shine forth; 四象 不形 則大象無以暢.	the Five Sounds did not take on notes, then the "Great Sound" would have nothing in which to come about 五音不聲則大音 無以至.

The notions of the Great Image and the Great Sound appear as "established sayings" quoted from elsewhere in *Laozi* 41.13ff in conjunction with the Dao:

> The Great Sound has an
> inaudible tone.

The Great Image is without form.

> [In short, all these "established sayings"
> mean to say:] The Way is hidden and
> nameless. In fact, [however], it is only
> the Way that is good at providing as
> well as good at completing.

Wang Bi comments that "all these 'great' things are made up by the Way. Among the images, [the Way] is the Great Image, . . . among the sounds it is the Great Sound." The *Laozi* repeats here the double feature of the Dao as being nameless and formless while at the same time being "good at providing as well as good at completing," at being the "That-by-which" of the ten thousand kinds of entities. Thus there is an interaction between the ten thousand kinds of entities and the Way as their "That-by-which." The Way does not "exist" as a separate entity beyond other entities, as do Heaven and Earth; it exists only as their "ancestor," "principle," or "master." So it "shines forth" and "comes about" in and through the manifold specifications of the ten thousand kinds of entities. In a sense, it "depends" on the specificity of the specific entities in order to be as their "negative" "That-by-which"; without the specific entities, it "would have nothing" in which to "shine forth" and "come about."

The consequences of this interrelationship are ontological as well as epistemological. The ten thousand kinds of entities, insofar as they exist, and exist in an ordered fashion, manifest the traces of their "That-by-which." Their "That-by-which" does not appear there as one of them but as their radical difference.

The entities in themselves are structured. There are "great" entities, specific only in one feature such as Heaven, which "covers" all other entities, or Earth, which "carries" them. Their lack of specificity allows them to exert their function on all specific entities. The lower the level of their own specification, the closer they are to that which is beyond all specification. But there also are entities of a lower order that repeat, in their relationship with a more strongly specified multitude, the basic features of the relationship between the "That-by-which" and the ten thousand kinds of entities.

Wang Bi thus provides an ontological reason why it should be possible to get any cognizance at all of this "That-by-which" from specific and definable entities. This cognizance cannot be in the first order of language, namely, definable terms and grammatically closed statements, but can only come in a second order of language, which speaks in a tentative, heuristic, and terminologically unreliable manner. In Wang Bi's reading, the texts for which he writes commentaries and analyses contain a fairly systematic screening of the realm of entities as well as knowledge/perception/language for the hidden traces of this "That-by-which." They are read as a series of makeshift pointers to an elusive center. This eliminates the systematic treatise as a viable form of philosophy. The literary structure of the *Laozi* and the *Lunyu*, with their short, unrelated statements, and the formal organization of the *Zhouyi*, with its complex layers of structural, symbolic, and verbal communication, are read as conscious attempts to establish a viable if technically unreliable way of speaking about the "That-by-which." The focus will be on the *Lunyu* and the *Laozi*.

TRACES OF THE THAT-BY-WHICH FOUND BY THE CONFUCIUS TEXTS WITHIN THE STRUCTURES OF DISCERNIBLE ENTITIES: ANTINOMY AND NEGATION

Wang Bi discovers that the Confucius texts make philosophic use of two different types of opposites, namely, antinomy and negation. *Lunyu* 7.37 runs:

> The Master [Confucius] was
mild, but stern
> authoritarian, but not brutal
> formal, but relaxed.

Wang Bi comments:

> He who is mild is not stern. He who is stern is not mild.
> He who is authoritarian is necessarily brutal. He who
> is not brutal is not authoritarian.
> He who is formal is not relaxed. He who is
> relaxed is not formal.

These [mild and stern, authoritarian and not brutal, formal and relaxed] are eternally [fixed] terms which are opposed to each other 此對反之常名也. However, if somebody

> is mild and nevertheless able to be stern,
> is authoritarian, but able not to be brutal,
> is formal, but able to be relaxed,

then this marks the perfection of the principle of unnamability 斯不可名之 理全矣.[117]

The *Lunyu* is describing Confucius here in contradictory terms. Wang Bi calls these "names," *ming*, that are "eternally fixed in opposition to each other." These terms are opposed to each other, *duifan* 對反; they mark two extremes from an imagined middle zero. They cannot be applied to the same person at the same time. Still, the *Lunyu* does apply them to Confucius. What might, on the surface, look like a fairly innocent exercise at describing the complex figure of Confucius is read here as a communication in the second order of language.

Wang Bi argues against what he sees as the shallow commentaries available hitherto, that this simple statement in the *Lunyu* implies an easily overlooked philosophical insight. Confucius is described in terms that exclude each other. The laws governing normal defining discourse collapse before the challenge of his person. It might be the implied purpose of the *Lunyu* statement to celebrate this collapse, or the statement might be a record of an unresolvable puzzle in the minds of Confucius' disciples, who note their inability to define their master in homogeneous terms without necessarily having understood the reasons for the collapse of their language. Confucius is a Sage beyond the reach of definite names. The communication of the phrase quoted does not come through the successful application of language but through the collapse of this effort in the form of contradiction. According to Wang Bi, the collapse of defining language in depicting

Confucius communicates to the reader that the Master has reached "the perfection of the principle of unnameability," which also applies for what he embodied, the Dao itself. The same collapse of language is celebrated for the Dao in the *Laozi*, where terms such as "big" and "small" (34.2, 3) and many more complex notions that exclude each other are applied simultaneously. Wang Bi goes through them in his *LZWZLL*.[118]

The discovery of this type of opposite that Wang Bi defines as *duifan*, "antinomy," opens the way for the discovery of another even more important type. While the concurrent use of antonym propositions for the Sage simply explodes the logic of cognizance and language and illustrates in the process the nature of the Sage and the principle he embodied, the second type of opposition repeats in a derived and recognizable form the structure of the relationship between the "That-by-which" and the ten thousand kinds of entities.

Commenting on the hexagram *fu* 復, "Return," of the *Zhouyi*, Wang Bi writes:

> *Fu* means returning to the root. Heaven and Earth take the root as their core. Generally speaking, once movement dies away, calm comes about, but calm is not the antonym of movement 靜非對動者也. Once talk dies away, silence comes about, but silence is not the antonym of talk 默非對語者也.[119]

Movement and calm and talk and silence are not antonyms on the same level, deviating in opposite directions from a median zero. Calm and silence are the negation of speech and movement. They are defined by the very absence of all the possible specificity of their opposites. The relationship between calm and movement and silence and talk is not static, however. Movement starts from the calm and "naturally" returns to it. Movement is manifold and specifically defined, while calm is simple absence of movement and thus not specifically or positively defined. The same holds true for silence and talk. In each of these two pairs, one is the point of departure, and of return. It is undefined and simple as opposed to the specificity and manifoldness of the other. It does not "exist" by itself, but only as the negative root of the specified forms. On an observable and specific level, these pairs repeat the relationship between the "That-by-which" and the ten thousand kinds of entities, which is why the terms *silent* and *calm* are used in these texts to indicate the nature of this "That-by-which."[120] Through his commentaries, Wang Bi reveals to the reader that these are not just helpless attempts to talk about the unsayable but philosophically reasoned terms based on an examination of the traces of the "That by which" within the structures of observable entities. The indicative, nondefining nature of the propositions about the "That-by-which" also is evident from Wang Bi's explanation. Both silence and calm come into view only *in* the rise and disappearance of their opposites. Relating his observation to the negative opposites of his original topic, the "root" from which Heaven and Earth arise and to which they "return," Wang Bi writes in his commentary to hexagram *fu* after the lines quoted above:

> Thus, even though Heaven and Earth are great and amply contain the ten thousand kinds of entities, even though the thunders roll, the winds race, and the ten thousand kinds of entities follow each other, their root is calm supreme negativity. That is why, when movement comes to rest "in Earth," [as the *xiang* 象 to this hexagram says with the words 雷在地中復也 "when thunder settles in the Earth, this is return"] the "heart of Heaven and Earth" becomes "visible" [as the *tuan* 象 to this hexagram says with the words 復其見天地之心乎 "return—that is the making visible of the heart of Heaven and Earth!"]. But were [Heaven and Earth] to take an entity as their heart, the different species would not manage to keep up their complete [and simultaneous] existence.[121]

Heaven and Earth belong to the category of "great" entities marked by one feature only, thus they are very "close" to the complete negativity of the "That-by-which." This enables them to "amply contain" 富有 the ten thousand kinds of entities, because they themselves are not partial to any one of them. Their "root," defined here as 寂然至無, calm supreme negativity, becomes "visible" in the thunder's coming to rest in the Earth, that is, in the very disappearance of the manifold manifestations of the specific.

Wang Bi began his statement on movement and language and silence and calm with a "generally speaking," *fan* 凡. In his language, this announces a general statement not restricted to the immediate passage commented upon. We are not restricted to this single passage, however. Having outlined the framework, I now document in more detail the fairly widespread use of language derived from negative opposites for the description of the "That-by-which." Wang Bi never fails to make this relationship explicit, thus imploding the multitude of propositions into one single argument.

This documentation is designed to support an argument. The examples are to substantiate Wang Bi's assumption concerning the basic unity of the Confucius texts as so many attempts to point, with the help of various structures within the realm of entities, to the same "That-by-which." With their interpretation, Wang Bi tries to prove that they do have a common agenda and understanding.

Laozi 26.1 runs:

The heavy is the basis of the light.	The calm is the lord of the impetuous.

Wang Bi comments:

Generally speaking with regard to entities,

the light cannot support the heavy, the small cannot press down the great.	that which [itself] does not act makes [others] act, that which [itself] does not move controls the movement [of others].

That is why

the "heavy" must by necessity be the "basis of the light."	the "calm" must by necessity be the "lord of the impetuous."[122]

In the specific context of this chapter, the chain on the left dealing with heavy and light refers to the relationship between the "heavy" baggage train and the "light" troops, where the baggage train with its provisions and arms forms the "bases" for the troops. Without entering here into a discussion of the political aspects of the second chain about the calm and the moving, it is obvious that in both cases the Laozi is read as operating with negating opposites, even if, on a formal level, they do not fit the mold entirely. The correspondence is achieved by applying this opposite to a real-life situation, where indeed the heavy train provides the wherewithal for the troops. As a consequence, the Laozi says, "The Sage never leaves it." In a variety of other expressions, Wang Bi discovers the same pattern. The term *muddy*, or *diffuse*, *hun* 混, in the first phrase of Laozi 25, 有物混成, "there is a thing that completes out of the diffuse," is in fact a negating opposite of another type. It marks the imaginary zero between the two extremes, in this case of the translucent and the completely impenetrable. Wang Bi comments: "Diffuse it is and [thus] undiscernible, but the ten thousand kinds of entities base themselves on it for their completion."

The statement "the Great Sound has an inaudible tone" 大音希聲 in Laozi 41.13 is interpreted by Wang Bi as follows:

[As Laozi 14.1 says] "That which [I] do not hear when listening for it, [I] call 'inaudible.'" It [the Great Sound] thus is a sound one is unable to hear. Once there is a [particular] tone, it will have specifications, and if it has specifications it will [let sound forth the note] *shang* if it does not [let sound forth the note] *gong*. Being specific it could [in this case] not encompass the entire multitude [of notes]. That is why that which has taken on a specific tone is not the Great Sound.[123]

The term *xi* 希, which means "hardly," and here the "in-" in "inaudible," is read by Wang Bi as the negation of all possible specific tones; only by being negative in this sense can the Great Sound encompass all possible specific tones. The "Great" in this context is beyond the confines of the antonym great/small. The surrounding propositions in this chapter of the *Laozi*, that the "Great Image is without shape," and that "the words uttered about the Dao are flat and without taste," are read in the same manner by Wang Bi. In this context, Wang Bi also can refer to the proposition of Confucius about the *zhong* 中, the "middle," which became the cornerstone of Confucian ethics in the *Zhongyong* 中庸.[124]

According to *Laozi* 15.1 ff., the description of "those in antiquity who were well-versed in the Way," that is, the Sages of old, is not possible in direct language. The *Laozi* uses a true avalanche of comparisons, all of which denote the zero middle between two specific opposites. These Sages are "hesitant," *yu xi* 豫兮, like someone who crosses a [frozen] river in winter, "undecided," *you xi* 猶兮, like someone who is afraid of his four neighbors and does not show against whom he will turn first in order to keep the others at bay; they are "formal," *yan xi* 儼兮, like a guest, "brittle," *huan xi* 渙兮, like ice that is about to melt, "genuine," *dun xi* 敦兮, like an uncarved block, "vast," *kuang xi* 曠兮, like a valley, and "diffuse," *hun xi* 混兮, like muddy water. Wang Bi comments:

> Generally speaking, these "they were like," *ruo* 若, all mean
> that one is incapable of [assigning a specific] shape and name to
> their countenance.

The terms already encountered in Confucius' admiring words for Yao in *Lunyu* 8.19, such as *tangtang* 蕩蕩, "vast," and *weiwei* 巍巍, "majestic," as well as the many statements by the disciples about the Master, belong to the same category. In a characteristic technique, Wang Bi implodes them into a single meaning, that one is incapable of assigning a specific shape and name to either the Dao or the Sage.[125]

The relationship underlying all of these examples as their common element is that between the One and the Many, the simple unspecified One and the multitude of specific entities. A number of passages in the *Laozi* are read as dealing explicitly with the relationship of the "That-by-which" with the ten thousand kinds of entities in terms of the One and the Many.

The text of *Laozi* 11.1 runs according to Wang Bi:

Thirty spokes share one hub. But it is the [latter's] negativity [vis-à-vis the specificity of the spokes] that is [the basis] for the usability of the existing carriage.

Wang Bi comments:

That-by-which a [= one] hub is capable of holding together thirty [different] spokes is its negativity [vis-à-vis their specific features]. Because of this negativity [the hub] is capable of taking in the points of origin of [many different] entities. That is why [the hub] is capable, being itself the minimum, to control the many [spokes]!

According to Wang's reading, this insight determined the feature in many hexagrams of the *Zhouyi*—that there is one line dominating the others.[126] The structure of the *Zhouyi* thus implies the same insight as the statements made by the *Laozi* and the *Lunyu*.

Wang Bi thus discovers and brings out through his commentary that, in addition to the overall form, the language and the comparisons of the texts he is working on are informed by an attempt to find structures in reality that mirror and manifest the relationship of the "That-by-which" to the ten thousand kinds of entities. He finds those structures in the use of negative opposites, middle zeroes between two opposites, and generally in all relationships between the One and the Many. These traces prove for him that these texts were written and crafted as attempts to circumvent the pitfalls of defining language while committed to an effort to prevent the collapse of philosophic communication into mystical silence. Thus these texts present for those who can read them a possible way of philosophic speech; they present "subtle words," while having to concede the tentative and heuristic nature of their pronouncements. Wang Bi does not restrict himself to noting and explaining these actual uses of language; he also tries to conceptualize them in a radically new exploration.

GRASPING ASPECTS OF THE
THAT-BY-WHICH

Although Wang Bi sees negativity 無 as the real philosophic issue in the texts he writes about, both these texts and Wang Bi himself repeat the impossibility of approaching this subject with *ming* 名, "definitions." The *Laozi* and the *Lunyu* consist of approximating, indicative statements, elucidating for Wang Bi various aspects of the "That-by-which." They achieve this end through the use of negations that still retain in their very negation of something specific an element of cognizance.

Wang Bi reduces the wealth of negative statements about the "That-by-which" and the Sage in the *Laozi* to a small number of basic aspects. Each of these aspects, he writes, "has its meaning, but does not exhaust the totality [of the 'That-by-which']" 各有其義未盡其極者也.[127] To differentiate between the operation delineating such an aspect and the act of definition, Wang Bi creates another artificial expression, *qu yu* 取於, "is taken for."[128]

In his commentary on *Laozi* 1.5, Wang Bi treats the word "Dark," *xuan* 玄:

> As to the "Dark," it is obscure, is silent without [any] entities, is that which lets the "beginning" and the "mother" emerge. It is impossible to give a definition [for this Dark], therefore [the *Laozi*] cannot say "their common [source] is defined as 'the Dark,'" but [only] says "[I] designate as . . . [the Dark]." The [term] "Dark" is taken for 取於 that [aspect of the ultimate principle] that it cannot be designated as being thus [and nothing else]. Should one designate it as being thus [and nothing else], it would definitely not be permitted to define it as one [specific] Dark. If one were to define it as being one [specific] Dark and nothing else, this would be a definition, and that would be far off the mark.

With the neologism *quyu*, "is taken for," Wang Bi stresses the provisional and makeshift character of the term then following. In his commentary to *Laozi* 25.5, "I give it the style 'Way,'" Wang Bi writes:

> It is a fact that a name is something to define the shape [of an object], while a style is something to designate what is sayable. The Way is taken 取於 for [the aspect of That-by-which all

entities are] that there is no entity which is not based on it. This is the greatest among the sayable designations concerning "that which completes out of the diffuse." 是混成之中 可言之稱最大也

Two aspects of the "That-by-which" thus emerge, *dao* 道 as the aspect that all entities are based on it, and *xuan* 玄 as the aspect that it cannot be discerned. As has been shown, these aspects condition each other. The other terms attached to the "That-by-which" in the *Laozi* in a seemingly random fashion are systematically grouped together by Wang Bi as subcategories of these two basic aspects. In his "Structure of the *Laozi*'s Subtle Pointers," Wang Bi writes:

"Dao" is taken for [its] [aspect] of being that on which the ten thousand kinds of entities are based. 道也者取乎萬物之所由也.

"Dark" is taken for [its aspect] of being that which lets the Recondite emanate. 玄也者取乎幽冥之所出也.

"Deep" is taken for [its aspect] that, [even] when "delving into the abstruse" [in which according to the *Xici* the yarrow stalks and tortoise shells excel,] it is impossible to get to the bottom of it. 深也者取乎探賾而不可究也.

"Great" is taken for [its aspect] that, [even if] one "fills it in and rounds it out [ever more]" [as the *Xici* says that the Yi does concerning the Way of Heaven and Earth], it is [still] impossible to get to the ultimate point. 大也者取乎彌綸而不可極也

"Distant" is taken for [its aspect] that it is so wide and remote that it is impossible to reach it 遠也者取乎綿邈而不可及也.

"Fine" is taken for [its aspect] that it is so recondite and fine that it is impossible to perceive it 微也者取乎幽微而不可視也.

Thus of the words

"Dao,"   "dark,"
                                           "deep,"

"great,"   "fine" and
"distant"

each has its meaning, but does
not exhaust its totality. 各有其
義未盡其極者也. Thus,

it is impossible to give to that which   it is impossible to give to that
one "fills in and rounds out [ever   which is fine and subtle and
more]" without getting to the   without form, the name "great."
ultimate point, the name "minute."

That is why the [*Laozi*] chapters [25.5
and 1.5] say:

"I give it the style 'Dao,' 字之曰道"

          and   "I designate it as the Dark,"
                                     謂之曰玄,"

but no *name* is given 而不名也.[129]

Wang Bi argues that the terms used in the *Laozi* for the different aspects of the "That-by-which" have a tentative and heuristic nature; they "are taken for" this aspect or another of the "That-by-which." In consequence of their not being definitions, *ming,* they can disregard the rule governing definitions, namely, that mutually exclusive qualities cannot be ascribed to the same subject at the same time. The "That-by-which" must be described as "great" in one aspect and as "minute" in another.

The argument itself repeats the regular structure of Wang Bi's analysis of the *Laozi.* He develops a theoretical and systematic argument that is fully reasoned out, and he concludes it with a phrase starting "that is why" and ending with a description of what the *Laozi* does. In this case, the *Laozi* says that the two main aspects of the "That-by-which" in Wang's analysis, Dao 道 and Xuan 玄, are described only in a tentative and nondefining manner, 字之曰, and 謂之曰. Accordingly, Wang Bi implies with the last words that all of the arguments he has made above were perfectly familiar to Laozi and were the very reason he should have used these formulae. Wang Bi only makes the implied logic underlying the *Laozi*'s statements explicit and understandable.

Wang Bi proceeds to extract from the *Laozi* a terminology for these different kinds of statements, calling the traditional definition a *ming* 名 and the heuristic proposition a *cheng* 稱 or *wei* 謂. The terms did exist in the language before him, but in a fairly loose, unspecific state.[130] From the existing record, it seems that Xiahou Xuan was the first to use them in a clearly distinct way, similar to that of Wang Bi. In the tract quoted above, he writes: "[But when Confucius] continues: 'Majestic' [Yao] is and 'completes achievements,' [this means that] 'forced to make up a name for him,' [Confucius] takes for a designation [something] familiar to the world" 取世所知而稱. From Xiahou Xuan's formulation, it is clear that the term *cheng* had not now become fixed and still needed explanation. Furthermore, Xiahou Xuan does not make a general statement, only a comment on Confucius' way of speaking. Again, Wang Bi transforms these terms into neatly defined philosophic notions that reduce a plethora of terms in the *Laozi* to single terms.

Just before the passage quoted above, Wang Bi writes in his *LZWZLL* about the *ming*—and I will extract the entire chain of phrases referring to it from a passage written in interlocking parallel style with the matching passages dealing with *cheng*:

> Giving *it* [the "That-by-which"] a name, *ming*, is unable to match it. 名之不當. A name necessarily has something that makes it specific. 名必有所分. Having a specification, there will, as a consequence, be something that is not included. 有分則有不兼. There being something not included, [the name], as a consequence, greatly deviates from its [the "That-by-which's"] true [essence]. 不兼則大殊其眞.[131]

The last sentence eliminates the *ming* as a proper instrument to grasp the "true nature" of the "That-by-which," as, by necessity, it "greatly deviates" from it.

About the heuristic proposition *cheng* 稱, Wang Bi says within the same chain of interlocked parallel statements:

> Giving it a designation is unable to fully grasp it [the "That-by-which"]. 稱之不能既. A designation necessarily has something on which it is based. 稱必有所由. Having a base, there will, as a consequence, be something that is not exhausted. 有由則有不盡. There being something not exhausted, [the designation], as a consequence, cannot be taken as a name. 不盡則不可以名.

The strict parallelism between the chains dealing with *ming* and *cheng*, respectively, seems to indicate an argumentative parallelism, eliminating both options, *ming* and *cheng*, from acceptable philosophic discourse. The specific contents of the two arguments, however, greatly differ, and while interlocking parallel style has the great merit of showing parallel structures, it operates more as an obstacle here, where the contents clearly are not parallel.

The all-important difference between the two chains is that the definition, *ming*, "greatly deviates from the true [nature]" of the "That-by-which," while the *cheng* only fails to "fully exhaust" the features of the "That-by-which." Thus while *cheng* do not qualify for *ming*, definitions, they establish the possibility of philosophy by preventing the philosopher from sinking into aphasia.

The term *cheng* is developed by Wang Bi from various elements given in the *Laozi* and the *Lunyu*. He begins his commentary to *Laozi* 25.5: "I give it [no name but only] the style 'Dao,'" with the words:

> It is a fact that a name is something to define the shape [of an object], while a style is something to designate what is sayable. 夫名以定形, 字以稱可言.

The formula *keyan* 可言 translates the *kedao* 可道 of *Laozi* 1.1: "A way that can be spoken of is not the eternal Way." Wang Bi merges the expressions *zi* 字, "style, personal name," *wei* 謂, "to call something" and *yan* 言, "saying," into a theoretical concept of the *keyan zhi cheng* 可言之稱, the "proposition that can be uttered." In this sense, he calls Dao the "greatest among the sayable designations" 可言之稱最大 directly after the statement quoted above from Wang's commentary on *Laozi* 25.5. This greatest of utterable propositions, however, remains a dangerous construct, because it might evoke the idea that the Dao is tied to being great. In the next commentary (25.6), Wang Bi writes, "If one puts too much weight onto the reason for which this style was determined, one would tie [the Way] down to being great" 責其字定之所由則繫於大. The analysis therefore cannot rely on and "put the weight on," *ze* 責, the term Dao; it is a makeshift device taken only for one aspect of the "That-by-which," as are the other "words" about which Wang Bi says in his *LZWZLL*, "thus the words 'way,' 'dark,' 'deep,' 'great,' 'fine' and 'distant' have each their meaning, but do not exhaust its totality" 各有其義未盡其極者也. In the commentary on *Laozi* 25.10, Wang Bi marks the limits of these *cheng* 稱 with a radical statement.

> Generally speaking, that of entities which has a name and has a designation is not their ultimate. 凡物有稱有名則非其極也. Saying "the Way" presupposes that there is a basis for [this expression]. 言道則有所由. Only as a consequence of there being

a basis for [this expression] will one talk about it as being "the Way." 有所由然後謂之爲道. Accordingly, "Way" is [only] the greatest among [aspects that can be assigned] designations, but that is nothing compared to greatness of the designationless. 然則是道稱中之大也不若無稱之大也.

Wang Bi does three things. First, he eliminates the possibility of thinking about the "That-by-which" in terms of a *ming* 名. Second, he establishes the *cheng* as a tentative, heuristic manner of speaking about aspects of the "That-by-which," a process that makes verbal philosophic communication about the "That-by-which" and thus philosophy as a discursive enterprise possible. And, third, he tries to counter the prevalent tendency to take these heuristic propositions as *ming* by stressing time and again their necessarily tentative nature.

The new term *cheng* also is used for describing the utterable propositions about the Sage. Even when the *cheng* in fact is only one Chinese character, Wang Bi still sees it as a complete, if condensed, proposition about one aspect of the "That-by-which."

The *Lunyu* 8.19 statement about Yao, which has already been quoted, runs:

Great indeed is Yao being the ruler! Majestic he is! Only Heaven is great, and only Yao was modeled after it. So vast he [Yao] is that none of the people were able to give a name to him. 大哉堯之爲君也巍巍乎唯天爲大唯堯則之蕩蕩乎民無能名焉.

Wang Bi comments:

[Only] a Sage has a capacity that matches Heaven;[132] that is why the heuristic proposition [here] "only Yao was modeled after it [Heaven]" means that at that time only Yao completed the Way of matching Heaven. 聖人有則天之德所以稱唯堯則之者唯堯於時全則天之道也.
    "Vast" is a heuristic proposition for "without form and name." 蕩蕩無形無名之稱也. Generally speaking, that which a name names arises from the good having something [specific] to become manifest, and [thus] kindness having something to attach itself to. 夫名所名者生於善有所章而惠有所存. Goodness and badness depend on each other, and [so] the specifications of names take on form. 善惡 相須而名分形焉. But if there is absolute [all-encompassing] love and absence of

personal preference, where should kindness [for particular indi-
viduals] have a place? And if there is ultimate goodness [善 for
美] without any one-sidedness, from what should a name arise?
That is why with being modeled after Heaven and completing
the transformation [for the betterment of other beings], making [his] Way identical with That-which-is-of-itself-what-it-is
he [Yao] did not give preferential treatment to his [own] sons
but made his minister [Shun] into the ruler [succeeding him].
[As a consequence], the evil-doers were punished automatically, and the good ones automatically gained merit [without
Yao's intervention], so that [as the next *Lunyu* passage says]
"achievements" [of the people] were "completed" without his
establishing his renown, and punishments were meted out without his applying the penal laws. As [in this manner] the "Hundred Families make daily use of [him and the Dao he embodies]
but do not know" That-by-which [this automatic order] came
about [as the *Xici* 上 40/4 says about the Dao], how, then,
could they give a name [to him]?[133]

The word "vast" might at first have looked like a negative term.
Wang Bi's commentary makes it quite clear that it is this very "unbound-
edness," interpreted as an "absolute love" for all entities without any
personal preferences for this one or that, that permits the self-regulatory
mechanism of society to realize its potential. What might have been read
as just a negation of specific features turns out in this very negation to be
a positive device characterizing the government of the Sage. For Wang Bi,
the statement "vast is he" refers to a governmental strategy and thus is a
legitimate if "unreliable" term for an aspect of the Dao of the Sage.

Through the *Xici* quotation in the end, Wang Bi also musters the
authority of this text for his argument. While the *Zhouyi* itself is coded
in a different manner [which will not be dealt with in any detail in this
book] and does not speak about the Dao or negativity, the *Xici* clearly
contains directly philosophic passages, which would have to run into the
same impasse as the *Laozi*. In fact, *Xici* 上 4, to which Wang Bi refers
here, does make a similar argument.

> Once Yin, once Yang—this is called Dao 一陰一陽之謂道. The
> humane sees it [the Dao] and calls it humaneness. 仁者見之謂
> 之仁. The knowledgeable sees it and calls it knowledge. 知者
> 見之謂之知. The Hundred Families make daily use of it and do
> not know [what it is they are making use of].百姓日用而不知.
> That is why the Dao of the Junzi is elusive. 故君子之道鮮矣.[134]

The *Xici* uses the same device as the *Laozi* to indicate the tentativeness of its terminology. "Once Yin, once Yang *is called* Dao." According to the personal emphasis of him who "sees it," it also may be called *ren* 仁, "humaneness," or *zhi* 知, "knowledge." Those who have humaneness or knowledge obviously grasp some aspect of the "That-by-which." The common folk, the "Hundred Families," have no such qualification. Although they "daily make use of it" they have no knowledge of what it is that secured the regularity of their lives. The word Junzi 君子 often is used synonymously with the Sage, *shengren* 聖人, or the *daren* 大人, the Great Man, in the *Xici* and other parts of the *Zhouyi* such as the *Wenyan* 文言 to hexagram 1, where all three are used in the same sense. The *Xici* itself, indicated with the repeated use of "is called," *wei* 謂, the tentative nature of its language, and the last phrase about the "elusiveness" of the Dao of the Gentleman, Great Man, or Sage, states this explicitly. With the authority of the *Lunyu* and the *Zhouyi*, Wang Bi can thus say that all of the arguments pertaining to the "That-by-which" of cosmic order also pertain to social order.

Wang Bi does not limit himself to general inserts into particular commentaries, nor to examples to define the difference between *ming* and *cheng*. In order to avoid later confusion, I have hitherto simply claimed that *cheng* 稱, "designation," must be understood as "heuristic proposition," but I have failed to provide the evidence. In *LZWZLL* 5.1ff., Wang Bi writes what must be read as the first systematic—and highly sophisticated—attempt in the history of Chinese philosophy to deal with the problem of the language of ontology:

A name is that which defines an object. 名也者 定彼者也.	A designation is that which is said by inference. 稱也者從謂者也.
The name is born from the object. 名生乎彼.	The designation comes out of the subject. 稱出乎我.

With the establishment of this basic difference between *ming*, definitions defining an object and emanating from the particular features of this object, and *cheng*, inferences based on the particular question or aspect pursued by the subject, Wang Bi opens the way for a more detailed treatment of these heuristic propositions.

That is why 故

when approaching *it* as that for which there is no entity which	when searching for *it* as that for which there is no subtlety which

is not based on it, he [Laozi] designates *it* "Dao." 涉之乎無物 而不由則稱之曰道.

As

the many are based on the Dao 眾由乎道,

thus 故

[the *Laozi* 10.7ff. statement] [that] "it generates them and rears them [the ten thousand entities]" [that is,] that it does not block [their source] and does not hem in [their nature] but permeates the nature of entities, is a proposition about the Dao, 生之畜之不禁不塞 通物之性 道之謂也.

[while]

is not emanating from it, he [Laozi] styles *it* "the Dark." 求之乎無妙而不出 則謂之曰玄.

the subtle emanates from the Dark, 妙出乎玄

[the *Laozi* 10.9 statement] [that] "while they come alive it has no [specific effort on its side] and while they act, it does not make them dependent, [that, in short,] while they grow there would be no lording it [over their growth on its side]"—that they have a receipt [from *it*] but that there is no dominance [from *it*],—this is the "Receipt [coming from] That-which-is-Dark" [spoken of by the *Laozi* in the end of 10.9]. 生而不有, 爲而不恃長而不宰有德而無主玄之德也.
"Dark" is the most profound of styles. 玄謂之深者也.

"Dao" is the greatest of designations 道稱之大者也.

The *cheng* thus arise from the "searching," *qiu* 求, and "approaching," *she* 涉, of the inquiring subject. The specificity of the resulting proposition is not determined by the specificity of the "That-by-which" but by that of the approach of the subject. As they show the "That-by-which" only in relation to this specific approach, these heuristic propositions—a term which in fact translates 從謂—do not and cannot form a coherent system of noncontradictory propositions, and in the mind of the presumed authors of the texts for which Wang Bi wrote his commentaries, they very consciously did not.

Wang Bi finds in the two core propositions about the "That-by-which" in the *Laozi* the articulation for the simultaneous presence and elusiveness of the "That-by-which," which makes it at once the true subject of the thinking of the Sages and prevents the cognitive grasp. That it is called "the Dao" is a proposition encompassing the aspect that it is the condition for the existence of the ten thousand kinds of entities, and that it is called the Dark is a proposition encompassing the aspect that as the basis of all entities it cannot share any of their specificities, and thus is cognitively and linguistically elusive.

It is the advantage of these propositions that they permit mutually exclusive statements about the "That-by-which" that can be argued with the rules of what is logically "necessary." The philosophizing subject cannot disappear in the objectivity of the logic of his or her proposition but remains present in the proposition through the particularity of the approach.

Wang Bi's inquiry into the cognitive aspects of ontology has a number of important implications. First, it establishes the philosophizing, "searching and approaching" subject in the rationality of its "necessary" conclusions as the only source of possible philosophic insights. The classical texts are not accepted on their own authority but on the authority of their conforming to the "necessary" insights to which each and every "subject," searching for and approaching aspects of the "That-by-which," must by necessity arrive. Thus while mustering the authority of the Sage and texts of the revered tradition for his own philosophy, Wang Bi established—the exceedingly modest form of the explanatory commentaries to the classics notwithstanding—the rationality of the philosophically autonomous subject as the only real touchstone for the validity of the thinking of the Sages.

Second, while accepting the insight into the impossibility of discerning the "That-by-which," which the *Laozi*, the *Lunyu*, and the *Zhouyi* have repeatedly stressed, his own commentary provides the philosophically reasoned basis for these assertions and in the process changes their meaning. It is not the incapacity of the human mind and language that prevents the full cognizance of the "That-by-which" (and leaves only meditative and mystical exercises as avenues for its discernment) but the necessary structure of the "That-by-which" as negativity. At the same time, insofar as the "That-by-which" does not have a separate realm of existence, it is, in modern terminology, *as* the Being of the entities, and in this manner its traces might be found in them.

Third, and most important, while Wang Bi concedes the argument made by Xun Can, he saves the bequests of the Sages as all-important philosophic sources and establishes the basis for an ontology. His inquiry into language establishes the possibility of a philosophy of Being while clearly delineating the possible validity of its statements. At the same time, this inquiry turns Xun Can's argument around. The reading of the texts left behind by the Sages has to be guided by their own indications concerning the nature of the language and the symbols they were using. The mistakes made in reading them are not caused by the ineptitude of their language but by the refusal of scholars to let themselves be guided by the indications inserted into these very texts about the proper strategies to be used for their reading. Instead, the scholars followed their own ill-advised preferences. Wang Bi's polemics against what he considers systematic misconstructions of the *Laozi* have been dealt with elsewhere.[135] If, in other words, the indications given in these texts are followed—and this also is true for the *Zhouyi* which we have left aside here—they turn out to be the very "subtle words" 微言 that seem to have so disappointingly disappeared. Wang Bi thus reinserts these texts into a cultural environment where the terse spoken word and nonverbal forms of cognition and communication have precedence over the written record as media of ontological thought.

While I have promised to refrain from a full-fledged analysis of Wang Bi's reading of the *Zhouyi* in this book, I cannot hold back with a development of Wang Bi's theory of philosophical language that came after his *Laozi* commentary and has had a very important impact on later thinkers, his rereading of the *Zhuangzi* simile of the hare-trap and the hare, and the fish weir and the fish. It will be recalled that the *Zhuangzi* did not really explore the meaning and the importance of the "forgetting" of the trap and the weir for the "getting" of the hare and the fish. Only in the last phrase "Where will I find a man who forgets about words to talk with him?" it becomes clear that the forgetting is not incidental, but essential. This is the point where Wang Bi comes in, combining references to the *Zhuangzi* and the *Xici* passages dealt with above. I will quote the relevant section in full.

AN EXPLANATION OF THE IMAGES [XIANG OF THE *ZHOUYI*]

Generally speaking it is true that

the image [in the *Zhouyi*] is what brings out the meaning [of a given hexagram];

the words [the *guaci* 卦辭 explaining the overall hexagram, and the *yaoci* 爻辭 explaining individual lines] are what explains the image [of a given hexagram].

For "fully exhausting the meaning" [of a given hexagram] [as the Master said in *Xici* 上 12] nothing surpassed the image.

For fully exhausting the image [of a given hexagram] nothing surpasses the words [explaining it].

The words arise out of the [given] image, and that is why it is possible to probe the words as a means to clearly perceive the image.

The image arises out of the meaning [of the given hexagram] and that is why it is possible to probe the image as a means to clearly perceive the meaning.

As

the meaning [of a given hexagram] is "fully exhausted" by the image, and

as the image [of a given hexagram] is brought out by the words ,
the words are [only] that by which the image [of a given hexagram] is explained, but once the image has been grasped, the words are forgotten;

and the image is only that by which the meaning [of a given hexagram] is arrested, but once the meaning has been grasped, the image is forgotten.

This compares

to the trap's being that by which a rabbit is arrested, but once the rabbit has been grasped, the trap is forgotten;

to a fish weir's being that by which a fish is arrested, but once the fish has been grasped, the weir is forgotten.

Accordingly

the words are the trap of the image [of a given hexagram],

the image [of a given hexagram] is the weir of [its] meaning.

This is why

someone clinging to the words [about the image] will not be the one who gets hold of the image [explained by them],

someone clinging to the image [of a given hexagram] is not the one who will get hold of [its] meaning.
The image [of a given hexagram] arises from [its] meaning, but, by clinging to the image, what one clings to is not indeed the image THEREOF [of the meaning of the hexagram].

The words [attached to the images] arise out of the [given] image, but, by clinging to the words, what one clings to are not indeed the words ABOUT IT [the image].

Thus only he who forgets about the image is indeed the one who will grasp the meaning,

forgets about the words is indeed the one who will grasp the [given] image.

Grasping the meaning [of a given hexagram] consists in/lies in forget-

ting the image [of it] 得意在忘象.   Grasping the image [of a given
hexagram] consists in/lies in for-
getting the words [illustrating it].

Thus [the Zhouyi] establishes images
so as to [as Xici上 12 says] "fully exhaust
the meaning" [of a given hexagram]
but the image may be forgotten, and it
duplicates the trigrams [into hexagrams]
so as to "fully exhaust the actual situation"
but the trigrams may be forgotten.[136]

Wang Bi here moves from the polemic against a reading of the Confucius texts that reduces them to the particular tenets of this school of
thought or the other to a more radical and more philosophical position.
The simile in his reading combines a theoretical statement about the sheer
instrumentality of language with regard to the thinking of the Sages with
the insight into the indispensability of "forgetting" the instruments if one
is to get at the meaning. A failure on this part and the ensuing attachment
to the reified surface verbiage will not only clutter up understanding, but
make it impossible. Grasping the meaning, his statement runs once gen-
eralised to encompass all the means of communication used by the Sages,
consists in/lies in forgetting and looking away from these instruments and
signposts, and only in this forgetting and looking away once might grasp
what they point at. As a basis for a strategy of reading, this means nothing
is of relevance but that which pertains to what the Sages are pointing at. In
this respect, reading has to rigidly adhere to and explore the hints given in
the text; all other aspects of the surface text, however, are but deflections
from the purpose for which these texts have been written and handed
down, and will end up in forgetting what these texts are all about.

The Buddhist doctrine of the language of the Buddha being but a
'convenient means', upâya, to guide the listeners towards an understanding
that by definition was beyond words, linked up with this discussion and
gave it a broader scope. Given the wide use especially of early Buddhist
thinkers such as Zhu Daosheng 竺道生 or Seng Zhao 僧肇 (384–414)
made of the concepts of the Scholarly Exploration of the Dark, Xuanxue,
in the centuries following Wang Bi's death, it is not surprising that Wang
Bi's reading of the Zhuangzi story became a stock reference concerning
the nature of Buddhist and from thence all philosophical language to the
point of the fish weir/hare trap ending up as a shorthand binome tiquan
蹄筌 for the instrumentality and necessary sign-post character of Sagely
language about the Dao. Wang Bi had transformed the simile into an
explicit and general hermeneutic strategy for dealing with the bequests of
the Sages.

Chapter 2

Wang Bi's Ontology

THE FRAMEWORK OF ANALYSIS

Tang Yongtong was the first scholar to claim a fundamental difference between the Han philosophers and Xuanxue 玄學, saying (with the English terms inserted in brackets) that the Han philosophers dealt with "cosmology" and "cosmogony," while the Wei Jin scholars such as Wang Bi pursued "ontology" or "theory of being." In a masterly survey "A Sketch of the Currents in the Philosophy of the Dark of the Wei and Jin," published in 1940, he wrote a passage that set the course for dozens of books and papers in recent years and deserves to be quoted and annotated in full:

> Since Yang Xiong (53 B.C.E.–18 C.E.), Han scholars and literati began to strive for the dark and recondite. Generally speaking, as Feng Yan 馮衍 said in [the preface to] his *Fu-poem Expressing My Ambition, Xian zhi fu* 顯志賦 [about himself], those who "set" their minds "upon the dark and subtle 玄妙" [which he said to be his own ideal][1] were "constantly devoted to the real issue which is Dao and De, but did not strive after [empty] fame in their time; they treated petty ritual rules with neglect, and freely left behind the concerns of the human world."[2] Or, in the words of Zhongchang Tong's 仲長統 (179–220) *Changyan* 昌言, they would "roam beyond their particular times and would look down with disdain upon things

going between Heaven and Earth, not accept responsibility for their times, and always secure their allotted life span."[3] In other words, they are remembered and known for the same features as are the personalities of the *zhengshi* 正始 (240–249) and *yongjia* 永嘉 (307–313) eras. The door for the twofold darkness, however, has been approached by the *Laozi* [a reference to *Laozi* 1], so that those holding forth about the Dark 玄 invariably had high esteem for the *Laozi*. That is why Huan Tan 桓譚 (43 B.C.E.–28 C.E.) said "as to Mr. Lao, his heart was dark and recondite and in unison with the Dao";[4] Feng Yan "had the constant purpose to pursue the Dark and recondite" 玄妙 and "greatly cherished Lao Dan's [= Laozi's] emphasis on the Dark";[5] Fu Yi 傅毅 (active between 85 C.E. and 76 C.E.) spoke in his *Qiji* 七激 of "letting [his] heart roam in the dark and recondite, and purify [his] thoughts in Huang/Lao [teaching],"[6] and Zhongchang Tong "let peace prevail in the inner chambers of [his] spirit and pondered the Dark and empty of Mr. Lao."[7] Thus, while it is true that emulation of dark words and taking Mr. Lao as one's patriarch reached a high point during the Wei and Jin eras, we already see the harbingers of this during the Eastern Han. However, there definitely is a fundamental difference between the Eastern Han and the Wei/Jin talk about the Dark. Huan Tan said: "In writing his *Book about the Dark* 玄 書 [now known as the *Taixuan jing* 太玄經], Yang Xiong considered 'the Dark to be Heaven, to be the Dao.' He said when the Sages and worthies publish laws and handle state matters, they all rely on Heaven and the Dao as their basic point of departure, and from there append the myriad regulations for the king's government and human affairs."[8] While it is true that what is called Heaven and Dao here rather rejects the supernatural and divinatory theories, it still cannot avoid basing itself on the idea of mutual influences between Heaven and man and to explain the ups and downs of human affairs on the basis of the rise and demise of material phenomena. They explored the ordering principles of nature to match them with the regulation of government affairs. What their minds were concerned with still did not get beyond the symbols and numbers [of divination books], and what they were after was still to find out good and bad luck. (In his *Fu on the Great Dark, Taixuan fu* 太玄賦, Yang Xiong wrote: "[I] observe the ups and downs [indicated by the] *Great [Book of] Changes*, and [I] peruse the happiness and calamity [as indicated] by Mr. Lao."[9]) Zhang Heng 張衡

(78–138) "wrote his *Fu on Pondering about the Dark* 思玄賦 because the ups and downs, happiness and calamity were so recondite and unfathomable as to be hard to understand."[10] In this respect, the philosophy of the Dark of the Wei and Jin period was different. It had gone beyond the narrow attachment to the external functions 外用 of cosmic movements and had proceeded to discuss the substance 本體 of Heaven, Earth, and the ten thousand kinds of entities. The Han dynasty reckoned Heaven and the Dao as part of physical nature; the Wei and Jin dismissed Heaven and the Dao and explored the substance 本體; for them the singular controlled the many and brought them back to the dark ultimate (see Wang Bi, *Zhouyi lüeli* 周易略例, section Ming tuan 明彖), [for them] it is in "forgetting the symbols" [of the *Zhouyi*] that "[the] meaning [to which they point] is understood" and they roamed beyond the material sphere (see Wang Bi, *Zhouyi lüeli*, section Ming xiang 明象). Thus they left behind Han cosmology [Tang himself offers the translations "Cosmology or Cosmogony" for 宇宙之論, R. W.] and focused on the 存存本本之眞 (ontology or theory of being [Tang's own English translation]). There was another Han scholar, Zhang Heng 張衡 (78–139), who in his *Plan for the Dark* 玄圖 said about the Dark: "The Dark belongs to the category of the formless and is the root of Ziran 玄者無形之類, 自然之根. It acts in the Great Beginning, and there is nothing that precedes it." 作於太始莫之與先.[11] But what is called the Dark here is still considered to depend on time; it is the subtle and elusive feature in which the ten thousand kinds of entities begin, is at the level of the Great Beginning, *taichu* 太初, and the Great Simplicity, *taisu* 太素. In his exploration, Zhang only discusses the construction of the universe and pursues the creation of the ten thousand kinds of entities, while the Wei and Jin managed to do away with the inquiry into physical things and proceed to the comprehension of substance, *benti* 本體. They discarded physical phenomena, transcended time and space, and studied the true limit, *zhenji* 眞際, of Heaven, Earth, and the ten thousand kinds of entities. They took the ten thousand kinds of entities, *wanyou* 萬有, for the dependent, *mo* 末, and empty negativity, *xuwu* 虛無 for the root, *ben* 本. This empty negativity is not a physical thing. It is not the shapeless original breath, *yuanqi* 元氣, at the time of the Great Beginning with nothing to precede it. Neither negativity, which is the root, nor the entities, which are the dependent, are terms referring to this physical thing and another, nor to an earlier and a later form. As the substance determining the ten thousand kinds of entities is called "empty negativity," *xuwu* 虛無, there is no entity that is not empty negativity, which also means that as long as there are no entities there is no empty negativity.[12]

Tang makes the following important points:

- Han philosophical thinking developed cosmogony, with the common point being a search for a primordial physical cause within space and time. Even the growing number of thinkers since Yang Xiong who defined this ultimate principle as "dark" 玄 and described it in ever more ethereal ways remained within the horizon of this approach.

- Xuanxue thinkers of the Wei and Jin made the important step toward ontology. They defined "empty negativity" as the "substance" 本體 of the ten thousand kinds of entities.

Tang's scheme has become the paradigm for most studies by Chinese scholars moving beyond philology and doxography. His studies were reprinted during the Hundred Flowers periods (in 1957 and 1962), after which philosophical inquiry in mainland China was replaced by mostly political analysis.[13] Since the early 1980s, when they were again reprinted, and when some previously unpublished studies came out for the first time (such as his seminal study on the relationship between Xuanxue and literature),[14] several scholars have taken up his basic paradigm, now explicitly defined as the transition from cosmology to ontology 本體論, and they have fleshed it out in many details.[15] Even occasional critics such as Feng Youlan in 1986 did not challenge the basic paradigm; Feng argued that in fact Wang Bi and others were not making as clear a separation between cosmology and ontology as Tang Yongtong had claimed.[16]

Scholars were mostly concerned, however, with inserting the available and often scanty material into this scheme of things and studying the different aspects and schools of Xuanxue. I think no scholar has gone back to the philosophic question of what ontology might mean here or has called attention to the difficulties in transferring the Greek transition scheme to third-century China.

In Tang's argument, further, but not very much more, developed in his subsequent pages on Wang Bi, a number of problems remain.

- Tang takes the basic historiographic scheme of a development from cosmology to ontology from his studies of early European philosophy, where the process is described as the transition from the pre-Socratic search for the ultimate matter of the universe to Aristotelian metaphysics. Aristotle himself had claimed that the philosophers before him were only physiocrats, and that he himself was the first to speak about Being.[17] In fact, Tang speaks of "Wang Bi's metaphysics" 王氏形上之學.[18] While the European historical model has provided an interesting and highly potent stimulus for perceiving the importance of the Han/Wei transition, it is evident that what Tang describes as Han "cosmology" or "cosmogony," with its emphasis on the Heaven/man analogy and the ensuing attempts at regulating human society, has little in common with the pre-Socratic atomists' search for the ultimate matter of the universe. We may infer that there might be as big a difference between the questions to which Aristotle's metaphysics tries to provide answers and the questions behind the Xuanxue endeavor as was between the answers.

• Tang does not explain what he means by "ontology," and the Chinese terms he uses do not shed much light on the issue. In the studies published at the time, Tang did not use the already established term for ontology, *benti lun* 本體論,[19]although it appears in an edition of his notes on Xuanxue for his 1940s' lecture in Kunming and Berkeley, edited by his son.[20] In the paper from which the above translation is taken, his terminology remains fluid; for example, *benti* 本體 is rendered "substance"[21] or "reality,"[22] and his Chinese explanation for ontology, namely, 留連於存存本本之眞, is a neologism based on a *Xici* phrase that would have to be translated "to focus on the true [substance] which makes existing things exist and makes the[ir] root rooting."[23] In another study on the period dating from around 1943, but published only in 1957, Tang uses still other terms, *goucheng zhiliao* 構成質料, "structured matter," for cosmology, and *benti cunzai* 本體存在 for ontology.[24] The only clear indication he gives about the meaning of the term is that the Wei Jin philosophers were no longer looking for an ultimate "outside" generating cause for the entities but for some ultimate principle involved in their very existence. Again, although Tang's paradigm is routinely referred to by scholars as the cosmology 宇宙論/ontology 本體論 transition, scholarship has not focused on the question of what "ontology" might mean and to what extent the philosophic endeavor of Wang Bi might fit this term.

Without reference to Tang Yongtong's argument, other scholars, above all A.C. Graham, have claimed a linguistic determinism, arguing that the terminology of *you* 有 and *wu* 無 used in this "ontology" is utterly incapable of dealing with ontological matters. Meaning "having" and "not having," respectively, they argue, these terms do not match the linguistic structure of the verb to be, *sein*, or *être*.[25] This argument was not proffered as a result of a close inquiry into the actual philosophical material but rather as a general observation derived from arguments suggested by Lee Whorf and others, which even in the field of linguistics they have not been able to hold sway. As the many new argumentative strategies and the neologisms of the Xuanxue scholars show, they were very much aware of the limitations of language and were willing as well as able to explore new avenues of inquiry. The same is in a way true for Tang Yongtong himself, who was grappling with a new Chinese terminology to express his views and research results.

I will give Wang Bi an open field to lay out his arguments, and I will not from the outset decide on speculative grounds what he might, and what he might not, be able to say. I shall thus first try to present the logic and structure of Wang Bi's philosophic inquiry with a fairly detailed documentation to make his own voice heard. As a second step, I shall try to set Wang Bi's inquiry into the context of earlier Chinese approaches. In the end, I will present my own findings in a critical discussion of the available scholarly models for conceptualizing Wang Bi's Scholarly Exploration of the Dark.

WANG BI'S INQUIRY INTO THE THAT-BY-WHICH

Wang Bi begins his structural analyses of the *Laozi* and the *Zhouyi* much in the same way. In his view, the *Laozi* explicitly and the *Zhouyi* implicitly deal with the only relevant question, namely, the necessary features of "That-by-which," *suoyi* 所以, the ten thousand kinds of entities are. To recall, the expression "That-by-which," as used in this chapter and book, refers to the Chinese term *suoyi*, in a phrase such as 萬物之所以生, "that by which the ten thousand kinds of entities are generated." The term has the advantage of clearly indicating the topic without prejudicing the reading of the Chinese materials as much as would be the case if "substance" or "Being" would be used.

The first pericope in the *Laozi weizhi lilüe* ends "the featureless and nameless is the 'ancestor of the ten thousand kinds of entities [mentioned in Laozi 4.1],'" and the first section of the *Zhouyi lüeli*, which explains the *tuan* 彖 statements, states at the outset concerning the six lines in the hexagrams: "It is a fact that the many cannot regulate the many; what regulates the many is the smallest in number. Movement cannot control movement; what controls [as *Xici* 下.1 says] 'the movements of All Under Heaven is pure Oneness'" 夫眾不能治眾治眾者至寡者也夫動不能制動制天下之動者貞夫一者也. The *tuan*, then, "are what sums up the core of a hexagram and explains the dominating principle on which it is based."[26]

Through his analysis of these two texts, Wang Bi sets a new philosophical agenda. Many comments were made here and there by earlier philosophers about the origin and/or base of entities, but with Wang Bi this becomes the only relevant philosophical problem. His treatment of this problem through the two texts claims that, in fact, this has been the only relevant problem all along; that it is at the core of the endeavor of the Sage (Confucius) and his close second, Laozi, but that their insights have been drowned out in the factional babble of the different schools.

The particular agenda of his inquiry is open. Wang Bi does not posit an ultimate base of the ten thousand kinds of entities and then deduce a cosmogony or ontogony. His inquiry is inductive and asks after the "necessary" features of that by which the entities are. In his work, this "That-by-which" is not defined either through revelation, mystical access, convention, or imposed government orthodoxy. Consequently, the question about the necessary features of the "That-by-which" is open. This radical openness at the very core marks a revolutionary turning point in the history of Chinese philosophy. Wang Bi, with his shocking youth and iconoclastic arrogance, born at a pivotal moment into the debris of a collapsed dynasty and its equally collapsed worldview, used this short breathing space to pioneer a discursive philosophy, that relied for its proofs on argument and not the authority of wisdom or the teacher's position. Such moments of a breathing space between two world orders are rare. They throb with an intellectual and artistic energy that defies the sober linearities of traditional doxography. The project of Wang Bi's generation, and above all he himself, made philosophy—for which there was no word beyond the general *lun* 論, "judgment"—a scholarly enterprise.[27]

There is a contradiction, however. Did not Wang Bi, as well as the other philosophers of the *zhengshi* era (240–249), use the form of the commentary for classical works, if they did not use the *lun* 論, which in turn often purports to prove the classics?[28] In Wang Bi's work, however, the classics, including the *Laozi*, have no intrinsic authority. They owe their authority to the fact that they, by implication or explicitly, dealt with the only relevant problem—the features of the "That-by-which"—and that their insights, whether spelled out or implied, could be proved by discursive philosophy in the form of commentary and *lun* to be arguably true. In this manner, they justified the story of these texts having been written by Sages or their close seconds. The common philosophic focus of the *Laozi*, the *Lunyu*, and the *Zhouyi*, as well as the particular insights of each of these three texts, however, had been lost in the ill-advised pursuits of the different philosophical schools that by definition lacked even the yearning for the openness of an unprejudiced scholar.

The revolutionary turn to discursive philosophy thus comes as the claim to rediscover what was both most clearly relevant and most radically forgotten in the hallowed texts handed down by tradition. This claim was made explicit in the status ascribed to the authors of the "classical" texts selected; in the choice, by Wang Bi, of the submissive form of the commentary and the *lun* as explanatory and not exploratory genres; and in his actual use of both these genres to discover the hidden philosophic argument and logic behind phrases long eliminated from the philosophical record through trivialization, mystification, factionalization, or decontextualization. The texts selected thus gain, it is true, a new authority and lease on life from the likes of Wang Bi, but the bargain has dramatically changed. They cannot claim the a priori authority of containing all relevant principle and insight and cannot place the burden on the reader to submit and understand what is by definition their truth. Their new authority is not theirs by inheritance but is granted on a condition. It hinges on their capacity to convince—phrase by phrase.

Wang Bi's *lun* and commentaries thus do two things; they spell out or elucidate what the texts imply or state and then show it to be valid. This has the double effect of proving their philosophic points, and of thus remaking them into philosophic texts deserving authority as coming from former thinkers of the highest caliber. The result of this check on their credibility is such that their authority is in fact undermined but reestablished on a much higher level. Confucius comes out as the Sage whose claim on this title is not that his students and their students venerate him as their master, but that his philosophic performance shows that he "embodies negativity"; Laozi comes out a close second.

"That by which" the ten thousand kinds of entities are does not present itself as such for empirical inquiry and thus cannot be handled with the traditional instrument of signifying language. The texts in question, aware as their "sage" authors were of the limitations of language, have thus turned to a variety of forms of oblique verbal and structural communication to expand the potential of language beyond straight talk. They are, therefore, hard to understand. Given the elusiveness of their object of inquiry as well as the (conscious) obliqueness of their linguistic devices, it comes as no surprise that both their object and meaning should be forgotten.

The result of Wang Bi's own reading of these texts was that their authors had been rare world events of or near the status of Sages. Their texts, accordingly, are not just some treasured heirlooms of a bygone age but are rare, rarefied, and neglected treasures. In fact, it is only by going through the linguistic maze of these texts that the unique level of insight into the "That-by-which" reached by their authors can be attained. Deciphering the meaning of these texts becomes the only avenue to the only relevant object of philosophy. The sober and sophisticated textual analysis of the *Zhouyi*, the *Laozi*, and the *Lunyu*, in short, philology, thus becomes the only possible medium for the new discursive philosophy. The spirit of scholarly openness of this new discursive philosophy finds its immediate expression in Wang Bi's philological openness and in the sophistication of his textual analysis.

WANG BI'S APPROACH

Wang Bi did not restrict himself to following his texts line by line in the commentaries; he also wrote structural analyses of the *Zhouyi* and the *Laozi*. All three texts for which he wrote commentaries have a loose structure of individual short sections, somewhat or entirely unrelated. They are not systematic expositions. In his *Zhouyi lüeli* and the *Laozi weizhi lilüe*, Wang Bi quotes freely from the respective texts and inserts these quotations into a systematic exposition focused on the metatext of their silent structures, but even the individual commentaries break through the walls surrounding each unit of meaning. As shown earlier, they get their analytical strategies and the criteria for the probability of a reading from data elsewhere in the text or from other texts such as the *Zhouyi*, which they implicitly allude to or explicitly quote. In the process, these commentaries build a thick network of philosophic, metaphoric, and terminological linkages among the different segments of the text in question and even between the different texts for which Wang Bi wrote commentaries. Such linkages create and evoke a textual homogeneity within a given text, which in turn finds its most radical expression in Wang Bi's writing a *lüeli* 略例 or *lilüe* 例略, a structural analysis and an exposition of the unified philosophical meaning of the text as a whole; the linkages create a philosophic homogeneity between these texts, which allows Wang Bi to discover their similar themes and approaches.[29]

This result did not come about naturally but is the product of specific analytical strategies. It is vital for us to learn about these strategies, because they show Wang Bi in the act of constituting a *Laozi* and tell us about his own agenda in contrast to that of the *Laozi*.

For economy, I begin with a detailed analysis of the introductory phrases of the *LZWZLL* so as to develop a first set of hypotheses to be tested against the rest of the oeuvre.

It is generally true with regard to

that by which things are created— that [things] are necessarily created out of the "featureless."	that by which achievements are brought about—that [achievements] are [necessarily] based on the "nameless."

The featureless and nameless is [what the *Laozi* calls] the "ancestor of the ten thousand kinds of entities."

[Being featureless,] it neither warms nor cools.	[Being nameless,] it neither [lets sound forth the notes] *gong* or *shang*. [Even when] "listening for it," one is [still] unable to "hear it."
[Even when] "looking for it," one is [still] unable to perceive it. [Even when] groping for it, one is [still] unable to identify it.	[Even when] going after its taste, one is [still] unable to get its flavour.

That is why [the *Laozi* says about the Dao]

"as a thing" it "completes out of the diffuse," as an "image" it is "without form";	as a "sound" it "has an inaudible tone," as a "taste" it is without flavor.

That is why it is able to be

the "principle" and

the "master"

of all [different] categories of entities, to cover and permeate Heaven and Earth so that there is nothing that it does not thread through.[30]

This stunning opening of what certainly is the most important philosophic treatise we have from the third century deserves close scrutiny.

First, Wang Bi begins his analysis by talking about the "necessary" features not of a text but of that by which the material things/beings and the immaterial achievements are. In other words, he begins his analysis of the *Laozi* with a hypothesis about a logical necessity prevailing in the relationship between the specific kinds of entities and their "That-by-which."

Their common "That-by-which," he argues, must by necessity lack all their specific features, that is, forms and names. By identifying this nameless and shapeless "That-by-which" with the "ancestor of the ten thousand kinds of entities" from the *Laozi*, he argues that the "necessary" result of this analysis is already contained in the *Laozi*. Nor does the *Laozi* resign itself just to mentioning this "ancestor"; in the proof for the hypothesis, Wang Bi again can identify certain compelling arguments in the *Laozi*, namely, the discovery that the "That-by-which" is not accessible to the senses. The beginning of the *Zhouyi lüeli* repeats this structure and reinforces our argument. We hypothesize that the authority of the *Laozi* in Wang Bi rests on the *Laozi*'s provable understanding of the necessary features of the "That-by-which" of the ten thousand kinds of entities.

Second, in the center of Wang Bi's philosophic inquiry is the relationship between the "That-by-which" and the ten thousand kinds of entities. As the features of the latter, namely, "forms" and "names," are accessible to the senses and to immediate cognition, while those of the "That-by-which" are not, Wang Bi infers from the verifiable structures of the ten thousand kinds of entities what the features of their "That-by-which" must be. His method is thus inductive. He does not deduce the structure and changes of the ten thousand entities from an assumed highest category such as *taiji* 太極, Dao 道, or Yin and Yang. He does not simply state and illustrate his insights in the manner of the *Laozi*, the *Zhuangzi*, or the *Wenzi* without proceeding to prove them. And he does not treat the *Laozi* phrases as a text with such unquestionable authority that a commentator is either reduced to illustrate their meaning, as do the *Wenzi*, the *Hanfeizi*, and the *Huainanzi*, or to translate them into mandatory guidelines of behavior for the adepts, as does the Xiang Er *Commentary*.

Third, Wang Bi makes use of a notion of logical necessity, expressed in the first phrase by the term *bi* 必, "necessarily." In the sequel to the quotation given above, Wang Bi tests the opposite case. What if the "That-by-which" were specific? "Would it be warming, then it would not cool; would it [be tied to letting sound forth the note] *gong*, then it would not be able to [let sound forth the note] *shang*" 若溫也則不能涼矣宮也則不能商矣. The negative counterpart to *bi* 必 is thus the "can not", *buneng* 不能. This is repeated in the beginning of the *Zhouyi lüeli*:

> What, generally speaking, are the *tuan*? 夫彖者何也 They are that which sums up the core of a hexagram and explains the dominating principle on which it is based. 統論一卦之體 明其所由之主者也.

Generally speaking,

the many cannot regulate the many. What regulates the many is the smallest in number; 夫 眾不能治眾 治眾者至寡者也;	movement cannot control movement. What controls [as the *Xici* says] "the movements of All Under Heaven is pure oneness." 夫動不能制動制天下之動者貞 夫一者也.[31]

That is why that by which

the many manage to persist simultaneously, is that [their] principle must by necessity pertain to the One. 故眾之所以 得咸存者主必致一也.	the movements manage to get around simultaneously, is that [their] origin must by necessity be without duality.[32] 動之所以 得咸運者原必無二也.

Philosophically, this notion of logical necessity establishes the reader's reasoning on an equal footing with the author. The author cannot legitimately refer to a precedent in the classics or to a saying of Confucius as a proof of the truth of his statement but submits his argument to the scrutiny of the reason of a highly educated, irreverent, and sophisticated implied reader. If the author can prove his proposition, the reader will be convinced; if not, not. In the process, the reader too comes under stress. He or she has to be willing to part with any idea previously formed if the argument presented here has logical stringency on its side. In the philosophic dialogue between text and reader in their common pursuit of the "That-by-which" it is not legitimate to claim adherence to any tradition, school, or authority.

The heavy artillery of logical necessity is not the everyday instrument of analysis for Wang Bi. It is introduced only at one crucial juncture. The features of the "That-by-which" can be found only through induction on the basis of accessible entities that are based on it. To free this induction from the randomness of guesswork or the need for direct revelation, the instrument of logically guided extrapolation of the kind "although it cannot be verified in itself it can be concluded on the basis of the verifiable material that it must by necessity 必 be so" is introduced; the conclusions are verified through the test of the opposite of the kind "were the opposite from the extrapolated assumption valid, it could not 不能 do or be what it does or is." Wang Bi's induction is guided by logical methods of proof and verification.

Sociologically, this reflects the demise of the teacher/student model of authority-guided philosophic communication and of family tradition as an intellectually binding force, of the *shifa* 師法 and the *jiafa* 家法. As Lu Shengjiang has shown,[33] this demise began with the competition for the state universities from huge private academies (often over a 1,000 students) since the beginning of the second century. Within the curriculum, greater diversity developed with scholars perusing texts from different traditions without the guidance of teachers. By the end of the second century, Ma Rong 馬融 would not only read and comment on all of the classics but also read the authors of the "hundred Schools" and comment on the *Laozi*. The end of the Han brought the end of teaching authority, which had already been withering away. Wang Bi himself engages in open argument against intellectuals whose mind-sets were predetermined by their school affiliation. In a clean sweep, he denounces all schools of thought in the *LZWZLL* because all of them are bound by preconceived ideas, and as a consequence they miss the main purport of the *Laozi*.[34] *Ad hominem* criticism is not excluded. Wang Su 王肅 is the classical example. A student of Zheng Xuan, he turned against his teacher and published a criticism of his master's erroneous views.[35] Wang Bi follows in Wang Su's footsteps; but while the former criticized certain particular interpretations of Zheng Xuan, Wang Bi ridicules his basic approach, his method of reading the *Zhouyi*.[36] The public shock of this irreverence is still felt in the story transmitted in Liu Yiqing's 劉義慶 *Youming lu* 幽明錄, where Zheng Xuan's ghost, enraged at the irreverence of young Wang Bi, bursts into his study to complain. Wang Bi, of course, died the next day, dead proof of the dangers of interpretation.[37]

Among the famous intellectuals of the *zhengshi* period, however, it was good form to bend to the superior argument. He Yan's gracious retreat before Wang Bi has been described elsewhere.[38]

Intellectually, this signaled the development of a critical spirit best documented in the work of Wang Chong (27–97), Wang Fu (ca. 76–ca. 156), Zhongchang Tong (179–220), and others, who would test intellectual opinions against standards of probability and consistency and social practices against moral norms. In all cases, a growing and irreverent "rationalism" 合理主義 (Kaga Eiji)[39] or "argumentativeness" 義理學 (Wang Baoxuan)[40] prevailed with schoolish and inherited opinion being ridiculed. There is, it is true, a certain arrogance and recklessness in this approach, which contemporaries noticed, but it did benefit philosophy. While Wang Bi here continues a tradition of rational criticism begun with scholars during the previous two or three generations, the author of the *LZWZLL* goes much farther. He gives the reader's reason a key role in the unprejudiced and unprecedented philosophic pursuit of the "That-by-which" of the ten thousand entities. Wang Bi argues from scratch with a skeptical and unreliable audience, overpowering them with the stringency of his logic, and he is saved from rational triviality by the texts for which he writes a commentary and a structural analysis, and by the focus of his endeavor.

Fourth, there is no linear relationship between the *Laozi* (or *Zhouyi*) text in Wang Bi's hands and his *Commentary*. Two points have been mentioned—the development of linkages across the borders of the *zhang* of the *Laozi*, and the writing of separate texts, the *Zhouyi lüeli* and the *Laozi weizhi lilüe*, respectively, in which Wang Bi himself sets the argumentative agenda while amply quoting from the *Laozi* and the *Zhouyi*. An analysis of these quotations in the introduction to the *LZWZLL* given above will show the manner in which Wang Bi establishes his own agenda.

Wang Bi's first proposition in the *LZWZLL* ends with the identification of the "That-by-which" in its formlessness and namelessness with *Laozi*'s "ancestor of the ten thousand entities." This reference makes the claim that the *Laozi* already contains the answer to the question asked in the first proposition. There is, however, no statement in the *Laozi* linking the "ancestor of the ten thousand entities" to the notion of being "without form and name." The first proposition is a case in point. *Laozi* 4.1 runs: "The Way is made use of by pouring out and is also not filled up—deep it is, [but still] resembling the ancestor of the ten thousand kinds of entities" 道沖而用之又不盈淵兮似萬物之宗. The "ancestor of the ten thousand kinds of entities" is a hesitant and tentative ("resembles," *si* 似") appellation for the Dao, far from the harsh logic of Wang Bi's "necessarily" 必. For the Dao, in turn, the *Laozi* explicitly claims that it is *wuming* 無名, "nameless." *Laozi* 32 begins: "The Eternal of the Way is namelessness" 道常無名, which is repeated in *Laozi* 41.15, "the Way is hidden and nameless" 道隱無名. One of the two attributes of the "That-by-which" thus explicitly occurs in the *Laozi*, but this text does not contain a straightforward statement that, "the Dao is formless and nameless." As to formlessness, Wang Bi refers to *Laozi* 41.14 for support: "The Great Image is without form 大象無形." This statement comes at the end of a series of parallel phrases with similar content, such as "The Great Sound has an inaudible tone," and it is followed by a summarizing statement, "The Way is hidden and nameless. In fact [however], it is only the Way that is good at providing as well as good at completing." Wang Bi comments on this last phrase:

> Generally spoken, all these "great" [things] are made up by the Way. Among the images [the Way] is the Great Image, but "the Great Image is without form."

In this manner, the "Great Image" becomes another name for the Way, and its attributes can be transferred. Wang Bi also subsumes a number of *Laozi* expressions indicating diffuseness under the theoretical category "formlessness."[41]

In short, Wang Bi argues that these "great" things are great beyond big and small, that their absolute greatness is in fact the Dao itself, and that in this absolute greatness they are immeasurable, and in the case of the

Great Figure, "without form." The evidence for his implied argument that the rigidly argued induction of the necessary formlessness and namelessness of the "That-by-which" can already be found as a statement in the *Laozi* comes from three places (*zhang* 4, 32, 41) and is in one case (*Laozi* 41) established only through Wang Bi's identification of the Great Figure with the Dao. There is no visible interpretive violence in this process, and Wang Bi is careful to stay within the realm of plausibility. Still, within the context of Wang's argument, the individual elements from the *Laozi* are endowed with an air of systematic analysis absent from the surface of Wang's *Laozi* text. We hypothesize that Wang Bi rearranges scattered elements of the *Laozi* (and other texts) into a systematically argued whole. We shall check this hypothesis with the passage immediately following the first proposition.

Wang Bi here argues that that by which all specific entities are cannot have any of their specificities. As a consequence, the sense organs able to perceive specificity will have nothing to attach themselves to. In his presentation, these organs are fitted into a binary construct with eye and touch perceiving the *xing* 形, "shape," of "material entities," *wu* 物, and ear and taste perceiving the *ming* 名, "names," of "achievements," *gong* 功, or "processes," *shi* 事. To prove that the *Laozi* already contained this insight, Wang Bi cites four *Laozi* statements from three different chapters. It should be kept in mind that it does not matter here whether Wang Bi or *Laozi* is speaking positively about something having form or negatively about something not having form, as long as they are speaking about form. In none of them is the system present into which Wang Bi cites them. In *Laozi* 35.3, it is said that "the words uttered about the Dao indeed are stale; they are without taste. Looking for it, one cannot manage to see it; listening for it, one cannot manage to hear it; making use of it, it is impossible to exhaust it." In this passage we have three, not four, senses—taste, sight, and hearing; the last item, "making use of it," does not refer to any sense and makes it clear that the text here has no intention to systematically go through the list of the senses.

In *Laozi* 14.1, another series of impossible sensual perceptions of the Dao is given, this time consisting of sight, hearing, and touch. In *Laozi* 41.14 ff., a pair is given with the "Great Sound" related to hearing and the Great Figure to seeing. This last pair fits best into Wang Bi's binary structure. Wang Bi arranges a series of individual *Laozi* statements that even stylistically do not fit together into a unified, systematic sequence for his binary arrangement. In this process of homogenization, the rigid laws of parallelism even force him to abandon a verbatim quotation and to reformulate it. This is the case where he talks about the *wu cheng* 無 呈, "tastelessness," of the "That-by-which" to fit the pattern of *huncheng* 混成, *wuxiang* 無象, and *xisheng* 希聲, and he abandons the *Laozi* 35.3

formula 道之出言淡兮其無味, that "the words uttered about the Dao indeed are stale; they are without taste!" A statement in two characters was needed about the intrinsic insipidness of the Way; as this statement was not to be found, Wang Bi supplemented it to complete the structure. There are other passages where he does the same.[42] We see here an energy at work which, while entertaining the highest regard for the *Laozi*'s insights, has no qualms about inserting their scattered sparks into a highly structured, thoroughly argued pattern. On the level of textual treatment, this handling reflects an important transition. It is the transition to a systematic philosophy.

THE BINARY STRUCTURAL ORGANIZATION OF ENTITIES

BEINGS AND ACHIEVEMENTS: THEIR FEATURES AND THEIR PERCEPTION

Wang Bi's focus is not on surveying the panorama of the ten thousand kinds of entities and mapping their subgroups, relationships, and processes. Still, as his object of inquiry is the "That-by-which" of the ten thousand kinds of entities, which in itself is abstruse, he proceeds in this inquiry through a strongly targeted analysis of the intrinsic laws and structures of the accessible entities themselves. The beginning of his two essays again provides us with the key evidence. We shall present the inner logic of his thinking first before investigating some of the intellectual developments preceding Wang.

The "ten thousand kinds of entities," *wanwu* 萬物, at the beginning of the *LZWZLL* come in two subgroups named here "beings" 物 and "achievements" 功. The former refers to physical objects mostly of the natural world, inanimate or alive, such as the "four images" 四象, a reference to metal, wood, fire, and water, or the "five things," 五物, probably the five kinds of grain,[43] but it also includes living beings and material wealth.[44] The "achievements" are normally called "processes," *shi* 事,[45] a term also used for government business and denoting here a large class of immaterial entities mostly in the human world, such as actions, processes, or social renown. The "five teachings," *wu jiao* 五教, dealing with the relationship between king and minister, father and son, teacher and student, husband and wife, and older and younger brother, are such *shi* 事. In one passage Wang Bi uses the older term "ten thousand kinds of entities and the ten thousand kinds of affairs" 萬物萬事.[46]

As the two categories together form the "ten thousand kinds of entities," they often are referred to in interlocking parallel style constructions, as in the above case. In Wang Bi on *Laozi* 1.1, they appear as 指事造形, "demonstrable processes and created shapes." In Wang Bi on *Laozi* 5.4, the *wu* and *shi* again appear as the totality of entities. In Wang Bi on *Laozi* 29.4, the simple term *wu* 物 in the *Laozi* is expanded to the complete *wushi* 物事 in the commentary. Wang Bi begins the commentary for the famous *Laozi* 47.1: "[Only when] not going out of doors [into All Under Heaven one has something] by means of which to cognize All Under Heaven" with the *wu/shi* pair: "As processes have a principle, things have a master" 事有宗而物有主. From the *Laozi* commentary as well as the *LZWZLL*, we see that the ten thousand entities are subdivided into two subgroups, each defined in its particularity by either "shape" 形 or "name" 名.

The beginning of the *Zhouyi lüeli* repeats this argumentative structure, but here the terms differ. Wang Bi talks of the "many," *zhong* 眾, instead of *wu* 物, and of "movements," *dong* 動, instead of *shi* 事. The many cannot control the many; what is in motion itself cannot control the many movements of others. What controls the many must by necessity be the one; what controls the movements must by necessity be calm. The relationship between the formless and nameless "ancestor of the ten thousand kinds of entities" and these *wu* and *shi* entities returns here in the relationship of the One with the Many, and the calm with the moving. In his comments on *Laozi* 16.2, Wang Bi uses still another pair of subgroupings of the ten thousand kinds of entities, namely, *you* 有 and *dong* 動, which must refer to materially existing entities and movements.

Wang Bi obviously treats the *Laozi* and the *Zhouyi* differently. The *Zhouyi* is read as a symbolic construct consciously crafted by the Sage,[47] and its features stand for categories of reality. Wang Bi's statement is directly related to this symbolic feature of the *Zhouyi*. The hexagrams of the *Zhouyi* have six lines, but one of them, described in the *tuan* 象 statements before the analysis of the individual lines, determines (in many cases) the overall thrust. Wang Bi's statement about the "many" and the "One" claims that the *Zhouyi* structure of one line controlling the "many" others in fact is an implied philosophic statement about the relationship of the One and the Many. The "movements" refer to the "movements of the six lines" 六爻之動 mentioned in the *Xici*, which deal with the changes. These movements have a "point where they converge," *huitong* 會通, which the Sage is able to observe.[48]

There are ample echoes in Wang Bi's work of this binary structure with no borders separating the *Zhouyi* and the *Laozi* in this respect.[49] Although there is some terminological fluctuation, Wang Bi generally implodes the variety of linguistic material at his disposition into these binary categories in an attempt to arrive at a well-defined philosophic terminology.

Why should the *wu* 物 and the *shi* 事 form the two categories into which the totality subdivides? Wang Bi bases this subdivision on their fundamentally different kinds of specification. The *wu* 物 are specified by their "shape," *xing* 形, the *shi* 事, by their "name," *ming* 名. Wang Bi writes at the end of *Laozi* 38.2:

	then indeed, as a name has something that specifies it,
. . . .	
then indeed, as a shape has something that limits it, it will, even if it maximizes its greatness, by necessity have something that it does not encompass.	it will, even if it [the name] makes its beauty abundant, by necessity have something worrisome and painful.
名則有所分雖極其大必有不周.	形則有所止雖盛其美必有患憂.[50]

We have to infer the meaning of these terms from the context of their usage.

Both of these terms are broad categories. The *xing* 形 encompasses the *xiang* 象, the "images," and the *ming* 名 encompasses the *sheng* 聲, the "sounds."[51] As we shall see, the *shi* 事 and *wu* 物 are an old pair, and so are *xing* 形 and *ming* 名. The latter's fundamental difference is based on the different modes of their cognition. Wang Bi links the *xing* 形 with the eye and touch, and the *ming* 名 with the ear and taste, the latter because of the *Laozi* statements about the taste of words on the Dao. The *xing* are visual and material, while the *ming* can be heard and spoken. We thus arrive at the following binary organization of entities themselves, their specifying features, and the modes of their perception:

萬物

ENTITIES	ten thousand kinds of entities	
	/	\
	物	事
	material entities	processual entities
SPECIFICATIONS	形	名
	shape	name
PERCEPTION	視, 體	聽, 味
	seeing, touching	hearing, tasting [speaking]

The structural arrangement above mirrors the rhetorical arrangement of the interlocking parallel style statements of the argument at the beginning of the *LZWZLL*. This arrangement in turn contains a further proposition: the internal structures of both sides, the *wu* and the *shi*, are rigidly parallel, their fundamental opposition notwithstanding. The parallelism of their structure is based on their common element, their specificity. "Shapes by necessity have something that specifies them; sounds by necessity have something to which they belong" 形必有所分聲必有所屬, writes Wang Bi in the *LZWZLL*. This specificity makes them recognizable. On the basis of this parallelism, statements can be made on their common "That-by-which," namely, that it is "without shape" and "without name." With his implosive technique of commenting, Wang Bi merges a great variety of literary expressions in the *Laozi* into the blunt "without form and name," which becomes a standard epithet of the Dao in his *Laozi* writings.[52]

In the context of the development of Chinese philosophy, this system at the beginning of the *LZWZLL* is a complete novelty. It is marked by its capacity to organize philosophic concepts on the basis of verifiable criteria, to link the entities, their discernible characteristics, and the instruments of specific cognizance in parallel chains—all this in great economy subordinate to the final purpose of finding the necessary features of the "That-by-which." The innovative analytic powers of Wang Bi in this marginal field of his endeavor become more evident once they are read in the context of the philosophic thinking within which he was operating. I shall now turn my attention to a short sketch of this context insofar as it pertains to the issues dealt with in the above section.

THE PREHISTORY OF THE PAIR WU 物 AND SHI 事

Wang Bi has not created any one of the pairs of terms used here but is the first to integrate them into a coherent system. The organization of the realm of entities into two large subgroups of *wu* and *shi* is not the fruit of a particular philosopher's labors but more the result of language's own silent ordering efforts.[53] The pair *wu/shi* 物/事 seems to have entered the common discourse separately as "the ten thousand kinds of beings" 萬物 and "the hundred kinds of affairs" 百事 or the "ten thousand kinds of affairs" 萬事, along with a fair number of numerical (Hundred Families 百姓, hundred kinds of beasts 百獸) or paired (Heaven and Earth 天地) terms, all denoting a given totality.

Both the "ten thousand kinds of beings" 萬物 and the "ten thousand kinds of affairs" 萬事 are relatively early members of this group.[54] While not attested in Zhou inscriptions and not listed in Schuessler, the *wanwu* occur frequently in the *Zhuangzi*, the *Guanzi*, the *tuanci* 彖辭 and the *xugua* 序卦 of the *Zhouyi*, the *Laozi*, and other texts with philosophic ambitions. The *wanshi* are attested in texts such as the *Mozi*, the *Guanzi*, and the *Liji*. They also occur as the hundred kinds of affairs 百事, which obviously are handled by the Hundred Officials in the *Yi Zhoushu* 逸周書, the *Zuozhuan*, and the *Zhouli* 周禮, with one marginal occurrence in the *Mozi*.[55] The term frequently occurs as one in a series with other numerical terms of the same order, which makes it clear that the hundred/ten thousand kinds of affairs are the totality of all affairs, but only a part of the totality of entities. There are rare occurrences of *shiwu* 事物 with the meaning of "things of both the *shi* and *wu* categories" in authors such as the *Guanzi* and the *Xunzi*, and the term survives in modern Chinese and Japanese. In these early occurrences, the *shi* and *wu* did not serve as argumentative and rhetorical structuring devices in the manner shown below.

These statements do not give clear explanations about what exactly counts among either the *wanshi* or the *wanwu*. The hundred kinds of affairs, however, have the traditional meaning of the manifold kinds of government business; the frequent use of reproductive terminology for the *wanwu*, like *sheng* 生, "to live, to be born, to be generated," carries the memory that *wu* 物 in fact frequently means a living being. *Laozi* 5.1, for example, describes the attitude of Heaven and Earth toward the *wanwu* as parallel to that of the Sage toward the Hundred Families. This seems to indicate a notion of nature versus society, with the *wanwu* as the ten thousand kinds of living beings insofar as their natural and physical existence is concerned, while the Hundred Families would refer to a subsection insofar as social life was concerned. In a similar vein, the *Xugua* 序卦 of the *Zhouyi* starts: "As, once there is Heaven and Earth, the ten thousand kinds of beings are born, it is the ten thousand kinds of beings that fill the space between Heaven and Earth" 有天地 然後萬物生焉 盈天地之間者 唯萬物. The *wanwu/wanshi* pair would thus originate in a government perspective of the two relevant kinds of matter to be attended to—living beings and government affairs—and evolve into a more abstract concept of the ten thousand kinds of beings, ending up in the completely abstract sense in which Wang Bi uses it in the beginning of the *LZWZLL*, where it denotes all kinds entities, whether specified by form or name.

The *Wenzi* 文子 is the first work where I could locate the *wanwu* and the *baishi* juxtaposed in parallel phrases, together denoting the totality of entities; they thus became part of an overall binary construction of reality, which has found other expressions in terms such as Yin and Yang or Heaven and Earth. The *Wenzi* writes: "Wenzi says: 'The control for the ten thousand kinds of beings altogether passes through one single hole; the root of the hundred kinds of affairs altogether comes out of one single door. That is why the Sage . . . " 萬物之總皆閱一孔; 百事之根皆出一門." The idea underlying the parallel structure of this kind of statement is that the two parallel sets together form the totality. In this sense, *shi* and *wu* in this phrase denote two "halves" of the totality of entities. In the explanation of this line, the *Wenzi* writes: "The ten thousand kinds of beings cannot help but be generated, the hundred affairs cannot help but be completed" 萬物不得不生百事不得不成, and concludes with another use of the pair "the ten thousand kinds of beings have something that generates them but he [the Realized Man 眞人] is only like their root; the hundred kinds of affairs have something from which they emanate, but he only keeps to their door [from which they emerge]" 萬物有所生而獨如其根百事有所出而獨守其門.[56]

In a similar sense, the *Wenzi* writes, after describing how the Sage floats with the Dao: "And as a consequence there is none of the transformations of the ten thousand kinds of beings that he is not matching, and there is none of the changes of the hundred kinds of affairs that he is not corresponding to" 如此則萬物之化無不偶百事之變無不應也.[57]

The *Huainanzi* uses a number of the *Wenzi*'s phrases, but adds one of its own, where again parallel structures are used, and the statement actually refers to the common structure of both parts, as well as their unified root.[58] The "Assorted Sayings," *tan cong* 談叢, in the *Shuoyuan* 說苑, which contains much pre-Qin material, lists one saying: "The ten thousand kinds of beings, insofar as they get hold of their root, live; the hundred kinds of affairs, insofar as they get hold of their way, are completed" 萬物得其本者生, 百事得其道者成."[59] The pair also occurs in the beginning of the Mawangdui text *Daoyuan* 道原.

From the above quotations it is clear that the ten thousand kinds of beings and the ten thousand or hundred kinds of affairs are part of an argumentative figure dealing with their unified root, and the fact that persons qualified by their insight into the structure of this world to regulate it—such as the Sage or the Realized Man—will hold onto this root as a way of dealing with all of them. The two terms do not come at the beginning of a detailed exploration of the particular features of either group, or of the subgroups into which they might be divided, but are the end.

The actual contents of this argumentative figure are in part verbalized, in part embedded in the parallel structure of Wang Bi's first proposition. The verbalized form establishes a general rule for both. Neither realm is randomly organized. The *wu* have a spatial hierarchy between essential and dependent elements; the *shi* have a temporal sequence in which they unfold. The silent statement, made through the parallelism of the two phrases, is that the two together form a whole, the totality of entities, and that their relative structures are essentially analogous, that is, parallel, so that unified statements about both sectors, their root, and the relationship of this root to these sectors become possible.

The awkwardness that "ten thousand things" appear in two different locations of this conceptual hierarchy—first as the totality of entities and second as one segment of them—is eliminated in a marginal use in the *Wenzi* and in the famous line from the *Daxue* 大學: "Things have their root and offspring, processes have their beginning and end" 物有本末事有終始.[60] Here the numbers have been dropped in the subsections so that the ten thousand—not mentioned here—things can continue in their well-attested role as the totality. This use is adopted by Wang Bi.

Wang Bi, however, writes a commentary to the *Laozi*. What basis, if any, is there in the *Laozi* for this pair? While the term 萬物 appears in the *Laozi*, the pair 物/事 discussed here does not occur in the textual surface. However, Wang Bi discovers the basic grid for this pair in a number of standard phrases of the *Laozi*. In his comments on *Laozi* 38, Wang Bi writes:

> That is why if only [the ruler]
> would obtain the mother bringing
> about the achievements,

"the ten thousand kinds of entities [as the *Laozi* says in 2.4] [would] "come about" "without their being given orders [by him as the *Laozi* says in 34.2]."	the ten thousand kinds of affairs [would] persist without [him] laboring.[61]

故苟得其爲功之母則

萬物作焉而不辭也.	萬事存焉而不勞也.

The *gu* 故, "that is why," at the beginning regularly introduces quotations from the *Laozi* that will prove that the *Laozi* contains the core of the conclusion for which Wang Bi has argued. There seem to be, however, only quotations dealing with the 萬物. Wang Bi added the second phrase for symmetry's sake. Through the juxtaposition with the 萬事, these 萬物 obviously are only one part of the entities, namely, the one described earlier as 物. The relevant passage in the *Laozi* 34.2 runs in Wang's reading:

> The ten thousand entities depend on it [the Way] for their being born, but it does not give orders. Achievements are completed [through it], but it does not take station [in them]. 萬物恃之而生而不辭功成而不居.

The section is not written in parallel style, and the parallelism between the two statements is modest at best, consisting of 生而不辭 and 成而 不居 at the end; but there is no formal parallelism between 萬物 and 功. Based on this weak parallel, Wang Bi created a *Laozi* phrase analogous to 萬物 dealing with 萬事. We see that Wang Bi, in his efforts to translate the insights of wisdom into a systematic argument, not only reassembles elements from different places of the *Laozi* into an imputed system but also is in some cases unperturbed by the seeming difference between his own terminology and that of the *Laozi*. In his own language, the *wanwu* are the ten thousand kinds of entities, which subdivide into *wu* 物 and *gong* 功. Based on a sophisticated reading of both style and content of the *Laozi*, he in this case homogenizes in the quotation the *Laozi* term *gong* 功 into the *wanshi* 萬事 to match the *wanwu*, and he then assigns to these *wanwu* and *wanshi* the place of *wu* 物 and *shi* 事 in his own terminology.

Furthermore, a number of *Laozi zhang* in interlocking parallel style seem to be structured by this pair. In *Laozi* 44, for example, two concepts are juxtaposed, the *ming* 名 or "social renown," and the *huo* 貨, the "material goods" of wealth. They are linked there to another pair, high social status and physical survival, a pair that appears again in *Laozi* 7.2, which deals with "being to the fore," *xian* 先, socially, and "lasting," *cun* 存, physically. *Laozi* 3 operates with the pair "honoring worthies" and "appreciating goods that are hard to get," and *zhang* 26 is structured by the mental calmness of the Sage, even when close to enemy watchtowers, versus his holding onto the heavy baggage trains that provide the support for the troops, a pair again repeating the *shi/wu* structure. Finally, the binary constructs *wu/shi* and *xing/ming* are present in Wang Bi's reading of the first two phrases of *Laozi* 1.

The *shi/wu* pair has considerable analytic potential. In the uses outlined above, however, it is not transformed into a defined philosophic term. Neither the structuring of the entities nor the particular criteria for it are being discussed. For this, Wang Bi turns to an important statement in the *Xici*, which ascribes the great ordering of the unending variety of entities to the Sages themselves and is the basis for his opening statement in the *Zhouyi lüeli*. The *Xici* write:

> It was the Sages who, endowed with the wherewithal to survey the multitudes of All Under Heaven, compared their shapes and forms and made images of the characteristics of the kinds of entities. This is why they are called "images." [And] it was the Sages who, endowed with the wherewithal to survey the movements in All Under Heaven, observed where they converged by

way of enacting their regulations, and linked up sentences by
way of determining whether they were auspicious or inauspi-
cious. That is why they are called "lines."[62]

We do not have a Wang Bi commentary for the *Xici*. The reading of
ze 賾 in the first phrase 聖人有以見天下之賾 is not clear. The standard
definition is "mysterious." However, the term stands parallel to *dong* 動
in the phrase 聖人有以見天下之動, and from the further context it is
clear that it must here mean a "multitude" of entities 物 with shapes 形.
As to Wang Bi's reading of the passage, his reference to it in the opening
of the *Zhouyi lüeli* juxtaposes the notions of 眾 and 動, of the "many"
and the "movements," and it is safe to assume that *zhong* 眾 translates
the *ze* 賾 from this *Xici* passage.[63] That is why I have translated the term
as "multitudes."

The *Xici* passage is important. It recognizes the confusing multitude of
beings and the complexity of relationships and movements as a philosophical problem and ascribes its solution to the Sages. It was their achievement
to discover the categories and classes of entities from their blinding variety,
to represent them through the structure of the *Zhouyi*, and to set up the
basic pair, many/movements, although the linkage to the *shi/wu* pair is
not made here.

On the level of the structuring of the entities, Wang Bi thus:

• makes use of the common language pair *wanwu/baishi* in pre-Qin
  political discourse;

• eliminates its numerical features to subordinate it to the single
  heading of *wanwu*, which originated with the meaning "the ten
  thousands kinds of beings" and is recast in Wang Bi into the abstract notion of the "ten thousand kinds of entities";

• links the *Xici* statement about the Sages' discovering and represent-
  ing symbolically the two great realms of *ze* 賾 and *dong* 動 to the
  shi/wu pair, so that 賾 with the meaning of "the many" fits *wu* 物,
  and *dong* 動 fits the notion of *shi* 事;

• proves the plausibility of his construct in terms of textual analysis
  through individual commentaries to the *Zhouyi* and the *Laozi*,
  which show this structure as being at the base of the *Laozi*'s arguments and the *Zhouyi*'s organization.

In short, the upper half of the structure given earlier synthesizes the
manifold and hardly systematic linguistic habits and argumentative forays
of earlier texts into a cohesive, argumentative structure. Wang Bi seems to
be the first to firmly establish the model

wanwu 萬物

wu 物   *shi* 事

and to translate the terminology inherited from the *Laozi* and other texts into this model.

Again, the Sage had stated flatly what in Wang Bi became an elaborately argued structure. In the *Zhuangzi* chapter "Old Fisherman," which we know was among the most popular at least in the two or three generations following Wang Bi, none other but Confucius says:

> The Dao, furthermore, is that which
> the ten thousand kinds of entities take
> as their base. 且道者萬物之所由也.

Those of the multitude of beings which lose it die; those who get it, live.	If the handling of affairs deviates from it, they fail, if it goes along with it, they will be successful.
庶物失之者死得之者生.	爲事逆之則敗順之則成.⁶⁴

Here we have, it seems for the first time, all of the core elements assembled in the proper hierarchy, the *wanwu*, the *wu*, and the *shi*. Graham counts the chapter among the late third century B.C.E. *Zhuangzi* chapters.[65]

In Wang Bi's scheme, the *wu* 物 are specified by their shape, *xing* 形, and the *shi* 事 by their name, *ming* 名. The pair *xing/ming* is well established before Wang Bi. It occurs in two different meanings, both used by Wang Bi. First, the *ming*, "name," is what describes the *xing*, "shape," of a being. Second, the *xing* 形 refers to the outward physical manifestations of social status, such as dress, or mutilation, while the *ming* refers to the "renown" or even "fame" associated with this social status.[66] Both establish social differentiation. They are used in discussions of society, not of nature. Wang Bi's use of the pair here is derived from the second variant. In his use, the thick social context of the terms is largely eliminated, and they have become abstract categories for the specificity of the two kinds of entities. Wang Bi thus inserts another inherited pair of notions into his binary structure. As his interest remains tied to political philosophy, he is not very radical in eliminating this social context from the pair, because in the translation of his philosophic discoveries to society it will resurface as the application of the abstract categories originally derived from its specific form.

In the last step, Wang Bi links the specificities of the entities to the instruments of perception and cognition. Again, he seems to be the first to establish this link. The effort and even intellectual violence in this attempt at arriving at a symmetrical and binary organization are felt at two points of this insertion of the senses into the overall structure. The traditional "five senses," *wuguan* 五官, being of an uneven number, have no place here. Wang Bi unceremoniously drops the "nose" from the list, because the *Laozi* does not mention it; it is supernumerary in a binary structure, and it senses neither of the two main kinds of specification. The "taste," on the other hand, stays in place, but in quite a different sense. It "tastes" the specificity of "words," *yan* 言, or "names," *ming* 名, as well as the "insipidity," *dan* 淡, of the words by the Way. It is described as an instrument of active linguistic cognition in conjunction with/opposed to the ear as the instrument of passive linguistic cognition, a constellation repeated in the touch/sight pair.

Wang Bi thus presents us with a homogeneous binary structure for reality, its specifications, and the instruments for their perception. The key element of this reality is specificity of the kinds of entities. Although the term *fen* 分 often used for this specificity has a social meaning of one's "proper place" in society, which implies an ordered structure, the specificity of the kinds of entities in itself does not necessarily imply order. Randomness and chaos might reign in the overall process of the entities' interaction as a consequence of their acting out their specificity. Wang Bi sees the problem and deals with the issue.

THE ORDER OF THE
TEN THOUSAND KINDS OF ENTITIES

The *Laozi* is not interested in the categories delineating the specificity of entities. In twenty out of thirty-seven cases, it treats the entities in their generality as *wanwu* 萬物—often with an implied anthropomorphic focus—and deals with that by which they are.[67] The simple *wu* 物 is only rarely the singular, "an entity," but comes in a host of contextually defined meanings such as "something," or "other people of lower status," which suggests that in the *Laozi* the *wanwu* had become a compound with its own meaning (and development of this meaning) fairly independent of the *wu*.[68]

The ten thousand kinds of entities are, however, not only "generated," *sheng* 生, by the Dao through mediation (*Laozi* 42.1), but each also has an intrinsic suchness and particularity, which the *Laozi* calls (64.9) 萬物之自然 "that of the ten thousand kinds of beings which is of itself what it is," which the Sage might "support," *fu* 輔, but with which he "will not dare to interfere," *bu gan wei* 不敢爲.[69] Without a specifier, this *ziran* 自然 appears in the hierarchy above the Dao in *Laozi* 25 and 23.

Wang Bi builds on the expression about a *ziran* of the ten thousand kinds of beings in *Laozi* 64 and ascribes to all entities a particularity. This particularity does not come to them individually but according to the class and species to which they belong, which is the reason the *wanwu* 萬物 are rather "ten thousand kinds of entities" than the totality of individual entities. The preset particularities of these ten thousand kinds of entities in fact are not random with a resulting entropy and chaos but fit into a predetermined order. The *Laozi* itself does not develop this thought explicitly, but its assumption that *wuwei* 無爲, "non-interference," will bring about order, *zhi* 治, may be read as an indicator of an internal spontaneous order among the ten thousand kinds of entities based on the integration of their preset particularities. Wang Bi develops this thought in his fresh commentary to *Laozi* 5.1 into a structure recalling Leibniz' *praestabilirte Harmonie*.

Laozi 5.1:
> Heaven and Earth are not kindly. For them, the ten thousand kinds of entities are like grass and dogs. 天地不仁以萬物爲芻狗.

Commentary
> Heaven and Earth let That-which-is-of-itself-what-it-is [of the ten thousand kinds of entities] come into effect. They are without interference and without creation [with the result that] the ten thousand kinds of entities spontaneously order and regulate each other. This is why [the *Laozi* says] "[Heaven and Earth are] not kindly"! 天地任自然無爲無造萬物自相治理故不仁也 . . . Heaven and Earth do not produce grass for the benefit of cattle, but the cattle [still] eat grass. They do not produce dogs for the benefit of men, but men [still] eat dogs. As they are without interference concerning the ten thousand kinds of entities, each of the ten thousand kinds of entities fits into its use, so that there is none that is not provided for. 天地不爲獸生芻而獸食芻不爲人生狗而人食狗. 無爲於萬物而萬物各適其所用則莫不贍矣.

The particular specificity of entities is determined by their "nature." Wang Bi implodes into the notion of this preset and prefitted particularity of the ten thousand kinds of entities a variety of terms, such as "nature," *xing* 性, "permanent nature," *changxing* 常性, "true essence," *zhen* 眞,

"core," *qing* 情, "ultimate," *zhi* 致, or "That-which-is-of-itself-what-it-is," *ziran* 自然. He explicitly identifies the "nature" 性 of the ten thousand kinds of things as identical with the highest concept in the *Laozi*, namely, *ziran*, "That-which-is-of-itself-what-it-is," when he says "the ten thousand kinds of entities have That-which-is-of-itself-what-it-is as their nature" 萬物以自然爲性 (Wang Bi on *Laozi* 29.3).[70]

With this implosion of many terms, Wang Bi engages in a dialogue not just with the *Laozi*. The terms *xing* 性, *zhen* 眞, *qing* 情 do not even appear in the *Laozi* or, as is the case with *zhen*, not in this sense.

In pre-Qin philosophy, the term *xing* 性 was mostly used for the invisible human "nature" endowed by Heaven, as opposed to the visible shape, but already in the *Wenzi* it appears as the "nature" of categories such as water, which "desires to be clean," or of the entire chain of metal, wood, water, fire, and earth.[71] *Zhen* 眞 has been introduced as a noun by the *Zhuangzi* in a sense of the true human nature that can find access to the Dao and appears in a similar sense in the *Wenzi* in phrases, such as "the man who pursues the Dao completes his nature and preserves his true [core]" 夫人道者全性保眞.[72] *Qing* 情, on occasion, is used synonymously with the others in passages of the *tuanci* of the *Zhouyi* and the *Xici*, as well as in other texts that talk of the *qing* 情 of Heaven and Earth, or of the Sage.[73]

This "nature" is defined not in relation to itself but in a functional, interactive way to other entities, for which the term *use*, *yong* 用, is used in the Wang Bi quotation given above. If this "nature" of entities, their preset, interactive characteristics, is not interfered with, then "each will fit into its use," and through this use, all are well provided for. The effect is a dynamic, interactive, preset order. It is not imposed by arbitrary rule but might be disturbed by interference. Accordingly, the "nature" of entities is not their trivial particularity but a part of the overall order secured by the Dao or by That-which-is-of-itself-what-it-is. In his commentary to *Laozi* 51, Wang Bi reads the term *de* 德, "capacity," as the homophonous *de* 得, "what someone or something receives," that is, as "the receipt." Among the things the entities "receive" is that they are "specified," *ting* 亭, and "completed," *du* 毒, and Wang Bi interprets these terms so: "'Specifies them' means it groups their shapes 品其形; 'completes them' means it perfects their substance 成其質," but I have not found further thinking on the issue in his work.

Wang Bi thus claims an intrinsic non-randomness for the interaction among the entities, a kind of prestabilized harmony as described in Leibniz' monadology. It does not come about through struggle or compromise, orders or planning, but it is encoded in the form of a functional relationship into the very "nature" of the entities and is tied not to them individually

but to the category to which they belong. Wang Bi sees this insight generally contained in the notion of *ziran* 自然 in the *Laozi* and encoded in
particular by the Sages into the structure of the *Zhouyi* hexagrams with
their basis in the relationship between the One [line] and the Many, but
also their regulated and thus predictable relationships between lines. In the
first section of his *Zhouyi lüeli*, Ming tuan 明彖, Wang Bi writes, ending
with a further reference to Xici上.6, which has already been quoted as
the origin of the many/movement pair:

> As entities are without randomness,
> they thus by necessity are based on
> their ordering principle.

> For the control of them [the
> movements] there is an ancestor,

for their [the many's] being held
together there is an origin.

> That is why [*Xici* 上.6 says]

> the [movements] might be com-
> plex, but they are "not chaotic."

the [many] might be manifold,
but they are not confused.

物无妄然必由其理.

統之有宗

會之有元

故繁而不亂眾而不惑.⁷⁴

Wang Bi introduces here the noun *li* 理. It is specified as *qi li* 其理,
"their ordering principle[s]," which means that each kind of entity has
its own ordering principle. These describe the aspects of their functional
interaction with other entities, their particular non-randomness. Forming
a totality of ordered interactions, these individual *li* have a common "great
purport" 理有大致 (Wang on *Laozi* 47.1) or "a single point where they
converge," 理有會 (Wang on *Lunyu* 4.15), and the overall prestabilized
harmony is then called "highest ordering principle," *zhili* 至理 (Wang on
Laozi 42.2, *LZWZLL* 3.10), "great order," *dazhi* 大治 (Wang on *Laozi*
58.7), or the "epitome of order," *zhi zhi ji* 治之極 (Wang on *Laozi* 63.1).
A key notion in this order is the term *zi* 自, "spontaneously," as in the
expression that the "ten thousand kinds of entities spontaneously order

and regulate each other" in the quotation from Wang Bi on *Laozi* 5.1. As long as this order is not disturbed, entities "spontaneously" or "of their own accord," that is, following their own nature and not some particular wish or desire, will fit into this ultimate order, which rejects the notion of a planned or managed order.[75] "That-[of the ten thousand kinds of enti-ties]-which-is-of-itself-what-it-is is [in itself] sufficient, interfering with it would destroy it," writes Wang Bi on *Laozi* 2.2 自然已足爲則敗也. Into this notion of order Wang Bi again implodes a variety of terms from the *Laozi* or the general philosophic discourse, such as *zhi* 治, *ji* 濟, *he* 和, *an* 安, *jun* 均, and *ping* 平.

Leibniz' monads live in a prestabilized harmony in which nothing can disturb them. This is not the case for Wang Bi's ten thousand kinds of entities. Their order is intrinsically unstable, and their "nature" on which this order is based is in constant danger of being lost or destroyed. With regard to the human world, this danger is evident from experience and has been properly dealt with. Here we find statements in pre-Qin philosophy that this true nature must be "protected," may be "completed," *quan* 全, but also can be "lost," *shi* 失, or "destroyed," *bai* 敗. There was a shared assumption during this time that the order of Heaven was by and large marked by regularity, for which the standard reference to the four seasons' sequence and the orderly reproduction of the ten thousand kinds of living beings was the visible proof. However, even in Confucius' famous reference to these two phenomena (*Lunyu* 17.19), their order was due to Heaven's particular way of letting them unroll and reproduce without giving orders, and not to the iron law of their own particularity and interaction with other things. The *Laozi* agrees with this assumption in the many *zhang* that refer to how Heaven deals with the ten thousand kinds of things as a consciously imitated model for the Sage, which presupposes a recogni-tion of the stable order of nature as a model for the unstable order of society.

It was the *Laozi*'s philosophic achievement to discover the dynamic and interactive character of this seemingly stable order of "nature," and Wang Bi discovered this discovery and developed it. *Laozi* 5.3 runs with and through Wang's commentary:

Text

	[The space] between Heaven and Earth is like a	
drum	or	flute,
	[that is,]	hollow it is, but inexhaustible [in the variety of sounds it can produce].

[the more] it is beaten, the more
[sound] comes out of it.

Commentary

. . . .

                          Inside

drum   and   flute

                          are

empty   and   hollow.

                                               [The flute] has no feelings [of its
                                               own to prefer one tone over the
                                               other].

[The drum] has no activity [of its
own to create this resonance rather
than another].

                          That is why [, as the text
                          claims,]

                                               [the flute] is hollow but it is
                                               impossible to exhaust it.

[the drum,] all the "beating"
notwithstanding, is
inexhaustible.

                          In the [space] between Heaven
                          and Earth That-which-is-of-
                          itself-what-it-is [of all entities]
                          is put grandly into effect. That
                          is why [the space between
                          Heaven and Earth] is inexhaus-
                          tible "like a flute and a drum."[76]

The statement of the *Laozi* comparing the space between Heaven and
Earth to a flute and a drum stresses its emptiness and inexhaustibility.
Wang Bi reads it in the context of *zhang* 39, to be discussed below, and
sees in the statement the outlines of a philosophic discovery. We have an
observable phenomenon: the flute can play many different tones; the drum
lends itself to different volumes. What enables them to be in this manner a
One containing and generating a multitude? The flute has no "feelings" of
its own, no preferences, and the drum does not create its own commotion
according to its own whims. It is this absence of particular and specific
preferences and desires that enables them to generate a great variety of

different sounds and volumes. In his next comment, Wang Bi makes this explicit: "Drum and flute 'keep to the middle' [without being specified in either way] so that they are inexhaustible to the maximum. They discard their selves and put themselves at the service of other entities so that there is none that is not well-ordered. If the drum or the flute were bent on making [a specific] sound [or volume], they would be unable to satisfy the requirements of flutists [and drummers]." What makes the flute and drum able to produce such a variety of sound and volume is their having no preferences for any of them; they themselves are unspecific with regard to the specificity of the tones that they effect. Clearly, the flute and drum cannot help but operate in this way, but they could not operate this way if their particular unspecificity was not intrinsic to their constitution. Wang Bi reiterates the same type of argument with regard to the potter. Only by neither being a pot nor being fixed to a particular kind of pot is the potter able to produce a great variety of pots.[77]

In a stunning turn, the *Laozi* itself hypothesizes in *zhang* 39 about what would happen to Heaven, Earth, the spirits, the valley, and the king if they would not "make use of the One." All of them are Ones covering, supporting, influencing, containing, or governing Many. Their capacity for taking care of a great variety of entities hinges on their not being one of them, but "making use of the One." The crisis ensuing in case of a failure to do this concerns not only the other entities, who would lose their cover, support, and so forth, but it would bode disaster for these Ones themselves: Heaven would "be in danger of being torn apart" 裂; the Earth would "be in danger of getting into commotion" 發; the spirit would "lose efficacity" 歇; the valley would "be drained" 竭; and the king "toppled" 蹶. The seemingly stable order of Heaven's covering the ten thousand kinds of entities and the Earth's supporting them is the result of a continuous dynamic process involving recourse by these "great" categories to some ultimate "That-by-which" as the basis for their interaction with the specific natures or particular ordering principles of the entities. Only by "making use," *yi* 以—which Wang Bi translates straight into *yong* 用—of the "One" can these "great" entities have an effect on and contain a variety of other entities and at the same time themselves survive intact.

In the *Laozi*, the line goes straight through from Heaven to the valley and the kings and dukes. There is no difference between those who cannot help but "make use of the One" and those able to blunder, namely, the kings and dukes. This lack of differentiation does not come from a lack of sophistication. It is a rhetorical device for the benefit of the only potential readers of this group, that is, the kings and dukes, who were sure to blunder, both when the *Laozi* was written and when Wang Bi lived, and might need advice. The valley can do its thing without the philosopher.

The dynamic and unstable order among entities is not maintained merely by their just being what they are. This argument was made a generation after Wang Bi by Xiang Xiu 向秀 and Guo Xiang 郭象 in their *Zhuangzi Commentary*, where they claimed the entities were "spontaneously such as they were," *zi er* 自爾, and "without a guiding principle," *wu zhu* 無主.[78] This challenge to Wang Bi highlights the core feature of his own analysis, namely, that the order among any multitude of entities depends on the relationship of a controlling One to them. The basic relationship One/Many is reproduced in the particular relationships of a given One like the flute, the potter, or the guiding line in a hexagram to the particular Many under its impact. In Wang Bi's terminology, these given Ones "make use" of the One itself in their relationship to their Many. The only real crisis—as opposed to the hypothetical ones—is described by Wang Bi for the social realm, where a particular One, the ruler, confronts the Hundred Families or simply the ten thousand kinds of entities. If he understands the basics of the relationship of the One and the Many or even is a Sage, his own position will be secure, and social order will be brought about and prevail; if he does not, he will not only be toppled but also "lose" and "destroy" the nature of the entities, with the effect that their prestabilized order is destroyed. The vocabulary used is on the negative side "to lose," *shi* 失, to "be destroyed," *bai* 敗, or to "be hurt," *shang* 傷, and to "be damaged," *hai* 害; on the positive side, it is "to complete," *quan* 全, to "preserve," *shou* 受, to "protect," *bao* 保, to "stabilize," *ding* 定, and "to achieve," *de* 得.[79]

We are at this moment primarily interested in the particular features of the order among entities and will return to the political science aspects of Wang Bi's philosophy further along. From what we have seen, the general relationship One/Many reproduced itself in a descending hierarchy of Ones and "Manies," from those "great" Ones that confront the entirety of entities but are specific in one point like Heaven and Earth, to those who with more specificity of their own confront a smaller group of entities like a potter his clay or the flute its tones. The overall order of the Many or the particular group of Manies depends on the One to bring to fruition and not to disturb the intrinsic orderliness of entities.

We shall now read Wang Bi's concept of ontic order in the context of the history of the concept of *li* 理, in which this order has been discussed.[80]

The notion of *li* 理, ordering principle, appears in the *Zhouyi lüeli* in the phrase "as entities are without randomness, they thus by necessity are based on their [respective] ordering principles." The term *li* does not appear in the *Laozi*, but it does in the *Xici*, *Shuogua*, and *Wenyan* of the *Zhouyi*, all of which share a strong, philosophic outlook.[81] There it occurs in its pre-philosophical meaning in the expression *dili* 地理, parallel to *tianwen* 天文, "[observable] patterns of Heaven," meaning "[observable] ordering principle of the Earth,"[82] which fixes *li* to the meaning of the ordering principle of a complex phenomenon such as Earth or a class of entities. In a more fundamental statement in the first *Xici* section, it is used to describe a more abstract structured order of the universe with Heaven and Earth in their respective places, movement and rest with their "permanent," *chang* 常, relationship, with "processes (?)," *fang* 方, "grouping together in accordance with their classes, and beings dividing in accordance with their particularities" 方以類聚物以群分 with the sun and the moon on their rounds, and cold and warm seasons alternating. The conscious reproduction in "All Under Heaven," that is, society, of this ordered universe is called here "the ordering principle[s] of All Under Heaven," *tianxia zhi li* 天下之理. The *Yueji* 樂記 chapter in the *Liji* 禮記 speaks of the "ordering principles of the ten thousand kinds of beings" 萬物之理[83] and of "Heaven's ordering principle" 天理, which can "perish" 滅 if the right Way is not enacted, and says that "ritual is the unalterability of the [respective] ordering principles [of entities]" 禮也者理之不可易者也.[84] From the uses quoted, it is clear that *li* is no general concept of order but the ordering principle of a particular realm or kind of entities. This must be true for the last-quoted phrase, and I have for this reason added the brackets.

The *Wenzi* is the first to use the notion of *li* 理 for the analysis of the *Laozi*'s philosophy, although the term has not yet developed into a fixed concept. In its verbal use, it occurs with *zhi* 治, "to regulate, to put into order,"[85] in the parallel position, which indicates a similar meaning. As a noun it often matches *jie* 節, as in "The Sage treats them [his body and mind] with respect and does not dare to exaggerate [their use]. As he responds by means of negativity to that which is, he invariably penetrates to the ordering principle[s] of it [of that which is]. As he takes in the real by means of the empty, he invariably fully penetrates the rule[s] of it [of the real]" 聖人遵之不敢越也. 以無應有必究其理以虛受實必窮其節.[86]

Here, that which is, *you* 有, altogether has such ordering principles, based on the Dao; otherwise, the Sage would not deal with it. *Li* also appears with, or parallel to, the *fen* 分 of things, their particular quality and place, and to the *zi* 資, the particular qualities.[87] The link between this *li* and the Dao is brought out in a phrase explaining the terms *tianwen* 天文 and *dili* 地理: "The Way of Heaven forms a [heavenly] pattern [天]文; the Way of the Earth forms an [earthly] pattern [地]理; the One makes for their [internal] harmony; time makes for their initiating [developments]; and in this manner they complete the ten thousand things; [I] call this 'the Way'" 天道爲文地道爲理一爲之和時爲之使以成萬物命之日道.[88]

Here the heavenly and earthly patterns are specific manifestations of their Dao.

In other places, the *Wenzi* uses the term as a noun synonymous with the Dao 道 or even in the binom *daoli* 道理, sometimes read as being "the structured order of the Dao" 道之理.[89] This denotes an objective structure of reality that a ruler has to understand and "follow," *shun* 順 or *xun* 循, instead of going after his personal interests and imposing his own will.[90]

Altogether, the term *li* 理 is used in the *Wenzi* as a noun for the structured order of the One, the Dao, for all that exists, 有, for Heaven, Earth, All Under Heaven, processes, human emotions 人情; as a verb it means the establishment of this structured order in human society where it does not come about on its own. In one passage quoted by Li Dingsheng and Xu Huijun as important for the development of the concept,[91] he says: "[As] the Yin and Yang, the Four Seasons, metal, wood, water, fire, and earth are identical with regard to the Way and different with regard to [their] ordering principles, the ten thousand kinds of things are identical with regard to [their] nature, but different with regard to their forms" 陰陽四時金木水火土同道而異理萬物同情而異形.[92] The somewhat diffuse context of this passage deals with the Sage adapting and having each one live out his potential. The Sage "establishes the law in order to guide the hearts of the people to have each one of them bring to bear [their] That-which-is-of-itelf-what-it-is" 聖人立法以導民心各使自然. The *li* 理 in this phrase refers to the constituent classes of objects and processes in the realm of nature. The Dao is common to them all, while the particular ordering principle of the four seasons or the elements differs. The passage seems to say that the fact that the ten thousand kinds of entities have a common basis in the Dao but differ in their outward appearance reflects the juxtaposition of *dao* and *li* in their constituent elements.[93] The expression *daoli* 道理 or *dao zhi li* 道之理 indicates that this structured order might be endowed by the Dao, but this thought is developed only in the *Hanfeizi* chapters dealing with the *Laozi*. Li Dingsheng and Xu Huijun argue convincingly that the *Wenzi* marks an important link between the *Laozi* and the *Hanfeizi* in the development of the concept of *li*.[94]

The *Hanfeizi* deals with the relationship of the Dao insofar as it is unspecific and *chang* 常, "eternal," and the *li*, insofar as they are specific and involve change in time. In a daring passage, he pleads for the impermanence of the Dao in its interaction with the ten thousand entities, for which it provides their particular ordering structure, and outlines the cognition of the Dao in the fine explanation of the origin of the word 象, which means both "elephant" and "image." The text runs:

The Dao is that which makes the ten thousand kinds of entities be so, and what fixes the ten thousand ordering structures. An ordering structure is the pattern of a completed thing; the Dao is that by which the ten thousand things are completed. Therefore it is said: "The Dao is that which gives them [the entities] the ordering structure." Things have an ordering structure and cannot overlap. As they have an ordering structure and cannot overlap, [the Dao as that] "which gives them the ordering structure" [is] the delineator of things. Each of the ten thousand kinds of entities has an ordering structure. As each of them has an ordering structure and as the Dao to the very last fixes the ordering structures of the ten thousand kinds of entities, it [the Dao] cannot but be involved in change. As it cannot but be involved in change, it has no eternal stance; as it has no eternal stance, it is endowed in the ether of life and death [of living beings], in the deliberations of the ten thousand kinds of knowledge, and in the rise and fall of the ten thousand affairs. Heaven gets it [the Dao] and is high through it; the Earth gets it [the Dao] and is hoarding through it; the Polar Star gets it and completes its majesty through it. . . . The Dao is knowledgeable together with [emperors] Yao and Shun, and mad together with Jieyu [who refused government service], went down together with [the evil emperors] Jie and Zhou, and was at the fore together with Tang and Wu [who deposed them]. If considered close by, it roams in the four cardinal points; if considered far off, it always is next to oneself. If considered dark, its brilliance is shining brightly; if considered bright, its material substance is obscure. Still [its] effects complete Heaven and Earth; it harmonizes and transforms the thunders, [in short] the things within the world owe their completion to it. Generally speaking, the Dao's own nature neither delineates nor gives shape; it is weak and soft and adapts to time; it is in mutual responsiveness with the ordering structures. The ten thousand living beings get it and die through it, and they get it and live through it; the ten thousand affairs get it and and fail through it, and get it and are completed through it. The Dao is comparable to water. A drowning person drinks too much of it and dies, while a dehydrated person gets to drink of it and lives. And it is comparable to a sword or a halberd. The fool will vent his vengeance with it, and calamity is born; the Sage will use it to punish the bully, and bliss will be completed. Thus getting it, a [living being] might die from it; getting it, a [living being] might live through it; getting it [an affair] might fail through it; and getting it [an affair] might be completed through it.

People rarely see a living elephant, but once they get hold of the bones of a dead elephant, they examine their layout by way of imagining its [the elephant's] living [shape]. Thus people call that by means of which they imagine something in their minds an "elephant" 象 [= an image]. Now, although one is neither able to see nor hear the Dao, the Sage holds on to its visible effects by way of envisioning its shape. That is why [the *Laozi* 14.2 says it is] "the shape of something shapeless, the image [= elephant] of a no-thing."[95]

The Dao manifests itself in all of the ordering structures. As all ten thousand kinds of things have such ordering structures, none is cut off from the Dao, not even death or the evil emperors Jie and Zhou. The visible ordering structures are the bones of the invisible Dao, and by *an qi tu* 案其圖, by "examining their layout," by *zhi qi jian gong* 執其見功, "holding on to [the Dao's] visible effects," that is by extrapolation and inference, the Sage "makes up its shape," *chu jian qi xing* 處見其形, although its actual shape is invisible. The Dao in its essence, 道之情, does not actively interfere with the ten thousand kinds of things but adapts itself to their *li* 理. Thus in having their ordered structure, in life and death, success and demise, length and shortness, they have the Dao. The Dao manifests itself in the order of the ten thousand things.

What, then, are the *li* that give evidence of the Dao's shape? The *Hanfeizi* continues:

Generally speaking, an ordering principle consists in the assignment of the square and the round, the short and the long, the coarse and the fine, the firm and the brittle. Therefore, only after this ordering principle is fixed is one possibly able to talk [about the Dao]. Therefore there is persistence and demise in the fixed ordering structures, death and life, rise and decline. However, one cannot call "eternal" things that now persist, now go under, now live and then die, first rise, and then decline. Only that which is born together with the separation of Heaven and Earth and will neither die nor decline until the disappearance of Heaven and Earth is called "eternal" 常. The eternal does not have . . . (corruption) and is without fixed ordering structure; as it is without ordering structure and is not in a fixed place, it cannot be spoken of.

The Sage, observing its [the Eternal's] darkness, *xuan* 玄, and emptiness, *xu* 虛, made use of its "getting around everywhere" [as the *Laozi* says in 25.3] and, "forced, gave it the style 'Way'," [*Laozi* 25.5], and only then it became possible to argue. That is why [the *Laozi* 1] says, "A way that can be spoken of is not the eternal Way."

The term *li* 理 describes the structured specificity of things. Insofar as they have shapes, *xing* 形, they can be defined as being either white or black, large or small. A *li* is not the specificity of an individual object but of a category; this also means it is not the particularity of an individual thing but the common feature of that class of things. The *Hanfeizi* expresses these features through a list of antonyms such as "short/long, small/big, square/round, hard/brittle, light/heavy, white/black—these are called *li*."[96] However, the processes involved in everything that is victim to time and not eternal, such as rise and fall, life and death, are not subsumed under the term *li*. The *Hanfeizi* says "the fixed ordering structures have persistence and demise, death and life, rise and decline" 定理有存亡有死生有盛衰, but these processes do not count among these structures. These *li* are manifest. The Sage is aware of the absence of definable ordering structures in the "essence of the Dao," is aware of its being "dark and empty," but in view of the fact that it *zhou xing* 周行, "gets around everywhere," as the *Laozi* 25 says, that is, makes itself felt through and in the *li*, he uses the metaphor of the Way, which also gets around everywhere. Now it is possible to talk, because the talk about the Way is the talk about all the places it gets to, that is, the *li*.

The *Hanfeizi* argument provides an avenue for talking about that which provides the ordering structures as one talks about the features of the elephant that can be extrapolated from the bones. The *Hanfeizi* is interested in the *li*, because they become the model for the *fa* 法, the order-enforcing structures set up in society within his political theory, an aspect also developed in the *Jingfa* 經法 of the *Huangdi sijing* 黃帝四經. After explaining the "seven methods" through which "Heaven ordains the fate of things" on earth, this text continues:

> If each thing is in unison with the Dao, [I] call it ordering structure, *li* 理. The [place] where the ordering structure is, I call "obedience [to the Dao]." If among the things there are those not in unison with the Dao, I call this [their] "loosing of ordering structure." The [place] where the loss of the ordering structure is, I call "rebellion [against the Dao]." 物各合於道者謂之理理之所在謂之順物有不合於道者謂之失理失理之所在謂之逆.[97]

Once the fact is established that it is the Dao that provides the *li*, the attention can shift toward the *li*. Both the *Huangdi sijing* 黃帝四經 and the *Hanfeizi* are interested in developing methods to enforce obedience to the Dao in the form of obedience to state rules.

Philosophically spoken, however, the story of the elephant opens induction from the categories visibly present in the ten thousand kinds of things as a viable avenue of thinking and arguing about the basis of these ordering structures. The *Hanfeizi* itself is not further interested in this option.

Wang Bi inherits the notion of a *li* from tradition. He accepts the dynamics and instability of the relationships among entities inherent in this notion as well as its linkage to the Dao itself. He lifts the notion of *li* from the aphoristic and unsystematic but, on this basis, he argues vehemently against attempts to make this notion the basis for state interventions to enforce conformity with the structures set up by the Dao itself. However, he certainly went along with the notion of induction and extrapolation as the only viable approach to the Dao.

Wang Bi thus claims to continue an exploration in which many philosophers and texts had taken part, not just the *Laozi*, and also claims to insert their insights into his own work. Aware of the limitations of language, which he greatly elaborates upon, Wang Bi does not impose a rigid new vocabulary—although attempts at standardization are visible—but rather a systematic new argumentative structure within which the terms find their common contextual place and definition, whatever the particular linguistic material being used.

THE ONE AND THE MANY

The two realms of entities are characterized by specificity. "Names have something that specifies them, shapes have something that limits them." Wang Bi introduces one single notion that he does not subject to further scrutiny, namely, that That-by-which-the-ten thousand-kinds-of-entities-are must be a One. This was a common assumption among all thinkers we know of up to his time, the open question being only what this One was. Was it *tian* 天, *qi* 氣, the *taiji* 太極, or the *dao* 道, and what were its characteristics and features? Again, it was the generation after Wang Bi with Xiang Xiu and Guo Xiang who questioned this basic premise, arguing that the entities "were what they were on their own," *zi er* 自爾, without any dominating principle lording it over them, *wu zhu* 無主.

Within Wang Bi's approach, the question was what the "necessary" features of this One were. For the One to be the One of all different kinds of entities, it has to be without all of their specific features. "Were it warming, then it would not be able to cool; were it [tied to let sound forth the tone] *gong*, then it would not be able to [let sound forth the tone] *shang*."[98] The features of the entities come in antagonistic opposites like cool and warm. Something that is to be the basis for both cannot be defined by either; otherwise, it could not be the basis of the opposite.

In the hierarchy of entities there are limited Ones confronting limited Manies. The examples of the flute, the drum, and the potter have been mentioned. In the highest order of this hierarchy are those categories that confront the totality of entities like Heaven, which covers all, and Earth, which carries all. Heaven alone or Heaven and Earth together have been described by earlier philosophers as the basis of the *wanwu*, the ten thousand kinds of entities. Already the *Laozi* rejects this notion with the introduction of the Dao as "anterior, *xian* 先, to Heaven and Earth." Wang Bi provides an argument for this rejection. Although Heaven and Earth confront the entirety of entities, they are still tied down by one feature: Heaven covers, and thus it does not carry; Earth carries, but it does not cover.[99] In a series of statements in the *LZWZLL* and his commentaries, Wang Bi cleans the notion of the One by which all entities are of all specificity, relying as usual on a systematizing and an argumentative interpretation of the *Laozi*. *Laozi* 41.13ff. runs:

> The Great Sound has an inaudible tone. The Great Image is without form.

The notion "great" here means "absolute," beyond the confines of great and small. Wang Bi reads these expressions as appellations for the Dao, which again is one of the appellations for the That-by-which. He comments on the Great Sound:

> [As the *Laozi* 14.1 says] "That which [I] do not hear when listening for it, [I] call 'inaudible.'" It [the Great Sound] thus is a sound one is unable to hear. Once there is a [particular] tone, it will have specifications, and if it has specifications, it will [let sound forth the note] *shang* 商 if it does not [let sound forth the note] *gong* 宮. If [the great sound] were specific, it could not encompass the entire multitude [of notes]. That is why that which has taken on a specific tone is not the Great Sound.

In the same manner, he deals with the Great Image (the Great Elephant of *Hanfeizi*'s statement).

If something has form, then it will also have specification. That
which has specification will be cooling if it does not warm, and
will be cold if it is not hot. That is why an image that has taken
on form is not the Great Image.

The *Laozi* provides Wang Bi with a rich and essentially negative vocabulary evoking the unspecificity of the That-by-which. The "eternal of
the Way is namelessness" 道常無名 (32.1) and "does not interfere" 無
爲; the Way is "hidden and nameless" (41.15); "the words uttered about
the Dao indeed are stale; they are without taste" (35.3), the *Laozi* writes,
and then adds a series of onomatopoetic "sighs," as Wang Bi calls them,
expressing the Way's diffuseness such as *hu* 惚, *huang* 恍 (14.3, 21.2 f), *yao*
窈, *ming* 冥 (21.4), *hun* 混 (25.1), *wei* 微, *xi* 希, and *yi* 夷 (14.1), while at
the same time speaking about its "eternal," *chang* 常, its "overflowing,"
si 氾 (34.1), and its generative, *sheng* 生, powers (42.1, 51.1). Wang Bi
merges all these expressions into his systematic neologism "without shape
and without name" 無形無名."[100]

The necessary feature of That-by-which the entities are is the absence
of any of their features, and it is in this sense that Wang Bi uses the most
radical of philosophic terms for the That-by-which, *wu* 無, which I translate here as "negativity." It is a cool, analytic construct with no tinge of
"nihilism" or abandonment of basic values. The merger of many different
terms within the *Laozi*, such as "way," *dao* 道, "the Eternal," *chang* 常,
of the Way or of the entities, the "beginning," *shi* 始, "mother," *mu* 母,
"root," *ben* 本, "one," *yi* 一, "ancestor," *zong* 宗, or "cover," *ao* 奧,"
and Wang Bi's own expressions, such as "highest thing," *zhiwu* 至物, or
even "absolute of highest truth," *zhi zhen zhi ji* 至眞之極, into the concept of "negativity," *wu* 無, has been described elsewhere.[101] They share
three features—the absence of any specificity, the notion that they are the
"That-by-which" of the totality of entities, and the notion that they can be
the latter only because of the former. As essentially heuristic appellations
often in metaphoric form for different aspects of the "That-by-which,"
they highlight different elements.

The term Dao, or Way, is a metaphor for something "traveling all
around" 周行 (*Laozi* 25.3), that is, something pertaining to all of the
entities. "The Eternal" of the Way, *dao chang* 道常, is defined in *Laozi*
32.1 in Wang's reading as "namelessness," is described as being "without
interference" in *Laozi* 37.1, and is used for the "eternal essence" of the
entities, which is without any particular features in Wang Bi on *Laozi*
16.6, 55.4 and 55.5. The term *beginning* refers to a cosmo- or ontogonic
function; "mother" refers to the continuing support that the entities receive

from the "That-by-which"; "root" is both the origin of the *mo* 末, the "outgrowth" of the unending specificities of the visible world, and that which gives them continuous support and nutrition. Both of these metaphors indicate the continuing dependence of the "child" or "outgrowth" on "mother" and "root," without which they would starve and wither.

"One" comes in as the basic unit from which the ten thousand start, but the One is not considered a number among others. It is the One as opposed to the Many, unspecific in its simplicity and thus the focal point to which all numbers refer back and which is contained in all of them. The "ancestor" links up with the notion of the "beginning" and with the metaphor of the clan, whose many present members trace their origin back to a single forebear and honor and worship him as their common origin. "Negativity" 無 finally, as the most sober and analytical appellation, is the term preferred by Wang Bi, stressing the featurelessness of the "That-by-which" as well as its radical difference with regard to the *you* 有, the realm of entities. Thus while these terms such as *mother* or *beginning* can be merged for good reason into the term *wu*, they still retain their analytic value because they stress different aspects. In his commentaries, Wang Bi proceeds to a careful analysis of this metaphoric and analytic value.

Wang Bi confronts this *wu* 無 with an equally radical counterpart, *you* 有, which I translate as "entities."[102] In a similar manner, Wang Bi groups the different kinds of entities mentioned in the *Laozi*, such as *wu* 物, *gong* 功, or *shi* 事 into a completely abstract notion, *wanwu* 萬物, "ten thousand kinds of entities" (in which the *Laozi*'s *wanwu* 萬物 only appear as the subcategory "living beings" of the *wu* 物), which he then occasionally addresses with the even more abstract notion of *you* 有, "Entity" or, to use the German term, *das Seiende*. Given the inability of language to accurately describe that by which the entities are in its featurelessness, the reduction of the plethora of different terms into a single hard notion would not be any gain but rather would lose the chance of bringing out the particular, if partial, insights contained in these statements and terms. Wang Bi's own concept of *cheng* 稱, "appellation," paves the way for understanding that, on the one hand, all of these terms and statements speak about the same thing while, at the same time, they "point at" it from different directions and contexts and thus describe different aspects.

We shall proceed in three steps: first, to extract from Wang Bi's work his own presentation of his argument about the That-by-which in its relationship to the entities; second, to subject this record to a philosophic analysis in which, among others, Tang Yongtong's cosmology/ontology paradigm will be scrutinized; and, third, to situate Wang Bi's language and argument in a historical context by highlighting his own contribution.

Wang Bi groups the numerous *Laozi* statements about the That-by-which into two main aspects, for which he uses terms of the *Laozi*, namely, *dao* 道 and *xuan* 玄. Both terms are *cheng* 稱, appellations of aspects of the "That-by-which." In an enclosed essay within his *LZWZLL*, Wang Bi writes:

"Dao" 道 is taken for [its aspect] of being that on which the ten thousand kinds of entities are based.
道也者取乎萬物之所由也.

"Xuan" 玄 is taken for [its aspect] of being that which lets the Recondite emanate.
玄也者取乎幽冥之所出也.[103]

With this dry definition, Wang Bi changes the rules of discourse. Both the Way and the Dark have a long history in the course of which they have become enriched with dimensions of meaning ranging from mystical intuition to dietetics, from philosophy of life to government technique. Both were categories defining all others but undefinable in themselves. This was true for the term Dao ever since the fifth century B.C.E., and for Xuan ever since Yang Xiong's *Taixuan jing* 太玄經. In Wang Bi's reading, neither term has an intrinsic value and authority but gets them only if and insofar as it can be shown that it contains a valid insight about the "That-by-which." He defines both as heuristic terms awkwardly "being taken for" one demonstrable aspect of the "That-by-which." They are stripped of their halo of mystical effusion and reduced to the hard core of a rational induction.

There are thus two main aspects in the relationship between the "That-by-which" and the entities: first, all of the entities are based on this "That-by-which"; second, they do not know what it is they are based on. The basis of the ten thousand kinds of entities does not show up as a separate thing, eludes cognition, and thus, while being the all-important basis for all that is, remains in the dark because it cannot have any features that could become the object of cognition.

THE DAO

The *Laozi* describes the Dao-aspect of the "That-by-which" with terms such as *sheng* 生 (*Laozi* 34.2, 42.1, 51.1), "to generate [the wanwu]," *cheng* 成, "to complete," *shi* 始, "to initiate [the wanwu]," *mu* 母, "being the mother [of the wanwu]" (*Laozi* 1, 25.3), *zong* 宗, "being the ancestor [of the wanwu]" (*Laozi* 4.1), "overflowing," *si* 汜 (*Laozi* 34.1), and "getting around" *zhou xing* 周行 (*Laozi* 25.3). It remains an appellation of an aspect, *cheng* 稱, because mutually exclusive statements are valid for it at the same time.[104]

With the exception of the last two, which focus on the capacity of the Dao to take care of all of the entities, these words imply a generative relationship in time where the Dao is the *causa efficiens* at the beginning and origin and creates and initiates the entities. In short, the language is cosmogonic, at least in its metaphors. However, *Laozi* 1.2 differentiates two functions of the Dao, that of being the "beginning" and that of being the "mother." The first, read by Wang Bi as "when there are not [now] names, it is the beginning of the ten thousand kinds of entities," is commented on with the words: "It will be at a time when there are neither shapes nor names, the 'beginning' of the ten thousand kinds of entities." This clearly refers to the traditional cosmo- or ontogenetic function. The second is read: "When there [already] are names, it is the mother of the ten thousand kinds of entities." It is commented: "It will be, when it comes to a time when there are shapes and names that which [as the *Laozi* says in 51.3] 'lets them [the entities] grow and nurtures them, specifies them and completes them,' [in short] it will be their 'mother.'" Wang Bi gives a general frame to the two specific commentaries on the *Laozi* 1.2 text by adding general statements before and after them: "Generally speaking, entities all begin in negativity" 凡有皆始於無 comes before, and "This means the Way begins and completes the ten thousand kinds of entities by means of [its] featurelessness and namelessness" 言道以無形無名始成萬物 comes after. Wang Bi thus formalizes these two aspects of "beginning" and "mother" in the new pair *shi* 始 and *cheng* 成.[105]

As evidence for the *Laozi*'s thinking along the same lines, he quotes a passage from *Laozi* 51.3 in his commentary on *Laozi* 1.2, which describes what the entities "get," *de* 得/德, from the Dao once they have been "begun," namely, to be grown, nurtured, specified, completed, protected, and covered. In this aspect, the relationship between the Dao and the entities is not one of momentary causation but one of continuous maintenance. This second aspect opens the way for an argument that the Dao is somehow permanently present with the entities as their existential base, although the "mother" metaphor smacks of breast-feeding the entities and remains a close relative of the ontogenetic "ancestor." The commentaries in both places, *Laozi* 1.2 and 51.4, show that Wang Bi had a hard time establishing a plausible reading of these passages. It is true that the *Laozi* in 52.1 said: "As All Under Heaven has a beginning, this may [also] be taken for All Under Heaven's mother," linking, in effect, the two notions of "beginning" and "mother" under the same heading. On this basis, Wang Bi establishes that the actual subject for both phrases in *Laozi* 1.2 dealing with the "beginning" and the "mother," respectively, must be the Dao, although the wording and grammar do not make this conclusion mandatory. In the *LZWZLL*, Wang Bi explicitly claims that the *Laozi* uses the ontogenetic or cosmogonic language of the "beginning" of the entities in order to discuss the ontological relationship between them and the[ir] That-which-is-of-itself-what-it-is. "He expounds the source of the Great Beginning in order to elucidate the nature of That-which-is-of-itself-what-it-is" 論太始之原 以明自然之性.[106] His comments, therefore, try to translate some of this metaphoric language into a newly formalized philosophic terminology.

After firmly linking both *shi* 始 and *cheng* 成 to the Dao, Wang Bi inserts a neologism into the relationship That-by-which/entities, namely, "to be based on," *you* 由. The term does not occur in the *Laozi*, and Wang Bi most probably took it from a hitherto hardly influential statement by Confucius in the *Zhuangzi*'s "Old Fisherman," which has already been quoted as the source for the *wanwu/wu/shi* hierarchy.

> The Dao, furthermore, is that which the ten thousand kinds of entities take as their base 且道者萬物之所由也.[107]

The formula looks close enough to Wang Bi's. Still, there is a marked difference. The statement is followed by: "Those of the multitude of beings who lose it, die; those who get it, live. If, in going about affairs one deviates from it, they [one's affairs] fail; if one follows it, they succeed. That is why the Sage honors those [beings and affairs] where the Dao is." The Dao is the base of the ten thousand entities only insofar as they "get" and "follow" it; it gives them a base for life and success, but not for their existence.

In the *Lunyu*, Confucius also uses the expression in a transitive sense "to base oneself on" or even "to make use of" with regard to the Dao. "Who would be able to get out [of the house] without making use of the door? How come that no one bases himself on this [my] Way?" 誰能出不 由戶何莫由斯道.[108] Wang Bi thus took this constellation from the Sage but inserted it into the logic of his own argument.

Within the *Laozi*, Wang Bi found a few statements describing a kind of relationship between the Dao and the *wanwu* that differed from the initiating/completing language. The most important term here is *men* 門, the "door," which clearly is not generative, although things might emerge from it. In his comments on *Laozi* 6.1 and 10.5, the term *men* 門, the "door" from which the entities emanate, is "translated" into *you* 由. In the comment on *Laozi* 34.2, Wang Bi renders the more indirect statement by the *Laozi* "the ten thousand kinds of entities depend on it [the Way] for their being born" 萬物恃之而生, with the words "the ten thousand kinds of entities are all generated on the basis of the Way," 萬物皆由道而生 but not, it should be repeated, "by" the Dao.

Wang Bi most decidedly highlights what he sees as the purely metaphoric nature of the *Laozi*'s generative and nutritive language in his comments on *Laozi* 10.7 and 10.8. He comments on *Laozi* 10.7: "He/it generates them [the entities]," 生之, with the words "that is, he/it does not block their source," 不塞其原也"; and on *Laozi* 10.8: "He/it rears them [the entities]," 畜之, with the words "that is, he/it does not hem in their nature" 不禁其性也. In other words, he bluntly "translates" the *sheng* 生, "generate," as meaning "not blocking the source," and the *xu* 畜, "nourishing," as "not hemming in the nature" of entities. He begins his commentary on *Laozi* 10.9 with the equally blunt statement: "As it does not block their source, the entities create themselves, and what achievement [from its side] should it 'have'? As it does not hem in their nature, the entities regulate themselves, and on what activity [on its side] should they 'depend'?" 不塞其原則物自生何功之有不禁其性則物自濟何爲之恃. In *LZWZLL*, Wang Bi quotes the same passages with the Dao as subject.[109] While Wang Bi continues to use the *shi/cheng* pair, his new term, *you* 由, actually reflects his own thought on the matter.

The introduction of *you* 由 into the genetic vocabulary of the *Laozi* changes the latter's meaning. While the *Laozi* 51.1 says, "The Dao generates them," 道生之, Wang Bi says in his comments on *Laozi* 34.2, "The ten thousand kinds of entities are all generated on the basis of the Dao"; and when the *Laozi* 25.1 says, "There is a thing that completes out of the diffuse," 有物混成, Wang Bi "translates" this "completes," *cheng* 成, into "the ten thousand kinds of entities base themselves on it [the Dao] for their completion" 萬物由之以成. This is an important change. The Dao in these phrases stops being the *causa efficiens* and becomes the condition for the possibility of the beginning and the completion of the entities. In a fine and terse formula on *Laozi* 51.2, Wang Bi fixes the relationship between Dao as the condition for the possibility and *de*, 德, as the specific features the entities "get," *de* 得: "Dao is that which is the basis for the entities. De is that which [the entities] receive. It is on the basis of this [former, the Dao that they] indeed receive [the latter, *de*]" 道者物之所由也德者物之所得也由之乃得. On 51.1, Wang Bi reduces the many terms describing what the entities "get" from the Dao to one single *you* 由: "Generally speaking, both that by which entities are generated and that by which achievements are brought about, have something that is the base [for them] 凡物之所以生功之所以成皆有所由. As they have something that is the base for them, there is none of them that is not based on the Way" 有所由焉則莫不由乎道也.

We have thus a separation of two kinds of relationships. The entities mutually manage their beginning and completion, but the basis, *you* 由, or in modern terminology, the condition for the possibility of this beginning and completion, is the "That-by-which." Again, Wang Bi finds evidence for this distinction between *you* 由 and *sheng* 生 in the *Laozi* itself. *Laozi* 40.3 runs:

> The entities of All Under Heaven have [their] life in [the realm of] Entity, [but] Entity has [its] life in negativity. 天下之物生於有有生於無.

Wang Bi comments:

> The entities of All Under Heaven all take [their being in the realm of] Entity as [the basis of their] life, [but] that which begins Entity takes negativity as the root. 天下之物皆以有爲生有之所始以無爲本.

The regular process of *sheng* 生 here takes place within the realm of *you* 有, of Entity, but the "root" that "begins" or "initiates" Entity is negativity. Wang Bi deepens the difference between the two by doing away with the seeming symmetry implied in the repetition of *sheng* 生 by keeping the *sheng* 生 for the interpretation of the first half, but then "translating" 有生於無, "Entity has [its] life in negativity," into the very complex 有之所始 以無爲本, "that which begins Entity takes negativity as the root," which corresponds to the notion of *you* 由. This switch also forces the difference in the translation of the particle 於, once as "in" and once as "from."

With his choice of the philosophic neologism *you* 由 as the key term describing the relationship between the "That-by-which" and the entities, Wang Bi again opts for the culturally least charged and analytically most sober term that does not involve a causative or generative relationship in his use.[110] Wang Bi signals that he reads the *Laozi*'s genetic and nutritive language as metaphor using biological relationships in time to describe structural relationships horizontal to the time axis, a type of relationship he sees indicated in other passages of the *Laozi*, especially in the descriptions of *de* 德.

The Dao aspect of the "That-by-which" is able to be the basis of the entities only because it does not specify itself into some particular generative action. Being the condition of the possibility of their ordered existence, their particular operations unfold only what is already in their natures. In this manner, as the famous expression of the *Laozi* says: "It does not interfere, and nothing remains undone" 無爲而無不爲. Such interference would in fact disrupt and destroy the self-regulatory process emanating from the natures of the entities. While it thus remains true that the One "controls" the Many, it exerts this control in the most complete way by not limiting itself to any particular controlling action.

What, then, is the necessity of this construct of the One as a logical construct if in fact the ten thousand kinds of entities proceed in their prestabilized harmony? The ordered existence of the entities is possible only insofar as they follow their natures. "The ten thousand kinds of entities have That-which-is-of-itself-what-it-is as their nature," 萬物以自然爲性, writes Wang Bi on *Laozi* 29.3. This "That-which-is-of-itself-what-it-is," however, is the One. The ordered existence of the entities does not come about through the battle for the survival of the fittest or through some negotiated settlement; in other words, it does not come about through their interaction but their collective "relating back" to the "That-by-which" that is present in them as their nature. The argument becomes clearer once we recall the negative case. In human society it obviously is a real possibility and a frequent reality that the ordered existence of the Hundred Clans or of All Under Heaven goes awry. This, the argument goes, is due to a disturbance in the relationship between the One and the Many in the human realm; as a consequence, people are "denatured," and with the destruction of their nature comes the destruction of the intrinsic harmony and order. The establishment of order in the realm of nature is thus the result of an undisturbed and a successful dynamic interactive process between the One and the Many, and Wang Bi's endeavor is to find the rules governing this relationship.

The overall relationship of the One as the basis of the Many is repeated in particular relationships that are governed by the same rule. In Wang Bi's reading, this rule is expressed in *Laozi* 25.12, which describes the "four Great Ones"—Dao, Heaven, Earth, and "also" the ruler, if indeed he is behaving as a Sage. In an ascending scale, they emulate each other or take each other as model: "The human being [= the lord of men] takes the Earth as model, Earth takes Heaven as model, Heaven takes the Dao as model, and the Dao takes That-which-is-of-itself-what-it-is as model." Only by emulating the next higher category up to the highest, Wang Bi argues, can these categories exist. "The Earth not deviating from Heaven and consequently managing it to completely carry [the ten thousand kinds of entities]—this is what '[Earth] takes Heaven as model' means."

The decisive term here is "completely," *quan* 全. To "completely" carry all entities is possible only by emulating the functional role of the One. At the highest level, the Dao's taking That-which-is-of-itself-what-it-is as model, the real principle is reached, which in the end they all take as their model, because this "that which is of itself what it is" is nothing else but the nature of the ten thousand kinds of entities. The Dao thus "taking That-which-is-of-itself-what-it-is as model means taking squareness as model when among squares and roundness when among round ones, and thus deviating in nothing from That-which-is-of-itself-what-it-is." It will not impose roundness on squareness, or vice versa. This means that these Great Ones can only cover all entities by not specifying themselves in terms of preference or action with regard to any of them. *Laozi* 5.1, "Heaven and Earth are not kindly; for them, the ten thousand kinds of entities are like grass and dogs," is in itself a paradox. Do not Heaven and Earth cover and support the ten thousand kinds of entities? Are they not the very paragons of kindliness? In a fine commentary to this statement, Wang Bi describes the prestabilized order among entities as maintained by Heaven and Earth without any particular interference:

> Heaven and Earth let [the entities'] That-which-is-of-itself
> come into effect. They are without interference and without
> creation, [with the result that] the ten thousand kinds of enti-
> ties spontaneously order and regulate each other. This is why
> [the *Laozi* says, Heaven and Earth are] "not kindly." Someone
> who is kindly will by necessity create and generate, have pity
> and interfere. Would they [Heaven and Earth, however,] create
> and generate, the entities would lose their true [nature because
> of the outside imposition]. Would they [Heaven and Earth]
> have pity and interference, the entities would not persist in their
> entirety [because this pity and interference would be partial and
> prefer some over others] . . . Heaven and Earth do not produce
> grass for the benefit of cattle but the cattle [still] eat grass. They
> do not produce dogs for the benefit of men, but men [still]
> eat dogs. As they are without interference concerning the ten
> thousand kinds of entities, each of the ten thousand kinds of
> entities fits into its use so that there is none that is not provided
> for. Would they [Heaven and Earth] confer kindness on their
> own [initiative], they would be unable to let [the entities' That-
> which-is-of-itself-what-it-is] come into effect.

It is in the nature of dogs to be eaten by men and of grass to be eaten by cattle, so they do not suffer any damage in the process but fulfill their nature in delivering their benefits to the general order of things. In his comments on *Laozi* 20.1, Wang Bi writes: "It is a fact that swallows and sparrows mate, pigeons and doves have hatred for each other, and people in cold areas inevitably know about furs and wool. That-which-is-of-it-self-what-it-is already suffices itself. If one adds to it, harm will come. In this sense, where is the difference between stretching a duck's foot and shortening a crane's neck?"

The drum and the flute cited at the end of *Laozi* 5 as comparisons with the way in which Heaven and Earth handle the entities can be "inexhaust-ible" in the variety of tones and pitches that they are able to generate, because they "discard their selves and put themselves at the service of other entities so that there is none that is not well-ordered 棄己任物則莫不理. If the drum or the flute were bent on having a [specific] sound [or volume], they would be unable to satisfy the requirements of flutists [and drummers]."

This self-abandonment is not only the precondition for these "Great Ones" to take care of all entities but also the precondition for their main-taining their role as the One of the Many. The *Laozi* 7.1 statement, "That by which Heaven and Earth are able to excel and persist [respectively] is that they do not live for their own interests," 天地所以能長且久者以其不自生, is commented on by Wang Bi: "Were they to live for their own interests, they would struggle with [other] entities. As they do not live for their own interests, the [other] entities relate back to them" 自生則與物爭不自生則物歸也. If they were to "struggle" with the other entities, they would be one among the many or even one against the many, and not the One of the Many, and their own existence among the undefinable "Great Ones" would be in danger. The evocation of this hypothetical danger serves the purpose of highlighting the fact that only by being modeled on the One are these Great Ones able to fulfill their function and preserve themselves.

In his handling of *Laozi* 39.1, Wang Bi further develops this thought.

The One is the beginning of the numbers and the ultimate of the entities. In each case it is the One by which the [great] enti-ties [mentioned below, such as Heaven, Earth, and the Spirits] are dominated. Each one of these entities attains this One for its completion, but [if], having once completed, [each] would discard the One in order to settle in [their] completed [state], they [would], having [thus] settled in [their] completed [state], as a consequence, lose their mother [that is, the One]; that is why [the text further down speaks of the danger of] [Heaven's] "being torn apart," [Earth's] "getting into commotion," [the spirit's] "becoming exhausted," [the valley's] "being drained," [and the dukes' and kings'] "being toppled."

All of the categories mentioned here are Ones confronting Manies. They are able to do so only by not settling in their completed state but by applying the principle governing the relationship of the One to the Many to their relationship with other entities. In Wang Bi's construction, the *Laozi* 39 uses the formula, "As long as Heaven attains the One, it will be clear through it; as long as Earth attains the One, it will be calm through it," and so forth 天得一以清, 地得一以寧. The translation "as long" might be replaced by "insofar as." The series ends with the *Laozi* statement: "It is the One that brings these [clarity, calmness, and so forth] about" 其致之一也. The *Laozi* then describes what would happen if they were not to fulfill their nature of being clear, calm, and so forth, "through the One": "Once Heaven is not clear through [the One], it is in danger of being torn apart" 天無以清將恐裂. In this case, it would not only be unable to "cover" the entities, it also would be threatened in its being high and enduring. This confirms the plausibility of our reading of Wang Bi on *Laozi* 7 above. As we shall see, through what appears in these *Laozi* statements as *de* 得, "attain," and *yi* 以, "by means of," the One is systematized by Wang Bi into the notion of 以無爲用, "taking negativity as [their] usability."

The four Great Ones discussed in *Laozi* 39 are, with the exception of the very real kings and dukes, traditional categories of cosmogony. Wang Bi is not much interested in their particulars, but reads them as illustrations of philosophic principles with a language familiar to readers. "He [Laozi] takes things external like Heaven and Earth in order to elucidate that which is inside the shape and bones [i.e., the body]," 取天地之外以明形骸之內, he writes in the *LZWZLL*.[111] Heaven, Earth, and so forth are at the top of the hierarchy of specificity; they are the Ones with just one single identifier confronting the entirety of entities. However, as the *Laozi*'s own comparison with the flute and the drum shows, their relationship to the Many is just a high-level application of the principles governing all One/Many relationships, including those between the hub of a wheel and the spokes, and so forth, discussed in *Laozi* 11. There is one condition for the ability of the Ones to be the basis for their Manies, to remain the Ones of these Manies without getting into conflict with these Manies and destroying their intrinsic order: only "by means of" negativity, that is, by making use of or "taking as model" the feature of negativity in themselves, do they fulfill their function as Ones, and they manifest their usability only insofar as they apply this feature with regard to the specificities of their particular Manies. In this sense, the particular One/Many constellations are only intermediate layers repeating the basic structural relationship of negativity as the ultimate One to the ten thousand entities as the ultimate Many.

Wang Bi's discussion does not end here. He takes up the challenge of formulating in general terms the relationship between the entities and negativity. Because his arguments are a fine illustration of his philosophic and linguistic daring and at the same time still present a formidable challenge for the modern reader, I shall go through the relevant texts in some detail.

Laozi 11 is occasion for further exploration. Elsewhere I have dealt with the various strategies used by commentators in reading *Laozi* 11.[112] Of the three examples given in this *zhang*, the hub/wheel, clay/pots, and walls/room, I shall only use the first. According to Wang Bi, *Laozi* 11.1 reads:

> Thirty spokes share one hub. But is it the [latter's] negativity [vis-à-vis the specificity of the spokes] that is [the basis] for the usability of the existing carriage. 三十輻共一轂當其無有車之用.

Wang Bi's commentary runs:

> That by which a [= one] hub is capable of holding together thirty [different] spokes is [its] negativity [vis-à-vis their specific features]. Because of its negativity, [the hub] is capable of taking in the points of origin of [many different] entities. That is why [the hub] is capable, being itself the minimum, to control the many [spokes]. 轂所以能統三十輻者無也以其無能受物之故故能以寡統眾也.

The hub is the point where the spokes come together to form a wheel "because of its negativity," 以其無, with regard to their specifics. The term *yong* 用 is not used in this commentary in the sense of the hub's "making use" of negativity but is used in the *Laozi* for the "use" the existing carriage, 有車之用, has due to the negativity of the hub. The three examples are summed up in the *Laozi* line:

> Therefore that [they are specific] entities makes for [their] being beneficial, while negativity makes for [their] usability. 故有之以爲利無之以爲用.

Wang Bi comments:

> The three [wheel, vessel, room] are made from wood, clay, and mortar, respectively, but all [depend] on negativity for their usability. This [*Laozi* statement] means: Entities in order to be

beneficial all depend on negativity for their usability. 木埴壁所
以成三者而皆以無爲用也言有之所以爲利皆賴無以爲用也.

In these extremely terse formulations, which push into uncharted ter-
ritory, one sees Wang Bi grappling with language and a precise expression
of a thought still in the process of formation. The difficulties in understanding and translating these passages are obvious from the many brackets as
well as the unusual terms forced on the translator such as "usability" for
the simple *yong* 用. All three items mentioned—the wheel, the vessel, and
the room—are characterized by their functionality, by their "benefit" or
usefulness, *li* 利. The benefit or functionality of a carriage (or rather the
spokes of the wheels) is that it can be driven anywhere, and of the vessel
and the room that they can contain or shelter an unending variety of things.
They are part of a functional order in which they have a particular place.
Wang Bi's question is what transforms them from a diffuse heap of wooden
spokes, clay, or mortar into a functional and functioning part of this structured order. The entity aspect of the carriage is that it is made of wood, of
the vessel that it is made of clay, and of the room that it is made of mortar,
but these in themselves cannot make anything that functions. The specific
you 有 "entities"—the wood of the spokes, the clay of the vessel, and the
mortar of the wall—are functional only through their opposite, negativity.
The clay and mortar become functional vessel and room through the emptiness within them; that means through the no-clay and no-mortar there.
The wooden spokes become a functional carriage through the emptiness
of the hub that holds them, that is, through the non-spoke quality of the
hub. Only this negative opposite, their negativity, enables them to become
part of a structured and functional order. In fact, the relationship of this
emptiness within them and the specificity of the materials of which they
are made is one between the One and the Many. Their emptiness is not
particular to them but a specific section of general negativity. The *Laozi*'s
very general formula about *you* 有 and *wu* 無 in this *zhang* beginning with
"therefore" clearly marks the carriage, room, and vessel as illustrations
of an overall structure. Wang, therefore, does have a point when recalling
this chapter to the reader's mind in other parts of his *Commentary*.

The second extensive treatment of the problem is in the beginning
of Wang Bi's commentary to *Laozi* 38 (if we disregard for the moment
the short commentary piece in the beginning transmitted only in Fan
Yingyuan).[113] Wang Bi comments on the first *Laozi* phrase, "He with the
highest receipt/capacity does not make anything of [his] receipt/capacity.
That is why he is in possession of the [highest] receipt/capacity," 上德不
德是以有德, with a theoretical introduction:

He who [has] receipt/capacity, *de* 德, receives [it]. 德者得也.
He constantly receives [it] and is without loss, has the advantage [of it] and [remains] without damage. That is why *de* 德,
receipt/capacity, is taken as a name for it.[114]

By means of what does one receive [one's] receipt/capacity?
何以得德 On the basis indeed of the Way 由乎道也. By
means of what does one make complete [use] of [one's] receipt/
capacity? 何以盡德 By taking negativity as [the basis of its]
usability. 以無爲用. Once negativity is taken as [the basis of
its] usability, there is no [entity] that will not be sustained. 以
無爲用則莫不載也. That is why, if something is negative with
regard to the [other] entities, there will be no entity that it does
not thread through; [but] if it is an existing [= specific entity
with regard to the other entities] it will not be able to maintain
their lives complete. 故物無爲則無物不經有爲則不足以全
其生. That is why Heaven and Earth, although they are wide,
have negativity as [their] heart, and that is why the Sage Kings,
although they are great, take emptiness as [their] principle. 是
以天地雖廣以無爲心聖王雖大以虛爲主.

This passage ends with the statement that he with the "highest receipt"
上德 will act like Heaven, Earth, and the Sage Kings and not reduce the
totality of his receipt by making particular use of it.

Wang Bi is again consciously using the very general terms *wu* 物,
"entity," *wu* 無, "negativity," and *you* 有, "entity," in this discussion to
arrive at general statements. The examples Heaven, Earth, and the Sage
Kings only push his case to the extreme. Even they, with their vastness and
greatness, would lose their control over the many and their own intactness
as Ones if they were not to take "negativity as their heart" and to make
"emptiness their principle." The "receipt," *de* 德, of an entity is characterized by the Dao's providing it "constantly" and by the recipient's becoming "functional, beneficial, or useful," *li* 利, in the context of a structured
order. In this structured order it is "functional" 利 not "harmful" 害 if
grass is eaten by cattle, and dogs are eaten by men. This functionality of
the receipt, of the particular capacities received from the Dao, comes about
in a complete way 盡 only if "negativity [and not the particular specific
features] is taken as the basis for usability." Examples of minor entities
such as wheels, vessels, and rooms have been given in *Laozi* 11. Here
the examples are the Great Ones; even their functionality has its base in
negativity.

In his comments on *Laozi* 40.1, "He who acts by way of the negative
opposite [i.e., the Sage] is the one who moves [in accordance with] the

Way" 反者道之動, Wang Bi develops the argument one step further:

> That [as *Laozi* 39.4 says] "to be elevated takes [acting as if] be-
> ing lowly as [its] base" and that [as it says in the same section]
> "to be esteemed takes [acting as if] being despised as [its] root";
> [in short,] that Entity takes negativity as that which [makes it]
> usable means "acting by way of" their "negative opposite." 高
> 以下爲基貴以賤爲本有以無爲用此其反也.

We shall return to the practical consequences of these phrases in a later
context. Wang Bi operates on the assumption of the *Laozi*'s homogeneity.
Laozi 11 does not deal with carriages, vessels, and rooms but with the
basics of the relationship of entities and negativity. In a quite different
metaphoric model the question arises on what a ruler's being "elevated"
and "honored" in a high position rests. In the same manner the question
arose in *Laozi* 39 as to what it is that lets Heaven be "clear" and Earth
be "calm." In all cases the answer was different in the specifics: a Sage
Ruler's being "elevated" rests on his acting "lowly"; his being "honored"
rests on his acting "despised"; Heaven's clarity and Earth's calmness are
"brought about by the One." The common denominator in all these examples is the negative opposite. Only "by means of" the emptiness and
hollowness in their very core have wheel, vessel, and room usability and
are thus functional. Only "by means of" negativity or the One within their
core can Heaven and Earth fulfill their clarity and calm.

In *LZWZLL* 4.1ff., Wang Bi finds the most radical and specific expression for this relationship:

Generally speaking,

that by which beings persist is the negative opposite indeed to their form.	that by which achievements are performed is the negative opposite indeed to their name.
凡 物之所以存乃反其形.	功之所以剋乃反其名.

Wang Bi illustrates this point with an application in the political realm
for the ruler, to which we shall return:

It is a fact that

he who persists does not take persistence for [the cause] of his persisting, but [his persisting is due]	he who is secure does not take security for [the cause] of his being secure, but [his security

to his not forgetting about [the danger of] perishing.	is due] to his not forgetting about perils.

That is why [to paraphrase the
Sage, Confucius, in Xici 下.4]

"he who guards his persistence" "perishes," while he who [like the Gentleman] "does not forget about [the danger of] perishing" "persists!"	"he who secures his position" "is in peril," while he who [like the Gentleman] "does not forget about peril" "is secure."

Wang Bi in fact makes the same argument in his comments on *Laozi* 39.3: "Once Heaven is not clear through [the One], it is in danger of being torn apart":

[Heaven] makes use of the One and thus achieves clarity, but does not make use of [its intrinsic] clarity to achieve clarity. As long as it preserves the One, [its] clarity will not be lost, but once it makes use of [its intrinsic] clarity [to achieve clarity,] it is in "danger of being torn apart."

The basis of the functionality of entities within a structured order is negativity as the absolute negative opposite. Only by means of it will their particular specificity be functional. As I have shown, the entities have their particular place and function within this structured order due to what Wang Bi referred to as their "nature," which he defined as That-which-is-of-itself-what-it-is 自然. It now turns out that the two strands of argument deal with the same problem; what is described as this "nature" of entities that makes them part of a structured order is in fact encoded in the notion of negativity as the basis for their functionality. *Ziran*, insofar as it is negativity, is the basis for the entities' functionality within a structured order.

In a last turn, we shall study the dynamics of this relationship as described in the terms *fan* 反, *fan* 返, *fu* 復, and *gui* 歸. Wang Bi uses the example of the relationship of movement and rest as well as speech and silence to illustrate the dynamic aspect of these opposites. Movement starts from rest as speech starts from silence, and both "return" to the original state. As movement and speech are diverse and multiple, and silence and rest are characterized by the absence of such diversity, it is a relationship between the One and the Many, a relationship between negativity and specificities. The relationship between the diversity of movement and speech emanating from their negative opposites, rest and silence, and "returning" there is described by Wang Bi with the general term of the Many and movement being "controlled," *zhi* 制, by the One and the calm. Commenting on *Laozi* 26.1, "The calm is the lord of the impetuous" 靜爲躁君, Wang writes: "generally speaking with regard to entities, that which [itself] does not act makes [others] act, that which [itself] does not move controls the movements [of others]" 凡物不行者使行不動者制動. As we saw earlier, calm and silence do not confront movement and speech on a horizontal level. They are characterized by the absence of the multiple specificities of movement and speech, by their negativity toward them. Evidently, theirs is not a control exerted through any particular intervention. Movement and speech quite naturally return to rest and silence as their core. It is this dynamic process of "return," *fu* 復, that "makes visible the heart of Heaven and Earth" 復其見天地之心, as the *Zhouyi* writes about the hexagram *fu* 復 in Wang Bi's construction. Wang Bi comments:

> "Return" is an appellation for relating back to the root. 復者反本之謂也. Heaven and Earth are of a kind to have the root as their heart. 天地以本爲心者也. Generally speaking, once movement dies away, calm comes about, but calm is not the antonym of movement; once talk dies away, silence comes about, but silence is not the antonym of talk. Thus, although Heaven and Earth are great and are richly endowed with the thousand kinds of entities, although the thunders roll and the winds rush, and the rotating changes go through ten thousand transformations, the calm highest negativity—that is their heart! That is why, when movement "comes to rest in the Earth,"[115] the "heart of Heaven and Earth" "becomes visible." Were they to take Entity [in its specificity] as their heart, the different kinds [of entities] would not have the benefit of all persisting simultaneously.

Nature thus provides the mind with a philosophic spectacle on a grandiose scale. When "movement comes to rest in the Earth," that is, when thunderbolts "come to rest" in the earth, and during the moment of the solstice, "the heart of Heaven and Earth becomes visible." This "heart" is negativity, the absence of all thunderbolting and glaring specificity, and it becomes visible only in the moment of the disappearance of this specificity into its calm and negative opposite. This heart alone enables Heaven and Earth to be "richly endowed" with the multitude of beings, and to be the framework within which the ten thousand transformations can roll on in an orderly manner.

Why is it so hard to catch a glimpse of the "heart of Heaven and Earth"? First, because of its negativity. The two examples of movement and speech offer glimpses of this "heart" in the very process of their specificity's dying away. Second, because the relationship between the That-by-which and the entities is one between the condition for the possibility and actuality, a dynamic relationship encoded into a structure present at all time, but not unfolding on the time axis. What is unique about the examples of movement and speech is that they unfold this structural dynamic of a "relating back" into the visible dynamic of a "return" on the time axis, where the two interlocked elements—silence and speech and calm and movement or, more generally, negativity and entities—momentarily separate and come together again so that in the [emergence and] disappearance of specificity, negativity "becomes visible." From here it becomes imaginable that Heaven and Earth, packed with entities and change as they are, have negativity as their heart; had they not and were they themselves in their "heart" marked by specificity, these entities and changes could not "all persist simultaneously."

In *Laozi* 16.1ff., Wang Bi discovers a close parallel to the *fu* hexagram—further evidence for the close links between the two texts in his mind. His construction of the *Laozi* passage can be quoted without the commentary:

[As the entities']

achieving emptiness is [their] Ultimate,

holding on to stillness is [their] true core,

[even while] the ten thousand kinds of entities all act at once, I [as opposed to others] by way of [emptiness and stillness] perceive that to which they return. Generally speaking, while the entities are of unending diversity, each one of them returns to its [common] root. 致虛極也守靜篤也萬物并作吾以觀其復凡物云云各復歸於其根.

The text describes a process of cognition by an "I," called here *guan* 觀, "to observe" or "to make out." The "root" of the entities is hidden in the flurry of their manifest diversity. The only way to observe not even their root but their "return" to it is through a mental process. This consists of mentally extending the fullness and movement of the entities to their utmost of emptiness and core of stillness to which they eventually must return. Wang Bi again gives the example of movement/calm as well as entity/emptiness:

It is by way of [their] emptiness and stillness that [I] perceive
their return. Generally speaking: Entity arises out of emptiness;
movement arises out of stillness. Therefore, even while the ten
thousand kinds of entities all act at once, their return in the end
to emptiness and stillness is the ultimate and the true core of
entities.

In certain observable processes the mind thus has something to go by
以 for its heuristic pursuit of the elusive That-by-which. These processes
are not necessarily processes in time such as the return of movement to
rest and speech to silence. *Laozi* 1.3 and 1.4 again use the the formula 以
觀 to say that there is "something by means of which to perceive" aspects
of the That-by-which:

1.3   1.4

Therefore,

while they [the ten thousand kinds   while they [the ten thousand
of entities] are [still] constantly   kinds of entities] are constantly
without desire, one has something   with desires, one has something
by means of which to preceive its   by means of which to perceive
[the ultimate principle's] subtlety.   its [the ultimate principle's]
                                           limiting.

Commentary

"Subtlety" means the ultimate of   "Limit" means the final point to
minuteness. The ten thousand   which [entities] return/relate
entities begin in the minute and   back. Generally speaking, for
then only become complete; they   entities to be beneficial, they
begin in negativity, and only then   have to get their
come to life. Therefore, while they   usefulness from negativity; that
are permanently without desires   on which desires are based will
and their concerns are being   be satisfied only as a consequence
emptied, it is possible, "by means   of adapting to the Way. That is
of this to perceive the subtlety [out   why, "while they are constantly
of which]" it initiates entities.   with desires," it is possible "by
                                           means of this to perceive the
                                           limiting" [in which] it finalizes
                                           entities.

Wang Bi relates the two *Laozi* terms *miao* 妙, "subtleness," and *jiao*
徼, "limiting," both of which share a meaning of "mysterious," to the *shi*
始/*mu* 母 pair of the previous line, "When there are not [now] names, it is

the beginning of the ten thousand kinds of entities; when there [already] are names, it is the mother of the ten thousand kinds of entities," and these two terms again are formalized into the *shi* 始/*cheng* 成 scheme. The irritating thought that a presence of desires 常有欲 should allow the perception of an aspect of the That-by-which is in this manner brought into harmony with other statements in the *Laozi*.[116] The period when the entities "have desires" (and from the formula 天下常無欲之時 in Wang Bi on *Laozi* 34.2, it is clear that the subject is All Under Heaven, not the perceiving subject) is thus the period when entities have unfolded into their specificity and do not "relate back" to that on which they are based. Wang Bi's definition of the *jiao* 徼 as the "final point to which [entities] return/relate back 徼歸終也" explicitly takes up the "return" language. Thus mentally following entities both "back" into a time "before" they had formed and become specific as well as from their developed and specified form "back" into the point where they converge, one has something to go by for perceiving the That-by-which in a heuristic pursuit of its aspects.

Thus particular processes and relationships within the realm of entities permit extrapolation of the basic negativity/entities relationship. But in most cases the relationship does not unfold in time. An example is *Laozi* 26.1, "The heavy is the root of the light," as well as the long list of examples such as Heaven, Earth, the Spirits, and the Valley in *Laozi* 39. Wang Bi therefore comments on the next phrase in *Laozi* 16.4 about the entities' "each one returning to its [common] root" 各復歸於其根 by translating the "returning," *fugui*, into the "structural" *fan* 反, "they all relate back to that which initiates them" 各反其所始也. The next *Laozi* line introduces a third term for "return" or "relating back," *gui* 歸, when saying "[their] return to [their] root means [reaching] stillness." In this manner, the entities finally "get hold of the Eternal of their innate nature and life endowment 得性命之常," which means that, through this relating back, they are fulfilling their function within a structured order.

This "relating back" of the Many to the One with the ensuing benefits, however, hinges on the One's playing its role. On *Laozi* 7.1, "That by which Heaven and Earth are able to excel and persist is that they do not live for their own interests," Wang Bi writes: "Were they to live for their own interests, they would struggle with [other] entities. As they do not live for their own interests, the [other] entities relate back to them" 不自生則 物歸也. In this manner, the language of "return," which operates on the time axis, is structured into an ontological relationship, as was the case with the generative language that Wang Bi transferred to the structural *you* 由. In fact, both speak about the same dynamics, and in one case, in his comments on *Laozi* 34.2 and 34.3, Wang Bi uses *gui* 歸 in exactly the same position where one usually would find *you* 由. His "each of the

ten thousand kinds of entities relates back to it for their generation" 萬
物皆歸之以生 neatly matches "the ten thousand kinds of entities all are
generated on the basis of the Way" 萬物皆由道而生 in the immediately
preceding commentary. The difference between the two terms is mostly
that the "return/relating back" terminology makes the dynamics of this
structural relationship more explicit, stresses the observability, *jian* 見, of
the process, and serves as a reminder that such a "relating back" might
very well not take place—with a crisis in That-by-which/entities relations
ensuing. The term *gui* 歸 also is used in political language in the sense of
scholars from afar "rendering allegiance to" or "taking abode in the realm
of" a Sage King. This relationship between the entities and Heaven and
Earth is factual and spontaneous, not the product of a decision on either
part. We shall see how its principles translate into conscious government
policy.

In short, the structured order of entities hinges on their relating back
to their "That-by-which" in its negativity, which thus becomes what Wang
Bi calls with another neologism "the mother bringing about the achievements," *wei gong zhi mu* 爲功之母.[117]

To sum up:

- Wang Bi reads the cosmogonic and ontogonic language in the *Laozi*
  as a metaphor for a structural relationship between the That-by-
  which and the entities.

- The "nature" or "eternal" of the entities, that through which they
  are what they are, is the "negative opposite" of their specificity; in
  the most abstract and general sense, it is "negativity."

- It is described as "That-which-is-of-itself-what-it-is," *ziran* 自然.

- It is through "relating back" to this negative opposite that entities
  gain usability, *yong* 用, as the condition for the possibility of their
  functionality, *li* 利, within a structured, overall order of entities.
  This is true for entities such as Dao, Heaven, Earth, and the [Sage]
  King, which are confronting as Ones the entire range of entities, but
  it also is true for all other entities.

- Certain processes among entities, such as the beginning of movement out of stillness and its return there, make the structural relationship between negativity and entities visible in a sequential fashion in time. In the process of movement's dying away or of speech's
  dying into silence, negativity becomes visible and observable. These
  processes can serve as proof and illustration of the overall relationship. The That-by-which thus "shines forth" and "manifests" itself

within the realm of entities in fleeting moments to the pursuing and investigating mind, which thus is enabled to grasp its aspects.

THE DARK

Xuan 玄, "the Dark," is a noun. It describes the feature of the "That-by which" that it cannot be discerned. It comes as a philosophic surprise that the non-discernibility of the That-by-which, its Darkness, should not evoke sighs about the ineptitude of human cognizance and ravings about the mysteries of the universe but should be a necessary and constitutive feature of the That-by-which. The Dao and the Dark together form a paradox that Wang Bi on *Laozi* 21.3 and *Laozi* 1.2, brings into the forms, "That the ten thousand kinds of entities are begun by it [the Dao] and completed by it, but that they do not know that through which these [their beginning and completion] come to be as they are, 萬物以始以成而不知 其所以然, is [its aspect of being] 'Dark-and-Dark-again'." Or on *Laozi* 34.2, "The ten thousand kinds of entities are all generated on the basis of the Dao. But, although they are born [on this basis], they do not know that which they are based on." Or on 51.5, "That [the entities] have [their] receipt, but do not know its master [on the basis of whom they obtain it] is [because] it [their receipt] comes forth out of the Recondite" 有德而不 知其主也出於幽冥. It puts the mind in the position of having to affirm both that this That-by-which exists and that it does not. "It persists, but is not an entity; it is not there, but is not nothing, whether it is or not is hard to make out" 存而不有沒而不無有無莫測, Wang Bi writes on *Laozi* 4.1. On *Laozi* 6.1, he says, "If one wished to state that it exists [the objection would be that] it does not show its form. If one wished to state that it does not exist, [it still remains true that] the ten thousand kinds of entities are generated by means of it," a formula repeated in the comment on *Laozi* 14.2. In all cases, he explains the *Laozi*'s use of fuzzy language to describe the Dao.

Wang Bi finds explicit evidence for this thought in *Laozi* 34.3: "[In-sofar as] the ten thousand kinds of entities go back to it but do not know the[ir] master, it [the Way] may be named among the 'great'" 萬物歸之 而不知主可名於大矣, which is the direct model for the statement on 51.5. Implicit evidence for this thought may be found in a key term of the *Laozi*, namely, *xuan de* 玄德, which Wang Bi reads as a short form of the above-mentioned paradox, that is, "the receipt from the Dark," in the sense that the entities "receive" from the Dao their existence, but do not know where it comes from, so that it comes from the "Dark." Both elements are linked in statements about the ontological paradox within the *Laozi* which, in a kind of self-commentary, defines the notions used in other *zhang*, especially the definition of *xuan de* 玄德 in *Laozi* 10.7ff. Wang Bi takes this up in his parallel treatment of the two main aspects of the That-by-which, Dao and Xuan, in *LZWZLL* 5.6ff.:

When approaching it as that for which there is no entity which is not based on it, he [Laozi] designates it as "Dao."	When searching for it as that for which there is no subtlety not emanating from it, he [Laozi] styles it "the Dark."
As the many are based on the Dao,	the subtle emanates from the Dark,
thus	
[Laozi's statement in *Laozi* 10.7] [that] "it generates them and rears them" [that is,] that it does not block the[ir source] and does not hem in [their nature] but permeates the nature of entities, refers to the Dao.	[Laozi's subsequent statement] [that,] "while they come alive, it has no [specific effort on its side] and while they act, it does not make them dependent, [that, in short,] while they grow there would be no lording it over [their growth on its side],"— that they have a receipt [from it] but that there is no dominance [from it]—this is the "receipt [coming from] That-which-is-Dark." 玄之德也.

This passage details the heuristic procedure in ontological exploration. The eventual designations come from the "searching and approaching" of the philosophical "I" and are answers defined in their particularity by the particularity of the question, not definitions of an object defined by its intrinsic specificity. Wang Bi here interprets the formulae in *Laozi* 10, 34, and 51, which juxtapose a generating and rearing of the entities by the Dao, with the statement that there is no particular interference from the Dao. Commenting on the term "the Dark" in *Laozi* 1.5, Wang Bi writes:

As to the "Dark," it is obscure, is silent without [any] entities, is that which lets the "beginning" and the "mother" [of whom *Laozi* 1.2 speaks] emerge. It is impossible to give a definition [for this Dark]; therefore [Laozi] cannot say "their common [source] is defined as 'the Dark,' but [only] says "[I] designate it as . . . [the Dark]." The [term] "Dark" is taken for that [aspect of the That-by-which] that it cannot be designated as being thus [and nothing else]. Should one designate it as being thus [and nothing else], it would definitely not be permitted to define it as one specific Dark. If one were to define it as being one [specific] Dark and nothing else, this would be a definition, and that would be far off the mark.

That the That-by-which "cannot be designated as being thus [and nothing else]" hinges on its necessary unspecificity and therefore is a constitutive aspect of the That-by-which. It should be remembered that it was not the generative aspect of Dao but the constitutive Darkness of the That-by-which that was considered the major discovery of Wang Bi and his peers. This later made their learning in the name of Xuanxue 玄 學—which is perhaps best translated as the German *Wissenschaft vom Dunklen*, because the English "science" does not include philosophical inquiry—the subject of teaching of a chair at the state university.

While by and large Wang Bi's explorations of the constitutive notion of the Dark are highly sophisticated and well argued, we also are left with a few intriguing passages. He speaks, for example, of "subtleties emanating," or "emerging," *chu* 出, from the Dark in the *LZWZLL* passage quoted above. Wang Bi does not use his own language here, but the terminology of *Laozi* 1.5: "Both ['beginning' and 'mother'] emerge from a common [origin 同出], but they have different names. Their common [origin] [I] designate as the Dark, the Dark-and-Dark-Again. It is the door [from which] the many and the subtle [emerge]." This *Laozi* statement means that both forms in which the Dao is the basis of the entities—namely, initiating and completing them, *shi* 始 and *cheng* 成—have their origin in the same Dao, which in this very initiating and completing remains completely "dark." The term *miao* 妙, here rendered as "subtle," refers to the still-invisible germs or sprouts of specific entities to come, mentioned in *Laozi* 1.3. Wang Bi's own language stands in a complex interaction with a *Laozi* language already preinterpreted.

Another passage is more intriguing. On *Laozi* 34.3, Wang Bi writes to explain the simultaneous application of the mutually exclusive epithets of "great" and "small" to the Dao "insofar as each of the ten thousand kinds of entities relates back to it for their generation, but a force causes them not to know that on which they are based 萬物皆歸之以生而力 使不知其所由, this is not 'small'." This notion of a "force"—if the text can be trusted—seems utterly unnecessary; still, the phrase stands as a challenge.

With his focus on the That-by-which, Wang Bi clearly pursues an inquiry into the basis of all entities. He makes a conscious break with

the cosmological line of pursuit by treating the *Laozi* passages about the Dao's relationship with the entities with their generative terminology as philosophic metaphors to be translated into a language of structural dynamics. His discovery and logical deduction of the necessity of the interlocked aspects of the That-by-which as both being the condition of the possibility of entities, *you* 由, and being "dark," *xuan* 玄, mark a major breakthrough in the history of Chinese philosophy.

Tang Yongtong is clearly right in noticing this innovation, and his suggestion that Wang Bi's philosophy is "ontology" has a point because, in Western terms, Wang Bi is indeed dealing with the ontological difference. However, the above analysis of one aspect of Wang Bi's philosophy notes a certain inadequacy in this definition. Ontology might by a good term to give a general idea to a reader reared in the Western philosophic idiom, but Wang Bi's agenda is quite different.

We have approached his philosophy from what must decidedly be called a marginal point within his own thinking, namely, the binary structure of the ten thousand kinds of entities, and we have pursued it to a point defined as central by the consensus prevailing in available scholarship with its strong preference for the universal validity of a European-style development of the history of philosophy, namely, the features of the That-by-which in its relationship with the entities. Within Wang Bi's own agenda, however, the investigation of the That-by-which might be a functional and an integrated part in quite a different inquiry, which has more to do with political science. Should this be true, the observation that his philosophy marks the transition to ontology—while remaining important in a writing of the history of Chinese philosophy along Western lines—might lose much of its relevance in understanding Wang Bi's own philosophic pursuit.

Chapter 3

Wang Bi's Political Philosophy

THE ACTUAL AND PERPETUAL CRISIS
OF HUMAN SOCIETY

In the previous chapter we discussed Wang Bi's discovery of the dynamics prevailing in the seemingly static *wu/you* 無/有 relationship. The natural order, it turned out, is not maintained through the particular interaction of entities but through the dynamic interaction between entities and their negative That-by-which. Wang Bi highlighted this by stressing, in the commentary on *Laozi* 39, that even Heaven and Earth would be in danger of being "torn apart" and "getting into commotion" if they were not operating "through the One." Against this hypothetical crisis, human society offers real crisis. The status of the king among the Four Great Ones, Dao, Heaven, and Earth is evident from his being counted last in *Laozi* 25. Only under certain conditions does he qualify. In fact, however, Wang Bi does not really emphasize in his commentary the difference between the king as the highest human being and the other three Great Ones. Only four entities qualify for being "great" according to *Laozi* 25.9, and this obviously because they pertain as Ones to the entirety of the ten thousand kinds of entities.

> The Way is great, Heaven is great, Earth is great. The king, too, is great. 道大 天大 地大 王亦大.

This text offers with the *yi* 亦, "also, too," the option to mark the difference between the other three and the king and, as a consequence,

148

between nature and society. The *Laozi*'s next statement runs: "In the Beyond there are four Great Ones, and the king has a place as one of them!" 域中有四大而王處其一焉 For the implied reader of the *Laozi*, it seems uncontroversial that the other three Great Ones should be in this realm "Beyond"; the new argument is that the king has a place among them. Wang Bi's comment about *wang yi da* 王亦大, "the king, too, is great," runs:

> [As Confucius says in the *Classic of Filial Piety*, *Xiaojing*, answering the question of Zengzi, "May I ask whether among the virtues of the Sage there is none superior to filial piety?"].
> "Among the natures [bequeathed to the ten thousand kinds of entities] by Heaven and Earth, the human being is the most exalted," but the king is the lord of the human beings. Although [the king] is not positionally great [by just having his office] he, "too," is great [if] matching the other three [Great Ones]. That is why [the text] says "the king, too, is great!" 天地之性人爲貴而王是人之主也雖不職大亦復爲大與三匹故曰王亦大.

The translation of 雖不職大亦復爲大與三匹 ("although [the king] is not positionally great") is tentative because the meaning of *zhi da* 職大 ("positionally great") and the punctuation of the last section are unclear.[1] One thing, however, is evident. Wang Bi was not interested in marking some fundamental difference between the other three Great Ones and the king. What might this mean?

The relationship between a One and a Many is not by necessity a mutually beneficial one. If Heaven operates through the One, it will be clear and able to cover the ten thousand kinds of entities. But if not, Heaven itself will collapse, and the entities will lose their cover. The same is true for the other Great Ones. Their being Ones in relationship to the Many entails that their impact on themselves and on the ten thousand kinds of entities is wholly beneficial if they act properly, but it also is disproportionately disastrous if they do not, in which case they will provoke a negative interaction between the One and the Many that will destroy both sides.

The king thus belongs to the Great Ones by his being the one lord of myriad men. Whether he acts in the sense of *Laozi* 39, "through the One" or not, he will have a dramatic impact on mankind's fate; there will be social peace in the first case, and mutually destructive battle between the One and the Many in the second case. Being the one lord of men, the king cannot help but have this impact, whatever course of action he might follow. Far from being a cheap, philosophic argument for the automatic legitimacy and positive function of the ruler *qua* ruler, insertion among the Great Ones burdens him with the responsibility of being potentially the greatest possible scourge for mankind, precisely because he is the One over the many men.

There is no indication in Wang Bi's writing that he considered phenomena such as eclipses of the sun or earthquakes as indicators that Heaven or Earth was not "relating back to negativity" and thus was about to be torn apart and shaken. His reading of the cosmos seems dominated by the notions of factual regularity and order, as in the sequence of the four seasons, his standard example. He thus rejects as invalid the main source of Han dynasty information concerning the human disturbance of the natural order—irregularities in Heaven's order—in favor of a rigidly philosophic analysis.

Is there, then, a philosophic reason for this disregard or forgetting of the That-by-which, or is it just the trivial result of the general decay of the emperors' moral caliber as amply documented by Ban Gu through the ever decreasing numbers of leaders qualifying for ranks such as "Sage," "Intelligent Man," or "Humane Man" as time went on, and the ever increasing numbers of inmates of the lower levels of his nine-tiered "Rankings of Personalities Old and New," *gujin renbiao* 古今人表? In his commentary on *Laozi* 39.1, which he reads, "That which [entities] attain as the [most] ancient is the One" 昔之得一者, Wang Bi deals with this problem:

> The "[most] ancient" is the beginning. The One is the beginning of the numbers and the ultimate of entities. In each case it is the One by which the [great] entities [mentioned below such as Heaven, Earth, and the Spirits] are dominated. Each one of these [great] entities attains this One for its completion, but [if], having once completed, [each] would discard the One in order to settle in [their] completed [state], they [would], having [thus] settled in their completed [state], as a consequence, lose their mother [i.e., the One]; that is why [the text further down speaks of the danger of] all of them
>
> "being torn apart" [such as Heaven],
>   "getting into commotion" [such as Earth],
>   "becoming exhausted" [such as the spirits],
>   "being drained" [such as the valley], or
>   "being toppled" [such as the dukes and kings][2]
>
> 昔始也一數之始而物之極也各是一物之所以爲主也物各得此一以成既成而舍一以居成居成則失其母故皆裂發竭蹶也.

Wang Bi's reading of this first phrase of *Laozi* 39, if I understand it correctly, is quite baffling. The consequence was that the copyists had trouble understanding his comment, and thus we have varying traditions for the phrase 各是一物之所以爲主也, with most editions reading the fairly incomprehensible 各是一物之生所以爲主也 with a break between 生 and 所. The more important problem, however, is the grammatical and logical linkage in the last section, which has been joined here into a single sentence. Wang Bi is not very clear in marking hypothetical sentences of the kind, "If they would not x, then y would happen." In the present case, the sentence formally runs like a regular indicative: "Once they have completed, they discard the One in order to settle in [their] completed [state]. Having [thus] settled in [their] completed [state] they, as a consequence, lose their mother [that is, the One]. That is why they will all 'be torn apart,' 'get into commotion,' 'become exhausted,' 'be drained,' and 'be toppled' [as the *Laozi* says about Heaven, Earth, the spirits, the valley, and the dukes and kings, respectively]." But this is not the regular path of events. The entities referred to all belong to the category of Ones containing, covering, enspiriting, or regulating multitudes by not sharing their particular features, that is, by their negativity toward them. They are used in the *Laozi* itself for illustrations of the relationship of the That-by-which to the ten thousand kinds of entities.[3] In order to have this impact on the Many, they must "make use of the One," *yong yi* 用一, as Wang Bi details in his comments on *Laozi* 39.3. And apart from the dukes and kings, who only might and should do so, the others all do so blindly; it is their very nature. Heaven, in fact (and this is Wang Bi's opinion), does not get torn apart; neither does Earth get into a commotion or the valley become exhausted. The king, however, might get toppled. In view of this factual information, the grammar has to be reconsidered, and the entire phrase has to be read as a hypothetical case, as I have done in the translation.

What is a hypothetical case for Heaven, Earth, the spirits, and the valley is a real one for the "dukes and kings." But why should they "discard the One," *she yi* 舍一, and *ju cheng* 居成, "settle in [their] completed [state]," with the result of "losing [their] mother," holding on to which alone enables them to maintain All Under Heaven in structured order? The argument is repeated throughout Wang Bi's *Laozi* work in various terms. With reference to human society, Wang Bi talks about "discarding the root in order to go after the stem and branches," *she ben yi zhu mo* 舍本以逐末也 (on 52.2, cf. *zhi mo* 治末 in Wang Bi on *Laozi* 57.4), "discarding the root and attacking the stem and branches," *she ben er gong mo* 捨本而攻末 (*LZWZLL* 6.29), "reject this [Great Way] and do not abide by it," *she zhi er bu you* 舍之而不由 (on 53.2), "discarding what supports them [the entities] and rejecting what generates them [the processes]," *qi qi suo zai she qi suo sheng* 棄其所載舍其所生 (on 38.2), and asks "as [the dukes and kings] take the One as [the entities'] master how can this One be dismissed [by them]," *yi yi wei zhu yi he ke she* 以一爲主一何可舍 (on 42.1)? The terms *she* 舍 and *she* 捨 (on 38.2, 39.3) are synonymous; another term is *qi* 棄, "to reject" (*LZWZLL* 2.57, Wang Bi on *Laozi* 20.15, 38.2).

In human society, the problem is not with the ruler alone. As opposed to the prestabilized harmony of nature, as depicted in Wang Bi on *Laozi* 5.1, the "people" have a spontaneous tendency to break out of the place allotted them. All the "Way's smoothness" notwithstanding, the "people" spontaneously discard the "Great Way" and "love the by-paths" (53.2). Wang Bi comments:

> This means: The Great Way is vast in its correctness and smoothness, but the people nonetheless reject it and do not abide by it. They rather follow the heterodox by-paths, and how much more [would they do this] were [I] in turn to interfere [with them] and to act on [them], thereby blocking the midst of the Great Way!

This spontaneous tendency of "the people" to go for heterodox by-paths is often addressed by Wang Bi. The people's "heart," *xin* 心, might be "depraved," *xie* 邪 (Wang Bi on *Laozi* 65.3); it has "cravings and desires," *ai yu* 愛欲 (*LZWZLL* 6.22), is prone to "competition," *zheng* 爭, and "robbery," *dao* 盜 (*Laozi* 3.1), and might be "deluded," *mi* 迷 (Wang Bi on *Laozi* 52.7), or generally "prone to chaos," *luan* 亂 " (*Laozi* 3.1). There is, in other words, no spontaneous order among the Hundred Families that would be restored through an elimination of the institution of the ruler altogether. There is a spontaneous drift into evil and chaos that might owe as much to Xunzi's (340–245 B.C.E.) sombre view of human nature as it does to the social turmoil marking the end of the Han-dynasty. This has to be consciously counteracted by the ruler if he does not want to exacerbate it by philosophically ill-advised measures, such as "interfering with" the people and "acting on" them as mentioned in the above quotation. As opposed to the realm of nature, usually referred to by *Laozi* and Wang Bi as *tiandi* 天地, "Heaven and Earth," as the One and the "ten thousand kinds of entities," *wanwu* 萬物, as the Many, order in "All Under Heaven," *tianxia* 天下, that is, in human society, is an artifact purposefully generated by the ruler's conscious application to the Hundred

Families of the general laws governing the relationship between the One and the Many.

Social reality in historical fact is for either Laozi or Wang Bi not marked by the presence of Dao-generated order but by the results of its destruction, which proceeds along the strict laws governing the dialectics between the One and the Many. While this destruction is constantly reenacted and particularized, it is not of recent origin. Wang Bi's *Laozi* 58.6 says, "The delusion of the people has definitely already been around for a long time," on which Wang Bi comments: "This means: The people's delusion and [their] loss of the Way definitely has lasted for a long time already." This is followed by a phrase of unified transmission, which nonetheless has been declared corrupt by various scholars: "It will not do [simply] to hold ruling [by means of] a standard and goodness responsible for it" 不可便正善治以責. I understand this to refer to the fact that any particular government by standards and goodness is already an attempt to bring the people back from an "old" delusion and in the process reaffirms and perhaps exacerbates this delusion, which is fostered by a spontaneous tendency of the people to "like the by-ways" instead of the Dao, smooth as it might be.

The main protagonist in "discarding" the root of order is the ruler, and it is he alone who is capable of "bringing" society "back" to it. The focus of Wang Bi's philosophic attention and consequently the ultimate worldly addressee of his philosophical project is therefore not "the people" but the ruler himself. Unaware of the laws governing the relationship between the One and the Many, he tries to establish order among the Many through tough government action and in the process organizes the destruction of the very order he wants to establish (*LZWZLL* 6.2ff., Wang Bi on *Laozi* 38.2).

THE CAUSES OF THE CRISIS

But what is the condition for the possibility and even probability of this forgetting the "root" beyond the deplorable tendency of "the people" to love byways and the equally deplorable inability of the "kings and dukes" to understand the dynamics between the One and the Many? How is it possible that the kings and dukes "discard" something as crucial as their "That-by-which" and "settle" in their "completed [state]," *ju cheng* 居成? This "discarding" in fact causes and greatly exacerbates the volatility of the social realm and thus is at the root of conflict and chaos.

The reason, I suggest, is the constitutional "darkness," *xuan* 玄, of the That-by-which. That by which the entities are does not show up as a separate entity. It eludes all of the senses, and it eludes language. In short, as Wang Bi reiterates, the entities "are initiated by it and completed through it, but they do not know that through which these [two, their beginning and completion] came to be as they are." (*Laozi* on 21.3). This intrinsic and necessary "darkness" of the That-by-which, that it is not "evident"—as opposed to the overwhelming and recognizable presence of the specific—is at the root of this "discarding." The awareness and understanding of the relationship of the That-by-which to the entities furthermore yield results strictly counter to the spontaneous assumptions of the human mind and lead to courses of action directly opposite to those assumed to be normal, reasonable, and effective. In the midst of his discussion of the dialectics of the opposite in the *LZWZLL*, Wang Bi suddenly quotes in 6.68 a "sigh of the people of old": "Indeed! Why are things so difficult to understand," *he wu zhi nan wu ye* 何物之難悟也. This locution registers some of the strain of this philosophical exercise for the human mind. Wang Bi had to make enormous efforts to rediscover what he felt to be the hidden philosophy of the *Laozi*, the *Lunyu*, and the *Zhouyi*. In fact, only the efforts of some rare philosophical commentators seem to be able to keep visible the strange traces of, and pointers to, the "That-by-which" in these texts, which even most other commentators fail to perceive. It is thus normal, and to be expected, that the entities' "That-by-which" should be forgotten and discarded.

Given the consequences in social reality of this discarding, however, the duty of the commentator/philosopher—who makes no personal appearance in these commentaries and essays—becomes even more crucial. It is only through him that the signposts to the That-by-which can be rediscovered and deciphered. To make matters worse, Wang Bi sees most previous commentators to the texts of his choice rather as part of the "discarding" problem than of its solution, so that what might be the only way out is effectively barred. In this argument we sense some of the tremendous youthful arrogance of Wang Bi as well as his pride in his philosophic discovery.

Wang Bi's *Laozi*, *Zhouyi*, and *Lunyu* all refer to this ongoing process of the destruction of order. In the analysis of this process, Wang Bi comes into his own as a political philosopher who analyzes the dynamics of a political process. The importance of this analysis in his own work is highlighted by his dealing with the dynamics of the "rise of depravity," *xie zhi xing* 邪之興, and the "upsurge of debauchery," *yin zhi qi* 淫之起, in a separate essay enclosed within his *LZWZLL* 6. Obviously Wang Bi felt that the indications given in his canonical texts were not sufficient, that a more systematic treatment from his own hand was called for.

The process of social destruction is engineered by the very One who might bring about social order, the ruler. *Laozi* 75.1 reads with Wang's commentary:

That people don't gather the harvest is due to their ruler's eating too much tax grain. That is why they don't gather the harvest!	That people are hard to rule is due to their ruler's practicing interference. That is why they are hard to rule!

[In short] that people accept death easily is due to their ruler's striving for the fullness of life. That is why they accept death easily! It is a fact that only the absence of appreciation of life is more worthy than the appreciation of life.

Wang Bi's commentary generalizes these particular statements into a rule of political theory, according to which the moral quality of the people as well as the status of social order depend solely on the ruler's action, because it will exacerbate a natural propensity among people:

This means that that by which people are turned wicked, and order is turned into chaos is all based on the ruler['s behavior] and not on [that of] those below [because] the people [only] follow [the precedent] of the ruler. 言民之所以僻治之所以亂皆由上不由其下也民從上也.[4]

Commenting on the Nine in the ruler's position, that is, the unbroken line on the fifth place counted from below, in the *Zhouyi* hexagram *guan* 觀, Wang Bi writes, interpreting the *xiang* 象 line, "to observe my [the ruler's] life, means to observe the people," *guan wo sheng guan min ye* 觀我生觀民也:

The lord's transformation of those below is like the wind's bending the grass. That is why [I, the ruler,] observe the people's customs by way of examining myself, and, if the Hundred Families commit transgressions, this is due to me the single human. 上之化下猶風之靡草故觀民之俗以察己之百姓有罪在予一人.[5]

These statements go much further than the texts on which they comment, although again Wang Bi can claim with some justification that the political theory he is spelling out underlies these statements.

Two features of the ruler's behavior in particular wreak havoc in society and undermine his own position—his attitude toward the amenities of life, and his exercise of political power. Wang Bi's *Laozi* 72 describes the process.

When the people are not in awe
of [their ruler's] authority [anymore],
then the Great Authority will come. [Only]

being without recklessness is what
makes him [the ruler] have rest.

being without repression is what
makes him [the ruler] have
[= keep] [his] life.

Wang Bi comments:

Having "purity" and "calmness"
[*Laozi* 15.4] and [thus] being
"without interference," [*Laozi* 2.2]
[Laozi] calls "having rest."

Being modest and "putting
[one's person as a ruler] in the
background" [*Laozi* 7.2, 67]
and [thus] "not to be filling [it]
up" [*Laozi* 15.6 ff.], [Laozi]
calls "having life."

If [the ruler]
leaves his purity and calmness and
acts out his excitements and
desires;

abandons his modesty and his
"putting [himself] in the background" and applies his authority and power,

then

the other entities will make
trouble

and
the people will become wicked.

Once

[his] authority is not capable
[anymore] to establish control
over the people,

and [once] the people are unable
to bear his authority [any longer],

then high and low are in great
turmoil: Heaven's death penalty
[for the ruler] will come. That is
why [the text] says: "When the
people are not in awe of [the ruler's]
authority [anymore], then the Great
Authority will come."

That [only]
"being without recklessness is
what makes him [the ruler] have
rest"   and   "being without repression is

> what makes him [the ruler] have
> [= keep] [his] life"

> means that he definitely should
> not apply the power of [his]
> authority.

The logic is thus that by the ruler's "acting out his excitements and desires" and "applying his authority and power," "high and low will be in great turmoil" and, for himself, "Heaven's death penalty will come." Wang Bi's *Laozi* 57.1 deals with the exercise of political power. It starts by juxtaposing a ruler who "rules the state by means of standards," *yi zheng zhi guo* 以正治國, and therefore will "with cunning make use of the military," *yi qi yong bing* 以奇用兵, with a ruler who does this "by means of not busying himself [with government] activity," *yi wu shi* 以無事, and thus is able to "get hold of All-under-Heaven," *qu tianxia* 取天下. The former ruler, Wang Bi writes, will "establish punishments as the means to take on the stem and branches [i.e., secondary phenomena]," *li pi yi gong mo* 立辟以攻末, instead of "emulating the root" and thus eliminating the root cause for disturbances. The *Laozi* text itself then asks for the dynamics involved: "How do I know that this [that the ruler who rules by means of standards will make cunning use of the military] is so? From the following." It then proceeds to spell out the logic behind the thesis: the effect of government action is the opposite of its intent. The ruler's "increase in taboos" of which the *Laozi* speaks, "had the purpose," so Wang Bi says, "of putting a stop to poverty, but [ends up with] the people's being even poorer." The ruler increases the number of "profitable instruments among the people" with "the purpose," so Wang Bi writes, "of strengthening the state," and the result is, as the *Laozi* says, that "the state will get paler," that is, weaker. He increases "knowledge among the people" with no other result but that more "depraved activities will arise." In his good intentions to eliminate poverty, strengthen the state, and make people more sophisticated, he ends up with in fact having engineered what the *Laozi* calls the "mushrooming of depraved activities," *xieshi zi qi* 邪事滋起.

The ruler's attempt, as Wang Bi says, "to put an end to depravity," *xi xie* 息邪,—a depravity that, of course, he himself has brought about— through the proclamation of ever-more "standards" backfires. The consequence of his good intentions, which are summarized in the expression "displaying beautiful objects", will be that "there will be more robbers and thieves." These in turn will have to be confronted with cunning military strategies. Therefore, a ruler ruling by standards will be reduced to the use of military repression. Wang Bi manages to read this *zhang* as a rigidly constructed description of the negative dialectics leading philosophically unguided good intentions in politics to disastrous results. In reading this *zhang*, we do not even need the popular criticism of the debauchery and waste of the court. Good intentions are quite enough to wreck both state and throne.

We have hitherto seen descriptions of the stages of social degeneration, but the particular logic that shows the necessity of this process has not been addressed. Wang Bi's *Laozi* 58 might serve as a beginning. It starts with another confrontation between the right and the wrong way of government with a listing of further elements in this process of inverse or negative dialectics. *Laozi* 58.2 reads: "He [a ruler] whose government is bent on surveillance, will see his people divided." Wang Bi comments:

> He establishes punishments and names [corresponding to social ranks], and publishes rewards and punishments in order to bring cunning and fraud under control. That is why the text says: "He [a ruler] whose government is bent on surveillance. . . ." The different categories [of people] are allocated and split [so that] the people are concerned with struggle and competition. That is why [the text] says "will have his people divided!"

In this manner, "it is disaster indeed on which luck rests, and luck under which disaster crouches."

The Wei government, under Mingdi (d. 239 C.E.), made an effort to develop codes and regulations to control not so much the "people" but the challenge coming from literati of the big clans that had formed during the Later Han. Although we have few sources on this, it seems from Wang Bi's reactions that government surveillance was very much a part of this system.[6] Wang Bi time and again returns to the catastrophic consequences of such surveillance. These passages also bring out the particular process through which these negative consequences occur. Wang Bi's *Laozi* 65.3 reads:

> That is why governing the state by means of intelligence is the plague of the state.

In his comment, Wang Bi writes:

> If [a ruler] gets the people moving by means of intelligence and tricks, what is [in fact] being moved will be their depraved hearts. If he then again with cunning and tricks blocks the de-

ceptions by the people, the people will recognize his tricks and will thereupon thwart and evade them. The more cunning his [the ruler's] devices become, the more exuberantly will falsehood and deceit sprout [among the people].

Wang Bi's *Laozi* 18.2 reads:

Once knowledge and insight have appeared [in the ruler's actions], there will be great deceit [among his subjects].

Wang Bi comments:

If he practices tricks and applies his intelligence to spy out cunning and deceit [among the people], his interests become apparent and his shape becomes visible, [and, as a consequence,] the others will know how to evade him.

Once the ruler specifies himself in particular actions and techniques such as laws and secret surveillance, these become perceivable, thus evadable, with the consequence that people develop their skills and cunning and are in this process deformed and torn away from their potential submission to their allotted role.

The same logic is described in the inverse process in Wang Bi's *Laozi* 3 and 64. *Laozi* 3.1 runs:

3.1

[As a ruler,]

not to shower worthies with honors induces the people not to compete	not to overly appreciate goods that are hard to get induces the people not to become robbers.

[In short, as a ruler,] not to display
[things] that might be craved for
induces the hearts of the people not
to become prone to chaos.

Spontaneously, the "people" have a tendency to "compete," "become robbers," in short, "to become prone to chaos," and have to be "induced," *shi* 使, not to drift in this direction. Wang Bi's commentary elaborates on the logic operative between the ruler's actions and the results among the people, arguing that this observation in the *Laozi* contains a political theory dealing with the dialectics prevailing between the top and bottom of the social scale, between the ruler and the people.

What is the purpose of showering [someone] with honors who is only capable of handling this [particular] assignment [and no others]?

If in granting honors to worthies and glorifying the famous, the emulation exceeds their assignment, those below will rush forward to compete, compare their [own] capabilities [to those of those honored], and outdo each other.

Why should [something] be overly appreciated which is useful only in this [particular] application [and in no others]?

If the appreciation of goods exceeds their use, the greedy will compete to rush for them; they will [as Kongzi says, in *Lunyu* 17.10, comparing "small men" to robbers who] "break through walls and search in chests," and will commit robbery without regard for their [own] life.

That is why [the text says] that, if [things] that might be craved for are not displayed [by those above], the hearts [of the people] have nothing to disturb them!

Wang Bi does not engage in a radical reading of this passage. In his reading, the passage is not directed against the employment of capable people by the ruler, nor against the use of goods that are hard to get, but against exaggerated appreciation. Such appreciation from the person at the top of the social ladder will set the standard for the rest. The consequence will be that all try to get out of their preset allotted space to compete for advancement and enrichment, resulting in competition and struggle and greed and robbery, in short, in their "hearts becoming prone to chaos." *Laozi* 64.7 drives home the lesson. On the *Laozi* text, "That is why the Sage desires [only] to have no desires, and does not put high value on goods that are hard to get," Wang Bi comments: "Even when [his] desires and preferences are [only] minute, competition and emulation [among the people] are called forth by them. Even when the goods [in his hands] that are hard to get are [only] tiny, greed and robbery are evoked by them." The particular form that this competition takes is the legal battle, *song* 訟. Wang Bi thus extracts from the *Laozi* a blind and statutory political, social, and moral dialectic of the One and the Many operative between the ruler and the ruled, which functions independently of the intentions and moral status of the particular players involved.

The negative dialectical process described here does not only have the government creating—with the best of intentions—a society ridden by social conflict, moral decay, government repression, and secret police surveillance, but ends up in overthrowing the ruler himself. *Laozi* 49 is the crucial chapter for this discussion. Wang Bi writes on *Laozi* 49.5:

Furthermore, what is the purpose of [the ruler's] exerting the intelligence of his single body to spy out the sentiments of the Hundred Families? It is a fact that, if

I were to spy out other entities by means of [my] insight, the other entities would compete with me by reacting to this with their own insight.

I were to spy out other entities by means of [my] distrust [of them], the other entities would compete with me by reciprocating with their own distrust [of me].

It is a fact that the minds of [people in] All Under Heaven are not necessarily [all] in agreement [with the ruler]. But if in their reactions [to me] they do not dare to differ [from me because of the pervasiveness of my security network], this would mean that no one would be willing to make use of his [own natural] feelings. Truly indeed! Among the things causing great damage, none is greater than [a ruler's] making use of his intelligence! It is a fact [as the *Huainanzi* 14.138.9 says,] that, "if [I] were to

rely on [my] knowledge, the others would litigate against [me]."

rely on [my] physical strength, the others would fight against [me]."

As [my own]

knowledge does not surpass that of [the multitude of] others, I am lost once I take a stand in litigation [with them].

physical strength does not surpass that of [the multitude] of others, I am in danger once I take a stand on the battlefield [against them].

The whole argument is couched in a hypothetical reflection of the Sage about what would happen if he were to use his intelligence. It is reinforced by an allusion to a statement by Kongzi, whom the *Lunyu* 12.13 quotes as saying that, in the reading of the *Lunyu jijie*, put together by He Yan,

"In hearing litigation, I am like [= not better than] the others. What I definitely would go after is bringing it about that there is no litigation to begin with." Wang Bi does not stop here. He gives a vivid depiction of the social cataclysm inevitable where the ruler stops being the One of the Many and becomes one among the many who crave his wealth and status and thus in their millions confront him alone:

> [Under these conditions] it is not possible anymore [for me] to prevent others from using their

knowledge   and   physical strength

> on me. Things being thus, [I] myself am alone in confronting the others as enemies, but the others confront me in their millions as an enemy. Were [I] indeed

to multiply the mesh of laws for   and to make the punishments
them   for them more vexatious,

to block their byways   and   to attack their hideouts,

> the ten thousand kinds of entities would lose their That-which-is-of-itself-what-it-is, and the Hundred Families would lose their hands and feet [through physical punishment]; [in short, as the *Zhuangzi*, 25/10/35 ff., says of the consequences of the ruler's cherishing knowledge,] "the birds would be in turmoil above, and the fishes would be in turmoil" below.

The pressure of Wang Bi's own agenda on the *Laozi* is particularly evident in this passage. While otherwise Wang Bi is very careful to bring out any speck of evidence showing that he is merely making explicit the philosophic implications of the *Laozi*, this is one of the few cases where he inserts a long, exceedingly important statement without any visible and textual link to the *zhang* under consideration. True, the *Laozi* polemicizes against the use of "knowledge," *zhi* 智, and "wisdom," *sheng* 聖, but no exertion of analytical skill will lead to the harrowing picture painted in Wang Bi's comment on the *Laozi* 49.5 statement "[while I, the Sage] make all of them [= the people] into infants." It also is one of the few chapters that allude for confirmation to texts outside of the *Laozi*, the *Zhouyi*, and the *Lunyu*, in this case, the *Zhuangzi* and the *Huainanzi*.

The passage ends with the *Zhuangzi* quotation in a picture of universal—not just social—chaos. Still, from the argument in this segment, it is quite evident to whom the *Laozi* commentary is speaking, namely, the ruler. The greatest danger is not general social turmoil, but the ruler's losing his position and his life. The text in the commentary on *Laozi* 49 is a threatening scenario that tells the ruler of the consequences ill-guided policies will have for himself. Happily, as he is himself the root cause of the destruction of the prestabilized order, he is also the main instrument for its re-establishment and preservation.

Wang Bi obviously felt that the genesis and dynamics of this social cataclysm had been inadequately covered by the *Laozi* as well as the other texts for which he wrote commentaries. It was an important topic for his political philosophy, and in its treatment he came to the limit of what could be done via commentary, which presupposes that all relevant topics have been covered by the main text in a definitive, if (by now) cryptic, manner. The passage quoted above was a clear sign of this, and in his *LZWZLL* 6, he inserted an essay formally marked as a philosophic contribution of his own, apart from the analysis of the *Laozi*.

Wang Bi sums up the political theory of the *Laozi* in a single phrase, to be discussed later. It outlines a way to *xi mo* 息末, "calm down the stem and branches," that is, to calm down and bring order to the affairs of the world and society. Against the many misunderstandings of this ultimate purpose of the *Laozi*'s philosophic inquiry, Wang Bi writes his enclosed essay. It begins with the words, "I shall venture to come to a judgment about this," *chang shi lun zhi* 嘗試論之, which became a stock phrase among later commentators to introduce this kind of inserted essay. Before this enclosed essay, Wang Bi outlines in *LZWZLL* 4.1 ff. with a radical precision and symmetry the general principle of negative dialectics in the human world, which is the direct opposite of what a spontaneous pre-philosophic understanding would have assumed. The structure and language still carry the thrill and excitement of a stunning and an important philosophic discovery.

Generally [speaking,]

that by which beings persist is the negative opposite indeed to their form.	that by which achievements are performed is the negative opposite indeed to their name.

Wang Bi then proceeds to apply this general rule to the specifics of the ruler's position:

It is a fact that

he who persists does not take persistence for [the cause] of his persisting, but [his persisting is due] to his not forgetting about [the danger of] perishing.

he who is secure does not take security for the cause of his being secure, but [his security is due] to his not forgetting about perils.

That is why [to paraphrase Confucius in the *Xici* 下 4]

"he who preserves his persistence" "perishes," while he who [like the Gentleman] "does not forget about [the danger of] perishing" "persists"!

"he who acquiesces in his position" "is in peril," while he who [like the Gentleman] "does not forget about peril" "is secure"!

That he who is [truly] good at strength [restricts himself to] lifting an autumn down   and

he who is [truly] good at hearing [restricts himself to] noticing the thunderclap,

this is the negative opposition between Dao and form.[7]

Chinese philosophy, since the days of Kongzi, Laozi, and Zhuangzi, has excelled and delighted in discovering paradoxes in the structures of reality that—against all spontaneous commonsense assumptions—would show the dependence of a visible object, process, or structure on its opposite, frequently its negative opposite. *Laozi* 2.1 gives a veritable catalogue of these discoveries. It even claims that "everyone in All Under Heaven knows" that it is nothing else "but the abhorrent that makes the agreeable agreeable; and they all know that it is nothing else but the unacceptable that makes the acceptable acceptable." He then proceeds to establish a general rule of the opposite, not the negative opposite: "That is the reason for the having and not having creating each other, the difficult and the easy forming each other, the excellent and the deficient comparing with each other." It is in imitation of this structure of reality that the Sage Ruler maps out his own strategy. "This is why the Sage [Ruler, his administrative and doctrinal monopoly notwithstanding] takes residence in management without interference and practices teaching without words." With his unmarked but often verbatim quotations, Wang Bi acknowledges these discoveries, but he goes beyond the simple paradoxes and establishes a philosophically reasoned theory that the relationship between the One and the Many is the negative opposite, not simply the opposite. He reports the earlier discoveries in the quotation above from his *LZWZLL* after the *gu* 故, "that is why," and he is exceedingly careful to select only those that illustrate the negative opposite. He himself will derive and formulate the general philosophic rule, and will then show how Confucius and Laozi were basing themselves on this rule in their underived statements.

The general rule established in the last phrase quoted above is not only valid for the ruler's maintaining his throne and life and his security and persistence but, as we have seen, it also is valid for the outbreak of social cataclysm if the rule is not understood. In the essays enclosed in this part of the *LZWZLL*, Wang Bi begins with the expected paradox:

The rise of depravity—how could it be the work of the depraved?	The upsurgeof debauchery— how could it be operated by the debauched?

[It cannot.]

The entire essay consists of a discussion of the paradox of *Laozi* 19, with its claim that, if the ruler "were to discard wisdom and reject intelligence, the benefit for the people would be a hundredfold." According to this chapter, the ruler is to discard all those instruments of government that political theory has hitherto considered most efficacious, such as wisdom, intelligence, kindliness, righteousness, cunning, and profit. In fact, these instruments continue to be used with the best of intentions. If the ruler does not keep out of the public view the "amenities of [his] predilections and desires," the general rule spelled out above rattles along in its ruinous dialectics, *LZWZLL* 6.24 ff.:

[The ruler] might

go to extremes with his wisdom and enlightenment in the attempt to keep them [the people] under surveillance	exhaust [his] intelligence and wit in the attempt to attack them [the people],

but

the more refined [his] skills are, the more variegated their [the people's] pretensions will become,	the more intensely his attacks on them proceed, the more efforts they will make to elude him,

and then, indeed, the dull-witted
and the intelligent will get the better
of each other, the [relatives in] the six
relationships will distrust each other,

the "Unadorned disperses" [*Laozi* 28.6],
and they become separated from the[ir]
true [nature], and there is debauchery
in [all] affairs. Once the root is abandoned and [its] outgrowth is attacked,

wisdom   and   intelligence

might be applied to the maximum, there
will only be more of sure disasters—and
how much greater [will they be] when
[a ruler's] art is inferior to this [maximum
wisdom and intelligence]!

Wang Bi then takes up the three main elements of *Laozi* 19. The emperor's "exertion of wisdom and intelligence," there "to control tricks and pretensions," actually makes the people more "perspicacious" in "eluding him" with the consequence that their "tricks and pretensions become deeper." His "promoting kindliness and justice in order to destroy the shallow and vulgar" ends up promoting the rush for social status and wealth, so that sincerity is lost in father/son relations and compassion in the relations between brothers. His "multiplying skills and profit interests in order to raise the utility of affairs" ends up promoting greed and robbery. In short, and Wang Bi again quotes Kongzi's statements in the *Xici*, by the ruler's "clinging to order, chaos is indeed brought about" and "by preserving his security, peril [for the ruler's person] is indeed brought about." The ruler's attempts at creating social order are the root cause for social disorder.

The general formula for the effects of this type of interventionist government on society is found only in Wang Bi's *Laozi Commentary*, not in the segments of the *LZWZLL* which have come down to us. It goes by the general name of *wei* 爲, "interfering," and it has the effects of "destroying," *bai* 敗, the entities' "That-which-is-of-itself-what-it-is" and creating "man-made falsity," *wei* 僞.[8] The entities, Wang Bi writes, have an "eternal nature," *chang xing* 常性, and by someone "acting on them and interfering with them," they would "necessarily be destroyed." In the same manner, they have a "coming and going 往來," and by "holding on to them" one "by necessity loses them."[9] On one occasion, on *Laozi* 17.5, Wang Bi uses a medical metaphor: "If one is reining in the body but misses [its original] nature, virulent diseases will spring up. If one is supporting entities but misses [their] true [essence], then transgressions will occur [committed by them]." Wang Bi, on *Laozi* 16.6, describes the entire process:

The Eternal [essence of the entities] as such is neither [inwardly] partial nor manifest [in its preferences]; it has an appearance without either brightness or darkness, and features without either warming or cooling. That is why [the text] says: "Having knowledge of [this] Eternal means being enlightened!" Knowing this [Eternal] he [the ruler] is able indeed to embrace and penetrate the ten thousand kinds of entities without there being anything that is not encompassed. Once he has lost this [knowledge of the Eternal], evil penetrates into the allotted role, *fen* 分, [of entities, which forms their life endowment], and as a consequence entities diverge from [their assigned] station [with chaos ensuing]. That is why [the text] says: "[But] if he [a ruler] does not know the Eternal, then, acting recklessly, he brings about a nefarious [outcome]!" 常之爲物不偏不彰無皦昧之狀溫涼之象故曰知常曰明也知此復乃能包通萬物無所不容失此以往則邪入乎分則物離其分故曰不知常則妄作凶也.

The particular expression of the "Eternal" in the entities is their *fen* 分, their "allotted role." Once government action fails to take their Eternal into account, *xie* 邪, "depravity," "penetrates into their allotted roles," destroying the order of their arrangement in the process.

As we have seen in the beginning of this chapter, the dynamics are highly specific. The essential feature is the public role of the ruler. If his "preferences and desires" are lived out publicly, they exacerbate—through a public display of his wealth and power—the fact that he is already at the top of the social hierarchy. In this manner, his preferences and desires set the standard for those of "the people," and once everyone starts craving wealth and power, he will be one among the many, and he alone will confront the millions as his competitors and enemies. The tersest symbolic expression for this ill-informed proceeding of the ruler comes as a silent text. The fifth position in the *Zhouyi* hexagrams is a strong one, a *yang* position, and normally stands for the ruler. As Wang Bi points out, if a strong, unbroken line is on this strong position, the effects are by and large negative. As a coded text on political theory, the *Zhouyi* thus points out the structurally deleterious effects of a man in a strong position making a show of his strength, or the arrogance of power.[10]

At the core of the ongoing social cataclysm is thus not a spontaneous craving of many people for the byways nor the lecherous appetites of some rulers fostered by their high position but a philosophic misconception concerning the dynamics prevailing between the One and the Many. The necessity of the ruler's proper philosophic understanding of his own position and role could not be more strongly emphasized. The same is true for the relevancy of Wang Bi's own philosophic enterprise, which promises nothing less than a completely new path to social order.

Wang Bi does not consider alternative options of political structure. The ruler and society are dialectically interlocked, but they are so as two distinct categories. There is no notion of a society happily regulating itself with some nominal head in the center, nor the notion of a society completely run by the state to the point of merging into the state. The state with the single ruler as its representative and society with its multifarious people manning it are clearly separate entities, eternally locked in a fateful dialectical relationship that operates blindly and independent of the particular status, situation, or understanding of each party. The existence of a single ruler over the multitude of the people corresponds to the basic constellation of the One and the Many, which is that of the That-by-which and the ten thousand kinds of entities and thus mirrors the ontic setup. In this sense the institution of the single ruler has the dignity of philosophic necessity. The absence of any explicit reasoning about the necessity of a single ruler or of arguments defending what then would be seen as a questionable legitimacy of such an institution shows that, within the cultural sphere where Wang Bi moved, there was no such discussion to which Wang Bi would have had to react. The philosophic problem was how the single ruler should act.

The actions of even ill-guided rulers in fact are determined by the use of the opposite. Against cunning they use surveillance; against robbers, penal laws. As described in Wang Bi's *Laozi* 57, these lead down the road to ever harsher and ever more counterproductive intervention. Inserted into the dynamics of the One and the Many, these actions engender the very turmoil they intend to prevent. These rulers have not understood that the One controls the Many, not by being their opposite, like one man fighting a thousand, but by being their negative opposite. This understanding can be gained, and can only be gained, from the blurred signposts left behind by the Sage and the *Laozi*. This is where the importance and relevance of Wang Bi's enterprise lies. He sets out to make these signposts again readable and thus to establish nothing less than the rationally understandable ontological basis of a practicable political philosophy.

Wang Bi does not simply set off the ideal ruler—who, like emperor Yao of old, would run the country without the "people's being able to assign a specific name to him" (*Lunyu* 8.19)—against the philosophically uninstructed ruler whose interventionist actions cause social conflagration. In the *Laozi*, Wang Bi discovers an entire sequence of ever-lower governmental principles that provide a far more sophisticated grid than ideal versus bad ruler, *shengren* 聖人 versus *yuren* 愚人. The motor driving this sequence is in fact the dialectical relationship into which the One and the Many are locked.

In the context of fourth- or third-century B.C.E. historical thinking, many writers have described a polity gradually deteriorating from the three Sage Emperors of old through the five Emperors to the hegemons of their day. The *Laozi* chapters (e.g., 17, 18, 38) take up this discussion, and Wang Bi reads them as attempts not just to name and describe the stages of this deterioration but to show the logic in this downward race of history. The language in these *Laozi* chapters is a time language. There is a sequence of emperor types in *Laozi* 17, listed as "the one after this one" or "those after these," a description that matches "after [a ruler] has abandoned the Great Way, there will be humaneness and justice" in *Laozi* 18, and a similar time notion in the words of *Laozi* 38, "Once the Way has been lost, there will be *de* 德; once *de* has been lost, there will be kindliness." These statements reflect a prevailing historical pessimism that sees the golden age in early times and a continuous deterioration to the present day.

This pessimism still finds its expression in the *Hanshu* "Tables of Personalities of Old and New Times," *gu jin ren biao* 古今人表, which graphically shows that the emperors of earliest times were Sages or worthies in the top categories, while the lower orders of this nine-tiered roster fill up ever more as one gets closer to the present, with the solitary last Sage, Kongzi, already gone a few hundred years at the time this list was compiled.[11] This view corresponds to the then-prevailing cosmogonic or ontogonic approach in philosophy with the Dao 道 or *qi* 氣 at the beginning. The philosophic consequence within the *Laozi* as well as in Confucius' *acta et gesta* is the assignment of philosophic authority to this utopian beginning. There and then, the Way prevailed, and the *Laozi* 15.1 and 65.1 quote "those in antiquity who were well-versed in the Way" as authorities of a life in conformity with the Dao, while Confucius (Lunyu 7.1) even considers himself superior to Laozi in his "veneration of antiquity," *hao gu* 好古.

Wang Bi reads all of this time sequence as a metaphor for logical sequence. This is most clearly visible in his handling of *Laozi* 14.4 and 14.5 which, in view of their parallelism, one might read together as

that holding [today] on to the way of antiquity it is possible [for a Sage Ruler] to regulate occurrences of the present and that [from these occurrences of the present] one [the Sage Ruler] has something by which to cognize the oldest beginning, this [I] call the continuity of the Way. 執古之道可以御今之有以知古始是謂道紀.

Sadly we have no evidence from texts such as the *Wenzi*, the *Hanfeizi*, or the *Huainanzi* of how this passage was read during the third and second centuries B.C.E.[12] Wang Bi's commentary runs:

> The featureless and nameless is the ancestor of the ten thousand kinds of entities. Although the present and antiquity are not the same, although times have changed and customs have changed, there definitely is no one who has not based himself on this [featureless and nameless] by way of completing their regulated order. That is why it "is possible" to "hold on to the Way of antiquity by way of regulating occurrences of the present" and although high antiquity is far away, its Way still persists. That is why, although one is existing today, it is possible "by means of this [present-day reality] to cognize the oldest beginning." 上古雖遠其道存焉故雖在今可以知古始也.

Because the Way is not, in Wang Bi's view, something belonging to the cosmic and social past, but is the That-by-which of all kinds of entities at any possible given time, the *gu* 古 in *gu zhi dao* 古之道, "the Way of antiquity," takes on a new meaning. In fact, the Dao is present in both antiquity and the present, so that *even though* it is a Way of a bygone period when times and customs were different, it is still valid today. For Wang Bi, the sentence does not stress veneration for things of antiquity but the timelessness of the insights of political philosophy. He manifests this by expanding a vague "by means of," *yi* 以, in the *Laozi* phrase 以知古始 into a full-fledged argument, "that is why, although one exists today, it is possible . . ." 故雖在今可以. This phrase is developed by Wang Bi in symmetry with the actual *Laozi* phrase about "holding on to the Way of antiquity." This operation, which builds on minimal indications in the *Laozi* text, transforms the entire *Laozi* argument from a nostalgic plea for the ongoing validity today of the "Way of antiquity" to an insight into the ever-same presence of the That-by-which. Extrapolating from this commentary, the *Laozi* text has to be supplemented with an appropriate bracket:

> That holding on [even] to the Way of antiquity, one [the Sage Ruler] has something by means of which to regulate occurrences of the present, and [even though living in the present] one [the Sage Ruler] has something [namely, present-day reality] by means of which to cognize the oldest beginning, this [I] call the continuity of the Way.

To stress that this is an option, not a reality, Wang Bi adds the *ke* 可, "it is possible," to both phrases in his commentary. We have seen in the analysis of Wang Bi's *Laozi* 47 that the two realms of nature and society operate according to the same philosophic principles, which can be understood without going out of doors or peeping through the window. Wang Bi now adds that the Dao is the ever-present That-by-which, so that present-day reality is as good a way to understand oldest antiquity as is the way of government of oldest antiquity for purposes of regulating present-day society. In fact, the commentary on *Laozi* 47.1 directly refers to the text of *Laozi* 14.4 ff. Wang Bi finds confirmation for the plausibility of this reading in *Laozi* 21.6, "from antiquity to the present its [the truthful essence's] name has not disappeared" 自古及今其名不去. It confirms that the *Laozi* thought of the ongoing presence of the That-by-which. In the *LZWZLL* 1.45 ff., Wang Bi restates his position in the clearest possible form:

> Therefore, that, as antiquity and present are connected, and as
> end and beginning have the same [structure], so that "holding
> on to . . . antiquity, it is possible [for a Sage Ruler] to regulate
> the present" and, taking the present as evidence, "[he] has
> something by which to "cognize the oldest beginning," is what
> [the *Laozi*] styles "the Eternal."[13]

There is no trace of the nostalgia for the wisdom of antiquity in Wang Bi's writing. True, he will write a commentary on Confucius' statement on Yao, but neither here nor elsewhere is there a confrontation in his own words between a real historic time when the Dao prevailed and a dismal present.

We return to the transformation of the possibly historic sequences of government techniques in *Laozi* 17, 18, and 38 into logical sequences in Wang Bi's *Laozi*. The sequence presented in Wang Bi's *Laozi* 17 is from the "Great One" of whom the people only "know that he exists," to the second, to whom the people are "close and whom they praise," to the third, whom they "fear" to the fourth, whom they "do not take seriously." In the commentary, Wang Bi links this descending order to certain government techniques. The Great One "takes residence in management without interference and practices teaching without words." The next one, "unable to reside in [his] affairs by way of non-interference and "establishes the good and spreads moral education." The third, "not anymore capable" again "of getting other beings to do something by means of kindness and humanness," "relies on might and power." The last, "unable to set the

law to treat people equitably by means of a correct standard," will rule
"by means of intelligence," that is, surveillance. *Laozi 65.3* describes this
last kind of rule as "the plague of the state," and Wang Bi adds here that
"those below know how to circumvent him so that his orders are not being
followed." Each of the steps is defined in a multiple way, through the attitude of the people, through a colloquial explanation of how this attitude
comes about, and through a restatement in other terms of the government
technique in the "unable to" phrases. The sequence is as follows:

RANK	POPULAR REACTION	GOVERNMENT TECHNIQUE	RESTATEMENT
1	知有之 People only know he is there	無爲, 不言 Non interference—teaching without words	無爲, 不言 *idem*
2	親而譽之 People get close and praise him	立善 施化 Establishing good—transforming	恩仁 Bestowing favors, kindness
3	畏之 People fear him	賴威權 Use of power and authority	法正 Use of laws and standards
4	侮之 People loathe him	以智治國 Manages state by means of knowledge	(智) *idem*

The last government technique marks the beginning of chaos, because
from then on social relations will be based only on deceit and violence.

Wang Bi's *Laozi* 18.1 and 18.2 simply list the first and last of these
transitions:

Once [a ruler] has abandoned the Great Way, there will be
humaneness and justice [guiding his actions].

Wang Bi personalizes the abstract text 大道廢焉有仁義, which could
read "once the Great Way has deteriorated, there will be humanness and
justice" by transposing the *fei* 廢, "deteriorate," to *shi* 失, "to lose" in
his commentary:

Once he [the ruler] has lost the "management without interference" [in which, according to *Laozi* 2.2, "the Sage takes residence"] he will in turn by means of the way of applying insight
and establishing good [deeds] further the other beings.

The *Laozi* continues:

Once knowledge and insight have appeared [in the ruler's ac-
tions], there will be great deceit [among his subjects].

Wang Bi comments:

If he practices tricks and applies his intelligence to spy out cunning and deceit [among the people], his interests become apparent and his shape becomes visible [and, as a consequence,] the other beings will know how to evade him. That is why [the *Laozi* says that,] once "knowledge and insight have appeared [in the ruler's actions,]" "great deceit" [among the subjects] will arise!

Adjusting the different argument structure to our table, the sequence here is:

RANK	POPULAR REACTION	GOVERNMENT TECHNIQUE	RESTATEMENT
1		大道 Great Way	無爲 Non-interference
2		仁義 Use of kindness and righteousness	施慧 立善 Apply insight and establish good
4	物知避之 Others know how to evade	慧智 Use of insight and knowledge	行術 用明 Practice tricks, apply intelligence

It is immediately evident that, in each of the three categories handled here, some of the core notions coincide with those used for the definitions in Wang Bi's *Laozi* 17.

In Wang Bi's *Laozi* 38, we have the most detailed hierarchy of government strategies. Wang Bi's comment to this *zhang* exceeds in length all of his other comments. According to Wang Bi, the *Laozi* here first makes a basic distinction between those with "superior receipt," *shang de* 上德, and those with inferior receipt, *xia de* 下德. The former quickly qualify as the "Great [Man]" of *Laozi* 17.1 by being able to be "without interference and leaving nothing undone" 無爲而無不爲. Those with "inferior receipt" generally "have interference," *you wei* 有爲, but on different levels of sophistication. In this "inferior-receipt" group three levels exist: "superior kindliness," *shang ren* 上仁, "superior righteousness," *shang yi* 上義, and superior ritual, *shang li* 上禮. The last is the result of the "wearing thin of truthfulness and credibility and [thus] the beginning of [social] chaos" because, "when no one is heeding [his orders,] he will roll up his sleeves and use violence [to enforce his will]." It is followed by the government technique "foreknowledge," *qian shi* 識, here read as a reference to a surveillance apparatus, which is the "beginning of stupidity." The word "stupidity," *yu* 愚, does not refer to a lack of intelligence but to the most unenlightened form of government. In Ban Gu's *Gujin ren biao* 古今人物表, the "stupids," *yuren*, are at the bottom of the nine-tiered ladder, and people such as the "bad last emperors" Jie and Zhou are listed in this category.[14] Wang Bi's commentary goes into some detail listing the particular governmental features of these various categories. I shall assemble them again here.

RANK	GOVERNMENT TECHNIQUE	RESTATEMENT
上德 1	無爲 Non-interference	唯道是用 Making use of Dao only
下德a 2	仁, 爲之而無以爲 Kindliness, interference dispensing kindliness, no ulterior motive	博施仁愛 "Broadly loving [entities]"
下德b 3	義, 爲之而有以爲 Righteousness, interference, ulterior motive	忿枉祐直 "Loathing the crooked and protecting the straight"
下德c 4	禮, 攘臂而扔之 Ritual; if unsuccessful, violence	尙好修敬, 不對之閒 忿怒生 Makes them show respect, but resentment grows
愚 5	前識 Foreknowledge	雖竭聖智而民愈害 Exhausting wisdom and knowledge increases damage to people

From a comparison, it is evident that we again have a hierarchy similar to that depicted in the two other *zhang*. The total numbers are not always the same, but the core terms in the government techniques match. At the top is *wu wei* 無爲, followed by "humaneness," *ren* 仁, and "righteousness," *yi* 義, which is combined with humaneness in the second example and defined as government by "law and standards," *fa zheng* 法正, in the first example. Ritual is mentioned only in Wang Bi's *Laozi* 38, but the last rank is shared by government by surveillance.

Wang Bi marks two fundamental breaks in this ranking: first, that between the top and all the rest; second, that between all of those government techniques still characterized via *de* 德 as having some "receipt" from the Dao on the one hand, and the government by surveillance, which is beyond salvation, on the other hand. The hierarchy corresponds to the assumptions of a tripartite hierarchy underlying Confucius' statement in *Lunyu* 6.21 about those "above the men in the middle," with whom one can talk, and those "below those in the middle," with whom one cannot talk. The hierarchy is repeated in *Lunyu* 16.9, where Kongzi puts those at the top, "who know from birth," those in the middle, "who know from studying" and "who are studying when pressured," and calls the "people" at the "bottom," those who "don't study even when pressured." This basic tripartite grouping also underlies Ban Gu's nine-tiered table.[15]

Once the capacity to follow the top government strategy is lost, the remainder goes into a deteriorating spin, with each of the techniques creating the problems that will force the use of the next lower one. This logical development from one of these middle techniques to the next lower one also was addressed in Wang Bi's *Laozi* 17 and 18. His description in the commentary to *Laozi* 38 is most detailed. As an example, the transition from kindliness to righteousness may be quoted. It is a fine specimen of Wang Bi's transformation of the *Laozi* from a text of philosophic statements into a text of philosophic arguments:

> Thus there will be one who with broadly and generally dispensed kindliness loves them [the other entities], but this love for them has nothing partial or self-interested; that is why [the text says,] "[He who possesses] the highest kindliness interferes with them, but has no ulterior motive [in this]!"
>
> As [this] love is incapable of being all-encompassing, there will be one who will regulate them [the other entities] with a [sense of] righteousness which is promoting [the one] and demoting [the other], corrective and straight; loathing the crooked and protecting the straight, he supports the latter and attacks the former, and with regard to things and affairs he has intentional interference. That is why [the text says], "He [who possesses] the highest sense of righteousness interferes with them [the other entities], but has ulterior motives [in this]"!
>
> As [this] straightening [through righteousness] is unable to be generous, there will be one . . .[16]

Once things have started to deteriorate, they have their intrinsic logic in deteriorating even further. "Kindliness," notwithstanding the best of intentions to spread its kind dispensation as far as possible, must remain specific and must be kinder to one entity than to another. It will be "incapable of being all-encompassing," which is why, as *Laozi* 5.1 says, "Heaven and Earth are not kindly," *tiandi bu ren* 天地不仁, because, as Wang Bi comments, they are not partial. As a consequence of some being preferred and others not, competition for imperial grace sets in, and "righteousness" will be needed to set standards. At this level, even the intent of impartiality is gone, which was still there in the exercise of "kindliness" with its being "without ulterior motive" or "without having an agenda," *wu yi wei* 無以爲. The government technique of righteousness will consist of "loathing the crooked and protecting the straight" and thus "have an agenda," *you yi wei* 有以爲. Again, Wang Bi draws strongly on other material within the *Laozi* and the other authoritative texts in his analysis. For kindliness, there is *Laozi* 5; for righteousness, *Laozi* 18 and 19, as well as the parallel in *Laozi* 17; for "foreknowledge," *qian shi* 前識, he drew on the polemics against using knowledge, *zhi* 智, as a government technique; only for ritual is there no other direct parallel.

Wang Bi explicitly points out in his commentary on *Laozi* 38 that the fundamental problem setting this downhill race in motion remains the ruler's misunderstanding the dialectics of the One and the Many and moving from one inept instrument of control to the next more inept one.[17] "Kindliness will turn into pretense, righteousness will turn into competition, and ritual will turn into struggle," Wang Bi writes in the commentary. By the principle of the negative opposite, the effects of kindliness do not come about through the application of kindliness or, in Wang Bi's words, "the abundance of the capacity of kindliness cannot be brought about by making use of kindliness."[18]

While this is powerful rhetoric to show to a ruler where his philosophical assumptions will eventually lead him, it also presents a much more sophisticated picture of actual governmental options, not just the stark black and white of those who do it right and those who do not. It allows for measuring the distance of a specific government from the optimum and the dangers that lie ahead if the course is continued. And, as a consequence, it allows a more sophisticated analysis of the implied addressees of text and commentary. They are not simply grouped into the category of "not having the Dao," *wu dao* 無道, and left to rot, but most of them might still be in the realm of "inferior receipt" from the Dao, operating their government with ever-smaller portions of this precious order-providing That-by-which. As a matter of fact, the little social order that they manage to establish is directly proportional to the size of the "receipt," *de* 德, that they can still activate. With the establishment of ritual as the main governmental instrument, the "credibility," *xin* 信, of entities in terms of giving evidence of the Dao is at its thinnest. Their nature is deformed to such a degree that they do not abide by their allotted stations, and this is "the beginning of chaos." With the establishment of "foreknowledge," the Dao has been completely "ornamentalized," *hua* 華; there is no substance left. As we know from the end of *Laozi* 38, this *hua* 華 is to be read as the opposite of *shi* 實. The *Laozi* here speaks of the Great Man, who "resides in its [the Way's] substantialness, and does not take residence where it [has become] an ornament" 處其實不居其華[19].

The starting point of Wang Bi's political theory is not a stable social order that might deteriorate at some future time and has to be maintained to prevent this. Instead, it is a human world whose ruler has "discarded" its That-by-which and is, along with his state, a helpless plaything in the inexorable logic of a dynamic structural relationship that he does not understand, fuels with his actions at the wrong end, and is heading for his and society's demise. It is a crisis perpetuating itself through the continuous attempts at overcoming it. Order in society does not have to be maintained but restored. The simple invocation of a utopian dream will not do; specific ways have to be found to get "back." The core parameters of these ways can be found only in the general dialectics of the One and the Many. In the last section, we shall turn to this endeavor.

OPERATING THE RETURN: THE SAGE

THE IMITATION PRINCIPLE

The result of the undisturbed interaction of the One and the Many and of negativity and entity in the realm of nature is order. Because negativity as the condition of their possibility "does not interfere with the ten thousand kinds of entities, the ten thousand kinds of entities each fit into their use, so that there is none not provided for" 無爲於萬物萬物各適其所用則莫不贍.[20] "That there is none not provided for" describes the achievement of order as a prestabilized harmony coming as a result of all entities "relating back," *fan* 反, *fu* 復, to their "That-is-what-is-of-itself-what-it-is," *ziran* 自然, or the One, which in fact is just the general form of their own "nature," *xing* 性, as classes of entities.

The One is thus the One of the Many by providing the general negative opposite of their positive features and in this way being "That-by-which" they are. The *wei* 爲 in *wu wei* 無爲 has been consciously overtranslated as "interference," because any particular action establishes a set of non-actions, so that differentiation among the entities comes about, and it becomes impossible that "there is none not provided for" by the That-by-which. In this manner, this particular action would tempt both the beneficiary and the non-beneficiary out of their place in the prestabilized harmony, and in this sense it would be "interference." On the other hand, the importance of the That-by-which for the entities is primordial, it is "on the basis of," *you zhi* 由之, negativity that they "are generated and are completed" 以生以成. In this sense, its non-interference is the condition for its providing the basis for all.

The same rule holds true for society, only there the establishment of order is a conscious act. "Someone who [only] supports the lord of men by means of the Way [i.e., a Sage] . . . will in his dealings [rather] emulate returning [or relating back] [All Under Heaven to the root]," says Wang Bi's *Laozi* 30.1/2, and Wang Bi comments: "'Someone who has the Way' will make efforts and desires [to make All Under Heaven] return and relate back [to the One] and [to himself practice] non-interference."

The human realm is not statutory in its order. Its volatility and constant drift into chaos is due to the fact that its order is not spontaneous but has to be established through the positive understanding and conscious application by the ruler, in his dealings with the people, of the universal laws governing the relationship between the One and the Many. The ruler is always a One but not by definition "great," as are Heaven, Earth, and the Dao. Being the One, he will, whatever he does, function within the dynamics of the One and the Many, but as long as he is not "Great," his attempts at creating order are the engine operating social chaos and his own demise through the inevitability of his becoming partial—and that in the real world means factional, nepotist, and vindictive—and thus derailing the prestabilized harmony of which he himself is to be the kingpin. Only by *fa* 法, "imitating" and "taking as a model," the Great Ones, who spontaneously fulfill their roles as Ones, will he himself be Great in the sense of "there being no one not provided for," and of the "entities [remaining] intact and fulfill [their] nature" 物全而性得.[21] Only then he will not simply be a "ruler," *wang* 王, but a Sage Ruler, *sheng wang* 聖王, or a Sage, *shengren* 聖人.

The analysis will proceed in two steps. We shall first contrast the perennial social crisis mapped out in the previous section with the model of a society whose ruler operates in conscious imitation of the general rules for the One and the Many; in a second step, we shall reinsert this model into the real world and study the pragmatics of Wang Bi's political philosophy.

This *fa*, this "being modeled after," referred to as *zetian* 則天, "taking Heaven as model," in the *Zhouyi* and the *Lunyu*, is explicitly mentioned only in *Laozi* 25, but it forms the structural backbone of many *zhang* of the *Laozi*. In *zhang* 5, for example, the first two *Laozi* statements run "Heaven and Earth are not kindly. For them, the ten thousand kinds of entities are like grass and dogs. The Sage is not kindly. He treats the Hundred Families like grass and dogs." Wang Bi explains the juxtaposition of Heaven/Earth and the Sage with his comment to the second phrase: "The Sage 'harmonizing [as the *Zhouyi* says of the Great Man] his capacity/receipt with [that of] Heaven and Earth'" 聖人與天地合其德 takes the Hundred Families as [something] like grass and dogs." There are two standard forms of this imitation structure.

The first takes the form "the spontaneously Great Ones (Heaven, Earth, Dao, and so forth) are/do X, that is why the Sage does x1," x1 being a derivative or imitation of x. The Sage's "taking Heaven as model" or "harmonizing his capacity/receipt with [that of] Heaven and Earth" is expressed through the "that is why" linking the sections about Heaven/ Earth and the Sage, respectively. This structure prevails in *Laozi* 2, 5 (no "that is why"), 7, 66, 77, and 81 (no "that is why").

The second states, usually as a paradox, some form of operation of the negative opposite, which is characteristic of the relationship between the One and the Many, and ends with "that is why the Sage . . . " This form prevails in *Laozi* 3, 12, 22, 26, 28 (no "that is why"), 29, 47, 57, 58, 63, 64, 71 (no "that is why"), 72, 73, and 79. In many other chapters, Wang Bi directly or indirectly inserts the Sage Ruler for an absent subject. Some, like *Laozi* 23, have this rhetorical structure, but most do not. Examples are chapters 3, 8, 10, 15, 16, 17, 18, 19, 20, 21, and 22. They go together with chapters explicitly dealing with the Sage outside of this structure, such as *Laozi* 49, 60, 70, and 78. Together, the Sage-related chapters in Wang Bi's reading of the *Laozi* form the majority of all chapters, although the term appears only in ten *zhang* of the *Laozi* text itself, an indication not only of Wang Bi's reading strategy but of the importance of the Sage in his thinking.

Wang Bi does not read the *Laozi* as a prescriptive but as an analytic text, although the results of his philosophic inquiry eventually lend themselves to a series of prescriptive and normative statements on the proper way of handling politics. In this reading, what comes after the "that is why the Sage," *shiyi shengren* 是以聖人, never describes how the Sage *should* behave. The opposite is true. What comes after this "that is why" is considered known. The thrust of the text in Wang Bi's reading is to explain not that but the reason why the Sage does what comes after the "that is why." It provides the general principles out of which the Sage's attitude and actions follow and can be understood.

How, then, is the Sage to model himself after and imitate negativity in his social role as the one ruler? In a very radical and youthful statement around 243, Wang Bi claimed that the Sage "embodies negativity," *ti wu* 體無.[22] This referred to Confucius. In his comments on *Laozi* 38, Wang Bi writes in a badly transmitted passage:

> It is a fact that the ultimate of greatness is only the Way! What is there from this [the Way] downward that deserves to be honored? [Nothing] That is why, although [as *Xici* 上5 says of the Great Men/Sages], "[their] capacity" might be "blossoming" and [their] "achievements" "great" [so that, although] they "richly endow" the ten thousand kinds of entities, they still each obtain their [particular] capacity and are not, by themselves, able to be "all-encompassing" [which according to *Laozi* 25.3 is the quality of the Way]. Thus Heaven [, which is able

to cover all ten thousand kinds of entities,] is [by itself] unable
to manage carrying [them]; Earth [,which is able to carry the
ten thousand kinds of entities,] is unable [by itself] to manage
covering [them]; and the [Sage Lords of] men [who might be
able to know all about bringing order to society,] are unable
[by themselves] to fully provide [for the ten thousand kinds of
entities]. Although they [Heaven, Earth, and the Sage Ruler]
highly esteem taking negativity as [the basis of] usability, they
are unable to complete negativity to make it [completely identical with] their [own] substance. 不能全無以爲體. As they are
unable to complete negativity to make it [completely identical
with] their [own] substance, they lose out on their being Great
[in the absolute sense in which the Dao is Great].[23]

Wang Bi here makes a difference between the Dao, on the one hand—
identified here with negativity and not reduced to the particular heuristic
meaning it had in the *LZWZLL* definitions—and Heaven, Earth, and
[the Sage Ruler of] men, on the other hand. The latter three are great in
the sense of *Laozi* 25, but the Dao is the "ultimate of Greatness!" 大之
極也. Their greatness lies in their being Ones with regard to the entirety
of the ten thousand kinds of entities. Their difference from the Dao is
their specificity in terms of one single feature. We know the particular
features for Heaven (covering) and for Earth (supporting), because they
often are stated, but we do not know the limiting feature of man, of the
Sage. Heaven can cover but not support, and Earth can support but not
cover, but there is no clear opposite to "fully providing for," *shan* 贍. The
only reasonable option would be that the Sage King cannot "generate and
complete," *sheng cheng* 生成, entities.

What then means *shan* 贍, "fully providing for"? According to various
Laozi statements, the Sage/Sage King is said to excel in understanding, in
being "enlightened," *ming* 明, which refers to his understanding the basis
of his own role as a One. This enables him to fully provide order, *zhi* 治, to
all entities in the manner of Heaven providing for them all. "That is why
even a human being [= ruler] who is knowledgeable about the establishment
of order among the ten thousand kinds of entities but does not proceed
in his ordering by means of the Way of the two principles [Heaven and
Earth] will not be able to fully provide [the ten thousand kinds of entities
with order]," Wang Bi writes on *Laozi* 4.1. The Sage Ruler thus is able
to fully provide order in imitation of the way Heaven and Earth provide
order for the realm of nature but remains limited in his capacity and is
unable to generate entities. (It is intriguing to note that mortality is never
mentioned as such a possibly specifying and limiting factor of the Sage.)

Due to this one specificity, however, neither of the three—Heaven, Earth, and ruler—can become fully identical with negativity in their substance. In short, the maximum the Sage can attain is to imitate negativity in his dealings with the people.

In this context, a passage from Wang Bi's *Solving the Difficult Points in the Lunyu, Lunyu shiyi* 論語釋疑, becomes relevant. The text in *Lunyu* 7.6 runs: 志於道據於德依於仁游於藝. It has been read at least since Huang Kan 皇侃 (Liang dynasty) as a prescriptive statement, meaning, as Waley translates, "Set your heart upon the Way, support yourself by its power, lean upon goodness, seek distraction in the arts!"[24] He Yan, to whose commentary Wang Bi is reacting, did not read it this way. For him the stress is on the difference between the terms *zhi* 志, *ju* 據, *yi* 依, and *you* 游. On the second phrase, for example, he comments 據杖也德有成形故可據, "*Ju* 據 means relying on. Capacity has a completed shape; therefore it is possible to 'rely on it.'" Extrapolating from this commentary, he read the entire passage: "While it is [possible only to] set one's mind on the Dao, it is [possible to actually] rely on capacity, it is [possible to actually] lean onto kindliness [of others], and it is [possible to actually] find entertainment in the arts." The reading of the first phrase is extrapolated from He Yan's commentary that "*zhi* 志 means "to aspire to." He comments: "The Dao cannot be embodied. Therefore one [only] aspires to it, and that is all." It is quite possible that He Yan read this text as referring to Confucius himself with an implied "I," which would prompt a translation "On the Way [I can only] set [my] mind, [but] on capacity [I can] lean, onto kindliness [I can] lean, and entertainment [I can] find." Wang Bi agrees with the basic orientation of this commentary but takes issue with it in that it does not explain why the Dao cannot be embodied. His commentary for this first phrase runs (no others have been transmitted):

> Dao is an appellation for negativity. There is nothing it does not penetrate, nothing that is not based on it. Moreover as it is said that the Dao is vacant and without substance, and that it is impossible to make an image of it, this [means] the Dao cannot be embodied. That is why he only "sets his mind on" and aspires to it, and that is it![25] 道者 無之稱也無不通也無不由也況之曰道寂然無體不可爲象是道不可體故但志慕而已.

Without further proof, I assume that Wang Bi read this passage as a statement by Confucius about himself. In this elevated meaning of the Dao meaning negativity, the statement was clearly not some general rule of behavior, but it was quite in tune with Wang Bi's perception of Confucius. Accordingly, Wang Bi read "[I only] set my mind on the Way, [but] rest on capacity, lean on kindliness [of others], and seek distraction in the arts." In serious speech, the Sage does not "embody" negativity, as Wang Bi had claimed in his discussion with Pei Xiu, but he certainly tries to emulate and imitate its features. He "sets his mind on the Dao." This puts him in the same category as Heaven and Earth but also lands on him the painful burden to translate the absolute negations of negativity into the relative mess of human affairs.

Laozi 32.1 will serve as a starting point:

The Eternal of the Way is namelessness. Even though the Un-adorned 樸 may be small, no one in All Under Heaven is able to put [it] to service. If only the dukes and kings were able to keep to it [the Unadorned], the ten thousand kinds of entities would submit [to them] of their own accord as guests.

Wang Bi comments:

The Way is without shape and attachment. [Its] Eternal cannot be named; [thus] namelessness is taken for [its] Eternal. That is why [the Laozi] says: "The Eternal of the Way is name-lessness." The Unadorned as such has negativity as its heart. [It], too, is nameless. That is why if one [i.e., a ruler] intends to achieve the Way, there is nothing better than to keep to the Un-adorned. It is a fact that the intelligent can be put to service for [his] ability; the brave can be employed for [his] warlike qual-ities; the dexterous can be put to use for [his ability to] handle affairs; the strong can be given assignments for [his capacity to handle] heavy loads. The Unadorned as such [, however,] is diffuse and not one-sided [and thus] close to not having [any specific feature at all]. That is why [the Laozi] says: "No one is able to put [it] to service [for a particular quality]!" If [only the dukes and kings] would [as the Laozi says in 19.1] "embrace the Unadorned," be without interference, and would not let their true [nature] become fettered by [particular] entities nor let their spirit be hurt by [their] desires, the other "entities" would [as the text says] "submit [to them] of their own accord as guests," and the Way would automatically be achieved.

The argumentative link here between the first phrase of the Laozi about the namelessness of the Eternal of the Way and the second about the smallness of the Unadorned is not evident. Wang Bi provides it by arguing that the Unadorned has the smallest of all, "negativity," "as its heart," *yi wu wei xin* 以無爲心, which means the Dao, and that it "too is nameless." As the Unadorned, *pu* 樸, is characterized by being the negative opposite of all specific ornamentation, it also cannot be well defined beyond this negative description and thus reproduces the core feature of the Dao—namelessness. All those listed have their particular strengths, which make them useful for a particular purpose; they can "be put to service." The person embracing the Unadorned is "not one-sided and is close to not having" 不偏近於無有 any specific features at all. Embracing the Unadorned is a political posture that can be assumed by a ruler who closely mimics the undefinability ("namelessness") of the Dao. It cannot fully match negativity, however, and it is only "close to" being altogether unspecific. That this refers to a political posture or even strategy is evident from the last phrase. If the dukes and kings were to hold onto the Unadorned and not let their desires and ambitions run wild by building big palaces and having scores of concubines, the people even from faraway regions would of their own accord submit. With this reading the dukes and kings are not told to become better men; they are not given moral advice; they are advised to imitate the negative features of the Dao in their own public behavior.

Wang Bi's commentary construes the text as a philosophically based statement on political strategy. His comment inserts this text into the context of *Laozi* 25 which, in general terms, states the imitation principle for the Great Ones. With the sigh of "if only" the dukes and kings would embrace the Unadorned, it marks the difference between Dao, Heaven, and Earth, on the one hand, and the dukes and kings, on the other hand, by making it clear that while the latter could and properly should follow this imitation principle, they usually do not.

This imitation and translation of absolute negativity into the specific circumstances of the human world shall now be studied in more detail. We first analyze some of the ways in which Wang Bi himself develops his arguments out of *Laozi* passages; we then see, in a second step, how he himself summarizes the core features in the *LZWZLL*; and eventually we try to define these in the framework of our rethinking and "translating" his philosophy.

Laozi 23.3 runs:

> That is why, if [a Sage] manages [all] affairs in accordance with the Way, he will make those who [practice] the Way, identical with the Way. 故從事於道者 道者同於道.

Wang Bi comments:

"Manages affairs" means that in [his] comings and goings [he] "manages [all] affairs in accordance with the Way." The Way completes and regulates the ten thousand kinds of entities by means of its being shapeless and without interference. That is why [the Sage] "who manages [all] affairs in [accordance with] the Way" is, by way of making [as *Laozi* 2.2 and 2.3 write about the Sage] "non-interference" his "residence" and the "unspoken" his "teaching," [like the "root of Heaven and Earth" in *Laozi* 6.1] "intangible but still existent" so that the other entities [all] attain their true [nature]. If they practice the Way, [the Sage's rule] will make them of the same substance as the Way.
從事 謂舉動從事於道者也道以無形無爲成濟萬物故從事於道者以無爲爲居不言爲教綿綿若存而物得其眞行道則與道同體.

That Wang Bi read the Sage as the implied subject here is evident from his quoting statements from *Laozi* 2.2 and 2.3, where the Sage is the subject. According to Wang Bi, the Sage's "managing [all] affairs in [accordance] with the Way" means a specific way of translating the features of the Way into human action. The Way is described here with two features: shapelessness and non-interference. By these it manages to "complete and regulate" the entities.[26] The Sage imitates the Dao's effect by managing that the other entities, that is, the people, "attain their true [nature]." The consequence of this handling things in accordance with the Way is that the other beings "[all] attain their true [nature]." In the context of this chapter, this means that those who practice the Way become identical with the Way; those who practice attaining it will be identical with this attaining; and those who practice losing it will be of the same substance as losing. All this happens in a self-regulatory manner as a consequence of the Sage's handling all things in accordance with the Dao.

The decisive dividing line between bringing about order in All Under Heaven and acting nefariously is the cognition of the Eternal. To recall: According to *Laozi* 16.3, the Sage's cognition of the Eternal is the conse-quence of a "perception," *guan* 觀, of the "emptiness" and "stillness" to which the entities "return" or relate back.[27] We have come to the turning point of this chapter. As we shall see, from this step of the cognition of the Eternal, everything else follows.

The Eternal is no mystical concept but another name for negativity. On *Laozi* 16.6 Wang Bi says it is "as such neither [inwardly] partial nor manifest [in its preferences]; it has an appearance without either brightness or darkness and features without either warming or cooling."[28] In short, it is hard to discern. That is why the person still managing to discern it by mentally following the entities back into their "empty" and "still" That-by-which is "bright" or "enlightened," *ming* 明."

The understanding of this eternal That-by-which of the entities means that the core and negative opposite of all entities have been grasped. It was Heaven's capacity to "cover" and Earth's to "support" all entities, and it is the Sage Ruler's capacity to "have knowledge of the Eternal" of all of the entities and thus to "embrace and penetrate them all." This capacity to "encompass," *rong* 容, qualifies him as being on a par with the other Great Ones of *Laozi* 25. His focusing on the common negative opposite of the ten thousand kinds of entities, and thus encompassing them all, renders their particular positive features without interest for him. Like Negativity or the Eternal itself, he is therefore "impartial," *gong* 公, as opposed to someone with "personal interest," *si* 私. This impartiality qualifies him for the position of the social One, "the king." As the king's domain impartially encompasses All Under Heaven, he is a match for Heaven, and as Heaven models itself after the Dao, he "embodies the great persuasiveness of the Dao," which in its turn is based on its negativity. As the Dao, due to its negativity, is eternal, he is secure in being "long lasting," *jiu* 久, in that "for all his life there will be no danger" because, as Wang Bi explains in a fine metaphoric passage at the end of his comment on *Laozi* 16, which shows the translation of the abstract concept of the eternity of negativity into the specifics of human life:

Negativity as such cannot be hurt by water or fire, and cannot be shattered by metal or stone. If use of it [negativity] is made in one's heart, "tigers" and "rhinoceroses" "will not find a place [on him] to thrust" "their claws" and "horns," "soldiers," and lances "will not find a place [on him] to insert their "point and blade" [as *Laozi* 50.2 says of those who are good at maintaining their lives]. What danger could there possibly be [for such a person]?

The meaning of this colorful illustration is of course that, owing to his philosophically guided impartiality, he will have no enemies. This ending marks the high point of the Sage Ruler's achievement, namely, the safety of his position and body. It involves a promise to the addressee as the passage from Wang Bi on *Laozi* 49, quoted in the previous section of this chapter, stressed the danger awaiting the ruler if he in the words of *Laozi* 16.6, "has no knowledge of the Eternal" and as a consequence "would recklessly bring about a nefarious [outcome]."

In terms of interpreting the features of the That-by-which into human dimensions, the two *zhang* studied hitherto, 23.3 and 16, yield the following results:

NEGATIVITY	SAGE
non-interference 無爲	"makes non-interference his residence," "practices teaching without words"
shapeless 無形	"intangible, but still existent"
not one-sided 不偏	"impartial" 公平
eternal 常	"long-lasting" 久
nameless 無名	"unadorned" 樸
taking negativity as core 以無爲心	taking emptiness as guiding principle 以虛爲主
Heaven excels by not living for its own interests 天長...以其不自生	keeps his own person in the background and his own person is in the fore 後其身而身先
Earth persists by not living for its own interests 地久...以其不自生	disregards his own person and his person lasts 外其身而身存
Heaven and Earth can only excel and persist because they are not living for their own interests 以其不自生	can only be in the fore and last because of absence of private interests 以其無私
rivers and seas are good at being low, therefore all rivulets (*Laozi* 66) flow into them	must put himself below people to be above them
Way of Heaven reduces excess, supplements deficiency, and thus covers everyone 天之道損有餘而補不足, 能包 [萬物] (*Laozi* 77)	Sage as opposed to other people 無身無私, 不欲見賢, does not wish to show off his capability
the Way of Heaven beneficial and not harmful 天之道利而不害 (*Laozi* 81.8)	way of the Sage to act but not to struggle 爲而不爭

The Policy of the Negative Opposite

Is there a time frame, a set of conditions, when the action of the Sage is needed and when a political science based on philosophic insight is needed? Various statements within the *Laozi* seem to imply some primordial time "before" when order prevailed; *Laozi* 1.2 speaks of a time "when there are not now names," which also is the time "while they [the entities] are [still] constantly without desire." However, a closer look at these passages shows that their context is that of the cognition of the That-by-which, not of cosmogony or sociogony.

Zhang 28 of Wang Bi's *Laozi* does not purport to describe a specific historical situation, but the structural relationship between the Sage and All Under Heaven. The multitude of entities are structurally and permanently in need of being "again returned to being babies" (28.1), of being made to "return to the unlimited," and of being made to "return again to the Unadorned." They are at any given time neither babies ignorant of the corruption of knowledge nor resting in the "unlimited" which is the Dao; nor are they unspecific, like the "Unadorned." As particular historic entities they are at any moment specified. In an extremely pointed commentary, Wang Bi explains the *Laozi* 28.6 statement (which very much looks like a historical narrative): "樸散則爲器 Once the Unadorned has dispersed, they [the entities] become instruments" in the following manner:

> The Unadorned is the "True" [nature of entities]. Once the True has dispersed, the hundred styles of action emerge and the different categories are born. These are like "[specialized] instruments." 樸眞也眞散則百行出殊類生若器也.

No date is given for this event. It does not appear as a historic disaster for which a particular ruler might be responsible. The existence of the "hundred occupations" and the "different categories" is the existence of a world consisting of specific entities, and there is no world that does not consist of specific entities. The notion that in some ontological or ontogenetic "prior" there was an "Unadorned" and a "True" that had not "dispersed" is a logical construct, not a historic reality. The "dispersion" marks the beginning of time, not an event in it.

Still, within the *Laozi* itself, Wang Bi finds the model for these two moments of "the True" and "the dispersal of the True" in *zhang* 1. The *Laozi* (1.2) there separates two moments of time, saying, "when there are not [now] names, it is the beginning of the ten thousand kinds of entities," and "when there [already] are names, it is the mother of the ten thousand kinds of entities." Within the *Laozi* it is not clear what "it" refers to, because *Laozi* 1.1 deals with both "Dao" and "Name"; it is not made clear which of the two, if either, is meant as the subject for the subsequent phrase. Wang Bi's commentary starts: "Generally speaking, entities all begin in negativity." He thus identifies "negativity," elsewhere identified with the Dao, as the hidden object of the first phrase ("A way that can be spoken of is not the eternal Way; a name that can be named is not the eternal name") and as the subject of the second one under consideration here. For both moments, that of "beginning" and that of the nourishing "mother," negativity is the core. Wang Bi formalizes the two moments with the terms *shi* 始 or *sheng* 生, and *cheng* 成. His commentary to *Laozi* 1.2 continues:

<blockquote>
That is why it [negativity] will be
</blockquote>

at a time when there are neither shapes nor names the beginning of the ten thousand kinds of entities,	when it comes to a time when there are shapes and names that "which [as the *Laozi* writes in 51.3] lets them [the ten thousand kinds of entities] grow and nurtures them, specifies them, and completes them"; [in other words,] it will be their mother.

The focus of the entire argument is on cognition of the Dao, not on delineating two moments in the relationship between the Dao and the ten thousand kinds of entities. The existence of these two moments seems rather a knowledge commonly shared, which needs no further proof.

Laozi 1.3 and 1.4 continue the argument with its focus on discerning negativity.

<blockquote>
Therefore
</blockquote>

while they [the ten thousand kinds of entities] are [still] constantly without desire, one has something by means of which to perceive its [the ultimate principle's] subtlety 妙.	while they [the ten thousand kinds of entities] are constantly with desires, one has something by means of which to perceive its [the ultimate principle's] limiting 徼.

The access to the cognition of negativity remains open in either state. In Wang Bi's *Laozi* reading, the two moments are not consecutive in a linear time frame; rather, they are two different avenues for "perceiving" the That-by-which. His commentary fixes the meaning of *jiao* 徼 on the opposite end of *miao* 妙. *Miao* is the subtlety in which entities take their beginning, and it is perceivable in the unspecified simplicity of the entities. "*Jiao* is the final point of return" 徼歸終也, the point to which entities will go back from the state of having desires that would make them depart from their allotted places. We have thus a circular or pendular process between the simplicity of desirelessness, and the simplicity to which entities will be made to return from the state of having desires. Negativity is thus the "ultimate of minuteness" 微之極, and "the ten thousand kinds of entities begin in the minute and then only become complete; they begin in negativity and then only come to life" (Wang Bi on *Laozi* 1.3), and negativity is at the same time "the final point to which they return/relate back" (Wang Bi on *Laozi* 1.4). In this construction, time is not measured on a linear axis but in terms of distance from that by which the ten thousand entities are.

But we are still dealing with a historical narrative of the relationship between the That-by-which and the ten thousand entities. In order to ensure that this is understood as just an awkward way of speaking, while what is actually being conceptualized is a structural and dynamic relationship, Wang Bi uses in his commentary on *jiao* 徼 in *Laozi* 1.4 a curious device. After having defined *jiao* 徼 as *gui zhong* 歸終, "final point of return," he proceeds:

> Generally speaking, for entities to be beneficial, they have to get their usefulness from negativity; that on which desires are based will be satisfied only as a consequence of adapting to the Way. 凡有之爲利必以無爲用欲之所本適道而後濟.

With the "generally speaking," *fan* 凡, he announces a statement of principle beyond the particular context. The reference in this statement is to the last phrase of *zhang* 11, which Wang Bi reads: "That [they are specific] entities makes for [their] being beneficial, while negativity makes for [their] usability." The relationship between a pot and the hollowness ("negativity") inside, which in *Laozi* 11 serves to illustrate the principle, is not a historic but a structural one. Wang Bi thus reads the awkward historical narrative of "beginning in" and "ending in" negativity as an attempt to catch the dynamics and dialectics of an essentially structural, that is, ontological, relationship between negativity and the ten thousand kinds of entities.

This detour was prompted by the inquiry about the character of Wang Bi's political theory. Was he dealing with issues of his own time and developing a political theory to provide guidance for the solution of these issues, or was he analyzing the philosophical problem of the origin and character of order that then would find its particular manifestation in a given historic setting? From the argument developed out of Wang Bi's reading of *Laozi* 1, it is probable and plausible that Wang Bi is following the second road and analyzing the structural relationship between the ruler and society that finds a specific manifestation at any given historic time; this does not exclude, but also is not reduced to, a focus on its applicability to his own time.

The One/negativity/the Dao in the realm of ontology finds its counterpart in the One/the Sage/the Ruler in the realm of "politology," if I may use this term here. The two realms differ in that the Dao *is* as the common condition of their possibility the negative opposite of all possible entities, while the ruler will fulfill his analogous role in society only if and insofar as he is a Sage "setting his will on the Way." The deleterious effects of the absence of this enlightenment have been described.

We return to *Laozi* 28.6. After "Once the Unadorned [nature of entities] has dispersed, they [the entities] become instruments," the *Laozi* continues: "Making use of them, the Sage makes officials and elders for [them]." Wang Bi comments on this phrase:

> Responsive to [the fact] that their [the people in All Under Heaven's] allotments have dispersed, the Sage [does not cut and trim them but] purposely sets up officials and elders for them. "Making the good ones into teachers . . ." and "the not good ones into [their] material . . . ," [as *Laozi* 27.6 and 27.7 says] changing [in this manner] the[ir] habits and altering the[ir] customs is [his way] of "returning [them] again to the" One [as the *Laozi* said in 28.5]. 聖人因其分散故爲之立官長以善爲師 不善爲資移風易俗復歸於一也.

This statement takes for granted a rather surprising element in the understanding of the *wuwei* doctrine, namely, that the Sage takes on the management of the state by setting up officials and elders. Its focus is on the fact that he will not impose harsh disciplinary measures to make people "return to the One" but will "be responsive to [the fact] that their allotments have dispersed." This reading of Wang Bi's finds support in the last phrase of this *zhang*, "the Great Regulator [i.e., the Sage, regulates] without [any] cutting off."

In the *LZWZLL* 6.29 the "dispersal of the Unadorned" and the "becoming separated from the True" mark the end of the nefarious process in which the activist interference of the ruler destroys the prestabilized order of his subjects.[29] In this order, there still are the "intelligent and the stupid," and there are the "six kinds of relations," who are supposed to have a trusting relationship with each other. The latter must be reckoned as the natural lot, *fen* 分, in which entities find themselves, like the grass and the dogs in Wang Bi's *Laozi* 5. This action of the ruler is not depicted as momentary or even exceptional but as the result of the normal course of an enlightened mind. The Sage does not preside over the original paradise, but he enters a polity where at any given moment the "allotments have dispersed," so that the "people are concerned with struggle and competition," as Wang Bi writes on *Laozi* 58.2, where there "is debauchery in all affairs." As in *Laozi* 1, for the relationship between negativity and entities, we have thus a historical narrative of the polity written into a philosophical framework. Within the basic framework of the relationship between ruler and people, as that between the One and the Many, we have inscribed historic moments determined by the level of philosophical understanding on the side of the ruler of the dialectics of this relationship, and the ensuing beneficial or nefarious effects.

The general purpose of the Sage's action in society is thus the "restoration" of the link between the entities and their "root," "mother," "beginning," their That-by-which. The terminology is that of "return," *fu* 復, *fan* 反, and *gui* 歸, as well as combinations of these terms.[30] What is the "natural" and logical relationship of the ten thousand entities to negativity becomes a conscious construct in society. Evidence for this is the reading of "return" as "make return," seen above; the people will not simply "return" to the One, but the Sage "will make them return."

While the efforts to make the people relate back have mostly to do with the enlightened ruler himself, they do, as we have seen, include the setting up of an administration. Wang Bi's *Laozi* 32.3 reads:

With the beginning of [my social] regulation [I, the Sage will] have names. Once the names are there, [I, the Sage] set out to have an understanding about [how to] put a stop [to the ensuing developments]. [Only] having an understanding about [how to] put a stop [to them] is what gets [me] out of danger.

Wang Bi comments:

"The beginning of [the Sage's social] regulation" is the time [referred to in *Laozi* 28.6] when "the Unadorned has dispersed" and [the Sage as the Great Regulator of *Laozi* 28.7] begins "to make officials and elders." With the beginning of [his social] regulation with officials and elders it is impossible [for Him] to do without setting up names and classifications by way of determining the honored and the lowly. That is why [the text says]: "With the beginning of [my social] regulation I [the Sage] will have names." Going beyond this would [mean the emergence of] [what the *Zuo zhuan* refers to as] "struggle [even] for [trifles as minute as] the point of an awl or a knife."

That is why [the text] says: "Once the names are there [I, the Sage] will set out to have an understanding about [how to] put a stop [to the ensuing developments]." The subsequent use of names to mark entities [would] engender a loss of the mother of [social] order. That is why [the text says]: "[Only] having an understanding about [how to] put a stop to [these developments] is what gets [me] out of danger [from the resulting social conflicts]!"

The business of the Sage being one of restoration, he first establishes officials including the establishment of "names" to define the social hierarchies. With this he "is responsive," *yin* 因, to the dissolution of the allotments of the different kinds of entities and the appearance of different levels of morality. Going beyond this initial stage of recognizing the facts and developing these "names" beyond what was necessary at this stage would mean an extreme exacerbation of social conflict exactly in the manner as is brought about if the regulator is not a Sage. Thus he attempts to "stop" such development, and proceeds in his business of having the entities "relate back" to the One.

The establishment of officials and elders over the people has the purpose of "changing the[ir] habits and altering the[ir] customs" and is his way of "returning [them] again to the One." It is carefully set off against any preferential treatment for the capable and knowledgeable. Commenting on *Laozi* 3.1, "Not to shower worthies with honors induces the people not to struggle," Wang Bi writes:

What is the purpose of showering [someone] with honors who is only capable of handling only this [particular] assignment [and no others]? . . . If in granting honors to the worthies and glorifying the famous, the emulation exceeds their assignment, those below will rush forward to compete, compare their [own] capabilities [to those of those honored], and outdo each other.

If those qualified are used for their qualification in the overall design of return, the "Hundred Families all make the best of their ears and eyes," or, in Wang's comment, all "make use of their intelligence" (*Laozi* 49.4). Then those whose "capabilities are great" "will be great," and those whose "qualifications are eminent" "will be eminent" (Wang Bi on *Laozi* 49.5), but they will not be particularly honored and promoted, but all be made into "infants" without "desires" to go beyond their allotted station (ibid.). At this stage of things, the Sage will make "the good ones into the teachers of the not good ones, and the not good ones into the material of the good ones" but "neither honor" the teachers "nor love" the material (*Laozi* 27.6, 27.7).

The starting point of the Sage and the unenlightened ruler is the same. Both are confronted with a social situation where, at any given historic moment, the entities have already dispersed from their allotted place. Both share the same intention—to have their subjects return to their lots. Both operate within the same structural dialectics, the One and the Many. Both are therefore the structural kingpins on which order or disorder depends and are granted the subjective wish and motivation to establish social order. The villains on the throne are—philosophically—freaks and much less interesting than the ruler who wreaks havoc with the best of intentions by applying what common sense would advise—namely, rewards for the good and punishments for the bad—and by instituting a surveillance apparatus for his own security.

The Sage Ruler operates with the pointed non-use of those very instruments he is authorized, and expected, to use. The results of this pointed and highly specific inaction are described in the end of Wang Bi on *Laozi* 49.5:

As there definitely is nothing that [I] spy out [with my insight], what should the Hundred Families evade?	As there definitely is nothing [I] go after [with distrust], against what should the Hundred Families reciprocate?

As [the Hundred Families]

neither evade [me by using their own insight]	nor reciprocate [against me by their own distrust]

there will be none among them
who does not make use of his [natural]
feelings. Not one will discard what he
is capable of and do what he is not
capable of, discard what he excels
in and do what he cannot handle.

無所察焉百姓何避無避	無所求焉百姓何應無應

則莫不用其情矣人無爲舍其所能而
爲其所不能舍其所長而爲其所短.

Wang Bi is conventional in his assumptions about where the classes of people get their particular stations and capabilities. He quotes in the beginning of his commentary on *Laozi* 49.5 the authority of the *Xici*, according to which, "Heaven and Earth establish the positions [of entities] and the Sage [in accordance with these] completes the[ir] capabilities. Other people he consults, the spirits he consults, and to the Hundred Families he gives [their] capabilities" 天地設位聖人成能人謀鬼謀百姓與能. The particular endowments for the kinds of entities are givens, determined in some unclear way by Heaven and Earth. It is decisive, however, that the different kinds of human beings find their proper stations in society so that they may be content in its order.

Obviously, within this system, different kinds of capabilities continue to exist as part of different lots in life, *fen*. They are not seen as being in conflict with the intended "relating back to the One," but as being part of the "natural feelings," *qing* 情. With this differentiated non-act usage of the different types of people, the Sage manages to take care of all, without exception. Wang Bi has good authority from the *Laozi* for this argument. His *Laozi* 27.5 states that, "the Sage is constantly good at saving other people, and for this reason there is no rejecting other people [by him]" 聖人常善救人而無棄人, and Wang Bi's commentary to this passage links it directly to the general formula of *Laozi* 64.9, where the Sage "boosts the ten thousand kinds of entities' That-which-is-of-itself-what-it-is but does not dare to interfere [with them]." 輔萬物之自然而不敢爲也. This capacity of the Sage to accommodate *all* members of society, and in some formulations even all of the entities into his scheme of self-regulating order, that is, of actually being the One of the Many, puts him into the same category with Heaven, Earth, and the Dao. As the person who is "enlightened," *ming* 明, through his "knowledge of the Eternal," *zhi chang* 知常 (*Laozi* 16.6), he alone is, as Wang Bi comments, "able indeed to embrace and penetrate the ten thousand kinds of entities without there being anything that is not encompassed" 乃能包通萬物無所不容.

Wang Bi extracts from the *Laozi* those elements that make it operative as a philosophically based theory for running a state's machinery with "officials and elders" performing their particular duties and a society of people with different skills and qualifications, all to be brought to fruition. This differentiation is not the forceful establishment of social order but rather corresponds to the structures of nature described in Wang Bi's *Laozi* 5.1, which he reads as implying that the "ten thousand kinds of entities each fit into their use [i.e., with their particular features], so that there is none not provided for." Still, while accepting the actual state of society and state as a starting point for the Sage's endeavor, the fact remains that the groups and classes of this human world are at any given moment in the process or danger of "discarding the root" and forgetting their That-by-which, thus "losing their true [nature]," leaving their place in the prestabilized order, and engaging in a battle for status and wealth. The symptom of this loss, and ensuing focus on the surface conflict is the overstepping of the lot, referred to with expressions such as *guo* 過, "to exceed/transgress" (*Laozi*

64.8), *shen* 甚, "excess," *she* 奢, "exaggeration," and *tai* 泰, "extremes" (*Laozi* 29.4), in Wang Bi's *Laozi*. Wang Bi links these oversteppings of the human lot to the *Laozi* notion of people's delusion. In a very radical statement, the *Laozi* 58.6 claims—and again, the language of historical narrative stands in for that of structural principle—"as to the delusion of the people, it has definitely already been around for a long time" 民之迷 也其日固已久矣. Wang Bi thus comments on the Sage's "doing away with excess, doing away with exaggeration, and doing away with extremes" (*Laozi* 29.4):

> He [only] wipes out what might cause them to be deluded, and does away with what might make them beguiled. Consequently, [under his guidance] their "hearts do not become prone to chaos" [as the *Laozi* 3.1 says of "the people" under the guidance of a Sage Ruler], and the nature of the entities is automatically fulfilled. 除其所以迷去其所以惑故心不亂而物性自得 之也

The two core notions here of what *Laozi* 3.1 calls the "people's hearts" "becoming prone to chaos," *luan* 亂, namely, *huo* 惑, "beguilement," and *mi* 迷, "delusion," have defined objects in Wang Bi on *Laozi* 20.3, the first referring to "glory and profits," *rong li* 榮利, the second to "beauty and promotion," *mei jin* 美進. They are not just occasional afflictions.

The primary activity within the Sage's ontological project is therefore to "reduce," *gua* 寡 (*Laozi* 19.1, *LZWZLL* 6.22) and "eliminate," *qu* 去 (*LZWZLL* 6.8) these desires in himself so as to "calm down," *jing* 靜, the people's desires (*LZWZLL* 6.15) and to "permanently prompt the people to be without knowledge and desires" 常使民無知無欲 (*Laozi* 3.4).

With the Sage Ruler engaging in the specific non-acts of his government, society takes care of the differences in quality among, and the moral fickleness of, its members in a self-regulatory process set in motion by this very form of government. Wang Bi describes this process in his comments on *Laozi* 36, and in a surviving comment on *Lunyu* 8.19. Wang Bi's *Laozi* 36.1 runs:

> Having the intention to make them contract, to definitely expand them; having the intention to weaken them, to definitely strengthen them; having the intention to do away with them, to definitely bring them to flourish; having the intention to take away from them, to definitely add to them: This I call "insight into the minute."

The governmental non-acts are here developed into governmental reverse acts, which do the opposite of what is expected and thus help society, as Wang Bi reads it, to more clearly perceive its own problems and to proceed to solve them. Wang Bi comments:

If [a ruler] intends to wipe out the "violent and brutal" [who, according to *Laozi* 42.3, "will not meet their (natural) death"] and do away with upheavals and riots, he has to proceed according to these four [precepts] and adapt to the nature of entities to have them self-destruct instead of relying on the magnitude of the physical punishment to eliminate violent entities. This is why [the text] calls this "insight into the minute [i.e., the nature of entities]!"

If, the expansion [of the violent] being sufficient, [the ruler with the insight into the minute] prods them to crave for further expansion beyond this sufficient [level], they will be made to contract by the multitude [of those envious of their powers who will cooperate to attack them]. If, [on the other hand, a ruler] contracts what is [already] deficient in their expansion and attacks their craving for expansion [by means of punishments], he will, the more he does this, in turn put himself into danger [because of the growing hostility of the violent].

In this manner, the Sage props up the self-regulatory mechanism of society and avoids being drawn into the situation of being One among the Many. The next section elaborates again on the negative effects of the inverse procedure. *Laozi* 36.2 runs:

[This is] the soft's overcoming the hard, and the weak's overcoming the strong. A fish cannot be taken out of the deep water. [In the same manner] the state's useful instrument cannot prevail by showing it to people.

Wang Bi comments:

"Useful instrument" is an instrument useful to the state. If [the ruler] only adapts to the nature of entities and does not rely on physical punishments to regulate the other entities so that the instruments [of government] cannot be perceived, but the entities still each attain their place, then [government truly is] "the state's useful instrument." "To show it to people" means applying physical punishment. If physical punishments [are applied] to be useful to the state, it will be a failure. If a fish is taken out of the deep water, it will necessarily be lost. If, [as] an instrument useful to the state, [the ruler] sets up physical punishments to show it to people, this inevitably will also be a failure.

In his comments to Confucius' praise for Yao's rulership in *Lunyu* 8.19, the process of constant social self-regulation under a Sage Ruler is spelled out more explicitly. On Confucius' statement, "Great indeed is Yao as a ruler! Immense he is! Only Heaven is Great, and only Yao lives up to this model. Vast he is to such a degree that none among the people is able to make up a name [for him]," Wang Bi writes:

As [Yao] has total love [for all entities] without any personal [preferences for any one of them], where should [particular] favors have a place? As he is supreme beauty without any one-sidedness, from where should a [particular] name [for him] arise? That is why, in his living up to the model of Heaven and completing the transformation [of the Hundred Families], [his] Way accords with [the entities'] That-which-is-of-itself-what-it-is; he does not give preferential treatment to his [own] sons but made his minister [Shun] into the ruler [succeeding him]. [As a consequence of his Way] the wicked drew punishment upon themselves, and the good acquired merit automatically; [but], while the merits [of the latter] formed, it was not he [Yao] who established their renown; and while the punishment [to the former] was applied, it was not he [Yao] who had their sentences executed. [In this manner, as the *Xici* 上4 says of the Way, while] "the Hundred Families make daily use [of him], they do not know" that by which this [self-regulatory order] comes about. What [specific element] then would there be that could be named [in Yao]?[31] 若夫大愛無私惠將安在至美無偏名將何生故則天成化道同自然不私其子而君其臣凶者自罰善者自功功成而不立其譽罰加而不任其刑百姓日用而不知其所以然夫又何可名也.

The non-acts of the Sage Ruler in fact set in motion the self-regulatory process among the entities, in which the wicked are duly punished, and the good get their merit. The social dynamics implied in the first quotation suggest that the wicked would evoke enough irritation and the good enough admiration among their fellow men that these would apply the proper treatment, guided by those whose "nature" qualifies them as teachers and local leaders, without the direct and particular involvement of the ruler. This would work in the same manner in which the absence of kindliness in Heaven and Earth in *Laozi* 5 secures the self-regulatory order with the cattle eating the grass and men the dogs.

The *ziran*-based specificity of entities in the human realm differs from that in the realm of nature by being largely of a moral character. In the above case, this is expressed in the terms "wicked" and "good," but Wang Bi reconstitutes on the basis of *ziran* 自然 the entire set of traditional forms of positive behavior, such as "filial piety," *xiao* 孝, "humanness, *ren* 仁, "loyalty," *zhong* 忠, and "consideration," *shu* 恕, which for the Han dynasty Ru had to do with blood bonds, human nature, or the Heavenly mandate.[32] As opposed to the Ru ("Confucian") attitude, which was to use the social position as encoded in the "name," *ming* 名, as an instrument to enforce behavioral standards on people, the *ming* in Wang Bi's thinking is a dependent derivative, and these forms of behavior flow directly out of a *ziran* brought to fruition through the Sage Ruler. As we have seen in the analysis of *Laozi* 38, even the much-maligned notion of "ritual," *li* 禮, as the proper mode of intercourse between persons of different levels is kept as the lowest form of "interfering," *you wei* 有爲, government. Wang Bi inserts it into his "sequence of interfering government," *you wei zheng zhi ci xu* 有爲政之次序 in his commentary on *Lunyu* 8.8.[33] The result of the Sage Ruler's rule is thus not the abolishment of these "Confucian" forms of behavior but their effortless prevalence, unenforced by any positive act of the ruler.

As Liu Zehua has pointed out in his fine paper on Wang Bi's political philosophy, Wang Bi does not accept the rigid separation, present for example in the *Zhuangzi* as well as in many texts associated with the Ru and "Legalists," between the innate nature of entities and external social regulations and controls. Quite the contrary, he deduces the mechanism of social regulation normally associated with the Han dynasty Mingjiao 名教 school directly from the notion of *ziran*, from the notion of the entities' That-which-is-of-itself-what-it-is.[34] The seemingly unavoidable bifurcation between the two realms of "root," *ben* 本, and "outgrowth," *mo* 末, with the ensuing bifurcation between the Daojia 道家, which is focusing on the "root," and the Mingjiao 名教, which is focusing on the "outgrowth," is thus overcome in favor of a system of philosophy that establishes ontology and politology on the very same fundaments.

The Sage's performance of specific non-acts in lieu of the expected acts of rewarding, punishing, and supervising is a condition for the success of the project, but it is not sufficient in itself. This is so because any given historic situation is already characterized by the people's delusion and the exacerbating efforts of the rulers to curb their ensuing unruliness. The Sage, therefore, is not called upon to maintain a status quo but to make the people "return" to the One. Something has to be done by the Sage, which might seem to be in conflict with the often-repeated statement that he engages in "non-interference," *wuwei* 無爲.

SAGELY POLITICS AS PUBLIC PERFORMANCE

Wang Bi again deduces the Sage's strategies in establishing social order from the general law of the negative opposite pertaining between the One and the Many outlined in the previous chapter. This general law starts in the *LZWZLL* 4.1ff.: "Generally speaking, that by which entities persist is the negative opposite indeed to their form; that by which achievements are performed is the negative opposite indeed to their name." Wang Bi extracted this general law philologically from statements in the *Laozi* dealing with the relationship of the One and the Many in its multiple variations; in this sense, the law claims the authority of only restating in more abstract form the insight encoded in the *Laozi*. Wang Bi, however, like his *Laozi* itself, is primarily interested in the possible applications in human society flowing from this law. This becomes visible in the neat juxtaposition of two parallel chains of arguments pertaining to Heaven and Earth, on the one hand, and the dukes and kings, on the other hand. These chains immediately follow the general law quoted above.

It is a fact that

he who persists does not take persistence for [the cause] of his persisting, but [his persisting is due] to his not forgetting about [the danger of] perishing.	he who is secure does not take security for [the cause] of his being secure but [his security is due] to his not forgetting about perils.

That is why [,to paraphrase Confucius in *Xici* 下.4,]

"he who guards his persistence" "perishes," while he who [like the Gentleman] "does not forget about [the danger of] perishing" "persists."	"he who secures his position" "is in peril," while he who [like the Gentleman] "does not forget about peril" "is secure."

That

he who is [truly] good at strength [restricts himself to] lifting an autumn down,	he who is [truly] good at hearing [restricts himself to] noticing the thunderclap;

this is the negative opposition
between Dao and form.

夫存者不以存爲存, 以其不忘亡也; 安者不以安爲安, 以其不忘危也.
故保其存者亡, 不忘亡者存; 安其位者危, 不忘危者安. 善力舉秋毫, 善
聽聞雷霆, 此道之與形反也.

That by which the entities persist in their entirety is by necessity devoid of all of their particular features and is their negative opposite. As a
consequence, the language dealing with the Dao states only the absence
of specific features and actions. The same is true for the *gong* 功, the
"achievements." In the following statements, Wang Bi finds little explicit
language in the *Laozi* on which to base himself, and thus he relies on the
Sage's statements in the *Xici*. They make an important turn by moving from
an analytic to a prescriptive mode. From the phrase "he who guards his
persistence" "perishes," while "he who does not forget about [the danger
of] perishing" "persists," and "he who secures his position" "is in peril,"
while "he who does not forget about peril" "is secure," it follows that the
ruler who wants to guard his persistence and secure his position has to do
so not by settling into the comfort of a reinforced surveillance machine
and security apparatus but by not being forgetful of the "dangers" to his
life and position. In terms of the law of the opposite, his life and position
are secured by rejecting and abandoning the very means that common
sense would dictate as appropriate for this purpose. Wang Bi again has
the *Laozi* as a witness:

He who is secure is secure
indeed but [the *Laozi*] says he is
secure through his refusal to
[treat] security [as a given].

He who persists persists indeed but
[the *Laozi*] says he persists through
his refusal to [treat] persistence [as a
given].

Dukes and kings are elevated
indeed but [the *Laozi*] says this
[= their status] is brought about
by their] rejecting elevation.

Heaven and Earth are great indeed,
but [it is] said that it [their greatness]
is achieved through [their] rejection
[of acting] great.

The achievements of [a ruler's]
wisdom persist indeed, but [the
Laozi] says they are established
by [his] "discarding wisdom."

The capacity of benevolence is manifest
indeed, but [the *Laozi*] says it persists
through "discarding benevolence."

安者實安, 而曰非安之所安; 存者實存, 而曰非存之所存;
侯王實尊, 而曰非尊之所爲; 天地實大, 而曰非大之所能;
聖功實存, 而曰絕聖之所立; 仁德實著, 而曰棄仁之所存.

The dynamics of the negative opposite have been extracted from a fair number of paradoxical statements by the *Laozi*, none of which has an abstract definition such as the one contained in Wang Bi's general formula in the beginning of the above quotation. The *Laozi* paradoxes are alluded to as proof of the compatibility of Wang Bi's formula with the *Laozi*'s argument. They range from a reference to *Laozi* 39.4, "To be esteemed takes [acting as if] being despised as [its] root, and to be elevated takes [acting as if] being lowly as [its] base," to *Laozi* 42.1, "What other people abhor is indeed to be orphaned, lonely, and needy, but kings and dukes refer to themselves with these [terms,]" to *Laozi* 19.1, "If [the ruler] were to discard wisdom and to reject intelligence, the benefit for the people would be a hundredfold," and "if [the ruler] were to discard benevolence and to reject righteousness, the people would return to filial piety and parental love."

The common and often unmentioned subject of these and similar phrases is the ruler or other great entities such as Heaven, Earth, and the Dao. The phrases only make sense if pertaining to the Great ones, because only their action will have an impact on the many. The *Laozi* phrases unfold their paradoxical and philosophic potential only under these circumstances. On the most general level, the Dao "generates and completes" the ten thousand kinds of entities by "not interfering" with them, and it can do the former only by means of the latter. In human society, the conscious application of the law of the negative opposite requires a conscious and public strategy. In this line of thinking, the Sage does not appear as a cosmic historic event of great rarity but as someone who masters this law and consciously applies it. In this manner he becomes the ideal ruler who can be imitated by imitating the principles upon which he operates. The Wang Bi *Laozi* discusses this ideal ruler through the figure of the Sage, but Wang Bi himself proceeds in the *LZWZLL* to discuss the ideal ruler in terms of philosophic insight and political strategy without explicitly referring to the Sage. He thus dissociates the *Laozi*'s philosophic insights from the born savior of mankind into which the Sage had evolved, and he proffers a philosophically based political theory, whose application will make an actual historic actor match what has been attributed to the Sages of old, namely, bringing order to society and securing his own life and position.

What form could and should the conscious application of the Dao's interaction with the ten thousand kinds of entities take? What does it mean to "reject" and "abandon," to "discard" and "cut off" the very means that common sense would suggest as the instruments of securing the ruler's life and position and social order? Obviously there is as little question of the ruler's stepping down and actually being "lowly," "orphaned," "solitary," and "needy" as there is of the Dao's relinquishing its role as the origin and support of the ten thousand kinds of entities. The solution must lie in the ruler's remaining in his position but consciously projecting himself in a manner that would make him the One over the Many, and not One among the Many. In this exploration, Wang Bi has little to go by in the *Laozi* itself. The development of a political theory out of the *Laozi* that can be applied to and translated into practical policies must be considered one of Wang Bi's main intellectual contributions.

As we have seen, the principal factor in bringing to fruition the "people's" latent tendency to seek satisfaction for their "desires" through the small "byways" is a ruler at the top of the hierarchy who sets a model of conspicuous consumption and the equally conspicuous exercise of his powers. This will set into motion a process of imitation and competition, which destroys the prestabilized order of entities and eventually brings about the downfall of the ruler and the advent of social chaos. The philosophically well-advised application of the law of the negative opposite would therefore suggest "that he who is [truly] good at strength [restricts himself to] lifting a [bare] autumn down, and that he who is [truly] good at hearing [restricts himself to] noticing [huge noises that all can hear, such as] the thunderclap." The proper dialectics of having the ruler's position and of bringing it to full benefit therefore requires the ruler to simultaneously fulfill two conditions: to retain his person and position as the highest and most powerful figure in society, and at the same time to remain defined in terms of complete negativity with regard to the people.

Wang Bi finds the solution to this paradox by separating the ruler's institutional position from his public performance of this role. This separation is prefigured in the *Zhouyi* arrangement where, in Wang Bi's reading, for many hexagrams each line is doubly defined, first as an institutional "position," *wei* 位, in society and second as the individual "line," *yao* 爻, occupying this position. The fifth position from below in many hexagrams is read as being that of the ruler. As such, it is defined in terms of Yin and Yang, and it figures as a Yang position. The line occupying this position, however, might be broken or unbroken, might be "six" or "nine" in the terminology of the *Zhouyi*. The broken lines in turn are defined as Yin and the unbroken lines as Yang. Thus we can have, and often do have, a situation where an unbroken Yang line is sitting in a Yang position, for example, the fifth, or where a broken Yin line is occupying such a position. We may have a "weak" ruler in a "strong" position or a "strong" ruler in a "strong" position. This separation of the character of a position and that of a person is taken up in Wang Bi's analysis of the relationship between the ruler's position, on the one hand, and his attitude and action in this position, on the other hand, and it highlights the difference between a Sage Ruler and a person in the ruler's position ignorant of the laws determining the relationship between the One and the Many.

The negative dynamic through which a ruler's action will lead the people and eventually himself to ruin operates not through the ruler's personal character or feelings but through his acts as a ruler. As these acts pertain to the people, they are essentially public acts. A ruler who, in addition to being in a position of strength, publicly acts as the strongman (*Laozi* 30.1, 42.2, 69)—a ruler who, in addition to having the monopoly on discretionary powers, makes active and particular public use of them, a ruler who, in addition to being the owner of All Under Heaven, goes into lavish spending on his court—in each case, it is the public and specific acting out of the absolute potential vested in his position that reduces him to the specific and prevents his achieving what can only be achieved through the proper handling of his position.

We are thus dealing with government as public performance of the non-use of the government's powers and privileges. The public gestures and acts of the ruler in his position of complete power will determine the reactions of the people. While it is easy to specify the negative dynamics set in motion by a misguided ruler, it is difficult to specify in terms of public acts what it means to "not interfere" and to "teach without words," and thus to "bring back" the entities to the One.

The *Laozi* offers some indications. In the most general formula, the Sage "acts out non-interference" with "the consequence that there is nothing that is not well ordered" 爲無爲則無不治 (*Laozi* 3.6). The same *zhang* mentions two—negative—forms of this "acting out":

[As a ruler]

not to shower worthies with honors induces the people not to compete.	not to overly appreciate goods that are hard to get induces the people not to become robbers.

[In short, as a ruler,] not to display [things] that might be craved for induces the hearts of the people not to become prone to chaos.

Here we have non-acts that become pointed and public non-acts through the pervasive powers of the ruler. The ruler is expected to attract qualified people by "showering them with honors," to display his grandeur with precious goods of great value, in short, to set the standards to which people might aspire. Against these expected public acts, the ruler's actions described by the *Laozi* above become pointed and equally public non-acts. As specific non-performances of expected acts, as "displays" of non-acts, they definitely are public acts, but without the consequence of tying the ruler down to one specific posture and action. This pattern is pervasive for the Wang Bi *Laozi*'s talk about the Sage's government.

Grammatically, the *Laozi* time and again stresses the act-character of these seeming non-acts. The Sage "takes residence" in "management without interference" and "practices," *xing* 行, "teaching without words" (*Laozi* 2.2 ff.). He "puts his own person in the background, *hou qi shen* 後其身, and [manages in this way] that his own person comes to the fore; he disregards his own person, *wai qi shen* 外其身, and [manages in this way] that his own person will last" (*Laozi* 7.2). Already the Wang Bi *Laozi*, however, writes that this agenda of non-acts and counter-acts of "rejecting" and "discarding" is "insufficient," because in this way the people have nothing to "go by" or to "attach themselves to," *shu* 屬. The argument is made in *Laozi* 19.1:

If [the ruler] were to discard wisdom and to reject intelligence, the benefit for the people would be a hundredfold.
    If [the ruler] were to discard benevolence and to reject righteousness, the people would return to filial piety and parental love.
    If [the ruler] were to discard craftiness and to reject [lust for] profit, there would be no robbers and thieves.

    These three [pairs of values whose rejection by the ruler is advocated] are as statements still not sufficient. Therefore to let [his subjects] have something to go by [he would]
manifest simplicity,
    embrace the Unadorned, and,
        by way of minimizing [his] private interests, reduce [his] desires.

Again, the public nature of the Sage's performance is stressed. Beyond the specific non-use of government devices expected of him, he makes a positive public performance of non-acts. The terms used in this context, "manifesting simplicity," *jian su* 見素, "embracing the Unadorned," *bao pu* 包樸, "by way of minimizing [his] private interests," *shao zi* 少私, "reducing [his] desires," *gua yu* 寡欲, share the same agenda with the non-acts described above, but they give a more specific guidance to the public political performance congruent with this ontological agenda.

It is a common misunderstanding that the policy of *wuwei* 無爲, of non-interference, contains only a negative agenda, opposed to the activist stance of government doctrines such as those associated with the other "schools." I argue that, in fact, the doctrine of *wuwei* provides guidelines for dynamic and active policies. As indicators of the plausibility of such an argument, its repeated and successful applications at the hands of central and regional governments since early Han times may be pointed out.[35]

In the tradition of the *Laozi*'s being read in terms of political philosophy, *wuwei* is a doctrine for the exercise of the rule of the One over the Many, the ruler over his people. Wang Bi's *Laozi* 28 begins:

> He who knows that as its [All Under Heaven's] cock he [has to] keep to [being] its hen, will be All Under Heaven's valley. 知其雄守其雌爲天下谿.

Being the "hen" implies projecting a lowly posture and not taking the initiative and thus enacting *wuwei*. The condition for the Sage's being the "cock" and ruler of All Under Heaven is his maintaining the posture of its "hen." The phrase is not general advice to human beings, only to those who are in the position of ruling over All Under Heaven, and only under this condition does the logic of the phrase become operative. Wang Bi's reading of this phrase is supported by much evidence from similar statements, to some of which he alludes in the following commentary:

> A cock belongs to the category of those standing at the fore, a hen to the category of those standing in the background. He who knows how to be [the person] standing at the fore [in All Under Heaven] will by necessity keep in the background. That is why the Sage [as the *Laozi* says in 7.2] "puts his own person in the background and [achieves in this way] that his own person comes to be to the fore." A "valley" does not yearn for other entities; the other entities render themselves to it on their own.

The *Laozi* phrase links two similes, the cock/hen relationship and the valley in its relationship to streams and rivers. The projection of the lowly position of the hen makes the Sage into the valley of All Under Heaven so that, as rivers and streams naturally run into the low-lying valley, All Under Heaven naturally will render itself unto his benign rule. The dialectic of being in the ruling position and projecting the image of the negative opposite is treated in at least fifty-six of the eighty-one *zhang* of Wang Bi's *Laozi* (2, 3, 5, 7, 8, 9, 10, 12, 13, 15, 16, 17, 18, 19, 21, 22, 23, 24, 26, 28, 29, 30, 32, 35, 36, 37, 38, 39, 40, 41, 42, 43, 48, 49, 52, 53, 56, 57, 58, 59, 61, 62, 63, 64, 65, 66, 67, 68, 70, 72, 73, 75, 76, 77, 78, and 81). It mimics the relationship of the Dao or of Heaven and Earth to the ten thousand kinds of entities described in many of these *zhang* but is also discussed separately, for example, in *Laozi* 4, 6, 11, 21, 25, 34, and 51. It is the absolutely dominant theme of the *Laozi* in this reading.

In most of the above-mentioned *zhang*, the ruler is not explicitly mentioned as the subject, although the Sage [Ruler] often appears. Still, the context suggests that Wang Bi definitely is justified in assuming that the ruler is the general subject under discussion. Referring to the *Laozi* text alone, the subject's actions, as well as the objects of these actions, betray the ruler as the main protagonist, even where he is not explicitly referred to. It is he alone whose actions will have an impact on all the "ten thousand kinds of entities" (*Laozi* 2.3, 8.1, 16.2, 32.1, 37.3); on "All Under Heaven" (*Laozi* 22.6, 28.1 ff., 29, 30, 35.1, 39.2, 48.4, 56.10, 60.2, 63.2, 67.4, 78.2); on the entire "people" (*Laozi* 3.4, 10.4, 19.1, 53.2, 57.5, 58.1, 65.1, 66.1, 75.1, 80.3); on the "others" (*Laozi* 12.1, 27.5, 68.4); on the "Hundred Families" (*Laozi* 5.2, 17.6, 49.1); on the "state" (*Laozi* 10.4, 18.3, 59.5, 65.4); on the "men of the crowd" (*Laozi* 64.7). He "stands at the fore" (*Laozi* 7.2), can be "entrusted with All Under Heaven" (*Laozi* 13.6), or "takes All Under Heaven" (*Laozi* 57.1).

The government doctrine of *wuwei* is operative only under the conditions of the statutory dialectics reigning between the One and the Many. The policy of *wuwei* receives its effectiveness from being enacted by the person who in fact could do everything and has all the power to do so vested in himself. *Wuwei* is thus the demonstrative, public non-use of these powers by the ruler.

In his commentaries, Wang Bi makes it clear that these non-acts and acts of negation are the form that the imitation of the Dao takes in the human world. On *Laozi* 32.1, he writes:

> The Unadorned as such has negativity as its heart. [It], too, is nameless [like the Dao]. That is why if one [i.e., a ruler] intends to achieve the Way, there is nothing better than to keep to the Unadorned. 樸之爲物以無爲心也亦無名故將得道莫若守樸.

In Wang Bi on *Laozi* 37.3, the performance of simplicity is an active policy of establishing social order in imitation of the Dao in direct opposition to the ruler's "playing the boss," *wei zhu* 爲主.

The Eternal of the Way is without interference,

Commentary
It adapts to [the entities'] That-which-is-of-itself-what-it-is.

Text 2
and still leaves nothing undone.

Commentary
There is none among the ten thousand kinds of entities that
does not base itself on it [the Way] to be begun and perfected.

Text 3
If dukes and kings were only able to hold on to [the Eternal of
the Way], the ten thousand kinds of entities would change [for
the better] of their own accord. If, this change notwithstanding, desires should arise [among them], I [the Sage] would quiet
them down by means of the Unadorned of the Nameless [of
myself],

Commentary
"If, this change notwithstanding, desires should arise" means
"if desires form." "I would quiet them down by means of the
Unadorned of the nameless" means [in the words of *Laozi*
34.2] "[I would] not become [their] overlord."

Text 4
and would also make [them] be without desire.

Commentary
[That is,] to be without desire for competition.

Text 5
Being without desire, [they] would therefore be calm, and All
Under Heaven would go about regulating itself.

Given the spontaneous growth of desires among the people, there is
never a static order. To "return" the people to the One is a permanent

effort based on the continuous projection of "unadornedness" or "simplicity" by the ruler. It is his philosophical and political duty to make visible
through his demonstrative non-acts the elusive and "dark" That-by-which,
so that the people might relate back and "return" to it as a way of fitting
themselves into their fate-assigned lot.

The fragments of the *LZWZLL* that have survived contain Wang
Bi's enclosed essay on the "rise of depravity and the development of debauchery," as well as the ways to do away with them. The essay is highly
polemical and takes the government doctrine to task that had dominated
thinking at least since the early Han Huang/Lao thinking gave way to a
more activist, interventionist and centralist policy, which the Cao Wei
continued.[36] These polemics bypass the cheap criticism of the ineptitude
of many rulers. In true philosophic fashion, they proceed from exactly
the opposite premise, namely, a ruler who disposes of the maximum of
"insight," *sheng* 聖, and "knowledge," *zhi* 智, and they study what the
application of these qualities might bring. Wang Bi writes (*LZWZLL*
6.23–29), concluding from the essay's arguments:

It is a fact that if the Dao of the plain
and unadorned does not shine forth
while the amenities of predilections
and desires are not hidden, [the
ruler] might

go to extremes with his wisdom and enlightenment in the attempt to keep them [the people] under surveillance	exhaust [his] intelligence and wit in the attempt to attack them [the people],

but

the more refined [his] skills are, the more variegated their [the people's] pretensions will become,	the more intensely his attacks on them proceed, the more efforts they will make to evade him,

and then, indeed, the dull-witted
and the intelligent will get the
better of each other, the [relatives
in] the six relationships will distrust
each other, the "Unadorned disperses"
[*Laozi* 28.6], and they become
separated from the[ir] true [nature],
and there is debauchery in [all] affairs.
Once the root is abandoned and [its]
outgrowth is attacked,

wisdom	and	intelligence

might be applied to the maximum;
there will only be more of sure disasters
—and how much greater [will they be]
when [a ruler's] art is inferior to this
[maximum wisdom and intelligence]!

The destruction of social order, the "rise of depravity and the development of debauchery," is not the work of the depraved and the debauched
but of the countermeasures by rulers with the best qualifications and mo-
tives. How much worse will things be with rulers of even lesser insight and
knowledge? The strategy for the restoration and maintenance of the ontic
order is developed out of exactly the same logic of the law of the negative
opposite, which here is turned to practical political use. Against the ruler's
"exertion of wisdom and intelligence" to "regulate cunning and fraud,"
his "promotion of benevolence and justice" to "destroy the shallow and
vulgar," and his "multiplication of skills and profit interests" to "raise
the utility of affairs," Wang Bi has his ideal ruler "manifest simplicity and
plainness to calm down people's desires," "embrace the Unadorned to
perfect the sound and unadorned," and diminish in himself "egotism and
desires to bring the competition for adornments [among the people] to
rest." In this sense, the ultimate negative acts—the "cutting off of surveillance and the submerging of [the ruler's] intelligence," the "elimination of
encouragement and promotion" of others by the ruler and the "cutting off
of adornments and eulogies," the "dismissal of skills and utility, and the
despising of precious goods"—become the most effective instruments of
government (*LZWZLL* 6.15–21). Through the dialectics of the negative
opposite only, "once wisdom is cut off [in the ruler], the achievements of
wisdom will be completed" and only, "once benevolence is discarded, the
capacity of benevolence will be ample."[37]

With this turn of the argument, what began as a highly sophisticated
philological and philosophical inquiry into the That-by-which, with its
double characteristics of being the condition of the possibility of the
ten thousand kinds of entities and being utterly elusive and "dark," has
developed into a philosophically guided politological analysis of societal
dynamics and an applicable set of policies. In immediately practical terms,
these policies of the almighty ruler would primarily consist of:

- his dismantling of the state's surveillance and security apparatus;

- his reducing the laws and ordinances on the basis of which legal
  battles might be fought;

- his abandoning policies of special promotion and encouragement
  for specially skilled people;

- his non-granting of special imperial favors to individuals;

- his projecting an image of simplicity and parsimony; and

- his lowering himself under his neighboring states and reducing the use of military force to the absolute minimum for the shortest possible time.

The promised outcome of such policies would be the achievement of the very results envisaged by the activist policies actually used. Within the general framework of people having their allotted place and keeping to it, the particular promised outcome would be that:

- The security of the ruler's position and person would be enhanced.

- The divisiveness of legal strife would be reduced.

- The competition and intrigues among courtiers to be promoted would be reduced.

- The envy and divisiveness accompanying the selective receipt of imperial favors would be avoided.

- The competition to match the ruler in conspicuous consumption and the concomitant impoverishment of the populace would be reduced.

- The costly battles with smaller neighboring states would be avoided, and they would on their own initiative render themselves as retainers to the larger state.

The political application of his philosophic inquiry was not extraneous to Wang Bi's project but was its driving force. This is easily visible in the economy of Wang Bi's pursuit. His philosophic focus is strictly on the relationship between the One and the Many, with its evident importance for that between the ruler and his subjects. He took none of the possible detours into other interesting areas of philosophy but held on to this central topic, because his eventual interest was in a philosophically based political science. His own summary of *Laozi*'s thinking shows both where his focus was and his eagerness to prove the applicability of his insights for a real-life ruler. The *LZWZLL* contains two such summaries. Although they contain elements of the *Laozi*'s language here and there, they in effect present Wang Bi's own formula of the key points of the *Laozi*'s philosophy. The first of these two summaries is:

Thus it is the [*Laozi*'s] great purport to expound the source of the Great Beginning in order to elucidate the nature of That-which-is-by-itself-what-it-is, and to hold forth on the ultimate of the recondite in order to settle the delusions of doubt and deception.

- To respond to, and not to act upon;
- to adapt and not to initiate;
- to emulate the root by way of bringing to rest its [the root's] outgrowth;
- to keep to the mother by way of maintaining [her] offspring;
- to hold lightly indeed skill and arts [of government as a means to control the people];
- to "act" [on dangers to one's life and position as a ruler] while "they have not now come about";
- not to "put the blame on others" but necessarily to seek all [mistakes] in oneself [as the lord])

—these are its [the *Laozi* text's] key points.[38]

Eventually, Wang Bi claimed that the *Laozi*'s entire teaching could be "summed up in one phrase" in the manner that Kongzi had claimed for the *Shijing*. But, as opposed to Kongzi's summary, which most commentators read as straight moral advice ("do not have any heterodox thoughts"), Wang Bi's summary of the *Laozi* comes as the highly condensed paradox of the law of the negative opposite:

Emulating the root [by way] of bringing to rest the stem and branches [growing from it]—that is all! 崇本息末而已矣.[39]

This tersest of possible summaries makes quite clear the ultimate political purpose of the *Laozi*'s philosophy in Wang Bi's reading, namely, *xi mo* 息末, "to bring to rest [the root's] outgrowth." The term *mo* 末 describes all that grows out of the root, such as the stem and the branches of a tree. They receive their origin and continuous support from this root but are in fact the visible world whose regulation is the purpose of government. The entire analytic and philosophic enterprise of Wang Bi, and his reading of *Laozi*, remains tied to the ultimate purpose of bringing rest and order to the world, and his main discovery in this respect is the law of the negative opposite, which encapsulates and theorizes observations on the dynamics of the body politic that can be found to this day in sources ranging from proverbial lore about cunning political strategies, such as the Chinese 36 stratagems,[40] to structuralist analyses of political power.[41]

The *Laozi* has multiple, and parallel, existences. They range from its being the utterances of the Dao about moral improvement and life prolongation, including detailed prescriptions on sexual practices (Xiang Er), to a treatise on the maintenance of the body and the state (Heshang gong); from the philosophic fundament of a terrorist state that would shock the population into such fear by threats of coercion that no further application of the coercive measures would be necessary (*Hanfeizi*), to the philosophical foundation of a government trying to restore civilized behavior after the ravages of war (Huanglao thought). It has continued to have new and newer existences from being a treatise on military strategy (Tang Lan) to a collection of proverbs serendipitously connected by an occasional "therefore" and "that is why" (Kimura Eiichi); from being a book by an Indian (Mair) to a book written by someone who then went to India to found Buddhism (*Laozi huahu jing*).

What, then, is the Wang Bi *Laozi*? It is a book whose implied reader is the ruler. In idealized ("Sage") or real form, he appears explicitly or through Wang's *Commentary* in the large majority of the chapters of the *Laozi*. It is a book that deals with the relationship between the ruler and All Under Heaven. This is a double relationship. The ruler has the institutional position of being the One of the Many. This gives him complete "control" over the Many, that is, the option to decide, do, and take care of everything. This option follows from his institutional position and is codified in the social prerogatives of his power, which in theory is unlimited. From this option it does not necessarily follow that in fact he has to decide, do, and take care of everything. How he actually should behave in his institutional role of the One is a matter of considerable controversy among various political philosophers. The Wang Bi *Laozi* (and the Wang Bi *Zhouyi*) propose that the ruler look at the fundamental dynamics governing the relationship between the One and the Many, between the Dao or Negativity and the ten thousand kinds of entities, in order to understand the laws of this relationship and map out a course of action that consists of imitating and translating into the human world the way in which the One actually manages to be and remain the One of the Many, their "That-by-which."

The Wang Bi *Laozi* therefore deals with the problems of ontology, the relationship of Being and Entity, the One and the Many, and Negativity and the ten thousand entities only because and insofar as it is necessary in order to extract these laws. These can be and are to be translated into a successful course of action by the ruler. The Wang Bi *Laozi* is prescriptive political philosophy based on analytic ontology. When summarizing the essence of the *Laozi*, Wang Bi does not talk about Negativity, the Dao, or the Sage. The grammatical form of his summary—and he claims that the *Laozi* can be summed up in one phrase—is prescriptive, not analytic.

WANG BI'S PHILOSOPHY: AN IDEOLOGY?

It has become fashionable to infer from the fact that any given historic actor is moving in a specific historic field and in one way or the other reacts to it, that his intellectual contribution is nothing but an attempt indirectly and perhaps unwittingly to defend, attack, legitimize, or question certain policies, factions, interests, or phenomena of his day. The fashion has been fueled, on the one hand, by the mass production of works of this kind in the socialist world in which the cheap subordination of even fairly esoteric research under the policy requirements of the day has become commonplace and, on the other hand, by many studies in intellectual history that have extended the records of such subordination deep into the past. From the self-interest of the approach a lack of intellectual honesty and argumentative credibility has been inferred.

The question, in my opinion, cannot be whether philosophers, artists, or other intellectuals interact with the world around them or not; they certainly do. The question is, however, whether their contribution can be reduced to a simple, legitimizing ideology with all of its unhappy side effects of sloppy and slippery argument, closed-circuit logic, unfalsifiability (not to mention unverifiability), selectiveness, and the ill-lit corners of the bad conscience of thoughts whose results are fixed beforehand.

Wang Bi is perfectly explicit on his relations with the intellectual and political life around him. He takes to task the philosophers of all schools for misreading the *Laozi* and the *Zhouyi* and thus contributing to the downward spiral of philosophical ignorance and destructive policies. He takes on the policy measures of the Cao Court with its surveillance system, heavy-handed state intervention, and constant military campaigns against the other two states, and argues that they are self-defeating and with all their good intentions of propping up the stability of the dynasty in fact they are undermining it in a highly dangerous manner. He went to the regent Cao Shuang to "talk about the Dao," that is, to offer himself with his meager twenty or so years as a philosophical and political advisor, which earned him quite a bit of hilarity at the court.[42]

At the same time, the question might be asked, *cui bono*? Whose interests does Wang Bi's line of argument serve? As I have shown elsewhere,

Wang Bi came from one of the newly emerging, large provincial clans of the Later Han dynasty. The social status of his family was such that his grandfather refused to marry the daughter of his superior, General He Qin, the powerful brother of the empress, because He Qin and his sister were the children of lowly butchers. Liu Biao, the Han scion who helped many scholars survive the end of the Han in his academy in Jingzhou, also wanted marital relations with the Gaoping Wangs. When Wang Bi, who at the time had not even been capped as an adult, visited He Yan, grandson of He Qin, who had grown up in Cao Cao's house and easily was the most elegant man of his time, quite apart from being the prime minister in charge of all appointments during this time of the *zhengshi* 正 始 era (240–249), He Yan was so flustered at the arrival of this illustrious youngster that he famously put the left shoe onto the right foot, and vice versa, when he rushed to the door.

The Cao Wei leadership consisted of an alliance between provincial upstarts such as the Caos, who had made their careers through military actions during the collapse of the Han, and members of the large Later Han clans, most prominent among them the Sima, led by Sima Yi. Many of them had not played an active military role during the preceding decades, but with the return of relative peace and some economic prosperity in Wei, their fortunes improved; by the late 230s, their offspring began to demand a greater political role in the capital and a voice in the development of government doctrine. Among this younger group were members of the "magnate," *haozu* 豪族, clans of the Later Han, as well as younger members of the founding families of the Wei. Against these attempts, the Wei emperor, Mingdi, decreed a positive employment ban for all those known to belong to this intellectual and political current, among them such lights as He Yan and Xiahou Xuan.

With Mingdi's death in 239 and the installment of Cao Shuang as co-regent with Sima Yi, this group managed to get hold of the levers of power in Wei and began an ambitious reform project. The effort was ended by Sima Yi's coup in 249 and the successive execution of all those leaders who owed their rise to their association with the Cao. Eventually the Jin was founded by the Sima and families from the old *haozu* clans, while the upstarts from the Cao entourage were eliminated. As a consequence of this development, the reforms of the *zhengshi* era have been strongly underreported in the historical works written during the Jin, such as the *Sanguo zhi*, and their particular content is hard to figure out. There is no question, however, that the reduction of the Center's activist policies and repressive machinery was among the demands of the large clans. In the analysis of the Huanglao current during the early Han, scholars have argued that these policies in fact favored the relative independence of the regional nobility that had been subdued by the Han central Court. At the same time this current came out against an offensive military stance against the Xiongnu in the West. Very much in the same manner, it might be argued that Wang Bi's philosophic enterprise was not oblivious to the interests of the segment to which Wang himself belonged, and that the reduction of government interference and military activity that he advocated was quite in tune with the aspirations of his social peers.

At the same time, little is explained by the reference to the particular historic circumstances of Wang Bi's philosophy. Its historic importance long outlasted the particular circumstances of its development. The very clan that executed a fair number of the people with whom Wang Bi had had closest contact, such as He Yan, namely, the founding clan of Jin, the Sima, did not only preside over a dynasty where the philosophers of the *zhengshi* era were considered the highest achievement since Confucius' time, but where even the reforms begun during the *zhengshi* seem to have been continued.[43] As a philosophically grounded doctrine of government, it has articulated a government performance style that has remained important and influential for centuries, especially during times when not war and civil strife but the development of civilized institutions of social intercourse, *wenming* 文明, was the order of the day. This indeed had been the reform program of the *zhengshi* era, which set out to "enhance *wenming*," *xing wenming* 興文明.

Notes

NOTES–INTRODUCTION

1. See R. Wagner, *A Chinese Reading of the Daode jing. Wang Bi's Commentary on the Laozi. With Critical Text, and Translation* (Albany: State University of New York Press, 2003), 82–106, for a full edition and translation of this text.

2. R. Wagner, *The Craft of a Chinese Commentator: Wang Bi on the Laozi* (Albany: State University of New York Press, 2000), 21.

3. R. Wagner, *A Chinese Reading of the Daode jing.*

4. R. Wagner, *The Craft of a Chinese Commentator.*

NOTES–CHAPTER 1

1. Feng Youlan, *Zhongguo zhexue shi* (Shanghai: Shangwu Press, 1934), 492.

2. Pi Xirui, *Jingxue lishi* (orig. published in 1907, with annotations by Zhou Yutong 周予同 in 1929); I used the Zhonghua Press edition (Beijing 1981); id., *Jingxue tonglun*, orig. 1907; I used the Commercial Press edition (Shanghai, 1936).

3. Ishida Kōdō, "Chūgoku ni okeru chūshakushu no hattatsu," *Hokkaidō jōshi tenki daigaku kiyō* 4:1–73 (1971).

4. Feng Youlan, *Zhongguo zhexue shi* (Shanghai: Shangwu Press, 1934), I.20 ff.; Yu Dunkang, *He Yan Wang Bi xuanxue xintan* (Jinan: Qi Lu Press, 1991), 144 ff.

5. Kaga Eiji, *Chūgoku koten kaishaku shi. Gi Shin hen* (Tokyo: Keiso Press, 1991).

6. *Zhouyi yinde, Xici* 44 上/12.

7. Although I describe the options here as they presented themselves to Wang Bi, a note might be added about the *Xici*. Often assumed to be a text as late as

the Former Han, the finding of a text in the Mawangdui tomb has confirmed that it is most likely a late Warring States text. The close links of the *Xici* to what is sometimes referred to as the "Taoist" tradition have been remarked on by various scholars and have most recently been carefully restudied by Chen Guying; cf. Chen Guying, "'Yizhuan. Xici' suoshou *Laozi* sixiang de yingxiang," *Zhexue yanjiu* 1: 34–42, 52 (1989); id. "Yizhuan. Xici suoshou *Zhuangzi* sixiang de yingxiang," *Zhexue yanjiu* 4:51–58 (1992); id. "'Tuanzhuan' yu Lao Zhuang," in id. *Lao Zhuang xin lun*, 277–93; id. "'Yizhuan' yu Chuxue Qixue," *Daojia wenhua yanjiu* 1:143–56 (1992); id., "Lun 'Xicizhuan' shi Qixia daojia zhi zuo -- Wu lun 'Yizhuan' fei rujia dianji," *Daojia wenhua yanjiu* 2:355–65 (1992). Wang Baoxuan, "Cong Mawangdui boshuben kan 'Xici' yu *Laozi* xuepai de guanxi," *Daojia wenhua yanjiu*, 1:175–87 (1992), has in the main confirmed Chen's assumptions and contributed important additional information concerning the formation of the *Xici* as visible from the comparison of the textus receptus of this text and the Mawangdui ms., where some parts of what is now the *Xici* appear in a text apparently entitled "The Meaning of the [*Zhou*]*yi* 易之義."

8. Wang Baoxuan, *Zhengshi xuanxue* (Jinan: Qi Lu Press, 1987), 322.

9. *Lunyu yinde* (Taipei: Ch'eng-wen, 1996) 8.19; see Lou Yulie, ed. *Wang Bi ji jiaoshi* (Beijing: Zhonghua Press, 1980), vol. 2, 626, for Wang Bi's commentary; see p. 197 for a translation.

10. *Lunyu yinde* 9.2; see Lou Yulie, ed., *Wang Bi ji jiaoshi*, vol. 2, 626.

11. *Lunyu yinde* 14.35.

12. *Lunyu yinde* 17.17.

13. All editions I have read punctuate 既求道中, 不可勝御. This does not seem to make sense. I read 御 as the object of 求 and 不可勝 as a composite adjective. It is used in this way in later Buddhist translations, but I presume that it must have existed already in Wang Bi's time. I have no hard proof for this.

14. Lou Yulie, ed., *Wang Bi ji jiaoshi*, 633 ff.

15. For economy, I refer only to the *Laozi* segment with the traditional numbering of *zhang*, and the phrase within the *zhang*, as cut by Wang Bi. The reader is invited to check the Chinese text, the context, and the translation in the appropriate place in my *A Chinese Reading of the Daode jing*, op. cit.

16. *Zhuangzi jishi* (Beijing: Zhonghua Press, 1982), p. 531. I cannot follow Graham, *Chuang-tzu: The Seven Inner Chapters and Other Writings from the Book Chuang-tzu* (London: Allen & Unwin, 1981), 133, in translating 人之難說 也, 道之難明邪? as "How intractable are the difficulties of making plain the Way." Watson, *The Complete Works of Chuang-tzu* (New York and London: Columbia University Press, 1968), 166, reads it as a simple parallel "How difficult it is to persuade others, how difficult to make clear the Way." This rendering does not take care of the interrogative 邪 at the end and makes two unrelated statements, while Confucius in fact talked to the princes about the Dao only in connection to the classics. I give a reference to Graham's regrouping of the *Zhuangzi* parts

only because it is used by many scholars. I believe the methodology used in this regrouping to be fatally flawed, and therefore cannot accept his results.

17. The reference to the six classics has been held as a clear sign of a Han dynasty date for this passage. This argument has to be abandoned, because we find explicit reference to the classics in the Guodian bamboo slips, which are dated around 300 B.C.E. See Yucong (Collected Sayings) 語叢 1, Jingmenshi Bowuguan, ed., *Guodian Chu mu zhujian* (Beijing: Wenwu, 1998), 195, slips 35–43.

18. *Zhuangzi jishi*, 532. Graham, *Chuang-tzu*, 133; Watson, *The Complete Works of Chuang-tzu*, 166. The Guo Xiang commentary is quoted from *Zhuangzi jishi*, 532.

19. *Huangdi neijing suwen* (Beijing: Renmin weisheng, 1978), 262.

20. *Zhuangzi jishi*, 488 ff.

21. Graham, *Chuang-tzu*, 139.

22. Watson, *The Complete Works of Chuang Tzu*, 152.

23. *Zhuangzi jishi*, 488 f.; see *Huainanzi zhuzi suoyin, A Concordance to the Huainanzi* (Hong Kong: Commercial Press, 1992), 111/1. Graham, *Chuang-tzu*, 139 ff; Watson, *The Complete Works of Chuang Tzu*, 152 ff.

24. Yu Dunkang, *He Yan Wang Bi xuanxue xintan*, 183.

25. *Zhouyi yinde* (Taipei: Ch'eng-wen Publishing Company, 1966); *Xici*, 44/繫上/12. See Peterson, "Making Connections: 'Commentary on the Attached Verbalizations' of the Book of Change," *HJAS* 42:1:98 ff. (1982).

26. Wang Baoxuan, *Zhengshi xuanxue*, 322.

27. The first statement about written and spoken words and about the thinking of the Sage might have originally been unrelated to the second statement about the strategies of the setting up and handling of the *Zhouyi*. As they shared with the terms *yi* 意 and *yan* 言 a common subject matter, they might have been put together here by the early editor(s) who produced what has become the standard textual setup. Wang Bi in fact treats only the matching elements and disregards the rest.

28. It is not quite clear to what these "words" in the second statement refer. It may be that the *Xici* meant by the "appended statements" the *tuanzhuan* 彖傳, which explain the short statement about the hexagram as a whole, and the *xiangzhuan* 象傳, which comment on the statements about the individual lines. In this case, the short statement about the hexagram as a whole, the *xiang* 象 of the entire hexagram, and the short statements about the lines would be the "words."

29. *Mengzi*, IV.II.ii.1–4. See my "Ein chinesisches Plädoyer gegen die autonome Person (A Chinese Plea against the Notion of the Autonomous Person)," in M. Welker, ed., *Die Autonome Person*, in press, for a discussion of the conflation of the Sages into a single, ideal type.

30. *Lunyu jijie*, Sibu beiyao (Shanghai: Zhonghua Press, 1930), 16.8.

31. Huang Kan 皇侃, *Lunyu jijie yishu* in Congshu Jicheng (Shanghai: Commercial Press, 1937), 234.

32. See R. Wagner, "Die Unhandlichkeit des Konfuzius," in Assmann ed., *Weisheit. Archäologie der literarischen Kommunikation III* (München: Fink Verlag, 1991), 455–64.

33. Yang Shixun commenting on the title of the *Guliang Commentary* for the first year of Duke Yin, Ruan Yuan, ed., *Shisan jing zhushu*, vol. 2 (Beijing: Zhonghua Press, 1987), 2365a; Ishida Kōdō, "Chūgoku ni okeru chūshakushu no hattatsu," *Hokkaidō jōshi tenki daigaku kiyō* 4:4 (1971), misquotes this statement as coming from the *Guliang Commentary* itself.

34. The most detailed and knowledgeable treatment of this passage is in Hachiya Kuniō, "Gen jin i ron to gen fu jin i ron," *Tōyō bunka kenkyūshō kiyō* 86:122 ff. (1981) and fn. 24–31. See also Liu Baonan, *Lunyu zhengyi*, in Zhuzi jicheng (Shanghai: Shanghai shudian, 1990), 98 ff.

35. Lü Youren, ed., Qian Daxin, *Qianyantang wenji*, in Qian Daxin, *Qianyantang ji* (Shanghai: Shanghai guji Press, 1989), 120 f.

36. Quoted in Liu Baonan, *Lunyu zhengyi*, 99.

37. See my "Ban Gu and the End of History," unpublished manuscript, 1995.

38. Ban Gu, *Hanshu*, vol. 6 (Beijing: Zhonghua Press, 1964), 30:1701. Also see my "Twice Removed from the Truth: Fragment Collection in 18th and 19th Century China," in G. Most, ed., *Aporemata* . . . (Göttingen: Vandenhoeck & Ruprecht, 1997). It should be noted that the standard reference to this passage as proving that the Qing burned the books "in order to stultify the people" is based, I believe, on a misreading not supported by the context.

39. *Hou Hanshu* (Peking: Zhonghua, 1965), 145.

40. See Chen Qiyou, ed., *Lüshi chunqiu jiaoshi*, vol. 2 (Shanghai: Xuelin Press, 1990), 18:1168; Wilhelm, *Frühling und Herbst des Lü Bu We* (Jena: Eugen Diederichs, 1928), 298. With minor variations, it also occurs in *Huainanzi* 12: 105.20 ff.) and *Liezi jishi* (Beijing: Zhonghua Press, 1985), 8:249 ff; Graham, *The Book of Lieh-tzu* (London: John Murray, 1960), 166 ff. In this account, I follow the *Lüshi Chunqiu* version. The Duke who plans to attack the neighboring state Zheng asks Confucius, "Is it possible to have subtle words [secret understanding] with others?" 人可與微言乎 When Confucius does not answer, he asks whether this might be done like throwing a stone into the water, but Confucius counters that even though not visible [on the surface], a skilled diver would find it; the Duke then asks whether it could be done like throwing water into water, but Confucius counters that a skilled cook would be able to tell the tastes apart. Exasperated, the Duke asks, "Is it then impossible to have subtle words [with others]?" Confucius answers: "Why should this be impossible? But it is only possible for someone who knows what words are hinting at" 唯知言之謂者爲可耳. The *Lüshi Chunqiu* then comments: "Once what is hinted at is understood, one is not in need of words 知謂則不以言矣. Words are appendages to what is hinted at 言者謂之屬

也. If someone who is after fish gets wet or someone who is going after game gets out of breath, this is not because he enjoys this [but because there might be no other way of getting what he is after, but they definitely would prefer to stay dry and not get out of breath if they could otherwise reach their goals. In the same sense, words are not used for their intrinsic value but as sometimes unavoidable instruments to convey a meaning]. That is why the highest words dispense with words 至言去言, and the highest action is absence of action" 至爲無爲. In this reading, Confucius identifies as the true "subtle words" 微言 those which manage to convey meaning without actually using any words whatsoever. The anecdote is told in a context where the wordless communication among Sages is discussed. It starts with the words, "The mutual recognition of Sages does not depend upon words; they have an understanding beyond words" ibid., 18.1167.

41. Cf. the uses of *ming* in *Laozi* 14.1 and 34.2 and 34.3. Cf. the commentary to *Laozi* 21.6 for Wang Bi's solution to this problem. The differentiation between *wei* and *ming* was first proposed by the Mohists. See Harbsmeier, *Science and Civilization in China. Vol. VII.1, Language and Logic* (Cambridge: Cambridge University Press, 1998), 332.

42. See Tang Junyi's 唐君毅 notes on silence as a philosophical statement in chapter 7 of his *Zhongguo zhexue yuanlun, Daolun pian* (Taipei: Taiwan xuesheng Press, 1986), 223 ff.

43. Du Yu, "Chunqiu xu," in Ruan Yuan, ed., *Shisan jing zhushu*, vol. 2 (Beijing: Zhonghua Press, 1987), 1703a ff. The approach chosen by George Kennedy in his "Interpretation of the Ch'un-ch'iu," *JAOS* 62:40–48 (1942), which is only interested in the traditions insofar as they might elucidate what he considers the original meaning of the *Chunqiu*, does help undermine the perhaps naive trust of Otto Franke in Part 1 of his *Studien zur Geschichte des konfuzianischen Dogmas und der chinesischen Staatsreligion: Das Problem des T'schun-ts'iu und Tung Tschung-schu's T'schun-ts'iu fan lu* (Hamburg: L. Friederichsen & Co., 1920) in the deep meaning of the *Chunqiu* as discovered by the traditions but contributes little toward the understanding of the actual role that either the *Chunqiu* or traditions played in China. For a detailed study of the Gongyang Commentary's commentarial strategies, see Joachim Gentz, *Das* Gongyang zhuan. *Auslegung und Kanonisierung der* Frühlings- und Herbstannalen (Chunqiu). (Wiesbaden: Harrassowitz, 2001.)

44. Its importance within the Chinese context notwithstanding, the *Great Preface* has not received much attention in critical scholarship. For some recent studies, see Steven Van Zoeren, *Poetry and Personality. Readings, Exegesis, and Hermeneutics* (Stanford: Stanford University Press, 1991); Hermann-Josef Röllicke, *Die Fährte des Herzens. Die Lehre vom Herzensbestreben (zhi) im Grossen Vorwort zum Shijing* (Berlin: Reimer, 1992); Haun Saussy, *The Problem of a Chinese Aesthetic*, chapter 3.

45. *Lunyu* 1.15. See also Confucius' discussion with Zixia about another *Shijing* passage in *Lunyu* 3.8.

46. *Lüshi Chunqiu jiaoshi*, 1:802. Chen, ibid., 807, note 12, argues that the statement by Xianqiu Mang and another reference to this poem in the *Hanfeizi*

with a similar reading indicate that the story of Shun's authorship must already have circulated during the *Zhanguo* period.

47. *Shijing* (Beijing: Zhonghua Press, 1987), 463b.

48. Jiao Xun, *Mengzi zhengyi*, in *Zhuzi jicheng* (Shanghai: Shanghai shudian, 1990), 9.377; see J. Legge, *The Chinese Classics, The Works of Mencius* (Hong Kong: Hong Kong University Press, 1960), II.353.

49. *Mengzi zhengyi* with the commentary by Zhao Qi, 9.377. Certainly the most radical antipode to the *lectio difficilior* rule, this has become the golden rule of many commentaries in their efforts to eliminate the irritation of certain unexpected words in a phrase by bluntly assigning to a character a meaning that corresponds to the expected meaning of the phrase but is highly unusual, and often unique. At the same time, the unreliability of the written word during the *Zhanguo* period is notorious. Many manuscript finds down to the second century have confirmed the high instability in the relationship between words and written characters, resulting in a large number of loan graphs.

50. Zhao Qi, ibid.

51. Ibid.

52. Strauss, *Thoughts on Machiavelli* (Glencoe: Free Press, 1959), 29. For another application of this strategy, see the chapter on Tian Han's reading Guan Hanqing's *Dou E yuan* in my *The Contemporary Chinese Historical Drama: Four Studies* (Berkeley: University of California Press, 1990), 29 ff.

53. Zhao Qi, *Mengzi tici*, in Jiao Xun, *Mengzi zhengyi*, 4.

54. Jiao Xun, *Mengzi zhengyi*, 565; Legge, *The Chinese Classics*, 479.

55. Zhao Qi, *Mengzi tici*, in *Mengzi zhengyi*, ed. cit., p. 11.

56. Ibid., 8.

57. Ibid., 11.

58. *Zhuangzi yinde* 75/26/48f; Graham, *Chuang-tzu*, 190; Watson, *The Complete Works of Chuang Tzu*, 302.

59. *Weimojie suoshuo jing*, T. 475.551c. E. Lamotte (tr.), *L'Enseignement de Vimalakīrti*, 317 ff.

60. See for the documentation further down, p. 81.

61. It should be mentioned that the *Zhuangzi* contains a classification of language and argumentative devices (Graham, *Chuang-tzu*, 25 ff., 106—a passage taken from ch. 27 and related, according to Graham, to the Inner Chapters), which also are said to have been used in the *Zhuangzi* itself; see also Graham, *Chuang-tzu*, 283 ff.,—a passage from the *Tianxia*, ch. 29. As the terms suggested in these passages do not seem to have been taken up by later authors, I shall not deal with them here, concerned as I am with depicting the origins of a third-century C.E. discussion.

62. Li Dingsheng and Xu Huijun, eds., *Wenzi yaoquan* (Shanghai: Fudan

daxue Press, 1988), 38 ff. *Wenzi zhuzi suoyin, A Concordance to the Wenzi* (Hong Kong: Commercial Press, 1992), 1/2/24 ff. The passage "having heard much" is not marked with the standard form of introducing a *Laozi* quotation, namely, *gu* 故, "that is why." Still, it appears in *Laozi* 5.4, where the *Huainanzi* and Wang Bi traditions read 多言, while the *Wenzi* and the two Mawangdui mss. read 多聞.

63. Li Dingsheng and Xu Huijun eds., *Wenzi yaoquan*, 61; Cleary, *Further Teachings of Lao-tzu: Understanding the Mysteries. A Translation of the Taoist Classic Wen-tzu* (Boston: Shambhala, 1991), 29.

64. *Huainanzi zhuzi suoyin* 12/110/17 f.

65. *Hanfeizi jishi*, vol. 1 (Peking: Zhonghua Press, 1962), 405.

66. Sun Xingyan, *Wenzi tang ji* in Sun Xingyan, *Dainange congshu* (Taipei: Yiwen, 1971), 4; *Wenzi xu* 文子序, in Sun Xingyan. *Wenzitang ji*, 2.1b. Cf. also the introduction to Li Dingsheng and Xu Huijun, eds., *Wenzi yaoquan*, 5.

67. Li Dingsheng and Xu Huijun, eds., *Wenzi yaoquan*, 192 ff.

68. *Huainanzi zhuzi zuoyin* 13/121/1 ff.

69. Dong Zhongshu, *Chunqiu fanlu*, Sibu congkan (Shanghai: Commercial Press, 1929–1934), 3.19b.

70. Ibid., 3.19a. The textual transmission here is fairly unanimous, but the editors of the Wuyingdian reprint in the Sibu congkan have changed *hua* 話 to *gu* 詁—in which case the first phrase would mean that the *Shi* "has no clear-cut interpretation"—and have changed *yan* 言 in the second phrase to *zhan* 占, which would mean that the *Zhouyi* does "not have clear-cut oracles." This attempt to smooth out an irritant in the text cannot be pursued to the third expression, namely, the *ci* 辭 for the *Chunqiu*, which function on the same level as speech and words but not as interpretation and divination.

71. Ibid. The text has 奉人 at the end; the conjecture 奉天 has been suggested by Yu Dunkang, *He Yan Wang Bi xuanxue xintan*, 151.

72. Dong Zhongshu, *Chunqiu fanlu*, 10, sec. 35, 55a.6.

73. Ibid., 10, sec. 35, 54b.12.

74. Ibid., 1.2, 7b. For the role of this "intention" as a Han dynasty legal category authorized by the *Chunqiu*, see Benjamin E. Wallacker, "The *Spring and Autumn Annals* As a Source of Law in Han China," *Journal of Chinese Studies* 2:1:59–72 (1985).

75. Dong Zhongshu, *Chunqiu fanlu*, 3.5, 19b.

76. Su Yu, ed., *Chunqiu fanlu yizheng* (Peking: Zhonghua Press, 1992), 97.

77. Dong Zhongshu, *Chunqiu fanlu*, 1.2, 8a ff.

78. Yu Dunkang, *He Yan Wang Bi xuanxue xintan*, 153.

79. Su Yu, ed., *Chunqiu fanlu yizheng*, 50ff.

80. Cf. Tjan Tjoe Som, *Po Hu T'ung: The Comprehensive Discussions in the White Tiger Hall. A Contribution to the History of Classical Studies in the Han Period*, vol. 1 (Leiden: Brill, 1949), 167 n. 626.

81. Xu Kangsheng, "Lun Wei Jin shiqi de zhuzi baijia xue," *Zhongguo zhexueshi yanjiu* 3:31–42 (1982).

82. See p. 49.

83. This date is based on the fact that in He Shao's *Xun Can bie zhuan* 荀餐別傳, as quoted in Liu Xiaobiao's *Commentary to the Shishuo xinyu* IV.9, 200 (Mather, *Shih-shuo Hsin-yu* [Minneapolis: Minnesota University Press, 1976], 96), an event taking place around 227 is narrated after the report about this controversy.

84. The option to translate the Dao in the phrase 好道言 as referring to the Daojia 道家 (with a translation "was in favor of talking about the Daoist'[s arguments]") is ruled out by a quotation of the same passage in Liu Xiaobiao's *Commentary to the Shishuo xinyu*, IV.9, 200, where this phrase runs, "he was a capable speaker on the Dark and elusive 能言玄遠."

85. All editions of Chen Shou's *Sanguo zhi* with Pei Songzhi's *Commentary*, vol. 2, 319, write here 通于意外. In view of the formula 象外之意 in the next phrase, which refers back to the above formula, one should expect 通於象外. Yang Shen's 楊愼 (1488–1559) *Danqian zalu* 丹鉛雜錄, which assembles interesting tidbits from encyclopedias, cites (10.6b) the lost *Jin yang qiu* 晉陽秋 (misspelled here as 晉春秋) by Sun Sheng 孫盛 (299–369), which gives this correct reading. Wang Baoxuan, *Zhengshi xuanxue*, 325, was the first to discover this.

86. He Shao, *Xun Can [bie] zhuan*, quoted in Pei Songzhi's commentary to Chen Shou, *Sanguo zhi* vol. 2, 319 ff.

87. See p. 20.

88. *Jin yang qiu* 晉陽秋, quoted in Pei Songzhi's commentary to Chen Shou, *Sanguo zhi*, vol. 2, 319.

89. For a more detailed discussion of the term *li* 理, see pp. 108–121.

90. Xun Can might not have known the *Zhuangzi*, which at this juncture was not widely available.

91. He Shao, *Xun Can biezhuan*, quoted in Liu Xiaobiao, *Commentary to the Shishuo xinyu* (Shanghai: Guji Press, 1982), IV.9.200 (Mather, *Shih-shuo Hsin-yu*, 96).

92. *Jinshu*, vol. 4 (Beijing: Zhonghua Press, 1974), 1243.

93. *Wei Jie biezhuan* 衛玠別傳, quoted in Liu Xiaobiao's *Commentary to the Shishuo xinyu*, 8.51, p. 450. The translation of this commentary is missing in Mather, *Shih-shuo Hsin-yu*, 226.

94. Jiao Xun, *Mengzi zhengyi*, 397.

95. Wang Baoxuan, *Zhengshi xuanxue*, 329.

96. See *The Craft of the Chinese Commentator*, 16–20.

97. Wang Baoxuan, *Zhengshi xuanxue*, 327.

98. He Shao, *Xun Can biezhuan*, quoted in Liu Xiaobiao on *Shishuo xinyu* IV.9, 200.

99. R. Wagner, "Lebensstil und Drogen im chinesischen Mittelalter," *T'oung Pao* LIX:79–178 (1973).

100. Tang Yongtong, "Wei Jin xuanxue he wenxue lilun," *Zhongguo zhexueshi yanjiu* 1:37–45 (1980), ms. based on talks given in Kunming in 1942 or 1943 and at the University of California, Berkeley, in 1947 or 1948, edited by Professor Tang's son, Tang Yijie, first published in *Zhongguo zhexueshi yanjiu* 1: 37–45 (1980). The paper has inspired a fair number of mainland Chinese scholars to pursue research in this direction. See also Wang Baoxuan, *Zhengshi xuanxue*, 350 ff.

101. Yuan Jixi, *Liu chao meixue* (Beijing: Beijing daxue Press, 1989), 96 ff.

102. Wang Baoxuan, *Zhengshi xuanxue*, 347–49.

103. A good summary of the relevant research is given by Wang Baoxuan, *Zhengshi xuanxue*, 334–56.

104. *Jin zhugong zan*, quoted in Liu Xiaobiao on *Shishuo xinyu* 4.12, 202 (Mather, *Shih-shuo hsin-yu*, 97).

105. Ding Guanzhi, "Ruan Ji," in Fang Litian and Yu Shoukui, eds., *Zhongguo gudai zhuming zhexuejia pingzhuan, xubian*, 2:106 ff.

106. *Liezi*, 4.121. See Graham, *The Book of Lieh-tzu*, 78. Graham translates "he does not govern, yet there is no disorder" and similarly for the subsequent phrases. This translation might fit a pre-Qin text when the provocation of the wu-wei theory was still to be felt. By the time the *Liezi* was compiled, the argument had shifted. It was exactly through his non-governing that chaos was avoided, not despite his non-governing.

107. The quotation is written in interlocking parallel style and is appended to the *Liezi* phrase taken from the *Lunyu*. Thus the main thrust is to explain this phrase about the Sage. Xiahou Xuan, however, explains it in parallel to statements in the *Laozi* about the Dao. The conclusion is explicitly given only for the Sage, but as the expression "forced to give it a name" from the *Laozi* in this section proves, it in fact refers to the Dao as well as the Sage. That is why I have treated the subsequent statement as a *pars pro toto* construction and have written it into the c section, which refers to both chains, a and b.

108. *Liezi*, 4.121.

109. See Wang Baoxuan, *Zhengshi xuanxue*, 131, for the detailed argument.

110. Conjecture proposed by Feng Zengquan, Jiang Hongzhou, and Lu Xueyi in their article "He Yan," in Fang Litian and Yu Shoukui, eds., *Zhongguo gudai*

zhuming zhexuejia pingzhuan, xubian 2, 75, on the basis of the parallel to the subsequent sentence.

111. The two conjectures are necessitated by the content; the punctuation proposed by Feng et al., op. cit., 76, to put a semicolon after 象, does not seem to provide a legible and meaningful text.

112. Zhang Zhan on *Liezi*, 4.121. Sadly, Yang Bojun has not edited the texts quoted in this commentary, and the editing by Feng Zengquan et al. is not rigorous enough. Most authors have had troubles with this passage. He Changqun, *Wei Jin qingtan sixiang chulun* (Shanghai: Shangwu Press, 1946), 66, and Tang Changru, *Wei Jin nan bei chao shi luncong* (Beijing: Sanlian Press, 1978), 324, break off after 象 without further indication and continue with excerpts from Xiahou Xuan's essay. Wing-tsit Chan translates the entire passage in his *A Source Book in Chinese Philosophy*, 324 ff. As only a few passages survive from He Yan's hands, these have to be treated with special care. A few critical remarks may be in order. The passage 此比於無所有故有所有矣而於有所之中當與無所有相從而與夫有所有者不同 is translated here, "It is like possessing nothing and thereby possessing everything. However in possessing things one should be in harmony with possessing nothing, and be different from those who possess what they have." From the subsequent analogy to the relationship of Yin and Yang to things of the same category, it is clear that the text does not intend to give moral advice, but that it deals with the fact that the Dao, even though being manifest within that which has what is has (the specific features), remains linked to the nameless. The passage 而同於遠 is translated, "They are all different while nearby, but similar while far away," although from the context it is quite clear that they are different "from what is nearby" and the same with "what is far away." This changes the meaning of the entire passage, which is to illustrate how the Dao is within the specific entities without losing its characteristic of not possessing any of the specificities of these entities. The difficult passage 故處有名之域而沒其無名之象由以在陽之近體而忘其自有陰之遠類也 Chan translates: "Therefore, though [Chan leaves the 雖 before the 處 in place], it dwells in the realm of the nameable, it shows no sign of the nameless. It is like a substance at a distance [Chan leaves 陽之遠體] characterized by Yang forgetting that it has a distant counterpart in Yin." This seems quite incomprehensible.

113. Lou Yulie, ed., *Wang Bi ji jiaoshi*, vol. 2, 609. See also pp. 80ff. of the present study.

114. Wagner, *The Craft of a Chinese Commentator*, ch. 2.

115. Wang Bi, "Laozi weizhi lilüe," in R. Wagner, *A Chinese Reading of the Daode jing*, p. 83. A text with translation and notes will be found there.

116. Cf. Wagner, *The Craft of a Chinese Commentator*, 129–30, for a full translation and discussion of this *Shishuo xinyu* anecdote.

117. Wang Bi, *Lunyu shiyi*, in Lou Yulie, ed., *Wang Bi ji jiaoshi*, vol. 2, 624 ff.

118. For the texts and translations, see Wagner, *A Chinese Reading of the Daode jing*, 88–89.

119. Wang Bi, *Zhouyi zhu*, in Lou Yulie, ed., *Wang Bi ji jiaoshi*, vol. 1, 336.

120. Cf. *Laozi* 16.1ff and 26.1 for the notion "calm" and *Laozi* 73.6 for "silent."

121. Wang Bi, *Zhouyi zhu*, in Lou Yulie, ed., *Wang Bi ji jiaoshi*, vol. 1, 337.

122. See R. Wagner, *A Chinese Reading of the Daode jing*, 207.

123. Ibid.

124. He Changqun, *Wei Jin qingtan sixiang chulun*, 67 ff., is, I believe, the first to have pointed out the similarity between the notion of *zhong* 中 and the *Xuanxue* notion of negativity. An example is *Laozi* 5.4.

125. For this technique of terminological implosion, see Wagner, *The Craft of a Chinese Commentator*, 281–98.

126. Wang Bi, *Zhouyi lüeli*, section Ming tuan 明彖 , in Lou Yulie, ed., *Wang Bi ji jiaoshi*, vol. 2, 591; see footnote 1 to my translation of *Laozi* 11, *A Chinese Reading of the Daode jing*, 433.

127. Wang Bi, *Laozi weizhi lilüe* 2.28; Wagner, *A Chinese Reading of the Daode jing*, 89.

128. The expression appears in *Zhuangzi jishi*, 22.763, in a statement by Confucius; there, however, Guo Xiang's reading suggests that the phrase 取於是者 也 has to be translated "is taken from this," in the sense that "the Sage's capacity to love men in the end is endless" is "taken from 取於 this," that "things exist without beginning."

129. *LZWZLL*, 2.21 ff.; Wagner, *A Chinese Reading of the Daode jing*, 88–89.

130. Tang Yongtong has pointed to the beginning of the *Yinwenzi* 尹文子 as a possible precedent, but the parallels do not go beyond the two terms appearing in the same line. Cf. *Yinwenzi*, in Wang Qixiang, *Zhou Qin mingjia sanzi jiaoquan* (Beijing: Guji Press, 1957), 22. In a similarly vague manner, the two terms appear in Liu Yi's 劉廙 *Zheng lun* 政論, as quoted in Tang Yongtong and Ren Jiyu, *Wei Jin xuanxue zhong de shehui zhengzhi sixiang lüelun* (Shanghai: Shanghai renmin Press, 1956), 12, n. 5. See also Harbsmeier, *Science and Civilization in China*, 355. This vague use remained possible even after Wang Bi, as Ouyang Jian 歐陽建 (ca. 265–300) used *ming* and *cheng* synonymously in his "On Words Fully Expressing Meaning 言盡意論," quoted in *Yiwen leiju* vol. 3, p. 541, line 7.

131. *LZWZLL*, 2.12 ff.

132. This statement refers to the *Wenyan* on hexagram 1 of the *Zhouyi*, which says "the Great Man merges his capacity with that of Heaven and Earth" 夫大

人者與天地合其德. Wang Bi, *Zhouyi zhu*, in Lou Yulie, ed., *Wang Bi ji jiaoshi*, vol. 1, 217.

133. Wang Bi, *Lunyu shiyi* in Lou Yulie, ed., *Wang Bi ji jiaoshi* vol. 2 (?), 626.

134. *Zhouyi yinde*, *Xici* 上, 40.4.

135. See Wagner, *The Craft of a Chinese Commentator*, 150–70.

136. Wang Bi, "*Zhouyi lüeli*," in Lou Yulie, ed., *Wang Bi ji jiaoshi*, p. 609. In the *Xici* 上 12, the formula for "fully exhaust the actual situation 盡情 " here in Wang Bi's text is "fully exhaust the actual and the false 盡情偽." Wang Bi retroactively imposed the rules of interlocking parallel style on this passage by reducing the triplet 盡情偽 to the couplet 盡情 so as to achieve strict parallelism with the couplet 盡意 in the preceding parallel phrase. For another translation, see Richard John Lynn, *The Classic of Changes, a new translation of the I Ching as interpreted by Wang Bi* (New York: Columbia University Press, 1994), pp. 31f.

NOTES–CHAPTER 2

1. Feng Yan, *Xian zhi fu*, *Hou Han shu* 18B, 1001.

2. Feng Yan, Preface to *Xian zhi fu*, quoted in his biography, *Hou Han shu* 18B, 985.

3. Zhongchang Tong, *Changyan*, quoted in his biography Hou Han shu 39, 1644.

4. Huan Tan, quoted from the Commentary to the Wenxuan in Yan Kejun, *Quan shanggu sandai Qin Han sanguo liuchao wen, quan Hou Han wen* (Peking, Zhonghua, 1985), 15.8b, 551b.

5. Feng Yan, *Xian zhi fu*, *Hou Han shu* 18B, 1001. Interestingly, the phrase is in a parallel construction with the parallel reading "he praised Confucius' understanding of the decrees [of Heaven]," which means that the easy juxtaposition of Confucius and Laozi was already quite widely accepted.

6. Fu Yi, *Qiji*, quoted from the *Yiwen leiju*, in Yan Kejun, *Quan shanggu . . . wen, quan Hou Han wen*, 43.4a, 706. The text is a dialogue written to satirize Emperor Ming's (reg. 58–76 C.E.) total lack of interest in the promotion of worthy scholars. The expression comes from the characterization of the first partner, who pretends sickness to be allowed to stay in seclusion.

7. Zhongchang Tong, *Changyan*, quoted in his biography Hou Han shu 39, 1644.

8. Huan Tan, *Xinlun*, quoted in Yan Kejun, *Quan shanggu . . . wen, quan Hou Han wen*, 15.8a, 551b.

9. Yang Xiong, *Taixuan fu*, quoted from the *Gui wenyuan*, in Yan Kejun, *Quan shanggu . . . wen, quan Han wen*, 52.3b, 408a.

10. Zhang Heng, Introduction to *Sixuan fu*, *Hou Han shu*, 59, 1914. Zhang Heng was not really pondering philosophical problems. Just before the quoted passage, he says that he "was constantly pondering matters that had to do with planning for his body."

11. Zheng Heng, *Xuan tu*, in Yan Kejun, *Quan shanggu . . . wen, quan Hou Han wen*, 55.9a, 759a. The passage continues: "It encloses Dao and De, includes Qian and Kun, contains the Original Qi, and is endowed with that which has no source."

12. Tang Yongtong, "Wei Jin xuanxue liubie lüelun" 魏晉玄學流別略論, originally published in *Guoli Beiping daxue sishi zhounian lunwen ji*, here quoted from Tang Yongtong, *Wei Jin xuanxue lungao* (1957), reprint, *Tang Yongtong xueshu lunwen ji*, 233 ff.

13. A good example of a primarily political reading is the treatment of Xuanxue in Hou Wailu et al., *Zhongguo sixiang tongshi*, vol. 3 (Beijing: Renmin Press, 1957). In fact, a study on the period focusing very much on the social and political implications with Tang Yongtong's name on the cover was published in 1956. Tang Yongtong and Ren Jiyu, *Wei Jin xuanxue zhong de shehui zhengzhi sixiang lüelun* (Shanghai: Shanghai renmin Press, 1956). According to Tang's preface to his *Wei Jin xuanxue lungao* (Beijing: Renmin Press, 1957), 194, the book was based on his own draft of a study on Xuanxue and political theory, but Ren Jiyu "used the new [Marxist] standpoint and added more research." Obviously, the editors of the bibliography of Tang's works felt that Ren Jiyu had fundamentally altered the orientation of the book, so they did not include this title. See "Tang Yongtong zhu yi mulu," in Tang Yongtong, *Tang Yongtong xueshu lunwen ji* (Beijing: Zhonghua Press, 1983), 419.

14. Tang Yongtong, "Wei Jin xuanxue he wenxue lilun," *Zhongguo zhexueshi yanjiu* 1:37–45 (1980).

15. See, among others, Wang Baoxuan, *Zhengshi xuanxue* (Jinan: Qi Lu Press, 1987); Xu Kangsheng et al., *Wei Jin xuanxue shi* (Xi'an: Shifan daxue Press, 1989); Yu Dunkang, *He Yan Wang Bi xuanxue xintan* (Jinan: Qi Lu Press, 1991); Wang Xiaoyi, *Zhongguo wenhua de qingliu—zhengshi zhi yin* (Beijing: Zhongguo shehui kexue Press, 1991), as well as many of the authors participating in the Xuanxue conferences during the 1980s. Tang Yongtong's *Wei Jin xuanxue lungao* also has come out in Taipei under the *zi* of Tang Yongtong, Tang Xiyi 湯錫予. Mou Zongsan, who was among Tang's students, accepts a three-stage model for the development of Chinese philosophy with the pre-Qin philosophers, Xuanxue, and Song Neo-Confucianism as the main turning points, but he does not conceptualize the Han/Wei transition. See Mou Zongsan, *Caixing yu xuanli* (Taipei: Xuesheng Press, 1985).

16. Feng Youlan, "Wei Jin xuanxue guiwu lun guanyu you wu de lilun," *Beijing daxue xuebao (Zhexue shehui kexue ban)* 1:11–18 (1986). See the rebuttal in Chen Lai, "Wei Jin xuanxue de 'you' 'wu' fanchou xintan," *Zhexue yanjiu* 9: 51 ff. (1986).

17. Cf. Wallace, comp., *Outlines of the Philosophy of Aristotle*. Translated by Tang Yongtong as "Yalishiduode zhexue dagang 亞里士多德哲學大綱," *Xueheng* 學横 17–19 (1923), reprint, *Tang Yongtong xueshu lunwen ji*, 127 ff.

18. Tang Yongtong, "Wei Jin xuanxue liubie lüelun," 236.

19. *Benti lun* 本體論, for "ontology," already has an entry in the main handbook for the "new culture"; see Tang Jinggao, ed., *Xin wenhua cishu* 新文化辭書 (Shanghai: Commercial Press, 1931), 707 ff.

20. In 1942 or 1943, Tang Yongtong taught a course on the "Philosophy of the Dark," Xuanxue 玄學, at the Southwestern Union University, Kunming. He dealt with a similar topic in Berkeley in 1947–48. The lectures were not published at the time but were reconstructed by Tang's son, Tang Yijie 湯一介, from Tang's own scanty and largely English notes, as well as from students' lecture notes. In the paper "Chongyou xuanxue yu Xiang Guo shuo" (On the Relationship of the [Current within] the Philosophy of the Dark Extolling Entity with Xiang [Xiu] and Guo [Xiang]), in Tang Yongtong, *Lixue, Foxue, Xuanxue* (Beijing: Beijing daxue Press, 1991), 345, Tang uses the term *bentilun* 本體論 with the explicit equivalent of "ontology." It is quite possible that the original on which this text is based was English and did not have the Chinese term at all.

21. Tang Yongtong, "Wei Jin xuanxue liubie lüelun," 235.

22. Ibid., 239.

23. Ibid., 233. See also *Xici* 上.5 in Lou Yulie, ed., *Wang Bi ji jiaoshi*, vol. 2 (Beijing: Zhonghua Press, 1980), 545.

24. Tang Yongtong, "Yan yi zhi bian," in *Wei Jin xuanxue lungao*, 214.

25. Graham, "'Being' in Western Philosophy Compared with Shih/Fei and Yu/Wu in Chinese Philosophy," *Asia Major*, n.s., 7:79–112 (1959).

26. Wang Bi, *Zhouyi lüeli*, in Lou Yulie, ed., *Wang Bi ji jiaoshi*, vol. 2, 591.

27. The term *lun* often is rendered as the noun "essay" or the verb "to discuss." Both suggest an openness which is not part of its meaning. Its core comes out best in its use in legal terminology, where it means "subsume a given action under the existing laws and pass a judgement." Liu Xie 劉勰 (465–522) writes "basically, the lun in its substance is the instrument to determine what is right and wrong," *Wenxin diaolong yizheng*, vol. 2, 696.

28. Liu Xie, probably under the impact of the Buddhist division between sūtra and śāstra, terms that in Chinese have been rendered as *jing* 經 and *lun,* respectively, writes that the *lun* "lay out the principles by holding forth on the classics" 述經 敘理, *Wenxin diaolong yizheng*, vol. 2, 665.

29. See Wagner, *The Craft of a Chinese Commentator*, ch. 4.

30. *LZWZLL* 1.1 ff.; Wagner, *A Chinese Reading of the Daode jing*, p. 83–84.

31. From *Zhouyi yinde*, *Xici* 下 1, 45. See Lou Yulie, ed., *Wang Bi ji jiaoshi*, vol. 1, 556. Extrapolating from Han Kangbo's Commentary and Wang Bi's phrase

here, the *Xici* statement 吉凶者 貞勝者也. 天地之道 貞觀者也; 明月之道貞明者也; 天下之動 貞夫一者也 has to be translated "As to luck and misfortune, it is the standard that [is able to] overcome [them]. As to the way of Heaven and Earth, it is the standard that [is able to] observe [it]. As to the Way of sun and moon, it is the standard that makes [them] clear. As to the movements of Heaven and Earth, it is the standard indeed that unifies them." Han Kangbo defines that "standard" 貞 means 正也一也, "the correct, the One," and makes it clear that only the "standard," by being the One unfettered by specificity, is able "not to be bound by either luck nor misfortune" and thus to overcome both of them. Still, the translation of this quotation within Wang Bi's opening lines to the *Zhouyi lüeli* remains awkward. Without knowledge of the *Xici* passage, the 貞夫一者 would have to be translated in accordance with the parallel phrase 至寡者 as "the ultimate One," with the result that the phrase would read "that which controls the moving of All Under Heaven is the ultimate One." The *Xici* phrase deals with "Heaven and Earth," while Wang Bi is interested in the affairs and processes that are "moving" in "All Under Heaven," thus he changes the wording.

32. *Wang Bi ji jiaoshi*, vol. 2, 591.

33. Lu Shengjiang, "Han Wei xuefeng de yanbian yu xuanxue de chansheng," *Nankai wenxue yanjiu*, 1987, 92ff. See also Jin Chunfeng, *Handai sixiang shi* (Beijing: Zhongguo shehui kexue Press, 1987), 559 ff.

34. *LZWZLL* 2.45 ff.; Wagner, *A Chinese Reading of the Daode jing*, 90–91.

35. See the record in *Sanguo zhi* section *Weishu*, 419 ff., concerning Wang Su's 王肅 *Shengzheng lun* 聖證論.

36. Cf. Wang Bi, *Zhouyi lüeli*, section Ming xiang 明象, in Lou Yulie, ed., *Wang Bi ji jiaoshi*, 609, where Wang Bi rails against what was known to everyone concerned to be Zheng Xuan's interpretation.

37. Liu Yiqing, *Youming lu* (Beijing: Wenhua yishu Press, 1988), 114. Wagner, *The Craft of a Chinese Commentator*, 19–20.

38. Wagner, *The Craft of a Chinese Commentator*, 14–18.

39. Kaga Eiji, "Chūgoku no gori shūgi ni kansuru ikkosatsu—Gi Shin ni okeru tenjin goitsukan o chūshin to shite," *Kambun kyōshitsu*, 56:1–9 (上) (1961), 57: 1–10 (下) (1961).

40. Wang Baoxuan, *Zhengshi xuanxue*, 277 ff.

41. Wang Bi on *Laozi* 21.3, 25.2, and 55.6. See also Wagner, *The Craft of a Chinese Commentator*, 297–98.

42. *Laozi weizhi lüeli*; see Wagner, *A Chinese Reading of the Daode jing*, 403 n. 3.

43. *LZWZLL* 1.34 ff. There, "Heaven generates the five things," and "the Sage enacts the Five Teachings," which stresses the association of the *wu* 物 with Heaven and thus the material world, and of *shi* 事 with the Sage and thus the human world. See Wagner, *A Chinese Reading of the Daode jing*, 85.

44. In Wang Bi's commentary on *Laozi* 10.2, the *wu* 物 in the formula 物全 而性得 primarily refers to human beings. The same is true for the expression *wu hua* 物化, in Wang Bi on *Laozi* 10.6. In Wang Bi on *Laozi* 13.6, the *wu* 物 in 無 物可以損其身 refers to both human beings and animals. In Wang Bi on *Laozi* 24.1 物 refers to human beings. In the last *Laozi* phrase in this *zhang*, it seems to simply mean "the others."

45. The two terms are used nearly synonymously in *Laozi* 17.7 功成事遂, although in most pre-Qin usages the "achievements" would have the form of successful "processes."

46. Wang Bi on *Laozi* 38.2; Wagner, *A Chinese Reading of the Daode jing*, 247. The meaning of these terms depends on their position in the hierarchy. The *wanwu* 萬物 in this pair thus are just the subsection *wu* of the *wanwu* 萬物 of the beginning of the *LZWZLL* which encompass both the *shi* 事 and the *wu* 物.

47. *Zhouyi, Xici* 上 2; cf. ibid., 6.

48. *Zhouyi, Xici* 上/6; cf ibid. 上/12. It should be mentioned that in Wang's own reading, a single line dominates in only twenty-three out of the sixty-four hexagrams, and he does not impose this argument if the textual basis looks different; see Wang Xiaoyi, *Zhongguo wenhua de qingliu*, 193 ff.

49. *Laozi* 26.1: "The heavy is the basis of the light. The calm is the lord of the impetuous," which is commented upon by Wang Bi: "Generally speaking with regard to entities, the light cannot support the heavy, the small cannot press down the great; that which [itself] does not act makes [others] act; that which [itself] does not move controls the movement [of others]." Similarly, Wang Bi on hexagram *heng* 恆 broken top line "the calm is the lord of the excited; the resting is the master of the movements" 靜爲躁君, 安爲動主, in Lou Yulie, ed., *Wang Bi ji jiaoshi*, 380. In his comments on *Laozi* 47.1 "[Only when] not going out of doors [into All Under Heaven one has something] by means of which to cognize All Under Heaven; [only when] not peeping out of the window [to Heavenly phenomena one has something] by means of which to cognize the Way of Heaven" Wang Bi writes "as processes have a principle and things have a master," reducing the diverse terminology of the *Laozi* to the standardized terminology. The statement is repeated, with inverted terminology, in Wang Bi on 49.5: "Things will have their principle and affairs will have their master." In other cases, Wang Bi himself will volunteer this vocabulary in his comments. The terminology remains slightly fluid in places. On *Laozi* 4.1, he says about the Dao: "A shape, even though it be huge, cannot contain its [the Way's] substance; a process, even though it be all-encompassing, cannot fill its measure." Here we have a juxtaposition of 形 and 事 instead of 形 and 名. In *Laozi* 6.1, the "spirit of the valley" 谷神 is described as the "Dark Female" 玄牝. Wang reads both as symbolic expressions enriching each other. He interprets the expression "spirit of the valley" as the "non-valley in the midst of the valley"; "the valley is constituted by it, but it does not show its form" 谷以之成而不見其形, and as a consequence it is "dark" or invisible. The expression "female" brings out the social status of the valley, which is lying

low. "It resides in a lowly position. . . . Its lowly position [notwithstanding] there is no way to define it" 處卑而不可得名. On *Laozi* 38.2, Wang Bi writes about the ideal ruler that, "in making use [of the material entities,] he [would] not go by [their] shape; in regulating [affairs] he [would] not go by [their] name" 用不以 形 御不以名. In the previous pair of sentences, Wang Bi introduces the notion of the "ten thousand [material] entities" and the "ten thousand kinds of affairs," to which the succeeding two phrases refer. The same pair is repeated further down in the same commentary.

50. Wang Bi on *Laozi* 38.2.

51. See *LZWZLL* 1.8, 8, 15, 18, 20, 23, 26, 29, and 32, where the *ming* 名 are referred to as *sheng* 聲.

52. Wang Bi on *Laozi* 1.2, 14.5; for the Sage's imitation of this pattern, see Wang Bi on *Laozi* 55.1.

53. Demiéville, "Langue et littérature chinoises," *Annuaire du Collège de France* 47:152 (1947), reprint, P. Demiéville, *Choix d'Études Sinologiques (1920–1970)*, 50, seems to be the first to have noted the pattern of dividing the entities into *shi* and *wu*, which he translates *êtres* and *activités*. While I generally agree with this translation, I do not see his evidence for the occurrence of this pair in the *Liji*.

54. Christoph Harbsmeier kindly suggested that the *wu* 物 in *wanwu* 萬物 are rather "kinds of things" than "things." The *wanwu* would thus not refer to the unending multitude of things or beings in their individuality but rather to the totality of classes of things or species of beings. The *Xici* 上 7 provides a simple proof for this proposition by giving the exact number of *wu* 物 as 11,520. "the [total number of] stalks in the two sections [of the *Zhouyi*] is 11,520 which corresponds to the number of the *wanwu*." Evidently, the *Xici* did not assume that the total number of individual living beings was 11520, but that there were so many kinds of them.

55. *Yi Zhou shu zhuzi suoyin* (*A Concordance to the Yi Zhou shu*) Hong Kong: Commercial Press, 1992), 29/13/2; for the *Zuozhuan*, see *Chunqiu jingzhuan yinde* (Taipei: Ch'eng-wen, 1966), 170/文18/9, 384/昭13/5; for the *Zhouli*, see *Zhouli zhuzi suoyin* (A Concordance to the *Zhouli*) *(*Hong Kong: Commercial Press, 1993), 1.28/11/8. For the *Mozi*, see *Mozi yinde* 43/27/37.

56. Li Dingsheng and Xu Huijun, eds., *Wenzi yaoquan*, (Shanghai: Fudan daxue Press, 1988), 42 ff. Irritatingly, the *Wenzi* edition by D. C. Lau, *Wenzi zhuzi suoyin: A Concordance to the Wenzi*, 4, line 12, writes 知 for 如 in the last phrase and adds 守 into the bracket reserved for emendations. No edition supports this reading of 知, and it is not marked as a conjecture. Obviously, the reading has been transferred here from *Huanainzi zhuzi suoyin: A Concordance to the Huainanzi* (Hong Kong: Commercial Press, 1992), 1/4/25.

57. Li Dingsheng and Xu Huijun, eds., *Wenzi yaoquan*, 82.

58. *Huainanzi zhuzi suoyin*, 2.13.12.

59. *Shuoyuan zhuzi suoyin*: *A Concordance to the Shuoyuan*. 16.36/126/1.

60. Li Dingsheng and Xu Huijun, eds., *Wenzi yaoquan*, 127.3. The expression *shiwu* 事物 for the two main categories of of entities appears in pre-Qin authors such as the *Guanzi* 管子, 226, and the *Xunzi* 48/12/100. For the *Daxue*, see *Liji zhuzi suoyin*, A Concordance to the *Liji* (Hong Kong: The Commercial Press, 1992). 43.1/164/25.

61. Wagner, *A Chinese Reading of the Daode jing*, 247.

62. *Zhouyi, Xici* 上 6.

63. Wang Bi, *Zhouyi lüeli*, in *Wang Bi ji jiaoshi*, vol. 2, 591.

64. *Zhuangzi yinde, A Concordance to Chuang Tzu* (Cambridge, Mass.: Harvard University Press, 1956), 88/31/49.

65. Graham, *Chuang-tzu: The Seven Inner Chapters and Other Writings from the Book Chuang-tzu* (London: Allen & Unwin, 1981), 28.

66. This use can be found in texts such as the *Zhuangzi* 天道 chapter, 34/13/30 ff., and in the *Hanfeizi*, 7/2/2 ff. and 8/3/19 ff.

67. The *wanwu* are juxtaposed with the "trees and plants" in *Laozi* 76, which suggests that they are animate beings. In *Laozi* 34.2, they are being "clothed and fed," which suggests human beings. In *Laozi* 32.1 and 37.3, they "render themselves as guests" 自賓 to the dukes and kings who "manage to hold on to the Dao," or "they transform themselves" 自化, which again suggests human beings. In *Laozi* 5.1 and 5.2, their treatment by Heaven is juxtaposed to that of the Hundred Families by the Sage, which suggests that they belong to nature and not to society with a similar juxtaposition of the "men of the crowd" 衆人 and the *wanwu* in *Laozi* 64.8 ff. In other contexts, the expression seems to refer to the sheer totality of entities, as in *Laozi* 42, where the Dao generates the One, the One the two, the two the three, and the three the *wanwu*. Wang Bi, on occasion, also uses *wu* 物 with the meaning of "human being," as in his comments on *Laozi* 50.2, where he says 故物苟不以求離其本不以欲渝其眞 雖入軍而不可害 "that is why [only] entities [i.e., human beings] which do not become separated from their root through cravings [and] which do not pollute their true essence through desires, cannot be hurt even when 'going into battle' [and] cannot run into adversity even when 'traveling over land'."

68. The term *wu* 物 is used as a vague "something" or "object of definition" in phrases such as 道之爲物, "the Way as a thing" (*Laozi* 21.2), or "there is a thing that completes out of the diffuse" 有物混成 (*Laozi* 25.1) but also comes in a variety of contextually defined meanings ranging from "other people" (*Laozi* 24.3) to entities that are strong and therefore "age," for which Wang Bi gives the examples of the military, and of a storm (*Laozi* 30.7).

69. In *Laozi* 17.6 the Hundred Families all say in view of the "achievements completed and affairs followed through" under an enlightened ruler "we are like this [have this bountiful life] spontaneously" 我自然. There is no *ye* 也 after this

that would translate "It is our Ziran." Therefore, the phrase has to be read as translated here. Accordingly, the term is not identical to the noun *ziran* 自然 here, but the *ran* 然 remains verbal. This is Wang Bi's understanding.

70. For *xing* 性, see Wang Bi on *Laozi* 10.2 and 10.9, 17.5, 21.5, 27.2 and 27.4, 29.2, 32.2, 36.1 and 36.2, 41.5, and 45.6; for *xingming* 性命, which is identical to *xing* 性, see Wang Bi on *Laozi* 12.1; for *qing* 情, see Wang Bi on *Lunyu* 4.15, on *Laozi* 29.3, 49.5; for *zhen* 眞, see Wang Bi on *Laozi* 3.4, 4.1, 5.1, 10.1, 17.5, 21.4, 22.5, 23.3, 45.6, and 65.5; see also *zhenxing* 眞性 in Wang Bi on *Laozi* 32.2, *changxing* 常性 in Wang Bi on *Laozi* 29.2, and *wu zhi zhi* 物之致 in Wang Bi on *Laozi* 47.3.

71. *Wenzi zhuzi suoyin, A Concordance to the Wenzi* (Hong Kong: The Commercial Press, 1992), 1/3/11, 12/60/17.

72. *Zhuangzi yinde* 4/2/18, 16/6/22, 44/17/53, and 87/31/32 ff.; *Wenzi zhuzi suoyin*, 2/6/27; cf. ibid., 9/45/2 and 2/9/2.

73. *Zhouyi yinde* 20/31 *tuan*, 20/32 *tuan*, 28/45 *tuan*, 21/34 *tuan*, and 45/繫 下 1.

74. Wang Bi, *Zhouyi lüeli*, in *Wang Bi ji jiaoshi*, vol. 2, 591. The reference to the *Xici* 上.6 is not easy to appreciate. The text there runs directly after the passage quoted on pp. 105–106: 言天下之至賾而不可惡 言天下之至動而不可亂. Han Kangbo's commentary starts by saying, "This means it is not acceptable to get away from the *Yi* as a book" 易之爲書 不可遠也. In this manner, the two *buke* 不可 of the *Xici* text become advice to the reader and the object of the verbs *wu* 惡 and *luan* 亂 becomes the *Zhouyi*. According to Han Kangbo, the *Xici* phrase has to be translated: "[Even in] the greatest multitude in All Under Heaven, one should not dispise [the *Zhouyi*], and [even in] the greatest turbulence in All Under Heaven, one should not misuse [the *Zhouyi*]." Wang Bi did not read it in this manner. From the wording *bu luan* 不亂, "not chaotic," in the *Zhouyi lüeli* it is clear that Wang Bi refers to this *Xici* passage. This means that the subject of being "not chaotic" are the movements. Accordingly, he must have read this *Xici* passage as meaning: "This [the previous statement about the *tuan* 彖] means that even the most extreme movement in All Under Heaven is not possibly chaotic." From this it again follows that as much as 繁而不亂 is a rephrasing of 至動而不可亂, 衆 而不惑 is a rephrasing of 至賾而不可惡, and in particular that 惑 either was in Wang Bi's text instead of 惡, or that it is his interpretation of its meaning. The translation of Wang Bi's reading of this item then would be, "This [the previous statement about the *yao* 爻] means that even the most multitudinous in All Under Heaven is not possibly confused." Regarding the punctuation of the phrase 物无 妄然必由其理, Lou Yulie, ed., *Wang Bi ji jiaoshi*, 591, writes 物无妄然，必由 其理, while the *Sibu beiyao* edition writes 物无妄，然必由其理. The expression *wangran* 妄然 does not seem to be attested and is not listed in either dictionaries or concordances, while the *wuwang* 无妄 is well attested, not least by being the name of a *Zhouyi* hexagram. Wang Bi reads the overall meaning of this hexagram as referring to the leading line, the unbroken line in the fifth, that is, the emperor's,

position. "The majestic hard [unbroken line] is upright and correct, and acts out none of its private desires, how should there possibly be randomness?" 威剛方正私欲不行何可以妄 My translation above is based on this parallel.

75. Wang Bi makes extensive use of this notion of "automatic," *zi*自, inter-active regulation. Cf. Wang Bi on *Laozi* 10.1 萬物自賓, 10.6 物自賓而處自安, 10.9 物自濟, 18.3 六親自和、國家自治, 28.1 物自歸之, 29.2 物性自得之, 32.1 物自賓而道自得, and 32.2 天地相合則甘露不求而自降. Again, he has a basis in the *Laozi*, which addresses such an automatism in *zhang* 32, 37, and 57.

76. Wagner, *A Chinese Reading of the Daode jing*, 116–17.

77. Ibid., 249, *zhang* 38.

78. The references for the use of these new terms are to be found in the index of Guo Xiang's *Commentary*, Kitahara Mineki, ed., *Sōshi Kaku Shō chū sakuin* (Hokyushu: Hokyushu Chūgoku shoten, 1990), 395, 87, with many examples in j. 2.

79. For *shi* 失, see Wang Bi on *Laozi* 5.1 物失其眞, on 17.5 失性, on 26.5 失本 (taking up a term in the *Laozi*), on 39 passim, and on 49. For *bai* 敗, see Wang Bi on *Laozi* 2.2 and 29.2. For *shang* 傷, see Wang Bi on *Laozi* 12.1, 35.1, and 51.4; for *hai* 害, see Wang Bi on *Laozi* 60.3.

80. Paul Demiéville has given a first sketch of the early development of the concept of *li* 理 in the report on his seminar on the formation of the Chinese philo-sophical vocabulary, "Langue et littérature chinoises," *Annuaire du Collège de France* 47.151–57 (1947), reprint, Demiéville, *Choix d'Études Sinologiques*, 49 ff.

81. Cf. *Zhouyi yinde* (Taipei: Ch'eng-wen, 1966), sub 理 in V.77874; ibid., 39/繫上/1, speaks of 天下之理.

82. *Xici Zhouyi*, 40, 上3.

83. *Liji zhuzi suoyin*, A Concordance to the *Liji* (Hong Kong: The Commer-cial Press, 1992), 19.13/101/10, 13. A similar position is found in the *Guanzi*: "Ritual is that which, in accordance with the feelings of men and basing itself on the ordering principles of righteousness, makes these into regulated patterns. That is why 'ritual' means having ordering principles. The ordering principles are what clarifies the specifications by way of illustrating the meaning of righteousness." See *Guanzi jiaozheng* (Shanghai: Shanghai Shudian, 1990), ch. 13, 219. Also see W.A. Rickett, trans., *Kuan-tzu: A Repository of Early Chinese Thought*, vol. 1 (Hong Kong: Hong Kong University Press, 1965), 175.

84. *Liji zhuzi suoyin*, 19.20/102/7; cf. 19.13/101/10, /13, where music "brings out the structured order of the ten thousand things."

85. *Wenzi zhuzi suoyin*, 2/9/17, 3.4/14/21, 4/19/23, and 8/42/7.

86. Li Dingsheng and Xu Huijun, eds., *Wenzi yaoquan*, 72.

87. For the *fen* 分, see *Wenzi zhuzi suoyin*, 4/23/21, 5/26/25; for *zi* 資, see ibid., 3/13/16, 8/41/15, and 8/43/1.

88. Li Dingsheng and Xu Huijun, eds., *Wenzi yaoquan*, 127.

89. *Wenzi zhuzi suoyin*, 1/5/12, 5/24/14.

90. Ibid., 4/19/24, 4/20/2, 4/21/7, 5/26/25, 7/39/4, 9/47/6, 9/47/2, and 9/48/16.

91. Li Dingsheng and Xu Huijun, eds., "Lun *Wenzi*," in id., *Wenzi yaoquan*, 20.

92. Ibid., 148.

93. Ibid., 20. The authors argue in this direction and say that the *dao* here is "the general rule" and the *li* "the specific rule," but they arrive at this meaning only by juggling the sequence of the parts of the phrase.

94. This assessment follows the argument by Li Dingsheng and Xu Huijun, eds., "Lun *Wenzi*," in id., *Wenzi yaoquan*, 22.

95. Chen Qiyou, ed., *Hanfeizi jishi*, vol. 1 (Peking: Zhonghua Press, 1962), 365 ff. His interpunctuation between 道盡 and 稽萬物 seems to break the argument. D. C. Lau, "Taoist Metaphysics in the Chieh Lao and Plato's Theory of Forms," in Chow Tse-tsung, ed., *Wen-lin: Studies in the Chinese Humanities*, vol. 2, 104 ff., deals with this passage. He also does not break the above-mentioned phrase. Cf. also W. K. Liao, *The Complete Works of Han Fei Tzu*, vol. 1 (London: Probsthain, 1939), 191 ff. It is not quite clear to which *Laozi* passage the first part before the elephant story refers. This story ends with a quotation from *Laozi* 14 and, as the *Hanfeizi* (as opposed to the *Wenzi*) seems to deal with one *zhang* at a time, it is probable that the two pieces belong together.

96. Chen Qiyou, ed., *Hanfeizi jishi*, vol. 1, 377.

97. *Jingfa. Lun*, quoted in Li Dingsheng and Xu Huijun, eds., *Wenzi yaoquan*, 20.

98. *LZWZLL* 1.17 ff.

99. Wang Bi, on *Laozi* 4.1: "The Earth is preserving its [material] shape, [but] its capacity is unable to go beyond its carrying [the ten thousand kinds of entities]. Heaven rests in its images 懍其象, [but] its capacity is unable to go beyond its covering [the ten thousand kinds of entities]."

100. The *Laozi* begins this merger of concepts through a kind of internal commentary. The long series of negative expressions about the One in the beginning of *Laozi* 14, such as 微 "fine," 希 "inaudible," and 夷 "smooth," 其上不皦, 其下不昧, 繩繩兮不可名復歸於無物, "its upper side is not bright, its lower side is not dark; dim it is and impossible to name. It returns and relates [the entities] back to the no-thing," ends in the *Laozi* with the interpretive statement, "This [I] call the shape of the shapeless, the appearance of the no-thing" 無狀之狀無物之象. On this basis, Wang Bi reads the "fine," "inaudible," and "smooth" as expressions for "without appearance," *wu xiang* 無象, "without sound," *wu sheng* 無聲, and "without echo," *wu yin* 無響. The *Laozi* continues in its self-definition by stating, "This [I] call undifferentiated and vague" 是謂惚恍, which Wang Bi

comments "that is, impossible to define" 不可得而定. Summing up all of these expressions, Wang Bi begins his comment for the last phrase: "The featureless and nameless is the ancestor of the ten thousand kinds of entities." He proceeds in a similar manner in *Laozi* 21, 25, 32, and 41.

101. See Wagner, *The Craft of a Chinese Commentator*, 281–97.

102. The plural is appropriate not only because of its equivalent *wanwu* 萬物 but also because Wang Bi indicates with the *jie* 皆 "all" in the phrase on *Laozi* 1.2 有皆始於無, "entities all have their beginning in negativity," that a general category such as the German *das Seiende* had not been formed.

103. *LZWZLL* 2.22 ff. See note 75 and 76 there for a discussion of the problems with this phrase.

104. *LZWZLL* 2.1 ff and 5.14 ff.

105. The pair *shi* 始/*cheng* 成 is different from the pair *sheng* 生/*cheng* 成. The latter refers to physical entities *wu* 物 and processes *shi* 事 or *gong* 功. Still, on the basis of *Laozi* 51.1, 51.4 道生之, and 34.2, the term *sheng* 生, "to generate," is used as a joint term for both *shi* 始 and *cheng* 成; for example in Wang Bi on *Laozi* 34.2, "the ten thousand kinds of entities are all generated on the basis of the Dao" 萬物皆由道而生. For the meaning of the term in a particular context, one has to look again at its opposite and its position within the conceptual hierarchy.

106. *LZWZLL* 2.44.

107. *Zhuangzi yinde*, 88/31/49.

108. *Lunyu yinde* (Taipei: Ch'eng-wen, 1966), 10/6/17. Cf. also id., 14/8/9.

109. *LZWZLL* 5.7. See also Wagner, *A Chinese Reading of the Daode jing*, 96.

110. *You* 由 is defined in early dictionaries and commentaries as *zi* 自 and *cong* 從 in the sense of "from." Cf. Ruan Yuan, *Jingji zuangu*, vol. 1, 366. More relevant for Wang Bi is the verbal transitive use, documented above from the *Lunyu*. In the *Lunyu*, however, *you dao* 由道, "to base oneself on the Dao," is a conscious act of humans. This use also occurs in Wang Bi on *Laozi* 51.2, where "the people" are not basing themselves on the Way, but wherever he uses it for the ten thousand entities, he describes a structural relationship between entities and the Dao independent of anybody's decisions. Wang Bi uses both the direct transitive form and the *suo* 所 construction. An example of the transitive form is his comment on *Laozi* 14.2: "One wishes to say it [the One] does not exist? [The fact still remains] that the entities are based on it for their completion" 欲言無邪而物由之以成. Cf. also Wang Bi on *Laozi* 21.4, and 21.6, 25.1, and 25.5, 34.2, 37.1, 38.1, and 51.1. The *suo* construction we find in Wang Bi on *Laozi* 51.2 道者 物之所由也: "The Dao is that which is the basis for the [ten thousand kinds of] entities; cf. also Wang Bi on *Laozi* 6.1, 25.6, 34.2, and 34.3.

111. *LZWZLL* 4.24; Wagner, *A Chinese Reading of the Daode jing*, 95.

112. Wagner, *The Craft of a Chinese Commentator*, 231–48.

113. Wagner, *A Chinese Reading of the Daode jing*, 242.

114. I am not sure that I understand this argument. Often in such cases there will be a phonetic pun providing an etiological explanation for the link in meaning of two characters related in sound. This also is the case here, but the claim "that is why 'receipt' is taken as a name for it" still remains unclear. I would suggest that Wang Bi here deals with the change in word class, although no such notion existed. *De* 得, "get, receive," as a verb, by necessity, is an event and it is characteristic of an event that it is temporary and not permanent. The *de* 德 is a noun, and Wang makes it clear that this is "permanent," *chang*. It thus denotes a "constant receiving."

115. This refers to the two trigrams out of which the hexagram *fu* 復 is composed. The lower trigram consists of an unbroken line at the bottom and two broken lines above it, and it has the meaning of *zhen* 震, "tremor," which also is defined as *lei* 雷, "thunder." The upper trigram consists of three broken lines, and it has the meaning of *kun* 坤, "female," which also is identified as "earth," *di* 地. The *xiang* 象 for the hexagram *fu* 復 describes the implied image with the words "the thunder [comes to] rest in the midst of the earth—this is *fu*, "return" 雷在地中復.

116. As opposed to the use of the term *desire* elsewhere in Wang Bi's *Laozi*, it does not carry destructive connotations here. The "desires" here refer to the preset, interactive dynamics of coming from the "nature" of entities.

117. The term recurs in the *LZWZLL* 6.77, see Wagner, *A Chinese Reading of the Daode jing*, 106, in the end of Wang Bi's commentary on *Laozi* 38, and in Wang Bi on *Laozi* 39.3.

NOTES–CHAPTER 3

1. Hatano Tarō, *Rōshi Ō chū kōsei*, A-3, No. 15 (1953), 26, follows Tao Hongqing in suggesting that the word order had been scrambled and restored it to 亦復與三大爲匹, "and thus again he [the king] too is a match to the three [other] Great Ones," which means he read this as one phrase, as I have done. Other scholars such as Lou Yulie and Shima Kuniō pause between 亦復爲大 and 與三 匹, but it is unclear what Wang Bi's argument would be in this flat statement.

2. Wagner, *A Chinese Reading of the Daode jing*, 254.

3. For Heaven and Earth, see *Laozi* 5, 16, and 25; for the valley, see *Laozi* 6.1, 15.3, 28.5, and 41.6; for the spirit, see *Laozi* 29.1; for the king, see *Laozi* 25.

4. Similar passages can be found in Wang Bi on *Laozi* 72.1; see infra. See also Wang Bi on *Laozi* 57.5: "What the ruler desires will be quickly followed by the people['s own ambitions]."

5. Lou Yulie, ed., *Wang Bi ji jiaoshi*, vol. 1, (Beijing: Zhonghua Press, 1980), 317.

6. See my "Lebensstil und Drogen im chinesischen Mittelalter," *T'oung Pao* LIX:94ff. (1973).

7. See *LZWZLL* 4.1 ff. Wagner, *A Chinese Reading of the Daode jing*, 94.

8. *Laozi* 2.2 ff. "This is why the Sage takes residence in management without interference and practices teaching without words." The first phrase is commented upon by Wang Bi: "[The other entities'] That-which-is-of-itself-what-it-is is sufficient [in itself]; interfering with it would destroy it." The second statement is commented on: "The [other entities'] intelligence is sufficient in itself; interfering with it would lead [them] to falsehood."

9. Wang Bi on *Laozi* 29.2.

10. Wang Bi reads the strong line in the fifth position in many hexagrams as a man in the ruling position who is in danger, or outright harmful in his actions. Inversely, the weak lines in this position generally are seen as embodying a proper understanding of the dialectics of politics. Evidence for this will be found, among others, in the first five hexagrams.

11. See Wagner, "Ban Gu and the End of History," unpublished manuscript, 1995.

12. There is a different textual tradition that reads 能知古始. Oddly, the transmitted Wang Bi texts all have 能, but Wang Bi's *Laozi* clearly had 以, while the Heshang gong texts all have 以, although the Heshang gong commentary clearly reads 能, which runs counter to the general trend of textual developments between these two families. With the *neng* 能, however, the parallelism is broken. The Heshang gong commentary links the 能知古始 phrase directly to the last phrase of this *zhang* 是謂道紀, by writing, "people are able to discern that at the fundamental beginning of oldest antiquity there was the One; this [One] is called the controlling principle of the Dao" 人能知上古本始有一是謂道之綱紀, which implies a reading of the *Laozi* phrase, "one is able to discern the oldest beginning. It is called the principle of the Way." It is not clear where this ability should come from.

13. *LZWZLL* 1.45. Wagner, *A Chinese Reading of the Daode jing*, 85.

14. Ban Gu, *Hanshu*, vol. 13 (Beijing: Zhonghua Press,1964), 20:863 ff.

15. See Wagner, "Ban Gu and the End of History."

16. Wang Bi on *Laozi* 38; Wagner, *A Chinese Reading of the Daode jing*, 244.

17. Ibid.

18. Ibid.

19. Ibid.

20. Wang Bi on *Laozi* 5.1.

21. Wang Bi on the *Laozi* 10.2. Wagner, *A Chinese Reading of the Daode jing*, 148.

22. See, for a full translation, Wagner, *The Craft of a Chinese Commentator*, 129–30.

23. Wang Bi on *Laozi* 38; Wagner, *A Chinese Reading of the Daode jing*, 245.

24. See Waley, *The Analects of Confucius* (London: Allen & Unwin, 1938), 123 f.

25. Wang Bi, *Lunyu shiyi*, in Lou Yulie, ed., *Wang Bi ji jiaoshi*, vol. 2, 624.

26. It is not entirely clear exactly how the Sage imitates these features of the Way. Three items are mentioned for the Sage instead of the two for the Dao. Because his "making non-interference his residence" and his "practicing teaching without words" are always mentioned together, these might form a single item, although it would clearly break the parallelism of the phrase. I therefore assume that these two are his way of emulating the Dao's two features. His being "intangible but still existent" is quoted from a statement about the "root of Heaven and Earth" in *Laozi* 6.1, which refers to the Dao rather than to the Sage, and there it is commented that, against an assumption that it exists, it may be argued that it does not show its form, while against an assumption that it does not exist, it may be argued that all entities are based on it. It is the Sage's elusiveness that enables the people to "attain their true [nature]."

27. The very first phrase of *Laozi* 16 is controversial and the commentary might be badly transmitted. This has resulted in different punctuations of modern editors, such as Shima Kuniō and Lou Yulie, as well as different emendations. It is unclear whether the Sage "brings about" their emptiness and "makes them hold onto" stillness, or whether he himself reaches emptiness and holds on to stillness, which then is defined in the commentary as the ultimate of the entities. It is clear, however, that the perception of the Eternal is based on the traces it leaves in the dynamics of entities.

28. A similar definition is in *LZWZLL* 1.17ff., see the translation in Wagner's *A Chinese Reading of the Daode jing*, 84.

29. *LZWZLL* 6.29. Wagner, *A Chinese Reading of the Daode jing*, 101.

30. See infra, 192ff.

31. Wang Bi, *Lunyu shiyi*, in Lou Yulie, ed., *Wang Bi ji jiaoshi*, vol. 2, 626.

32. Commenting on *Lunyu* 1.2: "It is rare that someone who is full of filial piety and does his duty as a younger brother would oppose his superiors, but it never happens that someone who does not oppose his superiors should enjoy rebelling! The gentleman focuses on the root, and, once the root is firmly established, his [entire] Way will come to life. As to filial piety and respect for the older brother—these are the root for his acting humanely," Wang Bi writes: "To be close and affectionate [out of one's] That-which-is-of-itself-what-it-is is filial

piety, spreading the affection to other beings is humaneness." 自然親愛爲孝推愛及物爲仁. In this commentary passage, filial piety is directly emanating from *ziran*, and humaneness again rests on filial piety.

33. Wang Bi, *Lunyu shiyi*, in Lou Yulie, ed., *Wang Bi ji jiaoshi*, vol. 2, 625.

34. Liu Zehua, "Wang Bi mingjiao chu ziran de zhengzhi zhexue he wenhe de jun zhu zhuanzhi sixiang" (Wang Bi's Political Philosophy of Social Regulations Emerging out of That-which-is-of-itself-what-it-is and His Thinking of a Moderate Autocracy), *Nankai xuebao* 4:24 (1993).

35. See Si Xiuwu, *Huang Lao xueshuo yu Han chu zhengzhi pingyi* (Taipei: Xuesheng Press, 1992).

36. Recently, Hans van Ess has argued that the early Han Huang/Lao thinking is more of a factional construct by Sima Qian than a historic reality; see van Ess, "The Meaning of Huang-Lao in Shiji and Hanshu," *Études Chinoises* 12:2: 162–77 (fall 1993). There seems to be some evidence, however, that the early Han established a pattern of moving to a less centralized, easier set of policies after the years of war and the establishment of a new dynasty, a pattern that has been repeated in Wei but kept alive at least into the Song dynasty, the earlier phase of which is again characterized by an emphasis on the *Laozi*'s political philosophy with the emperor himself coming out with a new commentary.

37. *LZWZLL* 6.72–73; Wagner, *A Chinese Reading of the Daode jing*, 105.

38. *LZWZLL* 2.44; Wagner, *A Chinese Reading of the Daode jing*, 90.

39. *LZWZLL* 6.1; Wagner, *A Chinese Reading of the Daode jing*, 98.

40. H. von Senger, *Strategeme*.

41. Luhmann, *Macht* (Stuttgart: Enke, 1975).

42. Wagner, *The Craft of a Chinese Commentator*, 16–17.

43. Wang Xiaoyi, *Zhongguo wenhua de qingliu—zhengzhi zhi yin* (Beijing: Zhonghua shehui kexue Press, 1991), 54 ff., argues this point. This book became suddenly popular and was quickly reprinted in 1992 because of some political double entendre. It argued that the coup of 249 against He Yan and Cao Shuang and their associates had been led by a band of hard-core conservatives and old military leaders around Sima Yi who tried to stem the tide of the reforms. In the end, while they crushed and killed the reformers, they still were forced to continue their policies, because these were what the times demanded. The echo with the events after 1989 is clearly audible, and this probably explains the inordinate amount of attention the book has received. Its idealization of the love of spiritual freedom of the *zhengshi* scholars has been implicitly criticized in the paper by Liu Zehua, quoted above in note 34.

Bibliography

Assmann, Aleida, ed. *Weisheit. Archäologie der literarischen Kommunikation III.* München: Fink Verlag, 1991.

Ban Gu 班固. *Hanshu* 漢書. 12 vols. Beijing: Zhonghua Press, 1964.

Chan, Wing-tsit. *A Sourcebook in Chinese Philosophy.* Princeton, N.J.: Princeton University Press, 1963.

———. *The Way of Lao-tzu.* Indianapolis and New York: Bobbs-Merrill, 1963.

Chen Guying 陳鼓應. *Lao Zhuang xin lun* 老莊新論. Hong Kong: Zhonghua Press, 1991.

———. "Lun '*Xicizhuan*' shi Qixia daojia zhi zuo—Wu lun 'Yizhuan' fei rujia dianji" 論 '繫辭' 傳是齊下道家之作——五論 '易傳' 非儒家典籍. *Daojia wenhua yanjiu* 道家文化研究 2:355–65 (1992).

———. "'Tuanzhuan' yu *Lao Zhuang*," '彖傳' 與老莊, in Chen Guying, *Lao Zhuang xin lun*, pp. 277–93.

———. "'Yizhuan. Xici' suoshou *Laozi* sixiang de yingxiang—Jian lun 'Yizhuan' fei rujia dianji nai Daojia xitong zhi zuo," '易傳. 繫辭' 所受老子思想的影響——兼論 '易傳' 非儒家典籍乃道家系統之作, in Chen Guying, *Lao Zhuang xin lun*, pp. 294–313. Originally published in *Zhexue yanjiu* 1:34–42, 52 (1989).

———. "'Yizhuan. Xici' suoshou *Zhuangzi* sixiang de yingxiang" '易傳. 繫辭' 所受莊子思想 的影響, in Chen Guying, *Lao Zhuang xin lun*, pp. 314–30. Republished in *Zhexue yanjiu* 4:51–58 (1992).

———. "'Yizhuan' yu Chuxue Qixue," '易傳' 與楚學齊學, in Chen Guying, *Lao Zhuang xin lun*, pp. 331–46. Republished in *Daojia wenhua yanjiu* 道家文化研究 1:143–56 (1992).

Chen Lai 陳來. "Wei Jin xuanxue de 'you' 'wu' fanchou xintan" 魏晉玄學的 "有" "無" 範疇新探. *Zhexue yanjiu* 哲學研究 9:51–57 (1986).

Chen Qiyou 陳奇猷, ed. *Hanfeizi jishi* 韓非子集釋. 2 vols. Peking: Zhonghua Press, 1962. Cf. Liao, *The Complete Works of Han Fei Tzu.*

———, ed. *Lüshi chunqiu jiaoshi* 呂氏春秋校釋. 2 vols. Shanghai: Xuelin Press, 1990.

Chen Shou 陳壽. *Sanguo zhi* 三國志. 5 vols. Beijing: Zhonghua Press, 1973.

———. *Sanguo zhi* 三國志. Bonaben 百衲本 ed. Taipei: Shangwu Press, 1967.

———. *Sanguo zhi* 三國志. (Photomechanical reprint of the Wuyingdian 武英殿 ed. of 1739), in *Ershiwu shi* 二十五史. Shanghai: Shanghai guji Press, 1991.

Chow Tse-tsung, ed. *Wen-lin, Studies in the Chinese Humanities*. Vol. 2. Madison: Department of East Asian Languages and Literature of the University of Wisconsin and NTT Chinese Language Research Center, Institute of Chinese Studies, the Chinese University of Hong Kong, Hong Kong, 1989.

Chunqiu jingzhuan yinde 春秋經傳引得. Reprint, Taipei: Ch'eng-wen, 1966.

Cleary, Thomas. *Further Teachings of Lao-tzu: Understanding the Mysteries. A Translation of the Taoist Classic Wen-tzu*. Boston: Shambhala, 1991.

Demiéville, Paul M. *Choix d'Études Sinologiques (1921–1970)*. Leiden: E. J. Brill, 1973.

———. "Langue et littérature chinoises. Résumé des cours de 1947–1948." *Annuaire du Collège de France* 47:151–57 (1947). Reprinted in P. Demiéville, *Choix d'Études Sinologiques (1921–1970)*, pp. 49–55.

Ding Guanzhi 丁冠之. "Lun Ji Kang de zhexue sixiang" 論稽康的哲學思想. *Zhexue yanjiu* 4:63–68 (1980).

———. "Ruan Ji" 阮籍, in Fang Litian and Yu Shoukui, eds., *Zhongguo gudai zhuming zhexuejia pingzhuan, xubian* 2, pp. 91–132.

Dong Zhongshu 董仲舒. *Chunqiu fanlu* 春秋繁露, in *Sibu congkan*. Shanghai: Commercial Press, 1929–1934.

Du Yu 杜預. *Chunqiu jingzhuan jijie* 春秋經傳集解. 2 vols. Shanghai: Shanghai guji Press, 1988.

———. "Chunqiu xu 春秋序," in Ruan Yuan, ed., *Shisan jing zhushu*, vol. 2, pp. 1703–09.

Fan Ye 范曄. *Hou Han shu* 後漢書. Peking: Zhonghua, 1965.

Fang Litian 方立天. "Han dai jingxue yu Wei Jin xuanxue—Lun woguo qianqi fengjian shehuizhong guanfang zhexue de yanbian" 漢代經學與魏晉玄學——論我國前期封建社會中官方哲學的演變. *Zhexue yanjiu* 3:48–59 (1980).

Fang Litian and Yu Shoukui 于首奎, eds., *Zhongguo gudai zhuming zhexuejia pingzhuan, xubian* 2 中國古代著名哲學家評傳, 續編 2. Jinan: Qi Lu Press, 1982.

Fang Xuanling 房玄齡. *Jinshu* 晉書. 10 vols. Beijing: Zhonghua Press, 1974.

Feng Youlan 馮友蘭. "Wei Jin xuanxue guiwu lun guanyu you wu de lilun" 魏晉玄學貴無論關于有無的理論. *Beijing daxue xuebao (Zhexue shehui kexue ban)* 北京大學學報 (哲學社會科學版) 1:11–18 (1986).

———. *Zhongguo zhexue shi* 中國哲學史. Shanghai: Shangwu Press, 1934.

Feng Zengquan 馮增銓, Jiang Hongzhou 姜宏周, Lu Xueyi 陸學藝, "He Yan" 何

晏, in Fang Litian and Yu Shoukui, eds., *Zhongguo gudai zhuming zhexuejia pingzhuan, xubian* 2, pp. 49–91.

Franke, Otto. *Studien zur Geschichte des konfuzianischen Dogmas und der chinesischen Staatsreligion: Das Problem des T'schun-ts'iu und Tung Tschung-schu's T'schun-ts'iu fan lu*. Abhandlungen aus dem Gebiet der Auslandskunde, Band 1. Hamburg: L. Friederichsen & Co., 1920.

Gentz, Joachim. *Das* Gongyang zhuan. *Auslegung und Kanonisierung der* Frühlings- und Herbstannalen (Chunqiu). Opera Sinologica 12. Wiesbaden: Harrassowitz, 2001.

Graham, Angus C. "'Being' in Western Philosophy Compared with Shih/Fei and Yu/Wu in Chinese Philosophy," *Asia Major*, n.s. 7:79–112 (1959).

———. *The Book of Lieh-tzu*. London: John Murray, 1960.

———. *Chuang-tzu: The Seven Inner Chapters and Other Writings from the Book* Chuang-tzu. London: Allen & Unwin, 1981.

Guanzi jiaozheng 管子校正. (Dai Wang 戴望, ed.), in *Zhuzi jicheng*. Shanghai: Shanghai shudian, 1990.

Hachiya Kuniō 蜂屋邦夫. "Gen jin i ron to gen fu jin i ron." 言盡意論と言不盡意論 *Tōyō bunka kenkyūshō kiyō* 86:105–51 (1981).

Hanfeizi jishi. See Chen Qiyou, ed., *Hanfeizi jishi*.

Hanfeizi suoyin 韓非子索引, Beijing: Zhonghua, 1982.

Harbsmeier, Christoph. *Science and Civilization in China, Vol. VII.1: Language and Logic*. Cambridge: Cambridge University Press, 1998.

Hatano Tarō 波多野太郎. *Rōshi Ō chū kōsei* 老子王注校正. Yokohama shiritsu daigaku kiyō 横濱市立大學紀要. Series A-2, No. 8 (1952); Series A-3, No. 15 (1953); Series A-8, Nō. 27 (1954).

———. "Rōshi Ō chu kōsei zokuhō" 老子王注校正續補, in Fukui hakushi shōju kinen rombunshū kankokai 福井博士頌壽記念論文集刊行會, ed., *Fukui Hakushi shōju kinen Tōyō bunka ronshū* 福井博士頌壽記念東洋文化論集. Tokyo: Waseda University Press, 1969, pp. 843–52.

———. "Ōchū Rōshi no fukugen ni tsuite" 王注老子の復原について. *Tōhō shūkyō*. 東方宗教 7:77–78 (1955).

He Changqun 賀昌群. *Wei Jin qingtan sixiang chulun* 魏晉清談思想初論. Shanghai: Shangwu Press, 1946.

Hou Han shu 後漢書. See Fan Ye.

Hou Wailu 候外盧 et al. *Zhongguo sixiang tongshi* 中國思想通史. 6 vols. Beijing: Renmin Press, 1957–1958.

Huainanzi zhuzi suoyin 准難子逐字索引. *A Concordance to the Huainanzi*. Hong Kong: Commercial Press, 1992.

Huang Kan 皇侃. *Lunyu jijie yishu* 論語集解義疏, in *Congshu jicheng* First coll. vols. 481–484. Shanghai: Commercial Press, 1937.

Huangdi neijing suwen 黃帝內經素問. Beijing: Renmin weisheng Press, 1978 (reprint of the 1963 edition).

Ishida Kōdō 石田公道. "Chūgoku ni okeru chūshakushu no hattatsu" 中國に於ける注釋書の發達. *Hokkaidō musashi joshi tenki daigaku kiyō* 北海道武藏女子短期大學紀要 4:1–73 (1971).

Jiao Xun 焦循, comm. *Mengzi zhengyi* 孟子正義, in *Zhuzi jicheng* vol. 1. Shanghai: Shanghai shudian, 1990.

Jin Chunfeng 金春風. *Handai sixiang shi* 漢代思想史. Beijing: Zhongguo shehui kexue Press, 1987.

Jingmenshi Bowuguan 荊門市博物館, ed., *Guodian Chu mu zhujian* 郭店楚墓竹簡. Beijing: Wenwu, 1998.

Jinshu 晉書. See Fang Xuanling 房玄齡.

Kaga Eiji 加賀榮治. *Chūgoku koten kaishaku shi. Gi Shin hen* 中國古典解釋史. 魏晉篇. Tokyo: Keiso Press, 1964.

———. "Chūgoku no gori shūgi ni kansuru ikkosatsu—Gi Shin ni okeru tenjin goitsukan o chūshin to shite" 中國の合理主義に關する一考察——魏晉における天人合一觀を中心として, part I: *Kambun kyōshitsu* 漢文教室 56: 1–9 (1961); part II: *Kambun kyōshitsu* 57:1–10 (1961).

———. "Gi Shin gengaku no sui-i to sono jissō (1) 魏晉玄學の推移とその實相 (一)," part I: Hokkaidō gakugei kyōiku daigaku Jimbun ronkyū 人文論究 18: 1–43 (1958); part II: 19:29–77 (1959).

———. "Gi Shin ni okeru koten kaishaku no katachi—Ō Hitsu no Shūeki chū ni tsuite" 魏晉に於ける古典解釋のかたち——王弼の '周易注' について. *Jimbun ronkyū* 人文論究 8:1–33 (1953).

———. "Gi Shin ni ukeru koten kaishaku no katachi—To Yo no 'Shunjū kyōden shukai' ni tsuite (1)—"魏晉に於ける古典解釋のかたち——杜預の '春秋經傳集解' について (1)—, part I: *Jimbun ronkyū* 13:15–34 (1955); part II: *Jimbun ronkyū* 14:24–74 (1955); part III: *Jimbun ronkyū* 15:32–58 (1955). (Parts II and III with subtitle "To Yo no 'Shunjū kaishaku' ni tsuite" 杜預の '春秋解釋' について).

———. "Ō Hitsu yori Kan Kohaku e—Ō Hitsu no Shūeki chū ni tsuite (zoku)" 王弼より韓康伯へ——王弼の '周易注' について (續). *Jimbun ronkyū* 9: 22–35 (1953).

———. "Shoshu koshiden no taidu" 尙書孔氏傳の態度, *Hokkaidō Gakugei daigaku kiyō 'Gakugei'* 北海道學藝大學紀要 '學藝', 3.1:28–38 (1951).

Kennedy, George. "Interpretation of the Ch'un-ch'iu." *JAOS* 62:40–48 (1942).

Kitahara Mineki 北原峰樹, ed. *Rōshi Ō Hitsu chū sakuin* 老子王弼注索引. Hokyushu: Hokyushu Chūgoku shoten, 1987.

———, ed. *Sōshi Kaku Shō chū sakuin* 莊子郭象注索引. Hokyushu: Hokyushu Chūgoku shoten, 1990.

Lamotte, Etienne, ed. and tr. *L'Enseignement de Vimalakīrti*. Louvain: Publications Universitaires, 1962.

Lau, D.C. "Taoist Metaphysics in the Chieh Lao 解老 and Plato's Theory of Forms," in Chow Tse-tsung, ed., *Wen-lin: Studies in the Chinese Humanities*, vol. 2, pp. 101–21.

Legge, James. *The Chinese Classics. The Works of Mencius.* Reprint, Hong Kong: Hong Kong University Press, 1960.

Li Dingsheng 李定生. "Wenzi lun dao" 文子論道, part 1: *Fudan xuebao (Shehui kexue ban)*, 3:80–85 (1984); Part 2: 4:41–48 (1984).

Li Dingsheng and Xu Huijun 徐慧君, eds. *Wenzi yaoquan* 文子要詮. Shanghai: Fudan daxue Press, 1988.

Liao, Wen-kuei. *The Complete Works of Han Fei Tzu: A Classic of Chinese Legalism.* 2 vols. London: Probsthain, 1939.

Liezi 列子. Commentary by Zhang Zhan 張湛. See Yang Bojun 楊伯峻, ed., *Liezi jishi.*

Liji zhuzi suoyin 禮記逐字索引. A Concordance to the *Liji*. Hong Kong: Commercial Press, 1992.

Liu Baonan 劉寶楠. *Lunyu zhengyi* 論語正義, in *Zhuzi jicheng* vol. 1. Shanghai: Shanghai shudian, 1990

Liu Xiaobiao 劉孝標, comm. *Commentary to the Shishuo xinyu Shishuo xinyu zhu* 世說新語注. See Liu Yiqing, *Shishuo xinyu.*

Liu Xie 劉勰. *Wenxi diaolong yizheng* 文心彫龍義證. Shanghai: Shanghai guji Press, 1989.

Liu Yiqing 劉義慶. *Commentary to the Shishuo xinyu* 世說新語. Shanghai: Shanghai guji Press, 1982. Cf. also Yu Jiaxi comm., *Shishuo xinyu jianshu*; Liu Xiaobiao. *Commentary to the Shishuo xinyu.*

———. *Youming lu* 幽明錄. Beijing: Wenhua yishu Press, 1988.

Liu Zehua 劉澤華. "Wang Bi mingjiao chu ziran de zhengzhi zhexue he wenhe de junzhu zhuanzhi sixiang" 王弼名教出自然的政治哲學和溫和的君主專制思想. *Nankai xuebao* 南開學報 4:22–31 (1993).

Lou Yulie 樓宇烈, ed. *Wang Bi ji jiaoshi* 王弼集校釋. 2 vols. Beijing: Zhonghua Press, 1980.

Lu Shengjiang 盧盛江. "Han Wei xuefeng de yanbian yu xuanxue de chansheng" 漢魏學風的演變與玄學的產生, Nankai daxue zhongwenxi 'Nankai wenxue yanjiu' bianweihui 南開大學中文系南開文學研究編委會, ed., *Nankai wenxue yanjiu*, 1987 南開文學研究, 1987, pp. 92–127.

Lü Youren 呂友仁, ed. *Qianyantang ji* 潛研堂集. Shanghai: Shanghai guji Press, 1989. See Qian Daxin, *Qianyantang wenji.*

Luhmann, Niklas. *Macht*. Stuttgart: Enke, 1975.

Lunyu, see Waley, Arthur. *The Analects of Confucius.*

Lunyu jijie 論語集解. Sibu beiyao. Shanghai: Zhonghua Press, 1930.

Lunyu yinde 論語引得. Harvard-Yenching Institute Sinological Index Series, Suppl. No. 16. Reprint, Taipei: Ch'eng-wen, 1966.

Lynn, Richard J., trans. *The Classic of Changes: A New Translation of the I Ching As Interpreted by Wang Bi.* New York: Columbia University Press, 1994.

LZWZLL see Wang Bi, "*Laozi weizhi lilüe*" and "*Laozi zhilüe.*"

Ma Guohan 馬國翰, ed. *Yuhan shan fang ji yishu* 玉函山房輯佚書. N.p., 1884.

Mao shi zhengyi 毛詩正義, in Ruan Yuan, ed., *Shisan jing zhushu* vol. 1, 259–630.

Mather, Richard. *Shih-shuo Hsin-yu: A New Account of Tales of the World.* Minneapolis: Minnesota University Press, 1976.

Mengzi. 孟子 Legge, James. *The Works of Mencius.* The Chinese Classics. Hong Kong: Hong Kong University Press, 1960.

Mou Zongsan 牟宗三. *Caixing yu xuanli* 才性與玄理. Taipei: Xuesheng Press, 1985.

Mozi yinde 墨子引得. Harvard-Yenching Institute Sinological Index Series, Suppl. No. 21. Taipei: Ch'eng-wen, 1966.

Peterson, Willard J. "Making Connections: 'Commentary on the Attached Verbalizations' of the Book of Change." *HJAS* 42:1:67–116 (1982).

Pei Songzhi 裴松之. *Sanguo zhi zhu* 三國志注, in Chen Shou. *Sanguo zhi.*

Pi Xirui 皮錫瑞. *Jingxue lishi* 經學歷史 (with annotations by Zhou Yutong 周予同; orig. published in 1929). Beijing: Zhonghua Press, 1981.

———. *Jingxue tonglun,* 經學通論 (1907) Shanghai: Commercial Press, 1936.

Qian Daxin 錢大昕. *Qianyantang wenji* 潛研堂文集, in Qian Daxin (Lü Youren, ed.), *Qianyantang ji.*

———. (Lü Youren 呂友仁, ed.). *Qianyantang ji* 潛研堂集. Shanghai: Shanghai guji Press, 1989.

Rickett, W. Allyn. *Kuan-tzu. A Repository of Early Chinese Thought.* Vol. 1. Hong Kong: Hong Kong University Press, 1965.

Röllicke, Hermann-Josef. *Die Fährte des Herzens. Die Lehre vom Herzensbestreben (zhi) im Grossen Vorwort zum Shijing.* Berlin: Reimer, 1992.

———. "*Selbst-Erweisung.*" *Der Ursprung des ziran-Gedankens in der chinesischem Philosophie des 4. und 3. Jhs. v. Chr.* Frankfurt: Peter Lang, 1996.

Ruan Yuan 阮元, ed. *Shisan jing zhushu* 十三經注疏. 2 vols. Beijing: Zhonghua Press, 1987.

———. *Jingji zhangu* 經籍纂詁. 2 vols. Beijing: Zhonghua Press, 1982.

Sanguo zhi 三國志. See Chen Shou.

Saussy, Haun. *The Problem of a Chinese Aesthetic*. Stanford: Stanford University Press, 1983.

Shijing 詩經. See *Mao shi zhengyi*.

Shima Kuniō 島邦男. *Rōshi Kōsei* 老子校正. Tokyo: Kyūkoshōin, 1973.

Shishuo xinyu. See Liu Yiqing, *Shishuo xinyu*.

Shuoyuan zhuzi suoyin 說院逐字索引. A Concordance to the *Shuoyuan*. Hong Kong: Commercial Press, 1992.

Si Xiuwu 司修武. *Huang Lao xueshuo yu Han chu zhengzhi pingyi* 黃老學說與漢初政治平議. Taipei: Xuesheng Press, 1992.

Strauss, Leo. *Thoughts on Machiavelli*. Glencoe, Ill.: Free Press, 1959.

Su Yu 蘇與, ed. *Chunqiu fanlu yizheng* 春秋繁露義證. Peking: Zhonghua Press, 1992.

Sun Xingyan 孫星衍. "*Wenzi xu*" 文子序, in Sun Xingyan, *Wenzi tang ji*, ch. 4, pp. 1a–5a.

———. *Wenzi tang ji* 問字堂集, in Sun Xingyan, *Dainange congshu*, contained in Baibu congshu jicheng. Taipei: Yiwen, 1971.

Tang Changru 唐長孺. *Wei Jin nan bei chao shi luncong* 魏晉南北朝史論叢. Beijing: Sanlian Press, 1978.

———. "Wei Jin xuanxue zhi xingcheng ji qi fazhan" 魏晉玄學之興成及其發展, in Tang Changru, *Wei Jin nan bei chao shi luncong*, pp. 311–50.

Tang Jinggao 唐敬杲, ed. *Xin wenhua cishu* 新文化辭書. Shanghai: Commercial Press, 1931.

Tang Junyi 唐君毅. *Zhongguo zhexue yuanlun, Daolun pian* 中國哲學原論, 導論篇. Taipei: Taiwan xuesheng Press, 1986.

Tang Yijie 湯一介. *Wei Jin nanbei chao shiqi de daojiao* 魏晉南北朝時期的道教. Xian: Shanxi shifandaxue Press, 1988.

Tang Yongtong 湯用彤. "Chongyou xuanxue yu Xiang Guo xue shuo 崇有玄學與向郭學說" (On the Relationship of the [Current within] the Philosophy of the Dark Extolling Entity with Xiang [Xiu] and Guo [Xiang]), in Tang Yongtong, *Lixue, Foxue, Xuanxue*, pp. 331–52.

———. "Guiwu zhi xue (xia)—Dao An he Zhang Zhan" 貴無之學 (下)——道安和張湛. *Zhexue yanjiu* 7:62–70, 48 (1980). Reprint, in Tang Yongtong, *Lixue, Foxue, Xuanxue* 理學.佛學.玄學, pp. 295–314.

———. *Han Wei liang Jin nan bei chao fojiao shi* 漢魏兩晉南北朝佛教史. 2 vols. Beijing: Zhonghua Press, 1955.

———. *Lixue. Foxue. Xuanxue* 理學.佛學.玄學. Beijing: Beijing daxue Press, 1991.

———. *Tang Yongtong xueshu lunwen ji* 湯用彤學術論文集. Beijing: Zhonghua Press, 1983.

———. "Tang Yongtong zhu yi mulu" 湯用彤著譯目錄, in Tang Yongtong. *Tang Yongtong xueshu lunwen ji*, pp. 417–20.

———. "Wang Bi shengren youqing yishi" 王弼聖人有情義釋, originally published in 1943, in *Xueshu jikan* 學術季刊 1.3. Reprint, in *Tang Yongtong xueshu lunwen ji*, pp. 254–63.

———. "Wang Bi zhi Zhouyi Lunyu xinyi" 王弼之周易論語新義, *Tushu jikan* 圖書季刊, n.s., 4.1, 2 (1943), reprint, in *Tang Yongtong xueshu lunwen ji*, pp. 264–79 (translated by W. Liebenthal as "Wang Pi's New Interpretation of the I Ching and Lun-Yu." *HJAS* 10:124–61 (1947)).

———. "Wei Jin xuanxue he wenxue lilun" 魏晉玄學和文學理論. *Zhongguo zhexueshi yanjiu* 1:37–45 (1980).

———. "Wei Jin xuanxue liubie lüelun" 魏晉玄學流別略論, originally published in *Guoli Beiping daxue sishi zhounian lunwen ji* 國立北平大學四十週年論文集, Kunming: Guoli Beiping daxue Press, 1940; reprint in Tang Yongtong, *Wei Jin xuanxue lungao*, pp. 48–61 and in *Tang Yongtong xueshu lunwen ji*, pp. 233–44.

———. *Wei Jin xuanxue lungao* 魏晉玄學論稿. Beijing: Renmin Press, 1957.

———, trans. "Yalishiduode zhexue dagang" 亞里士多德哲學大綱, *Xueheng* 學衡 17–19, (1923). Reprint, Tang Yongtong. *Tang Yongtong xueshu lunwen ji*, pp. 127–59 (translation of E. Wallace, comp, *Outlines of the Philosophy of Aristotle*).

———. "Yan yi zhi bian" 言意之辨, originally published in Tang Yongtong, *Wei Jin xuanxue lungao*, pp. 26–47. Reprint in *Tang Yongtong xueshu lunwen ji*. Beijing: Zhonghua Press, 1983, pp. 214–32.

Tang Yongtong and Ren Jiyu 任繼愈. *Wei Jin xuanxue zhong de shehui zhengzhi sixiang lüelun* 魏晉玄學中的社會政治思想略論. Shanghai: Shanghai renmin Press, 1956.

Tao Hongqing 陶鴻慶. *Du Laozi zhaji* 讀老子札記, in Yan Lingfeng. '*Tao Hongqing Laozi Wang Bi zhu kanwu' buzheng*. Taipei: Wuqiubeizhai, 1957.

———. "Laozi Wang Bi zhu kanwu" 老子王弼注勘誤, in Yan Lingfeng. '*Tao Hongqing Laozi Wang Bi zhu kanwu' buzheng*. Taipei: Wuqiubeizhai, 1957.

Tjan Tjoe Som. *Po Hu T'ung: The Comprehensive Discussions in the White Tiger Hall: A Contribution to the History of Classical Studies in the Han Period*. 2 vols. Leiden: Brill, 1949.

van Ess, Hans. "The Meaning of Huang-Lao in Shiji and Hanshu," *Études Chinoises* 12:2:162–77 (fall 1993).

Van Zoeren, Steven. *Poetry and Personality: Readings, Exegesis, and Hermeneutics*. Stanford, Calif.: Stanford University Press, 1991.

von Senger, Harro. *Strategeme: Der erste Band der berühmten 36 Strategeme der Chinesen-lange als Geheimwissen gehüet, erstmals im Westen vorgestellt.* Bern: Scherz, 1992.

Wagner, Rudolf G. *A Chinese Reading of the Daode jing. Wang Bi's Commentary on the Laozi. With Critical Text and Translation.* Albany: State University of New York Press, 2001.

———. "Ban Gu and the End of History." Unpublished manuscript, 1995

———. "Bei yiwangde weizhi, Wang Bi de 'Laozi' jieshixue 被遺忘的微指——王弼的老子解釋學." *Xueren* 10:313–44 (1996).

———. *The Contemporary Chinese Historical Drama: Four Studies.* Berkeley: University of California Press, 1990.

———. *The Craft of a Chinese Commentator: Wang Bi on the Laozi.* Albany: State University of New York Press, 2000.

———. "Die Unhandlichkeit des Konfuzius," in A. Assmann, ed., *Weisheit. Archäologie der literarischen Kommunikation III*, pp. 455–64.

———. "Ein chinesisches Plädoyer gegen die autonome Person (A Chinese Plea against the Notion of the Autonomous Person)," in M. Welker, ed., *Die Autonome Person.* In press.

———. "Exploring the Common Ground: Buddhist Commentaries on the Taoist Classic Laozi," in Glenn Most, ed., Commentaries—Kommentare. Göttingen: Vandenhoeck & Ruprecht, 1999, pp. 95–120.

———. "The Impact of Conceptions of Rhetoric and Style upon the Formation of Early *Laozi* Editions: Evidence from Guodian, Mawangdui, and the Wang Bi *Laozi. "Transactions of the International Conference of Eastern Studies* XLIV: 32–56 (1999).

———. "Lebensstil und Drogen im chinesischen Mittelalter." *T'oung Pao* LIX: 79–178 (1973).

———. "Twice Removed from the Truth: Fragment Collection in 18th and 19th Century China," in G. Most, ed., *Aporemata 1: Collecting Fragments—Fragmente Sammeln.* Göttingen: Vandenhoeck & Ruprecht, 1997, pp. 34–52.

———. "The Wang Bi Recension of the Laozi." *Early China* 14:27–54 (1989).

———. "Wang Bi: 'The Structure of the Laozi's Pointers' (Laozi weizhi lilüe)." *T'oung Pao* LXXII:92–129 (1986).

Waley, Arthur. *The Analects of Confucius.* London: Allen & Unwin, 1938.

Wallace, Edwin, comp. *Outlines of the Philosophy of Aristotle.* Cambridge: Cambridge University Press, 1908.

Wallacker, Benjamin E. "Han Confucianism and Confucius in Han," in D. Roy, Tsuen-hsuin Tsien (eds.). *Ancient China: Studies in Early Civilization*, Hong Kong: Hong Kong University Press, 1978, pp. 215–28.

————. "The *Spring and Autumn Annals* As a Source of Law in Han China."
Journal of Chinese Studies 2:1:59–72 (1985).

Wang Baoxuan 王葆玹. "Cong Mawangdui boshuben kan 'Xici' yu *Laozi* xuepai
de guanxi," 從馬王堆帛書本看 '繫辭' 與老子學派的關係. *Daojia wenhua
yanjiu* 1:175–87 (1992).

————. *Jin gu wen jingxue xinlun.* 今古文經學新論 Beijing: Zhongguo shehui-
kexue Press, 1997.

————. *Xuanxue tonglun.* 玄學通論 Taipei: Wunan Tushu Press, 1996.

————. *Zhengshi xuanxue.* 正始玄學 Jinan: Qi Lu Press, 1987.

Wang Bi 王弼. *Laozi weizhi lilüe* 老子微旨例略. *Zhengtong Daozang*, Shanghai:
Commercial Press, 1932–26, HY 1245, Schipper 1255.

————. *Laozi Daode jing zhu* 老子道德經注, in Lou Yulie, ed., *Wang Bi ji jiaoshi*,
vol. 1, pp. 1–193, in Wagner, Rudolf G., *A Chinese Reading of the Daode jing*,
pp. xx–xx.

————. "*Laozi zhilüe*" 老子指略, in Zhongguo Kexueyuan zhexue yanjiusuo,
Zhongguo zhexueshi zu and Beijing daxue zheshi jiaoyanshi, eds., *Zhongguo
lidai zhexue wenxuan, Liang Han Sui Tang bian*, pp. 308–315.

————. "*Laozi zhilüe*" 老子指略, in Lou Yulie, ed., *Wang Bi ji jiaoshi*, vol. 1,
pp. 195–210.

————. *Laozi zhu* 老子注. Published as *Ji Tangzi Laozi Daode jing zhu* 集唐字
老子道德經注, in *Guyi congshu*, Taibei: Yiwen yinshuguan, 1965.

————. "*Lunyu shiyi*" 論語釋疑, in Lou Yulie, ed., *Wang Bi ji jiaoshi*, vol. 2,
pp. 621–37.

————. "*Lunyu shiyi*" 論語釋疑, in Ma Guohan, ed., *Yuhan shan fang ji yishu*.
Taipei: Zhongwen Press, 1979, vol. 3, pp. 1769–1775.

————. "*Zhouyi lüeli*" 周易略例, in Lou Yulie, ed., *Wang Bi ji jiaoshi*, vol. 2,
pp. 591–620.

————. "*Zhouyi lüeli*" 周易略例, in *Zhouyi Wang Han zhu*, ch. 10, in *Sibu beiyao*,
vol. 9–10. Shanghai: Zhonghua Press, 1930.

————. "*Zhouyi zhu*" 周易註, in Lou Yulie, ed., *Wang Bi ji jiaoshi*, vol. 1, p.
211; vol. 2, p. 590.

————. "*Zhouyi zhu*" 周易註, in *Zhouyi Wang Han zhu*. Cf. Richard J. Lynn,
tr., *The Classic of Changes: A New Translation of the I Ching As Interpreted
by Wang Bi.*

Wang Qixiang 王啓湘. *Zhou Qin mingjia sanzi jiaoquan* 周秦名家三子校詮.
Beijing: Guji Press, 1957.

Wang Xiaoyi 王曉毅. *Zhongguo wenhua de qingliu—zhengshi zhi yin* 中國文化
的清流——正始之音. Beijing: Zhongguo shehui kexue Press, 1991.

————. *Wang Bi pingzhuan* 王弼評傳 (Nanjing: Nanjing daxue chubanshe,
1996).

Watson, Burton. *The Complete Works of Chuang Tzu.* New York and London: Columbia University Press, 1968.

Weimojie suoshuo jing 維摩結所說經 (trans. Kumārajīva). Taishō shinshū daizō-kyō, Taibei: Xinwen feng Press, 1983– , vol. 14, no. 475, pp. 532–37. 475. Cf. E. Lamotte, ed. and trans, *L'Enseignement de Vimalakīrti.*

Wenzi zhuzi suoyin 文子逐字索引. *A Concordance to the Wenzi.* Hong Kong: Commercial Press, 1992.

Wilhelm, Richard. *Frühling und Herbst des Lü Bu We.* Jena: Eugen Diederichs, 1928.

Xu Kangsheng 許抗生. "He Wang xuanxue guanjian" 何王玄學管見. *Wen shi zhe* 3:31–32 (1985). Reprint in *Zhongguo zhexue shi* 6:56–57 (1985).

———. *Boshu Laozi zhuyi yu yanjiu (zengding ben).* 帛書老子注譯與研究 (增訂本) Hangzhou: Zhejiang renmin Press, 1982.

———. "Lun Wei Jin daojiao yu xuanxue de guanxi" 論魏晉道教與玄學的關係. *Zhongguo zhexueshi yanjiu* 3:26–31 (1986).

———. "Lun Wei Jin shiqi de zhuzi baijia xue" 論魏晉時期的諸子百家學. *Zhongguo zhexueshi yanjiu* 3:31–42 (1982).

Xu Kangsheng, Li Zhonghua 李仲華, Chen Zhanguo 陳戰國, and Na Wei 那薇. *Wei Jin xuanxue shi* 魏晉玄學史. Xi'an: Shanxi Shifan daxue Press, 1989.

Xunzi yinde 荀子引得. Harvard-Yenching Institute Sinological Series, Suppl., No. 21. Reprint, Taipei, Ch'eng-wen Publishing Company, 1966.

Yan Kejun 嚴可均, *Quan shanggu sandai Qin Han sanguo liuchao wen* 全上古三代兩漢三國六朝文. Peking: Zhonghua, 1985.

Yan Lingfeng 嚴靈峰. *'Tao Hongqing Laozi Wang Bi zhu kanwu' buzheng* '陶鴻慶老子王弼注勘誤' 補正. Taipei: Wuqiubeizhai, 1957.

Yang Bojun 楊伯峻, ed., *Liezi jishi* 列子集釋. Beijing: Zhonghua Press, 1985.

Yi Zhou shu zhuzi suoyin 逸周書逐字索引. (*A Concordance to the Yi Zhou shu*). Hong Kong: Commercial Press, 1992.

Yiwen leiju 藝文類聚. Taipei: Xinxing shuju, 1960, 10 vols.

Yu Dunkang 余敦康. *He Yan Wang Bi xuanxue xintan* 何晏王弼玄學新探. Jinan: Qi Lu Press, 1991.

Yu Jiaxi 余嘉錫, comm. *Shishuo xinyu jianshu* 世說新語箋疏, edited by Zhou Zumo 周祖謨 and Yu Shiyi 余淑宜, rev. ed., Shanghai: Shanghai guji Press, 1993.

Yuan Jixi 袁濟喜. "You wu zhi bian yu ziran diaoshi zhi zheng—Wei Jin nan bei chao liang zhong shenmei qingqu de xuanxue genyuan" 有無之辨與自然雕飾之爭——魏晉南北朝兩種審美情趣的玄學根源. *Xueshu yanjiu* 學術研究 1: 105–09 (1986).

———. *Liu chao meixue* 六朝美學. Beijing: Beijing daxue Press, 1989.

Zhang Zhan 張湛. *Liezi zhu* 列子注. See Yang Bojun, *Liezi jishi.*

Zhao Qi 趙岐. *Mengzi tici* 孟子題辭, in Jiao Xun, *Mengzi zhengyi*, pp. 1–17.

———, comm. *Mengzi shisi juan* 孟子十四卷, in *Sibu congkan*, vol. 39–41. Shanghai: Commercial Press, 1929–1934.

———, comm. *Mengzi zhangju* 孟子章句, in Jiao Xun. *Mengzi zhengyi*, pp. xx.

Zhongguo kexueyuan zhexue yanjiusuo, Zhongguo zhexueshi zu 中國科學院哲學研究所, 中國哲學史組 and Beijing daxue zhexueshi jiaoyanshi 北京大學哲學史教研室, eds. *Zhongguo lidai zhexue wenxuan* 中國歷代哲學文選, *Liang Han Sui Tang bian* 兩漢隨唐編. Beijing: Zhonghua Press, 1963.

Zhouli zhuzi suoyin 周禮逐字索引 (A Concordance to the *Zhouli*). Hong Kong: Commercial Press, 1993.

Zhouyi Wang Han zhu 周易王韓注, in Sibu beiyao. Shanghai: Zhonghua Press, 1930.

Zhouyi yinde 周易引得. Harvard-Yenching Institute Sinological Index Series, Suppl., No. 10, Reprint, Taipei: Ch'eng-wen, 1966.

Zhuangzi jishi 莊子集釋. (Guo Qingfan 郭慶藩, comp., Wang Xiaoyu 王孝魚, ed.), in *Xinbian zhuzi jicheng* 新編諸子集成. 4 vols. Beijing: Zhonghua Press, 1982.

Zhuangzi yinde 莊子引得. *A Concordance to Chuang Tzu*. Harvard-Yenching Institute Sinological Index Series, Suppl., No. 20. Cambridge, Mass.: Harvard University Press, 1956.

Index

Antinomy: and negation, 62–68.
Authority: basis for acceptance of of classics, 78, 90; collapse of school at end of Han, 94–95.

Ban Gu: on deterioration of understanding after Confucius, 22. See also *Gujin ren biao*.
Ben: See Root.
Binary organization of entities, 98–108.

Calm: as negation of movement, 64, 66.
Chanwei texts, 43.
Cheng: See Designation.
Chinese philosophy: age of philosophers in, 5; age of the study of the classics in, 5; Feng Youlan on ages of, 5 – 6; history of and European models. 5.
Chunqiu: commentary reading strategy for, 26; Dong Zhongshu on encoding and decoding of, 41–42.
Classics: as dregs of Sage, 44, 48; as empty traces of Sages, 11–15; as relevant source for philosophy in Wang Bi, 79; basis for acceptance of authority of in Wang Bi, 78; Confucius on unity of meaning of, 20; conscious use of language in, 10; deterioration of understanding of, 23; incapacity of in defining Dao, 10–11; status of authors of

for Wang Bi, 90–91; Yang Shixun definition of, 20.
Cognition: instruments and objects of, 107–108.
Commentary: as preferred form of Chinese 'scholastic age' 6; Kaga Eiji on 6.
Confucius: and Lao Dan on language, 10–11; anticipating misunderstanding of his words, 10; hidden meaning of acta and gesta of, 19; in *Xici* on language, 7; on par with Heaven, 9; only wishing to be without words but talking, 9–10; non-writing of book by, 19–20; on Sage from West, 50; spoken of as 'master', 16; students of not comprehending him, 20; subtle words by not understood, 22.
Confucius texts: *Lunyu*, *Laozi*, and *Zhouyi* as, 56; language of in talking about the Dark, 57.
Crisis: cause of social, 153–177; *Laozi* 39 on hypothetical in nature, 114; ongoing social, 176–177; real in society, 151–153; 'Return' as solution to, 179–213.

Da: See Great.
Dao: as aspect of That-by-Which, 70, 77; catching of and catching of fish, 32–33; continuous presence of as That-by-which, 170–

171;inconstant nature of in *Wenzi*, 34–40; *Hanfeizi* story on and cognition of elephant, 117–120; He Yan on within entities, 53–55; language's capacity to define, 10–13; meaning of in Wang Bi/*Laozi*, 125–144; pervasive presence of, 123–124; *shi* (initating) and *cheng* (completing) as aspects of, 127; silence as speech act about, 33; Wang Bi on *Laozi* talking about, 73–74; *Xici* definition of, 75–76.

Dark(ness) (*xuan*): as appellation for Negativity, 181–182; as aspect of That-by-which, 70, 77; enactment of by ruler, 2; of That-by-which, 1, 2; of That-by-which as condition for forgetting root, 153–154; talking about in Confucius texts, 56; Tang Yongtong on origin of philosophic use of term of, 83–86; Wang Bi analysis of, 144–147.

Descartes, 5.

Designations (*wei*): and names, 71–79; meaning of in *Laozi*, 24; Xia Houxuan on and names, 51.

Dong Zhongshu: on difficulty to understand classics, 40; on seeming triteness of *Chunqiu*, 41.

Duke Huan: on classics in *Zhuangzi*, 14.

Elephant: *Hanfeizi* story on *Dao* and traces of elephants translated, 117–120.

Eternal (*chang*): 166–167; result of cognition of, 182,185.

Feng Yan: on Dark 83–84.

Feng Youlan: division of history of Chinese philosophy into ages by, 5; orientalism of, 6.

Fish weir and hare trap: as simile for language in *Zhuangzi*, 31–32; development of *Zhuangzi* simile about in *Zhouyi lüeli*, 79–82; Buddhist use of simile of, 82.

Fu (Return, *Zhouyi* hexagram): Wang Bi on, 64–65; parallel with *Laozi* 16.1, 140–141. See also Return.

Fu Jia, 49.

Fu Yi: on Dark, 84.

Government institutions: Sage's setting up of, 186–194.

Graham, A. C.: on linguistic impossibility of Chinese ontology, 87–88.

Great (*da*): and negativity, 179–180; and Way, 96–97; as 'absolute', 8.

Great Entities: defined by single feature, 61–62.

Gujin ren biao (Hanshu section): hierarchy in and *Lunyu* 16.9, 174; pessimism about leader qualities in, 169.

Hanfeizi: developing term *li* in comment on *Laozi*, 117–121.

He Yan: on definitory versus tentative language and its objects, 54–55; on *Lunyu* 5.13, 20–21; on presence of Dao within entities, 53–55; on words of Sages, 19; translation of *Wuming lun* by, 52–53.

Grass and dogs: Wang Bi reading of metaphor of in *Laozi* 5.1, 131.

Guo Xiang: on basis of order, 115.

Heart of Heaven and Earth: visibility of, 9.

Heaven: and negativity, 179–180; as model for Confucius, 9.

Histories: written and unwritten 6.

Huainanzi: juxtaposing *wanwu* and *baishi* (hundred kinds of affairs), 103; on burning books as way to signal their understanding, 35; on inconstancy of *Dao*, 37–39; on *Laozi* 1.1, 37–39; on *Laozi*

5.4, 35; relationship of to *Wenzi*, 34–36.

Huan Tan: on Dark, 84.

Huang Kan: defining meaning of 'words of the Sages', 19; on *Lunyu* 5.13, 20–21.

Jingfa: on *li* of entities, 120–121.

Kaga Eiji: commentary studies by, 6; on spread of 'rationalism' in Han 95.

Kang Youwei, 5.

Language: collapse of in defining That-by-Which, 64; Dong Zhongshu on of classics difficult to understand, 40; fish weir and hare snare as simile for function of, 31; forgetting of as indispensable condition for understanding That-by-which, 80–82; hierarchy written word/spoken word/thinking in *Xici*, 7; in *Zhuangzi*, 13–15; in *Wenzi*, 36–37; inability of to define Sages according to *Lunyu*, 8; limited viability of in discussing That-by-Which, 61; meaning of Sages being object of philosophy of in Wang Bi, 55–56; of *Laozi* and *Lunyu*, ch. 1; of *Zhouyi*, 17–18; on *LZWZLL* deducing inability of to define That-by-Which, 57–60; terms for non-defineability by means of in *Laozi* and *Lunyu*, 67; undefineability of That-by-Which by means of not deficiency of, 59; Wang Bi reading of generative and nutritive in *Laozi*, 128; warnings about unreliability of in *Laozi*, 24; *Xici* on abilities of, 7.

Laozi: 1.1, 41, and 32.1 on ineptitude of definitory language for *Dao*, 8; being analytic not prescriptive text, 179; *Huainanzi* reading of 1.1, 37–39; imposition of symmetry on by Wang Bi, 104–105; list of descriptions of use of negative opposite in, 206; multiple simultaneous existences of, 212; on undefinability of Sage, 10; rhetorical structure of, 24–25; ruler as implied reader of for Wang Bi, 212; time circumstances of compared to those of Wang Bi, 3; use of name (*ming*) and designation (*wei*) in, 73; use of terms of non-defineability in, 67; Wang Bi reading of generative and nutritive language in, 128; Wang Bi on 1.2, 126; on 1.2–1.4, 188–190; on 1.3–1.4, 141–142; on 1.5, 69, 143–144; on 3.1, 159–160, 192; on 3.6, 203–204; on 4.1, 163–164; on 5.1, 109, 131; on 5.3, 112–114; on 11.1, 68, 134–135; on 14.5 and 14.6, 169–170; on 16, 185–186; on 16.1, 140; on 16.6, 166–167; on 17, 171–173; on 18, 172–173; on 18.2, 159; on 19.1, 204–205; on 20.1, 131–132; on 23.3, 183–184; on 25.5, 69–70; on 25.9, 149; on 25.10, 73–74; on 26.1, 66; on 28.1, 205; on 28.6, 187–190; on 31.2, 182–183; on 32.1, 206; on 32.3, 191–192; on 36.1 and 36.2, 195–197; on 37.3, 206–208; on 38, 135–136, 173–177, 179–180; on 39, 113–114; on 39.1, 150–152; on 39.3, 138; on 40.1, 136–137; on 41.13, 66–67, 122–123; on 41.14, 96; on 49.5, 161–163, 193–194; on 57.1, 157–158; on 58, 158; on 64.7, 160; on 65.3, 158–159; on 72, 156–157; Wang Bi summarizing political philosophy of, 210–211; warnings about unreliability of its own language in as guide for reading of, 24–25; *Wenzi* reading of 1.1, 33–35.

Laozi weizhi lüeli: 1.1 1, 1.45, 171;
analysis of 2.21, 70–71; of 4.1ff,
137, 199–201; of 5.6 ff., 143;
analysis of essay on rise of depravity in 6, 154–155, 165–166, 208–
9; deduction of unnameability
of That-by-Which in, 57–60; on
names and designations, 76–78.
Leibniz: notion by of praestabilierte
Harmonie and Wang Bi's of order,
109.
Li (ordering principle): history of
term, 115–121; meaning of in
Zhouyi wings, 115–116; of entities as source for cognition of
Dao, 119–121; Wang Bi use of
term, 111–112.
Liezi: quoting Confucius in Sage
from West, 50.
Liji: use of term *li* in, 116.
Liu An, 5.
Lüshi chunqiu, 23.
Lunyu: controversy about reading
5.13, 20; rhetorical features of
and definitory language, 19; statements on language in as guide to
reading of, 21; terms for non-defineability in, 67; Wang Bi reading
of 4.15, 19; of 6.21, 174; of 7.1,
19; of 7.6, 181–182; of 8.19, 8,
197–198; of 9.2, 8; of 15.3, 24;
of 16.9, 174; of 17.17, 9; Xiahou
Xuan reading 8.19 on Yao matching Heaven, 50–51; Zhao Qi on as
model for *Mengzi*, 30.

Mengzi: on reading *Shijing*, 27–29;
reading of *Shijing* by as guide for
reading of, 29–30; Zhao Qi criticism of misreading of 30–31.

Name (*ming*): and designation
(*cheng*), 71, 76; He Yan on, 52;
Xiahou Xuan on, 51.
Nature of entities: *Laozi* and Wang

Bi on, 109–110.
Necessity: logical, of philosophical
deduction, Wang Bi on, 91–94.
Negation: as trace of That-by-which,
62–69; calm and silence as examples of, 64.
Negative dialectics: in social processes, 163–172.
Negative opposite: ill-guided use of
by ruler, 168; law of, 199–201; list
of use of in *Laozi*, 206; notion of,
137–138; use of policy of by Sage,
186–199.
Negativity (*wu*): as most radically
unspecific notion, 60, 123–124;
Dao as appellation of, 181; em-
bodiment of by Sage, 181–182;
Great ones and, 179–180; hub as
metaphor for, 134–135; invulner-
ability of, 185; parallel features of
and of Sage, 186, Sage's imitation
of, 177–186.
Non-interference (*wuwei*): as Sagely
performance, 203.

One: not a number among others,
124; use of as basis for simultaneous intactness of entities,
114–115.
One and Many: and relationship
between ruler and Hundred
Families, 1; disturbance in relationship as cause of chaos, 130;
relationship of as normative
guideline for ruler running society,
2, 202–213; stability in relationship of compared to relationship
ruler/Hundred families, 3; Wang
Bi analysis in comment on *Laozi*
39.1, 132–133; Wang Bi on,
121–125.
Ontology: as basis for political philosophy in Wang Bi *Laozi*, 212;
Graham on linguistic impossibility
of in China, 87–88; meaning of in

present work, 2; meaning of term in Tang Yongtong, 87; Tang Yongtong on in Xuanxue, 83–86, 147.

Order: as feature of universe, 150; as ultimate purpose of the *Laozi*'s political philosophy, 211; discovery of dynamic character of of nature, 112; features of as result of correct performance by ruler, 210; intrinsic of entities and Leibniz notion of harmony, 109; of ten thousand kinds of entities, 108–121. See also *Li*.

Pei Hui: 49; Wang Bi discussion with on Confucius's silence about That-by-Which, 60.

People: tendency of to veer off *Dao*,152–153, 195; Sage's policies with regard to, 195.

Philosophy: beginning of systematic, 51; explorations in through art, 49; of Wang Bi as scholarly enterprise, 89; privileging of oral against written, 47–48; Wang Bi's, 83–147; Wang Bi's political 148–215.

Pi Xirui, 6.

Qu yu (…is taken for…): as technical term introducing heuristic aspects, 69.

Rationalism: spreading of during Later Han, 95.

Return: as philosophic concept in Wang Bi, 138–143; as purpose of Sage's action, 177–213, 191–193.

Root (*ben*): forgetting of as cause for crisis, 150–153.

Ruan Ji, 50.

Ruler: as cause of social order and disorder, 151–152; as focus of Wang Bi's political philosophy, 153; as implied reader of Wang

Bi *Laozi*, 212; bringing about crisis through efforts to avoid it, 154–177; conditions for his being 'great', 149–150; deteriorating sequence of instruments to establish order used by, 156–177, 172–174; instability of, 3; performance of non-acts by, 204–205; list of *zhang* in *Laozi* with as hidden subject, 206; list of applications of law of negative opposite by, 209–210; relationship of with Hundred Families and that between the One and the Many, 1; Wang Bi on being of in fifth position in *Zhouyi* hexagrams, 167. See also Sage.

Sage: and language in *Lunyu* and *Laozi*,10; Confucius on from West, 50; government in time when hope of appearance of was given up, 3; governmental non-acts of, 196–198; imitating negativity, 177–186; non-verbal communication among in *Lüshi chunqiu*, 23; operating 'return' of society from crisis, 177–213; parallel features of and of negativity, 186; political acts of as performance, 199–213; setting up of government institutions by, 187–193; thinking of and language, 7; unnameability of in *Lunyu*, 8; Wang Bi on matching Heaven by, 50–51, 74, 177–186; words of being fearsome and unfathomable, 19; *Zhouyi* expressing meaning of, 16; See also Yao.

Scholasticism: Feng Youlan's transfer of European concept of to China, 5.

Schools: Wang Bi and, 1.

Shi (affairs): paired with *wu* (things), 101–108.

Shijing: *Mengzi* on reading strategy

for, 27–29; reading strategies for, 26–27.

Silence: as negation, 64; as speech act about *Dao*, 32–33.

Su (humming sound): as ultimate form of philosophic communication, 49.

Subtle words (*weiyan*): as form of communication among Sages, 220 n. 40; understanding of of Confucius, 22–24; Xuanxue scholars' creation of, 47–48.

Strauss, Leo: on strategy of reading Macchiavelli, 29.

Suoyi: See That-by-which.

Systematical: Wang Bi's approach in reading *Laozi*, 96–97.

Tang Yongtong: impact of on Xuanxue studies, 86; on Aristotle's and Wang Bi's metaphysics, 87; on Xuanxue ontology, 83–86; use of term ontology by, 87.

That-by-which (*suoyi*): and ten thousand kinds of entities, 1; darkness of, 1; deduction of unnameability of in *LZWZLL*, 57–60; grasping aspects of, 69–80; negation as trace of, 62–68; ontological reason for cognizeability of, 62; source for term, 1; terms for, 122–124; traces of in discernible entities discovered by Confucius texts, 62–68; Wang Bi analysis of, 91–93; Wang Bi analysis of as basis for political philosophy, 209. See also: Negativity, Dao, Eternal.

Ten thousand kinds of entities: consisting of *shi* (affairs) and *gong* (achievements), 57–58, 98–109; order of, 108–121; prehistory of subdivisions of, 101–108; qualities of That-by-which of, 57–60.

Truth: classics as only access to, 40.

Understanding: Ban Gu on deterioration of, 22; Chinese history of, 6 – 43.

Urtext: status of in protestant tradition, 6.

Wanwu: use of term in Laozi, 234 n. 67. See also: Ten thousand kinds of entities.

Wang Baoxuan: on *Xici* statement about language, 7.

Wang Bi: family and personal interest of in commenting *Laozi*, 213–215; *Lunyu* commentary, translation of 17.17, 9; strategy of reading classics of, 90; status of classics' authors for, 90–91; summary of reading of *Laozi* political philosophy by, 210–211; systematic philosophical exposition by, 91; That-by-which of entities as only relevant philosophical problem in, 89. See also: *Laozi*, *LZWZLL*, *Zhouyi lüeli*,

Wei ([I] call): meaning of in *Laozi*, 24. See 'Designations'.

Wei (interfere), 166–167.

Weiyan: See Subtle Words.

Wenzi: as link between *Laozi* and *Hanfeizi*, 117; on writing, words and *Dao*, 33–35; reading of *Laozi* 1.1, 33–35; relationship of with *Huainanzi*, 34–36; parallelism of *wanwu* and *baishi* (hundred kinds of affairs) in, 102–103; use of term *li* in, 116–117; use of term *xing* (nature) for entities in general, 110.

Wheelwright Bian: on classics and *Dao*, 14.

Wu: See Negativity.

Wu (things): paired with *shi* (affairs), 101–108.

Wuwei (non-interference): as performance, 205–209.

Xiahou Xuan: 49–52; date of *Da-ode lun* by, 49–50; on Dao and Yao, 50–51; on designations and names, 51; translation of *Daode lun* by, 50–51.

Xici: comments by Han Kangbo and Wang Bi on *Xici shang* 6, 235 n.74; on language's abilities, 7; on *Zhouyi* structure, 15–16; on *Dao*, 75–76; Wang Bi reading of on 'Many' and 'Movements', 106.

Xuan (Dark): See Dark(ness).

Xuanxue: as political philosophy, 2; meaning 'scholarly exploration of the Dark', 2; not 'Taoism', 2; university teaching of in six dynasties, 2.

Xun Can: on classics as dregs of Sage, 44–46, 48.

Yang Shixun: definition of classics by, 20.

Yang Xiong: on Dark, 84–85.

Yao, emperor: elusive definition of as Sage, 74–75; government strategies of, 197–198.

You (on the basis of): difference between and 'being born from', 129; Wang Bi use of term, 127–128.

Zhang Heng: on Dark, 85.

Zhangju commentaries: disregarding meaning of classics by, 23.

Zhao Qi: on reading *Mengzi* as he read *Shijing*, 29–30.

Zhongchang Tong: on Dark, 83.

Zhouyi: as created by Sages, 18; circumvention of limitations of language by, 8, 44–46; form of communication of, 17; hexagram *fu* [return] in 9, rhetorical structure of, 15–16; use of term *li* in, 115–116; Wang Bi on ruler in hexagram *guan*, 155; Wang Bi on ruler symbolized by fifth position in hexagrams of, 167, 202–203. See also *Xici*.

Ziran: as basis for conventional virtues, 197–198; of entities as basis of order, 109–111; Xiahou Xuan on Heaven and Sage making use of, 50.

Zhouyi lüeli: translation of *ming xiang* section of, 80–82.

Zhuangzi: fish weir as simile for language in, 31–32; on books and Dao, 12–15; *Tianyun* chapter on language and *Dao*, 10–11.